Human R

WITHDRAWN

Effective management of human resources is essential to the success of any organization. In this authoritative, sophisticated and engaging new text on Human Resource Management (HRM), an international team of leading analysts guides the advanced student through this fundamental discipline of management in all its complexity.

The book explores all the central themes and concepts of HRM theory and practice, and introduces the most important issues influencing contemporary practice in a wide range of organizational contexts. It systematically examines the main functional areas of HRM, and engages with a number of key contemporary issues for both scholars and practitioners. Topics covered include:

- Strategic HRM
- Ethics in HRM
- Knowledge management
- HRM and performance
- Outsourcing and implications for HRM
- HRM in small and medium enterprises
- Key functional areas of HRM practice
- International HRM

Adopting a critical perspective throughout that challenges the student to examine closely the fundamental purpose and practices of HRM, this book is essential reading for all serious students of Human Resource Management and for any HRM professional looking to deepen his understanding of the subject.

David G. Collings is Lecturer in International Management at the National University of Ireland, Galway and editor of the *Human Resource Management Journal*.

Geoffrey Wood is Professor of Human Resource Management at the University of Sheffield Management School, UK. He has authored seven books and published in a variety of journals.

Human Resource Management

A critical approach

Edited by
David G. Collings and Geoffrey Wood

LIS LIBRARY
Date 5/2
Fund BS
Order No 2075076
University of Chester

LONDON AND NEW YORK

First published 2009
by Routledge
2 Park Square, Milton Park, Abingdon, Oxon OX14 4RN

Simultaneously published in the USA and Canada
by Routledge
270 Madison Ave, New York, NY 10016

Routledge is an imprint of the Taylor & Francis Group, an informa business

© 2009 David G. Collings and Geoffrey Wood

Typeset in Times New Roman by Keyword Group Ltd.
Printed and bound in Great Britain by CPI Antony Rowe, Chippenham, Wiltshire

All rights reserved. No part of this book may be reprinted or reproduced or utilized in any form or by any electronic, mechanical, or other means, now known or hereafter invented, including photocopying and recording, or in any information storage or retrieval system, without permission in writing from the publishers.

British Library Cataloguing in Publication Data
A catalogue record for this book is available from the British Library

Library of Congress Cataloging in Publication Data
Human resource management: a critical approach / edited by David G. Collings and Geoffrey Wood.
p. cm.
Includes bibliographical references and index.
1. Personnel management. I. Collings, David G. II. Wood, Geoffrey.
HF5549.H78414 2009
658.3—dc22
2008053050

ISBN10: 0-415-46246-0 (hbk)
ISBN10: 0-415-46247-9 (pbk)
ISBN10: 0-203-87633-4 (ebk)

ISBN13: 978-0-415-46246-4 (hbk)
ISBN13: 978-0-415-46247-1 (pbk)
ISBN13: 978-0-203-87633-6 (ebk)

Contents

Figures

Tables

About the editors

David G. Collings is Lecturer in International Management at the National University of Ireland, Galway. Previously he was on the faculty at the University of Sheffield Management School. He was also a Visiting Research Fellow at Strathclyde Business School. His research interests focus on management in multinational corporations with a particular emphasis on staffing and industrial relations issues. His work in these areas has been published in outlets such as the *Journal of World Business, International Journal of Human Resource Management* and the *International Journal of Management Reviews*. His recent books include *Global Staffing* (with Hugh Scullion), published by Routledge, and *International HRM and International Assignments* (with Mike Morley and Noreen Heraty), published by Palgrave Macmillan. He is Editor of the *Human Resource Management Journal.*

Geoffrey Wood is Professor of Human Resource Management at the University of Sheffield Management School and visiting Professor at the Nelson Mandela Metropolitan University in South Africa. He has authored/co-authored/edited seven books, and over one hundred articles in peer-reviewed journals (including journals such as *Work and Occupations, Work, Employment and Society, Organization Studies, International Journal of Human Resource Management, British Journal of Industrial Relations, Human Resource Management* (US), etc.). Geoff's current research interests centre on the systematic testing and development of contemporary institutional theory in the light of large-scale survey evidence. This has encompassed assessments of variations in industrial relations in different institutional settings, the relative fortunes of organized labour in emerging markets, and developments and extensions of regulationist theories. The latter includes assessments as to internal diversity within specific varieties of capitalism, and the relationship between finance and HR practice.

Contributors

Corine Boon is Post-Doctoral Researcher at Erasmus University Medical Center and Tilburg University, The Netherlands.

Chris Brewster is Professor of International HRM, Henley Business School, University of Reading, UK.

Deirdre Curran is Lecturer in HRM at J. E. Cairnes School of Business and Economics, National University of Ireland, Galway, Ireland.

Tony Dundon is Lecturer in HRM at J. E. Cairnes School of Business and Economics, National University of Ireland, Galway, Ireland.

Mick Fryer is a Doctoral Student at Loughborough University Business School, UK.

Irena Grugulis is Professor of Employment Studies at Bradford University School of Management, UK, an AIM/ESRC Service Fellow and an Associate Fellow of SKOPE.

Patrick Gunnigle is Professor of Business Studies at Department of Personnel and Employment Relations, Kemmy Business School, University of Limerick, Ireland.

Richard Haines is Professor and Head of the Development Studies Department at the Nelson Mandela Metropolitan University (NMMU), South Africa.

Donald Hislop is Senior Lecturer in OB/HRM, Loughborough University Business School, UK.

Frank M. Horwitz is Professor and Director of Cranfield School of Management, University of Cranfield, UK.

Phil Johnson is Professor at the University of Sheffield Management School, UK.

Zsuzsa Kispal-Vitai is Associate Professor, University of Pécs, Hungary.

Gilton Klerck is Senior Lecturer at the Department of Sociology, Rhodes University, South Africa.

Wolfgang Mayrhofer is Professor at Interdisciplinary Unit for Management and Organizational Behaviour, WU Wirtschaftsuniversitaet Wien, Austria.

Anthony McDonnell is Research Fellow, Centre for Institutional and Organisational Studies, Faculty of Business and Law, University of Newcastle, Australia.

Kamel Mellahi is Professor of Strategic Management at Sheffield University Management School, UK.

Jaap Paauwe is Full Professor of Human Resource Studies at Tilburg University, and Professor of Organisation (part-time) at Erasmus School of Economics, Erasmus University, Rotterdam, The Netherlands.

Suzanne Richbell is Senior Lecturer in HRM at Sheffield University Management School, UK.

Hugh Scullion is Professor of International HRM at J. E. Cairnes School of Business and Economics, National University of Ireland, Galway, Ireland.

Rosalind Searle is Senior Lecturer in Occupational Psychology at The Open University, UK.

Adrian Wilkinson is Professor and Director, Centre for Work, Organization and Wellbeing and the Department of Employment Relations, Griffith Business School, Griffith University, Australia.

Stephen Wood is Research Chair and Deputy Director, Institute of Work Psychology, Professor of Employment Relations, University of Sheffield, UK.

1 Human resource management

A critical approach

David G. Collings and Geoffrey Wood

Introduction

Despite almost two decades of debate in the mainstream literature around the nature of human resource management (HRM), its intellectual boundaries and its application in practice, the field continues to be dogged by a number of theoretical and practical limitations. This book is intended to provide students with a relatively advanced and critical discussion of the key debates and themes around HRM as it is conceptualized and operationalized in the early part of the twenty-first century. Thus the current contribution is intended to be in the tradition of Storey (2007) and Legge (1995) and aims to provide students with a well grounded and critical overview of the key issues surrounding HRM from a theoretical and practical perspective. In doing so we draw on contributions from the leading scholars in the field who provide detailed discussions on key debates in their respective offerings.

In this introduction we provide the context for the book though considering a number of overarching themes within which key debates in the field of HRM are situated. Specifically, we provide a summary discussion of the theoretical and intellectual boundaries of HRM, consider its emergence in historical context and identify some of the pervasive contradictions and limitations which prevail in the literature. Finally we provide a short outline of the structure and content of this volume.

HRM defined

Our discussion begins by considering what HRM actually means. Given the importance of definition in understanding the boundaries of a field, this issue is clearly an important point of departure. However, this question is more difficult to answer than one would expect, since from its emergence HRM has been dogged by the still largely unresolved ambiguity surrounding its definition. As Blyton and Turnbull (1992: 2) note 'The ways in which the term is used by academics and practitioners indicates both variations in meaning and significantly different emphases on what constitutes its core components'.

One of the dominant definitions (in the UK at least) has been to define HRM as a contested domain, with rival soft and hard approaches. The soft approach to HRM is generally associated with the Harvard School and in particular the writings of Michael Beer and colleagues (see Beer *et al.*, 1984; Beer and Spector, 1985;

Walton and Lawrence, 1985). The soft school emphasizes the importance of aligning HR policies with organizational strategy, it emphasizes the role of employees as a valuable asset and source of competitive advantage through their commitment adaptability and quality (Legge, 1995; D'Art, 2002). It stresses gaining employee commitment to the organization through the use of a congruent suite of HRM policies. Soft HRM draws on behavioural sciences in particular, with strong resonance with the human relations school, while the concept of human growth, which is central to its theory, echoes 'all-American' theories of motivation, from McGregor's *Theory Y* to Maslow's *Hierarchy of Needs* (Legge, 1995). Hence it is sometimes conceptualized as 'developmental humanism' (Storey, 1989; Legge, 1995). HRM is operationalized in terms of strategic interventions designed to develop resourceful employees and to elicit their commitment to the organizational goal (Storey, 1992). However, sceptics have conceptualized soft HRM as the 'iron fist in the velvet glove', arguing that the theory of soft HRM 'reduced . . . the complex debate about the role of people in work organizations to the simplistic dogma of an economic model which even its "creator" Adam Smith would probably not have wished applied in such an indiscriminate manner' (Hart, 1993: 29–30). Another uncharitable definition of soft HRM is that it constituted a desperate rearguard action by liberal academics and practitioners, mostly writing in the United States, to sell more humane forms of managing people to essentially conservative owner interests that have in increasing numbers ruthlessly pressed for a maximization of short term profits, regardless of the cost to both employees and the long term good of the organization. In other words, soft HRM is about trying to encourage firms to be 'nicer' to their people, on the basis that such 'niceness' is likely to translate into greater commitment and productivity, and hence, even more profits.

Soft HRM stands in contrast with the hard variant. Hard HRM is generally associated with the Michigan School (Forbrun *et al.*, 1984). Its emphasis is on the use of human resource (HR) systems to 'drive' the attainment of the strategic objectives of the organizations (Forbrun *et al.*, 1984). While soft HRM emphasizes the human element of HRM, the emphasis of the hard approach is very much on the resource as a means of maximizing shareholder value over the short term. The duty of managers is quite simply to make money for owners, and a focus on other issues such as employee rights is simply a distraction: rather, by focusing on returns, the organization will perform most efficiently, which ultimately is in the interests of all.

It has been argued that, in the tradition of Taylorism and Fordism, employees are viewed as a factor of production that should be rationally managed and deployed in quantitative and calculative terms in line with business strategy (Tyson and Fell, 1986; Storey, 1992). However, rather different to classic Taylorism or Fordism, job security in the new hard HRM is seen as an unnecessary luxury, whilst pay rates are to be kept to the lowest level the external labour market would permit: there is little mention in the literature illustrating how hard HRM echoes Henry Ford's famous commitment to a 5 dollar/day wage. Human resource policies in the hard variant are designed to be both internally consistent and externally aligned with the organizational strategy. These interventions are designed to ensure full utilization of the labour resource (Storey, 1992). It is legitimized and finds its impetus from a market-responsive frame of reference

(Storey, 2007). At the extreme, implicit contracts regarding pensions and tenure are seen as hampering effective management: these should, if possible, be jettisoned, with employee rights being pared back as much a possible. Critics of this point of view have argued that such a focus is likely to make for higher staff turnover rates, with the inevitable loss of job specific skills and accumulated wisdom, low trust, low levels of organizational commitment, and hence, higher transaction costs (see Marsden, 1999). In other words, hard HRM is likely to make organizations less efficient. It could be argued that most successful incrementally innovative high value added manufacturing firms have shunned hard HRM. In contrast, it has been more widely deployed in more volatile areas of economic activity, such as financial services.

A second and simpler way of viewing things is that HRM in the narrow sense can be defined as a strategic approach to managing employees, which came to the forefront in the liberal market economies, particularly the US and the UK, in the 1980s. Whilst having both soft ('people friendly') and hard ('people as a resource to be deployed, utilized, and, if need be disposed of') variations, common to this approach was an emphasis on optimal shareholder outcomes, with enhancing outcomes for other stakeholders being at the best a secondary objective, and at worst, an unnecessary distraction. This 'two sides of the same coin' point of view argues that, since the end of the long boom that lasted from the post World War II period up until the 1970s, there has been a period of erratic and unstable growth and recession. This period has been characterized by employers gaining the upper hand over employees, on account of the very much weaker bargaining position of the latter (cf. Kelly 1998). Given this, managers – particularly in the liberal market economies, such as the US and UK, where workers have historically had fewer rights under both law and convention – have taken the opportunity to fundamentally change the way they manage people. This has taken the form of systematic attempts to undermine collective bargaining with unions, replacing this with weak forms of consultation with individual employees. Collective employment contracts – where workers performing similar jobs are rewarded according to a pre-agreed pay scale – are replaced with individual ones, with employees being rewarded on the basis of regularly appraised performance, and/or through pay rates simply being linked to outputs. In other words, the role of the employee in the firm is not a dynamic and, in some sense, negotiated relationship, but rather simply the deployment of a resource, in the same way a firm would deploy other physical resources, such as raw materials.

A third way of looking at things is to simply conceptualize HRM as little more than a renaming of personnel management. In this vein, writers such as Armstrong (1987) describe HRM as 'old wine in new bottles', while Guest (1987) pointed to the fact that many personnel departments changed their names to HRM departments, with little evidence of any change in role. In practice, this would suggest that much HR work really concerns the administration of systems governing the administration of pay, promotion and recruitment procedures, etc. In turn, this would imply that HR managers are likely to lack power within the organization and have little say in setting real organizational strategies.

Finally, HRM may be defined broadly in terms of including all aspects of managing people in organizations and the ways in which organizations respond to the actions of employees, either individually or collectively. The value of this catch all term is that it describes the wide range of issues surrounding both the employment contract, situations where an employment contract has yet to be agreed on (recruitment and selection), and ways in which employees may be involved and participate in areas not directly governed by the employment contract to make working life more agreeable and/or to genuinely empower people. In other words, it goes beyond simply 'industrial relations' or 'employment relations'. The terms 'personnel administration' or 'personnel management' would not provide a totally accurate label, given their administrative and non-strategic connotations.

Some insights into the different ways HRM has been conceived have been provided by the Keele University affair in 2007–2008. A conservative university administration resolved to restructure business and management studies in the university through the simple device of making academics that had formally specialized in 'industrial relations' redundant. In many respects, this was a surprising decision, given robust student numbers, and the fact that industrial relations research was one area where Keele had gained an excellent reputation. Backed up by the findings of a committee of external 'experts', university administration implied that industrial relations academics were likely to be less capable of teaching HRM, and, by implication, had skills sets not relevant to modern business education. Tellingly, a petition signed by many leading HRM and industrial relations academics in Britain, in response to this decision, included a statement that HRM could not be separated from industrial relations, and that the skills necessary to teach industrial relations could broadly be applied to understanding HRM. In other words, HRM was simply a collective noun describing work and employment relations in the broadest possible sense, and was not really about special new skills, or a new and different agenda (see www.bura.org.uk).

The preceding discussion highlights the ambiguity around the boundaries of HRM. These differences are summarized in Table 1.1. The tension around definition persists in the literature and a central theme in this volume is highlighting the contradictions between these two broad understandings of HRM. We argue that for ethical and sustainability reasons, more stakeholder orientated approaches to people management are preferable, with shareholder dominant approaches facing both quotidian micro-crises at firm (encompassing problems of human capital development and commitment) and at macro economic (encompassing problems of excessive speculation-driven volatility, industrial decline, and chronic balance of payments problems) levels.

HRM and personnel management compared

As noted above, a key point of reference in definitions on HRM is through comparing it with its predecessor – personnel management. Although this debate is somewhat dated, it remains important. Thus it merits summary discussion.

During the early days of HRM's emergence as a mainstream approach to people management a number of commentators were sceptical about the extent to which it represented something different to its predecessor – personnel management. Over time it has become apparent that there are substantive differences between the two,

Table 1.1 Definitions of HRM

Definition	*Implication*
Contested domain	HRM is a contested domain, with two rival paradigms, hard and soft HRM
Two sides of the same coin	Whether hard or soft, HRM is about the management of people in a particular, new way. This may involve the use of strategy to manage people, or simply reflect structural changes that have strengthened management at the expense of employees
'New wine in old bottles'	HRM is little more than the extension of traditional personnel management
Collective noun	HRM is a commonly reflected description for a range of practices associated with managing work and employment relations

at least at a theoretical level. In illuminating these differences a brief discussion on personnel management is merited (for a full discussion, see Legge, 1995).

While there are a number of accepted definitions of personnel management, some of which in the US context are closer to accepted definitions of HRM (see Kaufman, 2001; Strauss, 2001), there is a degree of consensus as to its key characteristics. First, personnel management is largely conceived as a downstream activity with a limited strategic role. And, despite the rhetoric, HRM is often not that strategic: after all, both hard and soft HRM ultimately depict HRM as a transmission belt, passing down an agenda of shareholder value. Further, personnel management is generally considered to be reactive and piecemeal with little integration between its various elements. One of the greatest management thinkers – if popular management writing can be considered thought at all – of the last century, Peter Drucker (1961: 269), neatly summarized the personnel role as 'a collection of incidental techniques with little internal cohesion. As personnel administration conceives the job of managing worker and work, it is partly a file clerk's job, partly a house keeping job, partly a social worker's job and partly fire-fighting to head off union trouble or to settle it'. This limited role is alluded to by Legge's (1995: 88) observation that 'in the UK "personnel management" evokes images of do-gooding specialists trying to constrain line managers, of weakly kowtowing to militant unions, of both lacking power and having too much power'. Indeed it has been argued that the perceived welfare role of the personnel function was one aspect of it that limited its credibility as a managerial function. It also resulted in females playing a key role in personnel in its formative years in the UK context (Legge, 1995). A scrutiny of the gender composition of classes at many Chartered Institute of Personnel and Development approved training centres provides some corroboration for the gendered nature of much HR work.

A further dimension of the broad personnel role in the UK was its key role in negotiating with trade unions, a characteristic which points toward the fire-fighting role of personnel. Indeed, it was this element of the role that bought increasing numbers of males into the profession (Gunnigle *et al.*, 2006). However, more recent evidence in the UK points to a shift in the balance towards a greater feminization of the HR function (Kersley *et al.*, 2006: 69). This engagement with trade unions points to a collectivist orientation and, owing to the historical prominence of trade unions, particularly in the UK and Ireland, personnel management became infused with a pluralist frame of reference (Flanders 1964). Given the importance of bargaining, managing the industrial relationship gained a distinct identity: it is worth noting that the divide between basic personnel management and industrial relations persists in the academic literature, with, as a general rule, those academic journals focusing on the former having low prestige, and on the latter, high prestige. Newer explicitly HR journals represent something of a cross over and incorporate aspects of both, as well as insights from, other disciplines.

The preceding discussion suggests that HRM and personnel management – and industrial relations – may differ in a number of substantive ways. The first is that HRM is conceived as having a more strategic role and hence elevated to the top management table, suggesting a more up stream role, even if, in practice, this has been little more than wishful thinking. Nonetheless, HRM does concern attempts to develop an integrated and congruent set of HR policies as opposed to the piecemeal approach apparent in the traditional personnel role. Furthermore, HR policy and practice is also targeted at the individual level. This is reflected in the preference for individual performance related pay, individual communication mechanisms, employee opinion surveys and the like. A final key distinguishing factor is that, reflective of the individualist orientation, HRM is premised on a unitarist understanding of conflict. Unitarism suggests that there are no intrinsic conflicts of interest in the employment relationship as all within the organization are working toward a common goal for the success of the organization. The common goal is reflected in the idea that there is a single source of authority within the organization – management. Given that there are argued to be no conflicts of interest within the organization – conflicts are caused by breakdowns in communication or by troublemakers. Conflict should be suppressed by improving communication or removing troublemakers from the organization. Unions are opposed on two grounds: (1) there are no conflicts of interest within the workplace and thus they are unnecessary and (2) they would represent an alternative source of authority. Alternatively, unions may be co-opted to the managerial agenda, through 'partnership', with unions trading off militancy for continued recognition, and the benefits that would arguably flow from greater organizational competitiveness. More critical strands of the HR literature suggest that this focus is mistaken, that employees often retain a collective identity, and that managerial power will inevitably continue to be challenged in ways that would make new accommodations necessary if the organization is to work in the most effective way.

HRM enters the mainstream

It is generally agreed that human resource management gained mainstream acceptance as an approach toward people management, particularly in the UK and the US, in the 1980s. However, it should be noted that the roots of the HRM approach can be traced some 20 years earlier in the US context (see Strauss, 2001). It was during the 1980s however that HRM became widely embraced by practitioners and academics alike. For practitioners, it offered a new agenda to replace the lacklustre image of personnel management and the adversarial rhetoric of industrial relations. While for academics it represented an opportunity for rebranding and reorientating careers away from industrial relations and personnel management, topics which many feared were losing their import as academic subjects (Guest, 2001; Strauss, 2001). The emergence of HRM is generally traced to a confluence of factors. The impact of the external context on HR function is reflected in Beer *et al.*'s (1984: 34) observation that 'HRM policies and practices are not and cannot be formed in a vacuum. They must reflect the governmental and societal context in which they are embedded' and it is generally recognized that a number of political, economic and social factors prompted the emergence of HRM at this time.

Guest (1990) argues that perhaps the most significant of these factors were external pressures on industry, of which the most important were increasing competition in the US and international marketplace combined with concerns over the retarded rate of productivity growth in the US. The greatest competitive threat, to the US in particular, at this time came from the rise of the Pacific economies, most notably Japan but also South Korea, Taiwan and Singapore, who competed through technological advantages and initially cheaper labour costs. These Japanese firms' entry into the US market threatened traditional strongholds of US industry, in particular the auto makers who had previously enjoyed an oligopolic position in the US marketplace. Japanese competitors could provide high quality products at a very competitive price. In the UK similar threats were experienced from other large European economies and the shift from 'command' to 'market' economies in central and eastern Europe (Legge, 1995). This increasing competition was reflective of the growing globalization of the marketplace, a trend which was facilitated by improvements in information technology and transportation, meaning that the barriers traditionally created by national borders were being broken down. Concomitantly, levels of technological differentiations became blurred as technological advances limited the potential of technology as a source of competitive advantage. Thus, as indicated above, firms were subject to far greater competitive pressures than they had been historically accustomed to. These factors influenced the shift in emphasis towards employees as a source of competitive advantage. This view was very much consistent with the 'excellence literature' in the US (Peters and Waterman, 1982). Their work traced the success of high performing companies to the motivation of employees through involved management styles which were responsive to market changes (Beardwell, 2001). This excellence literature was very influential and also influenced the shift toward HRM in organizations.

The increasing competition should also be considered in the context of the difficult economic conditions of the early 1980s. Specifically, the oil crises of the latter part of the 1970s and early 1980s precipitated a global economic recession which further influenced the climate in which organizations operated. At a political level the Reagan Government in the US and the Thatcher Government in the UK certainly facilitated the emergence of a new individualist approach to management of employees, which gave impetus to the declining role of trade unions in these countries. The free market ideology of these governments was most visible in Reagan's showdown with the air traffic controllers in the US which ultimately resulted in the dismissal of the striking employees. In the UK, Thatcher's high profile stand off with striking miners had broadly similar connotations. This led to mine workers being defeated, but also the wilful destruction of much of the mining industry, over-exploitation of North Sea oil and gas reserves, and an overvalued currency (with, in turn, seriously adverse consequences for manufacturing), reflecting the extent to which breaking organized labour – and the pursuit of a broader, right wing ideology – was prioritized over basic economic logic, and the well being of the country at large. Indeed, it has been argued that the policy of privatization of elements of the public sector, combined with a raft of anti-union legislation under Thatcher's Conservative Government in the UK, 'encouraged firms to introduce new labour practices and to re-order their collective bargaining arrangements' (Hendry and Pettigrew, 1990: 19). The unitarist underpinning of HRM certainly resonated more closely with these ideals compared with pluralist industrial relations traditions. The developments have left an enduring legacy in the UK context. Whilst union rights have increased under the New Labour governments of the late 1990s and 2000s, the government has been reluctant to extend comprehensive employment rights to the growing body of agency workers, and has ruthlessly privatized, partially privatized, or otherwise outsourced the provision of public infrastructure and services to politically well-connected private contractors, who have generally tended to practice far tougher HR than their public sector counterparts (Dibben et al. 2007). Again, efforts to reign in the gangmasters that supply cheap (and, in alarmingly many cases, coerced) labour to agriculture, catering and frontline service industries have been half-hearted at best.

A final factor which facilitated the emergence of HRM in mainstream management practice was a fundamental restructuring of economies in the UK and US. This shift was reflected in a decline in significance of traditional industries and a rise in new industrial sectors such as high tech industries and a significant shift in employment towards the services sector. Many of these industries were less tied to the established patterns of traditional old style industrial relations (Beardwell, 2001). More critical accounts have, as noted earlier, suggested that all these economic and industrial changes represented one of many historical periods where the relative power of management vis-à-vis employees had disproportionately increased; in time, this will be reversed, with employees fighting back, clawing back some of the gains of previous decades (Kelly, 1998). In this regard HRM is conceived to be the current incarnation of management's ongoing search for the 'best' method to manage the employment relationship (D'Art, 2002).

Thus, while the precise antecedents of the emergence of HRM can be very dependent on the analyst's interpretation of events (Beardwell, 2001), it is clear that a range of factors combined to facilitate the emergence of HRM as a mainstream approach to the management of employees. Notwithstanding the aforementioned examples of factors in the UK environment which facilitated the emergence of HRM there, for some HRM as a concept is rooted in US traditions (Brewster 2007; Guest, 1990) and hence may have limited applicability abroad. We now consider this perspective.

HRM: An American concept with little applicability abroad?

As we have demonstrated, HRM as an approach to people management is generally seen to have its roots in the US context. In this regard much of the heritage of HRM in the US context long predates the mainstream emergence of HRM in the 1980s. Particularly prominent in the US context has been the dominance of non-union industrial relations which clearly resonates with HRM. This anti-union ideology is generally attributed to the development of American industry. Most notable in this regard is, as Leidner (2002) notes, the fact that the balance of power in the US workplace favours capital more than in most other countries. Arguably this is most apparent in terms of the doctrine of 'Employment at Will' which underscores all aspects of the employment relationship in American industry. This widely accepted doctrine means that, in the absence of contracts or legislation, employment contracts are 'at-will', and thus can be terminated by either party without explanation or cause, thus workers have no ongoing right to employment and no legal obligation for fairness is placed on employers (Leidner, 2002). The evolution of the power relationship alluded to above can be traced to the evolution of US industry. In this regard, the lack of legislative support of worker collectives prior to the 1930s resulted in non-union practices prevailing for the majority of US employees (Kochan *et al.*, 1986). Guest (1990) posits that at this stage individualism became ingrained in US culture. This individualism is often characterized in terms of a meritocracy, where ambition predominates (ibid.). This is reflected in articulations of the 'American Dream', which Guest (1990) posits was first formally articulated in the context of the New Deal in the 1930s. While different variations have been presented over the years, Guest (1990) postulates that a number of common themes emerge. Most significant in terms of our consideration of the industrial relations context of US industry, is the view of America as a land of opportunity, where through self-improvement and hard work anyone can become a success. Thus, the emphasis in US culture is on individuals grasping opportunities as they present themselves and making the most of them, with government and employers aiding simply in terms of providing a context (Guest, 1990). This is significant for a number of reasons. First, it intensified managements' perceived right to manage and second, it amplifies individualistic tendencies and notions of meritocracy ingrained in US culture. Leidner (2002: 27), when examining the nature of employment relations in the US fast-food industry, highlights this cultural idiosyncrasy thus:

> The American values of individualism and meritocracy suggest that workers should improve their lot by moving out of fast-food jobs rather than by improving the compensation and working conditions of the jobs.

Thus, from a cultural point of view at least, the obligation is placed on the individual to improve their situation by exiting the unsatisfactory working situation and moving on to a more rewarding or satisfactory job. This highlights the individual focus in HRM theory and is consistent with the shift away from collective employment relations.

Clearly reflective of this ideology is the welfare capitalist movement which developed during the late nineteenth century. This involved America's large corporations developing a uniquely American response to the 'labour question', which was private and managerial as opposed to governmental and labourist (Jacoby, 1997). This movement viewed the industrial enterprise as the source of stability and security in modern society, as opposed to government or trade unions (Jacoby, 1997). These firms emphasized job security (achieved through an emphasis on internal labour markets), good rates of pay, a variety of welfare benefits and non-union forms of employment relations (ibid.). Clearly these characteristics, combined with the later influence of 'all-American' theories of motivation, from McGregor's *Theory Y* to Maslow's *Hierarchy of Needs* (Legge, 1995) referred to above, were also influential in the emergence of HRM in the US context.

For some (Guest, 1990; Brewster, 2007) the US heritage of HRM thinking and practice means that its application in practice in other countries may be questionable. As Brewster (2007: 771) notes 'Whether the US-derived visions of HRM apply everywhere in the world is an important question for both theory and practice'. On the basis of a large body of empirical work, Brewster (2007) concludes that many aspects of HRM practice are different in the European context. It is worth noting that, for example, how many UK employers chose *not* to get rid of unions in the 1980s, when they certainly would have enjoyed much government support: hence, to a degree at least, pluralist ways of doing things remain surprisingly embedded in many UK workplaces. The comparability of HRM systems across countries is a key theme in the literature and this is taken up by Chris Brewster and Wolfgang Mayrhofer in their contribution to the current volume.

The credibility gap?

A final theme which we explore in this introduction, is the challenge which HRM has long since faced with regard to establishing its value as a managerial activity. In Legge's (1995: 9) words this 'obsession with [establishing] their credibility' has dogged personnel, and more recently HRM, practitioners throughout their history. In this regard Tyson's (1985: 22) oft-cited comment is illustrative of this credibility gap:

> If all the managers were to write in their diaries each day 'What have I done today to make the business successful?' would the personnel manager have an embarrassingly short entry to make?

To a degree these credibility challenges relate to the traditional down-stream role which personnel management occupied in firms, combined with the established welfare role which the function performed in many organizations. Thus, as we noted above, practitioners were quick to embrace HRM as it offered the potential to replace the uninspiring image of personnel management. Further, rhetorically at least, it offered the possibility of bringing HRM to the top management table and a role in developing corporate strategy. In the UK context the Workplace Employee Relations Surveys have provided key insights into the changing role of the HR profession over recent decades. The most recent survey (WERS, 2004) concluded that 'HR managers are a new breed of managers, and that the increase in their numbers is not the product of a re-labelling exercise' (Kersley *et al.*, 2006: 70) as some early critics of HRM purported. Thus, the WERS studies provide evidence of substantial differences in role between those with HR in their job titles and their counterparts who retain Personnel. The former tended to spend more time on employment relations issues, were more qualified, were more likely to have responsibility for pay and pension and tended to have been in their posts for a shorter period than the latter. HR professionals also appeared to have a greater degree of autonomy, particularly in relation to pay (see Kersley *et al.*, 2006: 70). However, the picture presented by the WERS data with regard to the influence of the HR/personnel function at board level is less optimistic. Specifically, personnel representation at board level displayed a marked decline in the private sector from 1984 onwards – from 76 per cent in 1984 to 71 per cent in 1990 to 64 per cent in 1998 (Millward *et al.*, 2000: 76). While, similarly, the 2004 study found that HR managers were even less likely to be involved in the development of strategic business plans than in 1998 (Kersley *et al.*, 2006). However, it would be wrong to suggest that HR does not have a strategic role in any organizations and in the UK the decline of the strategic role of the HR function was largely confined to smaller firms. Board level representation remained relatively stable in UK based multinational corporations (MNCs), while it actually rose in the largest organizations and those recognizing trade unions (Millward *et al.*, 2000: 77). Indeed, large MNCs such as Yahoo, Procter & Gamble, Pitney Bowes, Goldman Sachs, and General Electric are often cited as truly embracing the potential of HR as a strategic partner within the organization (see Hammonds, 2005).

Notwithstanding the positive examples cited above, some feel that there is a significant gap between the rhetoric and reality of HRM in terms of its strategic contribution. As Hammonds (2005) neatly summarized in his recent contribution *Why we hate HR*:

> After close to 20 years of hopeful rhetoric about becoming 'strategic partners' with a 'seat at the table' where the business decisions that matter are made, most human-resources professionals aren't nearly there. They have no seat, and the table is locked inside a conference room to which they have no key. HR people are, for most practical purposes, neither strategic nor leaders.

Perhaps this outcome has something to do with how performance is conceptualized in the modern firm. This is illustrated in the tension between the hard and soft variants of HRM in the literature: a central theme in this volume is highlighting the contradictions between these two broad understandings of HRM. We argue that for ethical and sustainability reasons, more stakeholder orientated approaches to people management are preferable, with shareholder dominant approaches facing both quotidian micro-crises at firm (encompassing problems of human capital development and commitment) and at macro economic (encompassing problems of excessive speculation-driven volatility, industrial decline, and chronic balance of payments problems) levels. As Stephen Wood discusses in his contribution to the current volume, this search for legitimacy of the HR function has long since been premised on the illumination of a link between HRM and the firm's financial performance, as evidenced by Mark Huselid and colleagues' contributions (Huselid, 1995; Huselid *et al.*, 1997). While acknowledging the importance of the bottom line of financial performance, a broader conceptualization of the HR role in terms of, perhaps, social legitimacy (as advanced by Lees, 1997; Boxall and Purcell, 2008, etc.), emphasizing the moral legitimacy or ethical standing of the firm in the societies in which they operate (Paauwe, 2004), or on governance, 'the establishment of appropriate "rules of the game" involved in successfully managing the employment relationship' (as advanced by Sisson, 2007), may be more appropriate in establishing the credibility of the HR function.

The disciplinary foundations of HRM

Any introduction of HRM would be incomplete without some discussion as to the disciplinary foundations of HRM. Personnel management may have emphasized procedures, but it also emphasized processes, and objectivity. The latter included formal mechanisms for selection and recruitment, and in the deployment of individuals within organizations, that encompassed the use of tools and techniques from psychology such as aptitude testing, manpower planning formula, and the application of theories of motivation based on assumed human needs and concerns. The latter would include, of course, both Maslow's theories of motivation – including the infamous triangular depiction of his hierarchy of needs much beloved by intellectually challenged undergraduates – to more sophisticated developments, extensions and counter-developments. To its proponents, the use of scientific knowledge could ensure that the most suitable workers were allocated to the most appropriate jobs. To its critiques, the use of such tools often constitute 'pseudo science', with very ambitious claims of universal applicability being constantly belied by organizational reality and applied research. Nonetheless, psychological approaches remain influential in serious debates by both academics and practitioners. Many concepts have also been appropriated by pop management 'gurus', whose works, linking bowdlerized theory with homespun wisdom and wilful stupidity, remain alarmingly well represented amongst the 'twit lit' to be found in any airport bookstore.

In contrast, industrial relations has tended to draw on industrial sociology (itself a synthesis of sociology and aspects of thinking from the discipline of engineering), a critical discipline that has sought to understand work and employment in terms of social group formation and dynamics, the role of institutions, and the interface between humans and technology. Particularly influential political economy perspectives analyze work and employment relations from a basic starting point: that the employment contract represents an open-ended exchange with a readily quantifiable cash wage being exchanged for an ultimately indeterminate amount of labour power (Hyman, 1989). Employers will naturally try and quantify the latter, with a view to maximizing the amount of labour extracted, be it through structuring and routinization, measuring of the quantity and quality of output, and regularly reviewing performance, whilst trying to circumscribe wage rates. Employees will in turn naturally seek to maximize wages, and try and limit and/or enhance the pleasure of labour time. To its proponents, such a perspective provides both a realistic assessment of what really goes on in organizations, and critical tools for analysis.

However, aspects of the industrial relations literature – notably in the US – have also drawn on the tools and techniques of rational choice economics to understand dimensions of employment, such as the operation of labour markets. However, scientific claims are often belied by the complexities of social reality and the tendency of both managers and workers to view the world from both an individual and a communitarian (or social) perspective. Nonetheless, rational choice economics' emphasis on 'economic man', of society and organizations as being composed of rational profit maximizing individuals, has infused much of the thinking behind shareholder value conceptualizations of HRM. More recent developments in heterodox economics, that take account of the effects of social collectives (associations) and institutions, have resulted in the application of what has been termed 'socio-economics' to studying people management. In practice, however, proponents of such thinking have tended to be have close links to industrial sociology, with individuals often moving between such groupings.

It is worth noting that those approaching people management from these different perspectives are often antipathetic to each other, in theory if not in practice, and, with some notable exceptions, make little effort to engage with each other's ideas. A scrutiny of HR and related departments in the UK will find some predominantly composed of psychologists, others of industrial sociologists, and a few of rational choice economists. Each publish in their 'own' journals, and are dismissive of the quality of others. For example, the *British Journal of Industrial Relations* is widely held by industrial relations experts and industrial sociologists as one of the finest academic journals – if not the finest – in the field, but is routinely ranked as second flight in journal rankings listings compiled by psychologists.

The structure and content of the book

The book is structured in three distinct sections, each containing contributions of leading academics in the respective areas who engage with the respective topics in a critical way. Following this introduction, Section One, the context of HRM, is intended to introduce readers to some key overarching issues which should frame any discussion on HRM. Chapter 2 by Phil Johnson specifically considers the organizational context of HRM and argues that there is an array of social and economic influences which influence HR practice in organizations.

Chapters 3 and 4 engage with the strategic role of HRM in organizations. Jaap Paauwe and Corine Boon introduce the debate in Chapter 3 while Stephen Wood specifically considers the linkage between HRM and organizational performance in Chapter 4. Chapter 5, by Mick Fryer, engages with the key debates around the ethics underscoring HRM, a topic often neglected in mainstream texts. Similarly, the underexplored topic of outsourcing and the implications from HRM are discussed by Richard Haines. In Chapter 7, Donald Hislop considers the linkage between HRM and knowledge management – a key issue given the posited role of knowledge in developing sustainable competitive advantage. Given the significance of small and medium enterprises in economies globally, in the final chapter in this section Tony Dundon and Adrian Wilkinson consider the role of HRM in SMEs.

Section Two of the text focuses on the practice of HRM. This section reflects the management of HR flows within the organizations and looks at specific aspects of the HR practice. In the opening chapter of the section Rosalind Searle introduces the key debates around recruiting and selecting employees within organizations. Zsuzsa Kipal-Vitai and Geoff Wood then outline the nature of HR planning in organizations and introduce the role of institutions in influencing HR activities within the firm. Chapter 11 by Anthony McDonnell and Paddy Gunnigle considers some key debates which emerge in the context of performance management in organizations. The nature of reward in organizations is considered by Suzanne Richbell and Geoff Wood in Chapter 12. Chapter 13 by Irena Grugulis engages with human resource development, which managers emphasize as a means of developing individual competence in organizations. The final chapter in this section by Gilton Klerck presents a useful counterpoint to the unitary underpinning of HRM through an industrial relations critique of HRM.

The final section of the book examines HRM in an international context. Given the increasing prominence of emerging markets in the global economy, Chapter 15 by Frank M. Horowitz and Kamel Mellahi consider the nature of HRM in these emerging economies. Considering the more general nature of HRM across national borders, Chapter 16 by Chris Brewster and Wolfgang Mayrhofer engages with variation in HRM across national boundaries. The final chapter of the book, by Dave Collings, Hugh Scullion and Deirdre Curran, considers the nature of HRM in multinational corporations.

Conclusion

Around the time of the emergence of HRM many contributors were convinced that HRM was a 'fragile plant' which they predicted would not survive. However, within a short time the signs were that its position was more positive than such an interpretation would suggest (see Storey, 2007); others were quick to dismiss it as a noxious weed. However, despite the unresolved issues around its intellectual boundaries, HRM has endured and gained an important place in managerial practice in organizations, even if as little more than a collective noun to describe many practices. For Keith Sisson (2007: 79) HRM 'appears to have firmly established its supremacy over personnel management'. While another key UK contributor, John Story (2007: 17), eloquently summarizes the position of HRM in modern organizations thus:

> Clearly, HRM is no panacea; no set of employment policies ever will be. But, as a persuasive account (or narrative) of the logic underpinning choice in certain organizations and as an aspiration pathway for others, it is an idea worthy of examination.

We hope that the contributions in the current text go some way towards introducing students to some of the key debates in the field of HRM. Further, the leading edge contributors advance debates in this key area of management practice.

References

Armstrong, M. (1987). Human Resource Management: a case of the emperor's new clothes, *Personnel Management,* 19(8): 30–5.

Beardwell, I. (2001). An introduction to human resource management: strategy, style or outcome, in I. Beardwell and L. Holden (Eds), *Human Resource Management: A Contemporary Approach,* 3rd edition. Harlow: Prentice Hall.

Beer, M., Spector, B., Lawrence, P. R., Quinn Mills, D. and Walton, R. E. (1984). *Managing Human Assets*. New York: Free Press.

Beer, M. and Spector, B. (1985). Corporate wide transformations in human resource management, in R.E. Walton and P.R. Lawrence (eds). *Human Resource Management, trends and challenges.* Boston: Harvard Business School Press.

Blyton, P. and Turnbull, P. (1992). HRM: debates, dilemmas and contradictions, in P. Blyton and P. Turnbull (Eds), *Reassessing Human Resource Management.* London: Sage.

Boxall, P. and Purcell, J. (2008). *Strategy and Human Resource Management,* 2nd edition. Basingstoke: Palgrave.

Brewster, C. (2007). Human Resource Management: European views and perspectives, *International Journal of Human Resource Management*, 18: 769–87.

D'Art, D. (2002). Managing the employment relationship in a market economy, in D. D'Art and T. Turner (Eds), *Irish Employment Relations in the New Economy.* Dublin: Blackhall.

Drucker, P. (1961). *The Practice of Management.* London: Mercury Books.

Dibben, P., James, P., Roper, I. and Wood, G. (2007). Modernising Work in Public Services: Redefining Roles and Relationships in Britain's Changing Workplace. London: Palgrave.

Flanders, A. (1964). *Industrial Relations: What is Wrong with the System.* London: Faber and Faber.

Forbrun, C., Tichy, N. M. and Devanna, M. A. (eds) (1984). *Strategic Human Resource Management*, New York: Wiley.

Guest, D. E. (1987). Human resource management and industrial relations, *Journal of Management Studies*, 24: 503–21.

Guest, D. E. (1990). Human Resource Management and the American Dream, *Journal of Management Studies*, 27: 977–87.

Guest, D. E. (2001). Human resource management and the American dream, *Journal of Management Studies*, 27: 377–97.

Gunnigle, P., Heraty, N. and Morley, M. J. (2006). *Human Resource Management in Ireland,* 3rd edition. Dublin: Gill and Macmillan.

Hammonds, K. H. (2005). Why we hate HR, *Fast Company*, Issue 97, August 2005, page 40.

Hart, T. (1993). Human resource management – time to exorcise the militant tendency, *Employee Relations*, 15(3): 29–36.

Hendry, C. and Pettigrew, A. (1990). Human resource management: An agenda for the 1990s, *International Journal of Human Resource Management*, 1: 17–43.

Huselid, M. A. (1995). The impact of human resource management practices on turnover, productivity, and corporate financial performance, *Academy of Management Journal*, 38: 635–72.

Huselid, M. A., Jackson. S. E. and Schuler, R. S. (1997). Technical and strategic human resource management effectiveness as determinants of firm performance, *Academy of Management Journal,* 40: 171–88.

Hyman, R. (1989). *The Political Economy of Industrial Relations: Theory and Practice in a Cold Climate*. London: Macmillan.

Jacoby, S. M. (1997). *Modern Manors: Welfare Capitalism Since the New Deal*. New Jersey: Princetown University Press.

Kaufman, B. E. (2001). The theory and practice of strategic HRM and participative management: Antecedents in early industrial relations, *Human Resource Management Review*, 11: 505–33.

Kelly, J. (1998). *Rethinking Industrial Relations*. London, Routledge.

Kersley, B., Alpin, C., Forth, J., Bryson, A., Brewley, H., Dix, G. and Oxenbridge, S. (2006). *Inside the Workplace: Findings from the 2004 Workplace Employment Relations Survey*. London: Routledge.

Kochan, T. A., Katz, H. C. and McKersie, R. B. (1986). *The Transformation of American Industrial Relations*. New York: Basic Books.

Lees, S. (1997). HRM and legitimacy market, *International Journal of Human Resource Management*, 8: 226–43.

Legge, K. (1995). *Human Resource Management: Rhetorics and Realities*. Basingstoke: Palgrave Macmillan.

Leidner, R. (2002). Fast Food in the United States of America, in T. Royle & B. Towers (eds) *Labour Relations in the Global Fast Food Industry*. London: Routledge.

Marsden, D. (1999). *A theory of employment systems*. Oxford: Oxford University Press.

Millward, N., Bryson, A. and Forth, J. (2000). *All Change at Work? British Employment Relations 1980–1998, as Portrayed by the Workplace Industrial Relations Surveys Series*. London: Routledge.

Paauwe, J. (2004). *HRM and Performance: Achieving Long Term Viability*. Oxford: Oxford University Press.

Peters, T. J. and Waterman, R. H. Jr. (1982). *In Search of Excellence: Lessons from America's Best Run Companies*. New York: Harper and Row.

Sisson, K. (2007). Facing up to the challenges of success: putting 'governance' at the heart of HRM, in J. Storey (Ed.), *Human Resource Management: A Critical Text*, 3rd edition. London: Thompson Publishing.

Storey, J. (1992). *Developments in the Management of Human Resources*. Oxford: Blackwell.

Storey, J. (2007). Human resource management today: an assessment, in J. Storey (Ed.), *Human Resource Management: A Critical Text,* 3rd edition. London: Thompson Publishing.

Strauss, G. (2001). Human resource management in the USA: correcting some British impressions, *International Journal of Human Resource Management*, 12: 873–97.

Tyson, S. (1985). Is this the very model of a modern personnel manager?, *Personnel Management*, 17(5): 22–5.

Tyson, S. and Fell, A. (1986). *Evaluating the Personnel Function*, London: Hutchinson.

Walton, R. E. and Lawrence, P. R. (eds) (1985). *Human Resource Management, trends and challenges,* Boston: Harvard Business School Press.

Section I

The context of HRM

2 HRM in changing organizational contexts

Phil Johnson

Introduction

Human resource management (HRM) in contemporary organizations is usually prescriptively conceived as an interrelated set of activities aimed at systematically enhancing the task performance of employees in a manner commensurate with the strategic aims of senior management. Simultaneously, numerous researchers (e.g. Langbert, 2002; Townley, 2002; Mueller and Carter, 2005) have noted that how these managerial practices are accomplished varies in response to an array of social and economic influences of which one key source is the broader organizational context in which they take place. Here we are immediately confronted by the often rather optimistically presented forecast that work organizations are progressively changing through the evolution of what are described as post-bureaucratic, flexible, high performance forms of organization and management (HeckshER, 1994; Osbourne and Plastric, 1998; Volberda, 1998; Applebaum *et al.*, 2000; Maravelias, 2003; Hendry, 2006; Josserand *et al.,* 2006). These 'new' organizational forms arise out of the reordering roles, relationships and tasks within organizations at the expense of traditional bureaucratic modes of control over employee task performance. The aim of this chapter is to explore the implications of these developments for the practice of HRM. I shall set the scene for this analysis by first reviewing the key characteristics of the bureaucratic form and the conditions perceived as necessary for bureaucracy to successfully operate. I shall then proceed to consider the pressures faced by contemporary work organizations which are often taken to be undermining the viability of the bureaucratic form and ostensibly encouraging the evolution of the post-bureaucratic. The chapter will then outline the nature of the post-bureaucratic form of organization as presented by various commentators before moving onto the possible implications for HRM praxis. The chapter will conclude by considering alternative views of contemporary organizational change which cast some doubt upon the claims of this post-bureaucratic thesis.

The bureaucratic organizational form

It has long been noted that bureaucratic forms of organization arose on a large scale in Western Europe and the USA during the late nineteenth and early twentieth centuries, and replaced earlier forms of work organization (see Doray, 1988).

Weber (1947) thought that one of the most distinctive features of these bureaucratic administrative systems was a framework of intentionally established and impersonal rules to govern task performance. For Weber, this entailed the subordination of members to the precise calculation of the means by which specific ends might be achieved. Through the exercise of formal rationality, these rules, sometimes expressed as orders from above, are designed by hierarchical superiors who occupy their posts on merit because they have more knowledge, experience and expertise than their subordinates (i.e. they possess formal-legal authority). The creation of a body of rules and procedures, backed up by various means of monitoring, evaluating, rewarding and sanctioning members' compliance, serves to pre-programme members' task performance, remove from operatives any choice or discretion with regard to how to do their work, and increase the probability that perceived organizational requirements dominate that behaviour. The result is that 'the performance of each individual worker is mathematically measured, each man becomes a little cog in the machine (*sic*)' (Weber, 1920: 335). It is this dependency upon hierarchically imposed rules, grounded in rational-legal authority as an epistemologically legitimate means of command and control, that defines bureaucracy as an ideal type of organizational form. The result is that:

> The fully developed bureaucratic apparatus compares with other organizations exactly as does the machine with the non-mechanical modes of production. Precision, speed, unambiguity, knowledge of the files, continuity, discretion, unity, strict subordination, reduction of friction and of material and personal costs – these are raised to the optimum point in the strictly bureaucratic organization . . .
>
> (Weber, 1947: 973)

Whilst Weber thought that the development of bureaucracy was progressive in the sense that it swept away earlier forms of organization which he regarded as irrational, he was fearful of its potential for creating an imprisoning 'iron cage' (1904: 1264) and the danger he saw was that people whose aims were not for the social good could gain command of the bureaucratic machine and misdirect its purpose. Because in bureaucracies the routine application of discipline, through members' mundane compliance with the rules, becomes progressively sanctified and normalized (see Bos and Willmott, 2001) the danger is that means come to dominate ends and people fail to morally evaluate the ends to which their everyday activities in organizations are working towards. The result, for writers such as Bauman (1989), is that bureaucracies can enable, rationalize, distance and render banal the engagement of people in horrific acts such as those associated with the holocaust. In opposition to Bauman's portrayal of bureaucracy as dehumanizing, du Gay has pointed to how 'objectivity' required by the bureaucrat to follow frameworks of rules can result in the virtuous 'trained capacity to treat people as individual cases . . . . so that the partialities of patronage and the dangers of corruption might be avoided' (2000: 42).

As in the case of Taylorism, bureaucratic control of labour processes resulted in job fragmentation and specialization so as to simplify operatives' tasks in order to enable the measurement of effort expended and the administration of cash incentives to encourage greater effort. Hence, it is closely associated with the development of modern forms of work study and industrial engineering which use various techniques for: deriving standard times and methods for undertaking tasks; planning and standardizing work flows with detailed divisions of labour; creating precise job descriptions; the operation of piece-work payment systems (Hales, 1993). Often, as in Fordism and McDonaldization, bureaucratization entails the application of technology (e.g. the assembly-line and the use of single purpose machine tools) to simplify tasks and pre-programme the pace, the sequencing and the nature of labour processes (see Ritzer, 2006) where the rules governing task performance are built into, and operationalized by, the technology in use.

Despite having dominated workplace organization throughout much of the twentieth century, bureaucracy as a form of control over labour processes is considered to be no longer viable by many contemporary commentators (e.g. Heckscher, 1994; Osbourne and Plastrik, 1998; Volberda, 1998; Applebaum *et al.*, 2000; Maravelias, 2003). The underlying rationale for this presumed demise centres upon a key characteristic of bureaucratic superstructures: that they are dependent upon a hierarchical ordering of knowledge, in the form of 'task continuity', as the basis of ration-legal authority. Task continuity (see Offe, 1976) refers to the requirement that in order to be able to write and administer the rules necessary for pre-programming and standardizing their subordinates' tasks, hierarchical superiors must be able to priorly conceptualize what their subordinates should be doing, how, where and when, in order to complete their allocated tasks efficiently and effectively. Only through having expropriated this knowledge can those hierarchical superiors then reconfigure and standardize the execution of tasks by operatives. However, as Perrow (1967) originally argued, where operatives' tasks are complex, unpredictable and unanalyzable, for whatever reason, this knowledge regarding task performance is not readily available for acquisition, reconfiguration and regulation (see also Kallinikos, 2003). Therefore such tasks cannot be readily subjected to bureaucratic hierarchical ordering in order to identify the 'best' way of doing tasks and thereby enable the divorce of task conception from its execution. If such task-discontinuity exists, the argument goes, it becomes necessary to develop alternative forms of control that leave task conceptualization and the identification of how best to undertake tasks to the discretion and intuition of the experienced operative by (re)uniting all aspects of task performance into a coherent whole. This demand for such de-differentiation of tasks resonates often with the motivational language of the 1950s job-redesign literature (e.g. Argyris, 1957), where it was argued that in order to promote organizations that were congruent with the needs of healthy adults, managers had to start treating employees as if they are adults capable of independently taking decisions rather than treating them as passive and dependent, yet potentially wilful, infants in need of constant surveillance and direct bureaucratic control.

In sum, it has been argued that the application of formal rationality to mould collective behaviour is only viable in conditions of environmental stability where there is a relatively constant and homogeneous throughput of goods and services. In these circumstances task requirements and transformation processes are already known and therefore predictable: therefore it is possible to assert control through the use of hierarchically generated rules and procedures that standardize, pre-programme, monitor and enforce required employee task performance (see Ouchi, 1980). Regardless of the specific form of bureaucracy adopted, HRM, or perhaps to be more accurate with regard to these circumstances we should use the term Personnel Management (see Guest, 1991), is geared to servicing bureaucratic requirements. According to Guest (ibid.), in such circumstances, Personnel Management is primarily associated with external and instrumental 'compliance-based' systems of control, largely dependent upon collectively negotiated systems of extrinsic reward, so as to ensure efficiency and cost minimization within a centralized, mechanistic organization structure. Hence the management of personnel within bureaucracies is focused upon: the creation of detailed job descriptions and specifications; the negotiation and implementation of payment systems to support the effort-reward nexus; minimal operative training for undertaking de-skilled tasks; the administration of management development with a focus upon succession planning through the dissemination of requisite technical knowledge and the maintenance of related promotion and career structures; and the procedural regulation of industrial relations in concert with elected employee representatives.

However, an array of theorists have argued that control through the monitoring of subordinates' compliance with bureaucratic procedures and rules becomes increasingly difficult if tasks are, or become, non-routine (Perrow, 1967) and de-differentiated (Clegg, 1990), since the task-behaviour required for efficient and effective task performance becomes, unknowable to, and therefore unpreprogrammable by (Ouchi, 1980), those elevated in the meritocratic hierarchies of rational-legal authority. It is precisely the relatively recent emergence of these conditions that are thought to be threatening the viability of bureaucratic forms of work organization today and hence changing the form that the management of human resources should take.

Changing organizational environments: the demise of bureaucracy?

During the last twenty years, an array of commentators have claimed that the social, economic, political and technological environment in which organizations operate has fundamentally changed. Here it has been argued that the production, distribution, exchange and consumption of goods and services have dramatically accelerated and become increasingly diverse, specialized and temporary: a destabilized 'hypercapitalism' (Rifkind, 2000) characterized by 'intensified risk and reflexivity' (Beck, 1992, 2000a,b) and 'time-space compression' (Castells, 2000a,b, 2004). Regardless of the language used, their uniting axiom is that we have recently entered a new unstable socio-historical configuration which is necessarily pushing organizations towards new designs as managers try to cope with irreversible dramatic changes which are thought to be gaining speed. According to this 'fast capitalism' thesis, the main casualties here are, or should be, bureaucratic organizations, which are seen as incapable of coping efficiently with this new world order (e.g. Heydebrand, 1989; Hastings, 1993; Heckscher, 1994; Castells, 1996; Perone, 1997).

For instance, in his analysis of contemporary Western society Beck argues that we now live in a risk society because society has evolved into something inherently more complex, dynamic, and uncertain (2000b) where, with the continued accumulation of knowledge and its application through scientific and technological innovation, comes an awareness of 'the incalculability of their consequences' (Beck, 1992: 22). At the macro level Beck draws attention to the ecological implications of these developments and the unsettling consequences of globalization (2000b). At the micro level he is more concerned with the need for individuals to reconcile themselves to an enduring sense of biographical insecurity where individuals are required to create, live and take responsibility for their own lives (Beck and Beck-Gernsheim, 2002). At the meso level he draws attention to how institutions are developing in a society dominated by our collective awareness of the unintended consequences its institutions produce. This, in turn, calls into question the legitimacy of those institutions. His view is that social changes are occurring which are 'opening up Weber's bureaucratic iron cage' (2000a: 222) through the requirement to cope reflexively with risk that escapes bureaucratic control and to respond to a more chaotic and uncertain world. However, Beck is cautious here as he suggests that these processes have not seen an end to bureaucracy through its replacement by more responsive institutional configurations. Rather he sees that the displacement and restoration of bureaucratic features are outcomes of on-going political struggles in which institutions attempt to gain and maintain trust in authority and hierarchy.

The rise of post-bureaucracy?

In contrast, much of management literature is less circumspect regarding the institutional outcomes of these processes analyzed by Beck. For instance, as Osbourne and Gaebler summarized it in their highly influential book, bureaucratic organizations 'increasingly fail us' because what is demanded are institutions that are extremely flexible and adaptable, 'that lead by persuasion and incentives rather than commands; that give their employees a sense of meaning and control, even ownership' (1992: 15). The reasoning here relates directly to the argument outlined earlier: that knowledge and information are no longer hierarchically ordered and distributed in contemporary organizations because destabilization has made the world less comprehensible than it once was. Bureaucracies, because of their top-down mode of command and control, are therefore condemned as being sclerotic, especially when faced with contemporary demands for constant innovation and change caused by unstable and unpredictable organizational environments and other disturbances such as rapid technological change. These destabilizing forces are now taken to be endemic and thus affect all organizations

(Kanter, 1989a,b; Peters, 1992; Savage, 1996). Such an organizational situation, the argument goes, requires employees who are capable of using their intuition, discretion and often superior local knowledge to creatively and flexibly deal with unpredictable variations in production and service demands, as and when they arise, rather than merely complying with pre-formulated rules and procedures, or waiting for the direct supervisory commands and permission of managers. The result has been an emerging organizational literature couched largely in terms of post-bureaucracy which has direct implications for how the management of human resources should be undertaken.

Although the language used does vary, a key element of this argument has been to point to both the immanent demise of bureaucratic organizations and to celebrate their requisite replacement by an emergent alternative organizational form that goes 'beyond bureaucracy' (Laffin, 1998), to even 'banish bureaucracy' (Osbourne and Plastrik, 1998) to constitute an ostensibly 'new work order' (Gee *et al.*, 1996) – the post-bureaucracy. This alternative organizational form is presented as a necessary response to conditions of change and uncertainty: a flatter, more networked and flexible organization, wherein 'empowered' employees are vested with high degrees of 'responsible autonomy' and self-management so that they can immediately respond to unpredictable demands in an efficient and effective manner.

Indeed, the term post-bureaucracy is often used to signify a universalistic rupture with the organizational tenets of a bygone age. Here the bureaucratic 'paradigm' is presented as something obsolete and counterproductive rather than contingently viable according to circumstances (e.g. Barzelay with Aramajani, 1992; Hecksher, 1994). This condemnation even sometimes encompasses the moral dimension. For instance the presumed defunct bureaucracies are often presented as also being oppressive and patriarchal, whereas post-bureaucracies are supposed to empower and involve everyone in decision-making and hence are presumed to be inherently morally superior as they are more likely to meet the needs of healthy adults through how they are organized (e.g. Kanter, 1989a,b; Savage, 1996).

Implications of post-bureaucracy for HRM

So the post-bureaucratic organizational form, it is often claimed, liberates employees from the increasingly dysfunctional hierarchical constraints engendered by bureaucracies and enhances their ability to deal with the requirements of an increasingly destabilized working environment (e.g. Adler, 2001). As Castells typically summarizes, post-bureaucratic organizations have to cope with uncertainty through a 'greater need for an autonomous educated worker able and willing to program and decide entire sequences of work' (1996: 241). Thus the intention is to create a workforce capable of adaptation rather than dependent upon routinized repertoires (Stark, 2001) and which is customer-driven yet empowered to make judgements on how to improve customer service and value (Kernaghan, 2000). This is achieved by the creation of functionally flexible high performance work forces (Applebaum *et al.*, 2000; Kalleberg, 2003), where multi-skilled employees are empowered so as to be capable of exercising discretion and creatively cope with discontinuous change by continuously (re)developing their organizational roles in the face of shifting demands (Volberda, 1998; Wood, 1999) made increasingly unpredictable due to the destabilizing disturbances outlined above. This leads us to a central plank of the post-bureaucratic thesis. As Heckscher (1994: 24–88) indicates, this relates to how shared general principles, rather than rules, guide and integrate members' actions. The 'master concept' here is the replacement of bureaucratic controls with 'structures that develop informed consent' where command is replaced by feelings of mutuality and commitment, embedded in organizational processes that produce dialogue, persuasion and trust (see also Osbourne and Plastrik, 1998).

Thus a key characteristic of the post-bureaucracy is employee empowerment. This is usually defined in terms of management ceding to employees the capacity to determine cooperatively certain aspects of their work (Engelhardt and Simmons, 2002; Maravelias, 2003), without waiting for 'permission and direction from top management' (Quinn and Spreitzer, 1997: 45) whilst enabling senior managers to retain overall control. Thus empowerment is aimed at engendering employees' autonomous self-management anchored in a sense of purpose and direction often provided by the systematic dissemination of an entrepreneurial ethic articulated and propagated by senior management in relation to the strategic goals of the enterprise (Black and Porter, 2002). Thus the extension and reconfiguration of employees' roles is restricted to their local involvement in deciding the means by which the strategic agenda set by senior management may be more effectively implemented through their exercise of discretion and control over how tasks are undertaken (see also Hardy and Leiba-O'Sullivan, 1998; Menon, 2001; Kochan and Osterman, 2002; Wallach and Mueller, 2006). Through a range of HRM practices that stimulate, support and sustain self-discipline, self-determination and self-development, whilst instilling a sense of organizational commitment and enhancing motivation, it is claimed that an empowered work force will become a source of competitive advantage through improved employee task-performance (Pfeffer, 1995; Applebaum *et al.*, 2000; Patterson *et al.*, 2004), and job satisfaction (Seibert *et al.*, 2004).

This form of employee participation is not just about broader task-design but is also usually operationalized through the creation of autonomous teams that make decisions, implement them and are held accountable. The result is a workforce that is organized through temporary team-based and project-related hetrarchies (Ozaralli, 2003) that appear and disappear according to shifting requirements (Powell, 2001; Neff and Stark, 2003) with horizontal collaborations to improve communication and speed up decision making (Kellogg *et al.*, 2006). Advocates present such teamworking as a means of facilitating and enhancing amongst employees: lateral communication; information sharing between and within organizational levels; cooperative problem ownership and resolution through critical evaluation of existing organization processes channeled by a commitment to continuous improvement (see Brodbeck, 2002; Ozaralli, 2003; Seibert *et al.*, 2004; Beirne, 2006).

HRM and culture management

However, according to some commentators (e.g. Quinn and Spreitzer, 1997; Mills and Ungson, 2003) cascading power down the organization might create centrifugal tendencies and thereby the need to reconcile a possible loss of management control, with the requirement for integration of a loosely coupled system through ensuring goal congruence. The solution to this perceived problem is presented in the literature as requiring a shift from bureaucratic modalities of control to less obtrusive culturally based, normative, ideational, or clan, modalities as more viable means of disciplining employees by reconstructing employee subjectivity so that it is commensurate with senior management's perceived requirements (see Ouchi, 1980; Volberda, 1998; Adler, 2001; Menon, 2001; Sewell, 2001; Alvesson and Willmott, 2002; Hodgson, 2004; Beirne, 2006). Whilst cultural forms of control are often deployed alongside bureaucratic modalities to create chimerical forms of control, or to reduce reliance upon the bureaucratic (see Hales, 2002) it is the high level of reliance upon culture management as a mode of control that is usually presented as one of the distinguishing characteristics of the post-bureaucratic ideal-type.

As Kunda notes (1992: 2), instead of overtly focusing upon members' actual behaviour, or the outcomes of that behaviour, normative or cultural control is a more hidden and insidious form of formal control which focuses upon the basic value premises which surround members' behaviour and decision making so as to normatively regulate the employee's consciousness through establishing 'intense emotional attachment and the internalization of clearly enunciated company values' (ibid.:10). In a similar vein, Anthony (1994: 92) observes that 'bureaucratic control, from the perspective of the controllers, unfortunately leaves subordinates free, partly because they possess their own cultural defences. So the defences must be broken down'. Once these cultural defences are broken down, informal peer group pressure upon the individual member is redirected and begins to marshal management approved norms (see also Barker, 1999). A possible result is 'an overcoming of the division between the "personal life", values and beliefs of employees and the impersonal demands of corporations for greater productivity and quality' (Willmott, 1993: 523). So if the appropriate values are subscribed to, a common sense of purpose or 'moral involvement', activated through emotion and sentiment, develops which makes the constant surveillance and supervision of employees by managers, as a means of external control, redundant. Ironically, this alternative source of discipline and control over the employee through the management of culture could, in principle, reduce the need for some tiers of management, thereby contributing to the delayering of organizations. Moreover it also has some other significant implications for HRM practice.

An important means by which culture management may be attempted is through the deployment of sophisticated recruitment and selection procedures aimed at pre-emptively controlling the attitudinal and behavioural characteristics of new organizational members (Townley, 1994; Hardy and Lieba-O'Sullivan, 1998; Kochan and Osterman, 2002; Brannan and Hawkins, 2007). Thus, through the use of assessment centres, psychometric tests, personal history inventories and indices of loyalty, etc., a systematic attempt is made to ensure that the attitudinal and behavioural characteristics of new employees match the prescribed organizational culture, thereby trying to exclude the introduction of alternative sources of social influence deriving from, for instance, communities outside the organization, trade unions, professional groupings and so on. Simultaneously redundancy may be used to eliminate alternative values by removing those employees who are seen to be unable to, or unwilling to, embrace the specified culture (Dobson, 1989). Besides attempting to alter the composition of the workforce through the use of recruitment, selection and redundancy, there may also be concerted attempts by management to influence the value premises of members' behaviour by trying to restructure their attitudes and beliefs through the use of an array of related HRM practices (see Hope and Hendry, 1995; Guest, 1998). For instance, induction, training, appraisal and reward systems may be formally realigned to disseminate and reinforce displays of culturally acceptable behaviour.

Thus, HRM praxis may play a key role in attempting to resolve the control-consent dilemma created by employee empowerment programmes and their diffusion of some elements of management prerogative downwards, through directing employees' exercise of initiative and self-management through the development of 'responsible autonomy' that harnesses 'their loyalty to the firm's ideals (the competitive struggle) ideologically' (Friedman, 1977: 5; 1990; Harley, 2005). In this fashion, the control-consent dilemma is notionally resolved through the delineation of how, where and when employees exercise their autonomy and power through reconstructing their subjectivity in line with management's requirements (see Elemes and Smith, 2001; Knights and McCabe, 2001; Maravelias, 2003). Where this strategy is effective, the means by which employees constitute their own identities is merged with how they exercise self-regulation and, as Miller and Rose (1990: 26) suggest, 'the 'autonomous' subjectivity of the productive individual . . . [becomes] . . . a central economic resource'. The result is that employee performance evaluation then becomes a (contentious) matter of assessing members' organization behaviour through reference to the observable manifestation of sanctioned cultural mores and sentiments in the performance of their tasks and their relationships with other members, customers, clients, and so on.

By extending employees' participation in deciding the means by which strategic decisions are implemented certain management functions previously usurped through the development of bureaucracy are reappropriated by operatives and the traditional division between managerial and other forms of labour becomes blurred. No longer can management practice be founded upon their authoritative articulation of (usually incalculable and inevitably dysfunctional) rules aimed at the direct control of subordinates' work-place behaviours. Instead, what is required are managers capable of leading through establishing horizontal communication and dialogue with subordinates in mutually therapeutic relationships (Tucker, 1999). Therefore, new management roles such as coach (Kalinauckas and King, 1994), mentor (Garvey and Alred, 2001) and co-learner

(Marquardt, 1996) become crucial roles which require managers with a knowledge and skill base quite different to those required by bureaucracies (see Hendry, 2006).

Here there is also an increasing emphasis upon leadership at the expense of management, where leadership is construed in terms of articulating, promulgating and inculcating in others an organizational vision and mission, often driven by some form of strategic analysis of the 'big picture' that confronts the 'business' (see e.g. Dubrin, 2001). In essence, leaders are presented as strategic visionaries who courageously anticipate and initiate changes through communicating and sharing their visions and enthusing their subordinates. Management, on the other hand, is recast and construed as being much more mundane, if not virtually banal. Management is apparently now about interpreting the leaders' vision and practically implementing it through various organizational processes whilst maintaining and enhancing employees' productivity. So whilst leadership is the primary focus of senior managers, all individual managers are expected, to some degree, to undertake aspects of both leadership and management in performing their organizational roles. As Dubrin starkly puts it 'without being led as well as managed, organizations face the threat of extinction' (2001: 4).

Pattinson (1997) describes how the ascription of a special leadership status to managers often entails the deployment of quasi-religious metaphors whereby senior managers are somehow endowed with mystical capacity and of being akin to latter-day prophets – charismatic figures who have a mission to pursue unquestionable goals and inspire other organizational members to change their ways. Such a view sets the (senior) manager at the centre stage of organizations as a crucial influence upon organizational culture and performance: 'transformational' leaders who can invoke, and energetically disseminate to 'followers', a compelling image of an idealized future state for their organizations which, through stimulating emotional attachment to, and trust in, the leader, inspires followers to become highly committed to the leader's vision and prepared to make drastic personal sacrifices on its behalf (see Tourish and Pinnington, 2002).

Although the articulation of these new modes of management and leadership may entail the search for new bases of legitimacy when rational-legal authority is threatened, the ostensible reason for this reconfiguration is to support and facilitate the hallmarks of the post-bureaucracy: the participation of self-directed employees in decision-making and the dissemination of culturally approved values as a form of commitment-based control. As Hope and Hendry have observed, the required management behaviour also demands 'an investment of "self" rather dogged mimicry of behaviour and values set down in the corporate handbook. If the self is not engaged then power is reduced, for the required behaviour is distanced from the person itself' (1995: 63). Moreover, employees may be alert to any disparity between management's cultural rhetoric and their apparent everyday behaviour, to the extent that employees may use the espoused values underpinning prescribed cultural change to challenge and rectify the inauthenticity signified by such lapses in managers' performance of their corporate script (see Linstead, 1999). The dissemination of the prescribed culture often entails reorganization of the workplace to ensure that those with the required values (at least at the public level of testimony) are in positions of influence as role models, so that they can communicate with them both symbolically in their everyday leadership (see Grugulis *et al.*, 2000) and through their establishment of corporate rites, ceremonies, slogans, stories and myths that in effect tell employees how they should behave. Other processes of communication and social interaction might, as Dent (1995) observed, entail some spatial reorganization by physically locating managers close to those they wish to influence so as to enable them to informally nurture and sustain the desired cultural changes. Other means of cultural dissemination and maintenance might include team briefings, quality circles, house journals and the organization of various social activities that entail 'cultural extravaganza' (Deal and Kennedy, 1982: 74) inside and outside the workplace.

As I have discussed above, employee empowerment, the evolution of new managerial roles, etc., supported by an array of HRM practices, may be seen as potential post-bureaucratic solutions to the uncertainties created by an array of destabilizing disturbances. However, so far I have focused upon one key means of responding to these demands through the development of one type of 'labour-led' flexibility, where the emphasis is upon the development of a functionally-flexible and multi-skilled internal workforce capable of exercising their discretion so as to cope with high degrees of task uncertainty. An alternative and often complementary way of variably using labour is via the external labour market and relates to the ease with which the numbers of particular employees can be varied to meet fluctuations in demand through the use of temporary employment contracts (Kalleberg, 2001, 2003). The result may be a division of the workforce into 'peripheral' numerically flexible temporary employees, organized around a numerically stable 'core' of permanent employees, willing and able to learn new skills according to requirements. Thus, increasing levels of internal and external uncertainty, by demanding various forms of flexibility in organizations, may result in a mixture of bureaucratic and post-bureaucratic modalities of control within one organization. For instance, bureaucratic modalities may be still appropriate for numerically flexible peripheries doing relatively unskilled tasks, since the uncertainty of their tasks is around (e.g. seasonal) fluctuations in the amount of this work, rather than the nature of the tasks themselves being unpredictable. In contrast, the functionally flexible cores may exhibit 'post-bureaucratic' modalities. However, an alternative to labour-led flexibility is the market-led flexibility engendered by 'network organizations' (Miles and Snow, 1986) which have been associated with post-bureaucratic developments. These phenomena are characterized by disaggregated operations spread between loosely coupled clusters of firms distributed along the value chain, which are co-ordinated primarily through contractual arrangements for goods and services. Therefore the development of networks entail to varying degrees: the 'unbundling' of large vertically integrated organizations through 'downsizing' to a core of high added value competencies, which include a brokerage role for co-ordinating the network and the 'outsourcing' or 'externalization' of other activities that can be done more efficiently by contractors.

Here it is the network as a whole which is flexible rather than the individual participatory organization since it is the mixture of goods and services available which can be altered by varying the combination of participants by the broker. Thus networks are seen to constitute 'lean', 'flexible', low cost organization structures particularly suited to the ostensible demands of current organizational environments by 'unblocking' organizational learning, innovation and change through the creation of more porous interfaces with their environments (Child and McGrath, 2001; Josserand, 2004). Relationships with, and control over, contractors to whom specific tasks have been outsourced may vary according to the nature of the forms of contractual network governance in place (Powell, 1990).

Conclusions

As I have attempted to demonstrate in this chapter, at the heart of the post-bureaucratic thesis are issues of control and changes in how management exercise direction, surveillance and discipline over subordinates in response to increasing level of uncertainty experienced in organizations caused by an array of destabilizing disturbances. The thesis boldly claims that there is an ongoing shift in control modalities from those associated with the 'direct' control of subordinates to those more associated with the establishment of 'responsible autonomy'. This shift in control is usually idealized as the development of empowered, self-regulated members who; having internalized management derived cultural norms, then proceed to exercise 'commitment-based' self-control in a manner commensurable with senior management's strategic aims and objectives. These processes have direct implications for the practice of HRM as control moves towards purposefully shaping the identities and attitudes of employees, albeit often in a reactive manner (see e.g. Evans, 1999). This shift in control is illustrated and summarized by Table 2.1.

In this chapter the possible shift from bureaucratic to post-bureaucratic modes of organization and HRM has been presented largely as a demand that has to be accommodated if we accept that increasing levels of turbulence and uncertainty

Table 2.1 Bureaucracy and post-bureaucracy compared

Bureaucracy	*Post-bureaucracy*
Vertical hierarchy	Delayered with team-based hetrarchies
Low trust chains of command	High trust, dialogue/persuasion
Search for predictability and efficiency	Search for flexibility and effectiveness through members' commitment and empowerment
Low discretion tasks: obedience valued	High discretion tasks: creativity valued
Control through calculative compliance via rules and incentives	Control through responsible autonomy based on principles anchored in moral involvement
Leadership based rational-legal authority	Learning-leadership often based on charisma

mean that many organizational settings are becoming too complex and ambiguous to be managed through the use of bureaucratic modalities of control. Here there is a tendency in much of the contemporary literature to present post-bureaucracy as unproblematically superior because it is taken to generate, through emotional and sentimental manipulation, internalized self-discipline expressed as feelings of commitment to 'the organization': employee behavioural outcomes which bureaucratic forms of control, with their focus upon compliance to external sources reward and punishment, cannot systematically deliver. So, in relation to its bureaucratic alternatives, post-bureaucracy is often presented as generally, rather than contingently, more effective and efficient because they can reduce bureaucratic impedimenta, flatten hierarchies, cut administrative costs, increase productivity and, crucially increase the agility and responsiveness of organizations to an increasingly destabilized business environment.

Here there is a danger of overly rationalizing management decision making and the choices that are made with regard to different organizational forms: that senior managers, by deploying economically rational calculation, seek to consciously seek out and implement efficiency-optimizing solutions to secure unambiguous organizational goals in the discharge of their fiduciary responsibilities to shareholders, in the case of private sector (or elected representatives in the case of the public sector). Such assumptions about management behaviour are dubious as they treat managers as if they were all-knowing, yet servile, agents of capital's interests – a characterization that has been widely questioned (see e.g. Jackall, 1988). A result of this characterization is that description of changes in organizational form and prescription about these processes get entangled. Another result is that it theoretically explains the evolution of post-bureaucracy as a necessary, progressive, response to demands arising from the need for efficiency and competitive advantage in changing organizational circumstances propelled by the destabilizing disturbances noted above.

In contrast, Barley and Kunda (1992) eschew such determinism by pointing to how the propagation of managerial 'ideologies of control' come in repeated historical 'surges'. With reference to North America, Barley and Kunda use historical information to document how, since the 1870s, management discourse has oscillated five times between what they call normative and rational rhetoric of control. Here rational control is defined as bureaucratizing work processes and a utilitarian appeal to what was construed as the employee's economically rational self-interest. Rational modes of theorizing surged from 1900 to 1923 with Scientific Management, and again with Systems Rationalization from 1955 to 1980. In contrast normative control is defined as the idea that managers could regulate employee behaviour by attending to their thoughts and emotions through some form of culture management. Normative modes of theorizing surged from 1870 to1900 with Industrial Betterment, again from 1925 to 1955 with Human Relations and again from 1980 to the (then) present day with Organization Culture and Quality. During each surge to prominence, the particular ideology being propagated is considered to be at the cutting edge of managerial thought, *if not necessarily* at the level of management practice.

Barley and Kunda proceed to argue that the different ideologies of control themselves express culturally based assumptions which have conceptually constrained the imagination of managerial community to what amounts to a dichotomy. However they demonstrate how economic cycles have determined when new surges in management theorizing happen. While each surge in management theorizing was championed by specific groups 'whose interests were thereby advanced' (ibid.: 393), they conclude that in practice rationalist thinking is usually dominant, but normative factors receive more attention at certain points in time. Generally they hypothesize that '. . . one might argue that rational rhetoric should surge when profitability seems most tightly linked to the management of capital. Conversely, normative rhetoric should surge when profitability seems to depend more on the management of labour' (ibid.: 389). They suggest that managers will be 'attracted to rhetorics that emphasize rational procedures and structures when profits hinge easily on capital investment and automation' (ibid.: 391) but will shift to normative rhetorics, emphasizing the motivation of labour, when returns on capital seem to be in decline during economic down swings. However, they also emphasize that they do not claim that rational and normative ideologies alternately become dominant according to economic cycles, rather the rational has always tended to be theoretically prevalent and more closely linked to actual managerial practice. Moreover rationalism will sometimes fuel an interest in, and be tempered by, normative theorizing, as it may be seen to provide a means of reducing employees' negative reactions to Scientific Management or Fordism and other attempts at bureaucratizing labour processes.

Hence it is important to temper any consideration of the emergence of new organizational forms and their impact upon HRM with the possibility that we may be witnessing waves of shifting rhetoric, that confuse prescription and description, whose relationship to organizational praxis is ambiguous yet nevertheless legitimize and possibly energize an evolving array of HRM practices that, when implemented, impact upon social relationships within the workplace. Perhaps it is here that Beck's (2000a) caution, referred to earlier, gains even more power when he warns that the displacement, retention and restoration of bureaucratic organizational features are outcomes of an on-going political struggle in which vested interests attempt to maintain and justify our trust in authority and hierarchy.

References

Adler, P. (2001). Market, hierarchy and trust: the knowledge economy and the future of capitalism, *Organization Science*, 12, March–April: 215–34.

Alvesson, M. and Willmott, H. (2002). Identity regulation as organizational control: producing the appropriate individual, *Journal of Management Studies,* 39(5): 619–44.

Anthony, P. (1994). *Managing Culture.* Buckingham: Open University Press.

Applebaum, E., Bailey, T., Berg, P. and Kalleberg, A. L. (2000). *Manufacturing advantage; why high-performance work systems Pay off.* Ithaca, NY: ILR Press.

Argyris, C. (1957). *Personality and Organization.* New York, NY: Harper and Row.

Barley, S. R. and Kunda, G. (1992). Design and devotion: surges of rational and normative ideologies of control in managerial discourse, *Administrative Science Quarterly,* 37: 363–99.

Barker, J. R. (1999). *The Discipline of Teamwork: Participation and Concertive Control*, London: Sage.

Barzelay, M. with Armajani, B. J. (1992). *Breaking Through Bureaucracy*, Berkeley, CA: University of California Press.

Bauman, Z. (1989). *Modernity and the Holocaust*. London: Polity Press.

Beck, U. (1992). *Risk Society*. Sage: London.

Beck, U. (2000a). *Risk Society Revisited. Theory Politics and Research*, edited by B. Adam, U. Beck and J. van Loon. London: Sage.

Beck, U. (2000b). *What is Globalization?* Cambridge: Polity Press.

Beck, U. and Beck-Gernsheim, E. (2002). *Individualization*. London: Sage.

Beirne, M. (2006). *Empowerment and Innovation*. Cheltenham: Edward Elgar.

Black, S. and Porter, L. (2002). *Management: Meeting New Challenges*. New York, NY: Prentice-Hall.

Bos, R. T. and Willmott, H. (2001). Towards post dualistic business ethics: interweaving reason and emotion in working life, *Journal of Management Studies*, 38(6): 769–93.

Brannan, M. J. and Hawkins, B. (2007). London calling: selection as a pre-emptive strategy for cultural control, *Employee Relations*, 29(2): 178–91.

Brodbeck, P. (2002). Implications for organizational design: teams as pockets of excellence, *Team Performance Management: An International Journal*, 8(1/2): 21–38.

Castells, M. (1996). *The Rise of the Network Society*. Malden, MA: Blackwell.

Castells, M. (2000a). *The Information Age: Economy Society and Culture: Volume I The Rise of the Network Society*. Oxford: Blackwell.

Castells, M. (2000b). *The Information Age: Economy Society and Culture: Volume II End of Millenium*. Oxford: Blackwell.

Castells, M. (2004). *The Information Age: Economy Society and Culture: Volume III The Power of Identity*. Oxford: Blackwell.

Child, J. and McGrath, R. (2001). Organizations unfettered: organizational form in an information intensive economy, *Academy of Management Journal*, 44(6): 1135–48.

Clegg, S. R. (1990). *Modern Organizations: Organization Studies in the Postmodern World*. London: Sage.

Deal, T. and Kennedy, A. (1982). *Corporate Cultures: The Rites and Rituals of Corporate Life*. Reading, MA: Addison–Wesley.

Dent, M. (1995). *The New National Health Service: a case of postmodernism?, Organization Studies,* 16(5): 875–99.

Dobson, P. (1989). Changing culture, *Empoyment Gazette*, 647–50.

Doray, B. (1988). *A Rational Madness: from Taylorism to Fordism*. London: Free Association Books.

Dubrin, A. (2001). *Leadership. Research Findings, Practice and Skills,* Boston, MA: Houghton Mifflin.

du Gay, P. (2000). *In Praise of Bureaucracy: Weber, Organization and Ethics*. London: Sage.

Elemes, M. and Smith, C. (2001). Marked by the spirit: contextuatizing workplace empowerment in American spiritual ideals, *Journal of Applied Behavioural Science*, 37(1): 33–50.

Englehardt, M. and Simmons, P. (2002). Organizational flexibility for a changing world, *Leadership and Organizational Development Journal,* 23(3): 113–21.

Evans, P. A. L. (1999). HRM on the edge: a duality perspective, *Organization*, 6(2): 325–38.

Friedman, A. (1977). *Industry and Labour*. London: Macmillan.

Friedman, A. (1990). Management strategies, techniques and technology: towards a complex theory of the labour process, in D. Knights and H. Willmott (Eds), *Labour Process Theory.* London: Macmillan.

Garvey, B. and Alred, G. (2001). Mentoring and the tolerance of complexity, *Futures*, 33: 519–530.

Gee, J. P., Hull, G. and Lankshear, C. (1996). *The New Work Order*. St Leonards, NSW: Allen and Unwin.

Grugulis, I., Dundon, T. and Wilkinson, A. (2000). Culture control and the 'culture manager': Employment practices in a consultancy, *Work Employment and Society,* 14(1): 97–116.

Guest, D. E. (1991). Personnel management: the end of orthodoxy, *British Journal of Industrial Relations*, 29(2): 149–75.

Guest, D. E. (1998). Beyond HRM: commitment and the contract culture, in P. Sparrow and M. Marchington (Eds), *Human Resource Management: the New Agenda.* London: Pitman Publishing.

Hales, C. (1993). *Managing Through Organization*. London: Routledge.

Hales, C. (2002). Bureaucracy-lite and continuities in managerial work, *British Journal of Management*, 13: 51–66.

Hardy, C. and Leiba-O'Sullivan, S. (1998). The power behind empowerment: implications for research and practice, *Human Relations*, April: 451–83.

Harley, B. (2005). Hope or hype: high performance work systems, in B. Harley, J. Hyman, and P. Thompson (Eds), *Participation and Democracy*. Basingstoke: Palgrave Macmillan.

Hastings, C. (1993). *The New Organization*. London: McGraw-Hill.

Heckscher, C. (1994). Defining the post-bureaucratic type, in C. Hechsher and J. Hendry (2006), Educating managers for post-bureaucracy: the role of the Humanities, *Management Learning,* 37(3): 267–81.

Hendry, J. (2006). Educating Managers for Post-Bureaucracy, *Management Learning*, 37: 267–81.

Heydebrand, W. (1989). New organizational forms, *Work Employment and Society*, 16(3): 323–57.

Hodgson, D. E. (2004). Project work, *Organization*, 11(1): 81–100.

Hope, V. and Hendry, J. (1995). Corporate culture – Is it relevant for organizations of the 1990s? *Human Resource Management Journal*, 5(4): 61–73.

Jackall, R. (1998). *Moral Mazes: The World of Corporate Managers*. Oxford: Oxford University Press.

Josserand, E. (2004). *The Network Organization: The Experience of Leading French Multinationals*. Cheltenham: Edward Elgar.

Josserand, E., Teo, S. and Clegg, S. R. (2006). From bureaucratic to post-bureaucratic: the difficulties of transition, *Journal of Organizational Change Management*, 19(1): 54–64.

Kalinauckas, P. and King, H. (1994). *Coaching: Realising the Potential*. London: Institute of Personnel and Development.

Kalleberg, A. L. (2001). 'Organizing flexibly: the flexible firm in a new century', *British Journal of Industrial Relations*, 39(4): 479–504.

Kalleberg, A. L. (2003). Flexible firms and market segmentation: effects of workplace restructuring on jobs and workers, *Work and Occupations*, 30(2): 154–75.

Kallinikos, J. (2003). The social foundations of the bureaucratic order: bureaucracy and its alternatives in the age of contingency, *Organization*, 10(4).

Kanter, R. M. (1989a). The new managerial work, *Harvard Business Review*, Nov-Dec: 85–92.

Kanter, R. M. (1989b). *When Giants Learn to Dance: Mastering The Challenges of Strategy, Management and Careers in the 1990s*. London: Unwin Hyman.

Kellogg, K. C., Orlikowski, W. J. and Yates, J. (2006). Life in the trading zone: structuring coordination across boundaries in post-bureaucratic organizations, *Organization Science*: 17(1): 22–44.

Kernaghan, K. (2000). The post-bureaucratic organization and public service values, *International Review of Administrative Sciences*, 66(1): 91–104.

Knights, D. and McCabe, D. (2001). 'Ain't misbehavin?' Opportunities for resistance under new forms of quality management, *Sociology*, 34(3): 421–36.

Kochan, T. and Osterman, P. (2002). The mutual gains enterprise, in C. Mabey, G. Salamon, and J. Storey, *Strategic Human Resource Management*. London: Sage.

Kunda, G. (1992). *Engineering Culture: Control and Commitment in a High Tech Corporation*. Philadelphia: Temple University Press.

Laffin, M. (1998). Beyond bureaucracy: understanding recent changes in the public sector professions, in M. Laffin (Ed.), *Beyond Bureaucracy? New Approaches in Public Sector Management*. Aldersot: Avebury.

Linstead, S. (1999). Managing culture, in L. Fulop and S. Linstead (Eds), *Management: A Critical Text*. Basingstoke: Macmillan Press.

Langbert, M. (2002). Continuous improvement in the history of human resource management, *Management Decision*, 40(10): 932–7.

Maravelias, C. (2003). Post-bureaucracy – control through professional freedom, *Journal of Organizational Change Management*, 16(5): 547–66.

Marquardt, M. J. (1996). *Building the Learning Organization: A Systems Approach to Quantum Improvement and Global Success*. New York: McGraw-Hill.

Menon, S. T. (2001). Employee Empowerment: An Integrative Psychological Approach, *Applied Psychology: An International Review*, 50(1): 153–80.

Miles, R. E. and Snow, C. C. (1986). Organizations: new concepts for new forms, *California Management Review*, 28(3): 62–73.

Miller, P. and Rose, N. (1990). Governing economic life, *Economy and Society*, 19(1): 1–31.

Mills, P. K. and Ungson, G. (2003). Reassessing the limit of structural empowerment: organization constitutions trusts controls, *Academy of Management Review*, 28(1): 143–51.

Mueller, F. and Carter, C. (2005). The HRM project and managerialism: or why some discourses are more powerful than others, *Journal of Organizational Change Management*, 18(4): 369–82.

Neff, G. D. and Stark, D. (2003). Permanently beta: responsive organization in the internet era, in P. Howard and S. Jones (Eds), *Society On-line: The Internet in Context*. Thousand Oaks CA: Sage.

Offe, C. (1976). *Industry and Inequality*. London: Edward Arnold.

Osbourne, D. and Gaebler, T. (1992). *Re-inventing Government*. Reading, MA: Addison-Wesley.

Osbourne, D. and Plastric, D. (1998). *Banishing Bureaucracy: Five Strategies for Reinventing Government*. New York, NY: Plume.

Ouchi, W. G. (1980). Markets, bureaucracies and clans, *Administrative Science Quarterly*, March: 129–41.

Ozaralli, N. (2003). Effects of transformational leadership on empowerment and team effectiveness, *Leadership and Organizational Development Journal*, 24(5/6): 335–44.

Patterson, M. G., West, M. A. and Wall, T. D. (2004). Integrating manufacturing, empowerment and company performance, *Journal of Organizational Behaviour*, 25: 641–65.

Pattinson, S. (1997). *The Faith of Managers*. London: Cassell.

Perrone, V. (1997). The coevolution of contexts and structures: the N-form, in T. Clark (Ed.), *Organization Behaviour: Essays in the Honour of Derek S. Pugh*. Aldershot, Hants: Ashgate.

Perrow, C. A. (1967). A framework for the comparative analysis of organizations, *American Sociological Review*, 32: 194–208.

Peters, T. (1992). *Liberation Management*. London: Macmillan.

Pfeffer, J. (1995). *Competitive Advantage Through People*. Boston, MA: Harvard Business School Press.

Powell, W. W. (1990). Neither market nor Hierarchy: Network Forms of Organization, in B. Straw (ed) *Research in Organization Behaviour*. Greenwich, CT: JAI Press.

Quinn, R. E. and Spreitzer, G. M. (1997). The road to empowerment: seven questions every leader should consider, *Organizational Dynamics*, Autumn: 37–49.

Rifkind, J. (2000). *The Age of Access: The New Culture of Hypercapitalism where All Life is a Paid-for Experience*. New York: Tarcher Putnam.

Ritzer, G. (2006). *McDonaldization: The Reader*, 2nd edition. Thousand Oaks, CA: Pine Forge Press.

Savage, C. (1996). *5th Generation Management, Cocreating through Virtual Enterprising, Dynamic Teaming and Knowledge Networking*. Boston, MA: Butterworth Heineman.

Seibert, S., Silver, S. and Randolph, W. (2004). Taking power to the next level: a multiple-level model of empowerment performance and satisfaction, *Academy of Management Journal*, 47: 332–50.

Sewell, G. (2001). What goes around, comes around: inventing a mythology of teamwork and empowerment, *Journal of Applied Behavioural Science*, 37(1): 70–89.

Stark, D. (2001). Ambiguous assets for uncertain environments: Hierarchy in post-socialist firms, in P. DiMaggio (Ed.), *The 21st Century Firm: Changing Organization in International Perspective*. Princeton NJ: Princeton University Press.

Tourish, D. and Pinnington, A. (2002). Transformational leadership, corporate cultism and the spirituality paradigm: an unholy trinity in the workplace?, *Human Relations*, 55(2): 147–72.

Townley, B. (1994). *Reframing Human Resource Management: Power, Ethics and the Subject at Work*. London: Sage.

Townley, B. (2002). Managing with modernity, *Organization*, 9(4): 549–74.

Tucker, J. (1999). *The Theraputic Corporation*. New York: Oxford University Press.

Volberda, H. (1998). *Building the Flexible Firm: How to Remain Competitive*. Oxford: Oxford University Press.

Wallach, V. A. and Mueller, C. W. (2006). Job characteristics and organizational predictors of psychological empowerment within human service organizations: an exploratory study, *Administration in Social Work*, 30(1): 95–113.

Weber, M. (1920). Some consequences of bureaucracy, in L. A. Coser and B. Rosenberg (Eds) (1989), *Sociological Theory, A Book of readings*, 5th edition. Prospect Heights, IL: Waveland Press.

Weber, M. (1947). *The Theory of Social and Economic Organization*. New York: Oxford University Press.

Willmott, H. C. (1993). Strength is ignorance; slavery is freedom: Managing culture in modern organizations, *Journal of Management Studies*, 30(4): 515–52.

Wood, S. (1999). Human resource management and performance, *International Journal of Management Reviews*, 1: 367–413.

3 Strategic HRM

A critical review

Jaap Paauwe and Corine Boon

Introduction

Since the development of Human Resource Management (HRM) as a field of scientific research in the 1980s, many changes have taken place in this area. An important development has been the integration of HRM into the strategic management process. This growing area of research has been labelled strategic HRM in that it emphasizes the strategic role of HRM in meeting business objectives (Delery, 1998). Strategic HRM draws attention to the contribution of HRM to the performance of organizations, in other words, what is the added value of HRM for organizations? For achieving this, the integration between strategy and HRM is emphasized; the basic premise underlying strategic HRM is that organizations adopting a particular strategy require HR practices that may differ from those required by organizations adopting alternative strategies (Delery and Doty, 1996), assuming an important link between organizational strategy and HR practices that are implemented in that organization.

Therefore, we need to make sure that we shed some clear light on the issue of whether strategy matters (either at corporate or business level) and in what sense does it matter to (the effectiveness of) HRM. In this chapter, we start out to give an introduction about strategy and different strategy approaches that have been used. Then, we will explain the link between strategy and HRM, and the concept of 'strategic fit' is introduced. As existing approaches to strategic fit have been highly criticized, we will present an alternative approach in this chapter, taking into account implementation and dynamics besides traditional approaches focused on processes and content of strategy and HRM. This chapter concludes with a step towards a synthesis of strategic HRM research in a contextually based human resource theory (CBHRT), taking into account the different perspectives and interests of different stakeholders involved in strategic HRM.

Strategy

In the strategy field, many different meanings of strategy are used, resulting in an enormous variety of approaches to strategy. The most well known of these and still dominantly present in all the strategic management textbooks, is the rational planned approach, also referred to as the so-called classical approach. Its main characteristics show resemblance with the military setting (based on Mintzberg, 1990 and Whittington, 1993):

- A controlled and conscious process of thought directly derived from the notion of rational economic man;
- For which the prime responsibility rests with the chief executive officer;
- Who is in charge of a fully formulated, explicit and articulated decision-making process;
- In which there is a strict distinction between formulation and implementation.

The classical approach to strategy places great confidence in the readiness and capacity of managers to adopt profit-maximizing strategies through rational long-term planning, as Whittington (1993: 17) critically remarks. In the early notions on strategic HRM we find a striking similarity with the above-mentioned premises of the classical approach. For example Hendry and Pettigrew (1986) state that the call or plea for strategic HRM implies:

- The use of planning
- A coherent approach to the design and management of personnel systems based on an employment policy and manpower strategy, often underpinned by a philosophy
- HRM activities are matched to some explicit strategy
- The people of the organization are seen as a strategic resource for achieving competitive advantage,

In reality, however, the concept of strategy has many different meanings. Mintzberg was one of the first to demonstrate this. He distinguished five meanings of the strategy concept (based on Mintzberg, 1987 and see also Mintzberg *et al.*, 1998):

- Strategy as a plan (intended); a direction, a guide or course of action into the future, which implies looking ahead
- Strategy as a pattern (realized); consistency in behaviour over time, which implies looking at past behaviour
- Strategy as a ploy; a specific manoeuvre intended to outwit an opponent or competitor
- Strategy as a position; the way in which the organization positions its products and or services in particular markets in order to achieve a competitive advantage
- Strategy as a perspective; an organization's fundamental way of doing things, the way in which the members of the organization perceive their environment, their customers, etc.

In order to integrate the many available perspectives on strategy, Whittington (1993) proposes a categorization, distinguishing on the one hand the kind of

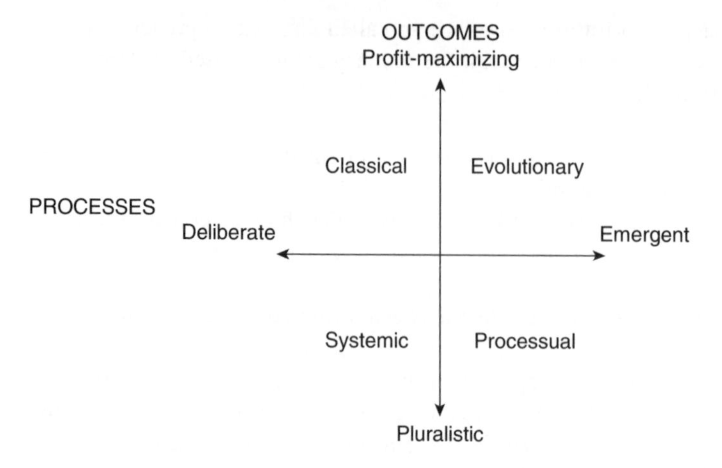

Figure 3.1 Generic perspectives on strategy (*Source*: Whittington (1993). Reprinted with permission of Thomson Publishing Services).

outcomes of strategy and on the other hand the *processes* by which the strategy has been made. Figure 3.1 gives a schematic representation on the generic perspectives on strategy.

The vertical axis indicates whether a strategy is aimed at producing profit-maximizing outcomes or also allows for more diverse/pluralist outcomes. The horizontal axis focuses on the way in which the strategy process takes place with, on the one hand, deliberate calculation and reasoning and, on the other hand, a more emergent approach based on coincidence, muddling through, etc. (Whittington, 1993). Based on Paauwe (2004) we link the different approaches of Whittington to relevant aspects of strategic HRM.

The *classic* approach considers strategy as a rational process of deliberate calculation and analysis, designed to maximize long-term advantage. In the HRM area this approach simply implies that the role of the HR-function is to maximize the contribution of human assets in order to achieve corporate goals. It encompasses approaches by which we attempt to link individual attitude and role behaviour to organizational performance in a logical and rational manner (see, for example Huselid, 1995; Koch and McGrath, 1996). This approach is especially popular in the US in order to justify that the chief HRM officer should have a seat on the board, by demonstrating that people make a difference to profit and generate added value.

The *evolutionary* approach considers businesses '... like the species of biological evolution: competitive processes ruthlessly select out the fittest for survival' (Whittington, 1993: 3–4). It is the market that decides and not the manager. The only thing the manager can do is to adapt the organization as optimally as possible to the demands of the market place. If this is not done, the organization will not survive. In the field of HRM we recognize this perspective in HR managers who want to keep their human resources as flexible as possible, embarking on core/ring strategies (Atkinson, 1984) and making use of transaction cost economics in order to decide on make or buy issues. Make or buy, both with respect to the employees themselves and in connection with the kind of HRM activities that should take place in-house or should be outsourced and/or delegated to line management or to autonomous work groups.

In the *processual* approach, strategy emerges in small steps based on a process of learning and adaptation. Related to HRM this approach refers to the incremental way in which strategic assets (among which patents, knowledge, culture, and organizational routines) gradually develop over time into core competences. The main role of the HRM function is to develop and maintain people-related competences over time. The HRM function can also be seen as responsible for contributing to the social fabric, which builds up over the long term, encompassing the less planned and intentional processes of skill formation, tacit knowledge, willingness to change and spontaneous co-operation among the members of the organization.

In the *systemic* approach, strategies reflect the social system in which they are enacted. Emphasizing the social embeddedness of economic activity, the objectives and practices depend on the particular social system in which strategy making takes place (Whittington, 1993). Social systems can be found at the national level, the branch or industry level, or in a certain region. Networks, in which economic activity is embedded, may include families, the state, professional and educational background, religion and ethnicity and these very networks influence the means and ends of action. The systemic perspective is very important, especially from an HRM point of view. It refers to the wider social context of the organization and how this influences and shapes HRM policies and practices. These settings differ by country, by branch of industry and even by organization. This perspective implies a plea for embracing the context of the organization, not only with respect to culture, legislation, institutions, etc., but also with respect to its technological and knowledge context (for example Silicon Valley or web based companies).

After having given an overview of strategy approaches and their implications for strategic HRM, we will then explain some traditional models used in strategic HRM.

Traditional approaches in strategic HRM

In describing the traditional approaches used in the area of strategic HRM we need to distinguish between process and content models. The *process* of strategy refers to the way strategies come about, whereas the *content* is concerned with the product of strategy in terms of the 'what' of strategy. In addition to this well-known distinction, de Wit and Meyer (1998: 5–6) also distinguish the context of strategy, which refers to the set of circumstances in which both the process and content of strategy are shaped, being developed or simply emerge.

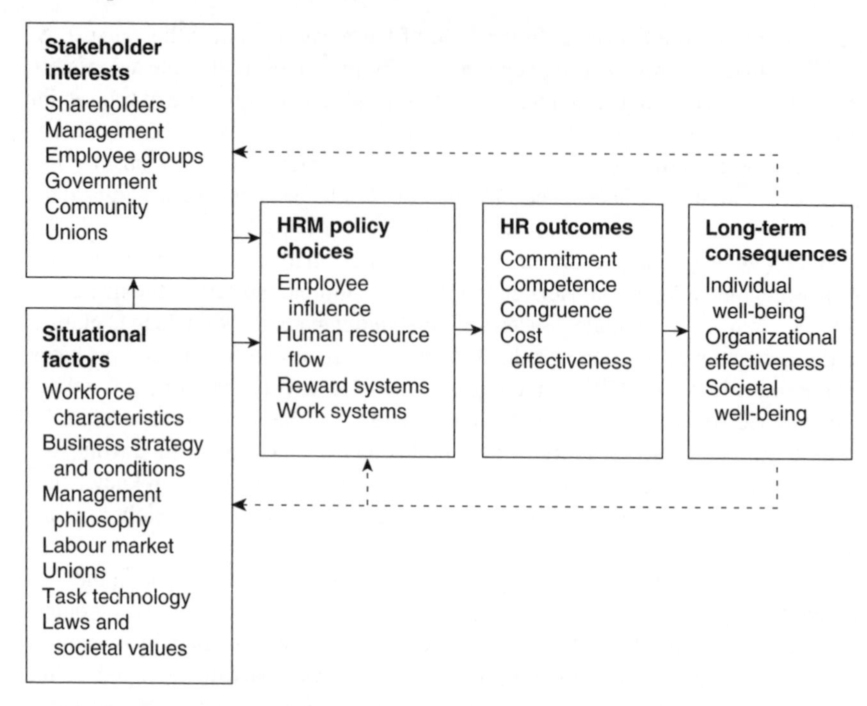

Figure 3.2 The Harvard approach (*Source:* Beer *et al.* (1984). Reprinted with permission of Michael Beer).

A mixture of both process and content is the so-called Harvard model by Beer *et al.* (1984), one of the most well-known models in HRM theorizing, which starts from a situational perspective (see Figure 3.2). Besides market and strategic considerations it takes into account the interests of the various stakeholders in both the external and internal environment. The emphasized outcomes do not only include performance in its strict economic sense, but also attention is given to individual well-being and societal consequences. The framework is both descriptive and prescriptive. It gives an overview of the factors that are important in shaping HRM policies, but at the same time it is quite conclusive in prescribing to what kind of outcomes these choices – once made – should lead.

Fombrun *et al.* (the competition from Michigan Business School) published their approach in the same year as their counterparts from Harvard (Figure 3.3). Achieving a tight fit between strategy, structure and HRM policies takes place amidst economic, political and cultural forces. More focused on the functional level of HRM itself, they emphasize the so-called human resource cycle, which can be considered as one of the first content models. In their cycle, performance is dependent upon selection, appraisal, rewards and development.

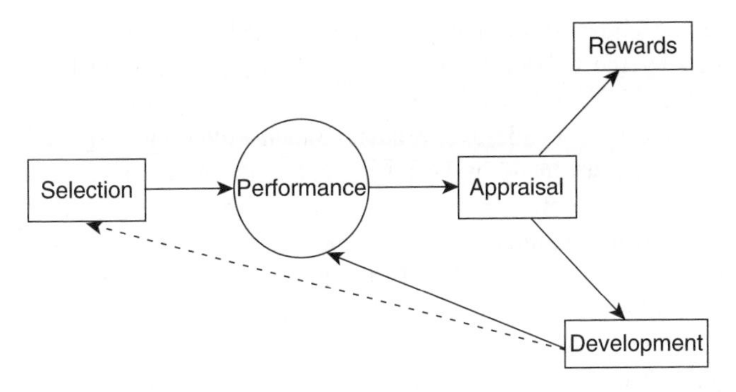

Figure 3.3 The Michigan approach – the human resource cycle (*Source:* Fombrun *et al.* (1984). Reprinted with permission of John Wiley & Sons Inc).

Strategic fit

As shown in the aforementioned conceptual models, the nature of the link between strategy and HRM has been a central issue to strategic HRM. The basic premise underlying strategic HRM is that organizations adopting a particular strategy require HRM practices that may differ from those required by organizations adopting alternative strategies (Delery and Doty, 1996), assuming an important link between organizational strategy and the HRM practices that are implemented in that organization. This alignment between HRM practices and competitive strategy has been labelled *strategic fit* (also *vertical fit*). Strategic fit stresses the importance of linking business objectives and HRM. The assumption is that HR systems, which 'simultaneously exploit the potential for complementarities or synergies among such practices and help to implement a firm's competitive strategy, are sources of sustained competitive advantage' (Huselid, 1995).

In testing strategic fit, most researchers use the 'classical' strategy typologies of Porter (1985) or Miles and Snow (1978) to operationalize strategy (e.g. Schuler and Jackson, 1987; Montemayor, 1996; Youndt *et al.*, 1996). For example, Schuler and Jackson (1987) were among the first to present how strategy and HRM policies could be related. They used a classic approach to testing strategic fit by using Porter's generic strategies (cost effectiveness, innovation and quality), and linked each of these strategies to a repertoire of role behaviours. Subsequently HRM policies and practices are used to reinforce the required role behaviours.

The role behaviours required for every distinct competitive strategy differ and can be stimulated by a consistent set of HRM practices. For example, for an innovation strategy, HRM practices are aimed at facilitating cooperative interdependent behaviour that is oriented towards the longer term and at fostering exchange of ideas and risk taking, such as variable pay rates and broad career paths. In sum, they offer a concrete insight in to the possible linkages between the content of a certain strategy and what kind of HRM policies would help to implement that strategy.

The models discussed above show that in strategic HRM the more classic models are dominated by the outside-in perspective. Many classic models of strategic HRM make use of strategy typologies from Porter (1985) or Miles and Snow (1978), which reflects an outside-in approach (Baden-Fuller and Stopford, 1994), as strategic decisions are made based on the external environment. This corresponds with the strategic contingency approach (i.e. Lawrence and Lorsch, 1967; Mintzberg, 1979) which emphasizes the influence of contextual factors inside and outside the organization on HRM. In the nineties a shift in strategic thinking was represented by the introduction of the resource-based view (RBV) (Barney, 1991), representing an inside-out perspective. The starting point in this approach focuses on the internal resources (like finance, organizational systems, and physical assets but also people) and how these contribute to a sustained competitive advantage. This shift in strategic management has had major implications on the field of HRM. Wright (who was then working closely together with Barney) states:

> This RBV of competitive advantage differs from the traditional strategy paradigm in that the emphasis of the resource-based view of competitive advantage is on the link between strategy and internal resources of the firm. The RBV is firm-focused whereas the traditional strategic analysis paradigm has had an industry-environment focus.
>
> (Wright and McMahan, 1992)

This approach uses (human) resources as a starting point. The unique strengths and capabilities of the employees determine the range of possible business strategies to be implemented. 'The resource-based view may demonstrate the fact that strategies are not universally implementable, but are contingent on having the human resource base necessary to implement them' (Wright and McMahan, 1992: 303). The RBV states that internal resources (like for example, human resources) which are scarce, valuable, inimitable, and non-substitutable, serve as the basis for a sustained competitive advantage. Table 3.1 presents an overview of the outside-in versus the inside-out perspective.

These two perspectives seem contradictory, but can both be relevant for strategic HRM. On the one hand HRM is dependent on the strategic positioning of the firm as it attempts to fit with the market environment, on the other hand (human) resources can be cultivated and developed in order to enable strategies that will result in a sustainable competitive advantage. An overview of HRM and performance research published between 1994 and 2003 by Boselie *et al.* (2005) shows that both perspectives are relevant for strategic HRM. Both contingency theory and RBV have been widely used as theoretical framework underlying strategic HRM models and rank among the top three theories being most used in strategic HRM and performance research (the third one is the so-called AMO theory, which draws our attention to the importance of a bundle of HRM practices which focuses on Abilities, Motivation and Opportunity to participate in order to improve performance).

Table 3.1 Outside-in versus inside-out perspective

	Outside-in perspective	*Inside-out perspective*
Emphasis on	Markets over resources	Resources over markets
Orientation	Market/industry-driven	Resource-driven
Starting point	Market/industry structure	Firm's resource infrastructure
Fit through	Adaptation to environment	Adaptation of environment
Strategic focus	Attaining advantageous position	Attaining distinctive resources
Strategic moves	Market/industry positioning	Developing resource base
Tactical moves	Industry entry and positioning	Attaining necessary resources
Competitive weapons	Bargaining power and mobility barriers	Superior resources and imitation barriers

Source: Wit, B. de and Meyer, R. (1998). Reprinted with permission of Thomson Publishing Services.

LIBRARY, UNIVERSITY OF CHESTER

Problems with 'fit'

Conceptually, the idea of fit is convincing, which is why it continues to play an important role in strategic HRM research (Gerhart, 2004; Becker and Huselid, 2006). However, to date, only limited empirical support for the impact of fit exists. Instead, more evidence has been found for the counterpart of the 'fit' approach, the 'best practice' approach. This touches on the issue of the universalistic approach of 'best practices' versus the contingent approach of 'best fit'. While the 'best fit' approach assumes that the effectiveness of HR practices is context-specific, the best practice approach assumes that certain HR practices universally outperform others and acknowledges that a set of 'best practices' exists which will lead to organizational effectiveness, regardless in which organization it is implemented. In the last two decades much attention has been paid to high performance high involvement work systems which have been successfully applied in a range of industries and which do not distinguish between different strategies.

Researchers who have tested both the 'best practice' and the 'best fit' hypothesis have consistently found stronger evidence for 'best practice' (e.g. Huselid, 1995; Delery and Doty, 1996; Becker and Huselid, 1998). Only modest evidence is found for 'best fit' so far, which is strange as the argumentation behind the best fit hypotheses seems to be stronger than the so-called best practice hypothesis. After all, human resource management is highly context dependent, based on differences in sector, industry, related institutional arrangements and difference in culture, both at the sectoral level as well as national level due to the embeddedness of HRM in the dominant system of industrial relations. So, how can we explain the lack of empirical support so far for strategic fit? The reason might be that measurement instruments used to test 'best fit' have a number of deficiencies, which entails that the real nature of fit is not captured in these research projects.

For example, most researchers use the 'classical' strategy typologies of Porter (1985) or Miles and Snow (1978) to operationalize strategy (e.g. Schuler and Jackson, 1987; Montemayor, 1996; Youndt *et al.*, 1996). While using these typologies, strategy is oversimplified in static constructs that do not capture the full breadth of business strategies in contemporary organizations (Paauwe, 2004; Boxall and Purcell, 2008). In reality, competitive strategies are not really that clear-cut. Organizational strategies are typically more complex and tend to consist of more elements than those captured in these classic strategy typologies (Paauwe, 2004). Moreover one company or one business can have more than one strategic orientation related to a variety of product market combinations, as Vloeberghs (1997: 77) notices. In such a case the required role behaviours are highly mixed. Strategy typologies are thus unable to capture the uniqueness of business strategies. Yet, this uniqueness is seen as the potential source of sustainable competitive advantage (Becker and Huselid, 2006).

There is a lot of criticism on the current operationalizations and measures of fit as they do not do justice to the complexity of the fit concept; the approaches used are seen as too superficial (e.g. Boxall and Purcell, 2003; Gerhart, 2004). Becker and Huselid (2006: 910) argue that fit is 'inherently multidimensional and not easily captured by simple bivariate statements'. Gerhart (2004: 10) notes a 'troublesome lack of progress on this front'. Boxall and Purcell (2003) formulate three main critiques on the 'classical' approaches for measuring strategic fit: they overlook employee interests, lack sophistication in their description of competitive strategy, and devote insufficient attention to dynamics. Moreover, empirical studies mainly do not take into account time lags; it takes 12 to 18 months for an HR strategy to be developed and implemented, and another 3 to 4 years before a relationship with performance could be observed (Paauwe and Boselie, 2005; Wright and Haggerty, 2005). Following these criticisms there is a need for a more advanced approach for measuring strategic fit, which will be described in the next section.

Towards a more advanced approach to strategic fit

Some steps have been made in developing more extensive strategic fit approaches. For example, Gratton *et al.* (1999a), using a content approach to strategy, use a set of strategic objectives unique to the organization instead of a predetermined typology of business strategies á la Porter.

They measure strategic fit as the alignment between the set of strategic objectives and 'people policies'. These people policies 'create and support the individual behaviour and competencies that have the potential to be a source of competitive advantage' (Gratton *et al.*, 1999a: 21). Gratton *et al.* (1999a) discern five levels of strategic fit, varying from a weak to a strong linkage. A strong link between individual objectives and business goals implies that the business objectives are transformed into clear individual objectives, which are agreed upon annually. A weak linkage implies no clear communication of the business strategy to individual employees, and no mechanisms through which individual tasks and behaviour are discussed and linked to strategic objectives (Gratton *et al.*, 1999a: 24).

Besides the content approach discussed above, establishing fit also involves a process dimension (De Wit and Meyer, 1998; Paauwe, 2004). The idea of process approaches is that the integration of strategy, HRM process and functions results in a fit between human resource needs (following strategy) and employee skills and behaviours (elicited by HR practices) (Bennett *et al.*, 1998). For example, Golden and Ramanujam (1985) focus on the process of strategy formation and the role of the HR department in this process and distinguish four phases of integration between strategy and HRM, varying from no link at all to full integration between strategy and HRM: administrative, one-way, two-way, and integrative linkage. An *administrative linkage* reflects the traditional and administrative role of the personnel management function. Human resources are not seen as assets, but as necessary costs for the organization. A *one-way linkage* implies that business goals are considered first, and HRM has no influence on strategy formulation. Only once the strategy has been formulated will the HRM department be involved in designing policies and practices that will help to implement the strategy, reflecting a reactive role of HRM (Kydd and Oppenheim, 1990). The *two-way linkage* involves a reciprocal relationship between strategy and HRM. Human resources are seen as important assets for the organization. Finally, the *integrative linkage* reflects a strong interaction between strategy and HRM, both formally and informally, and represents the strongest fit. The strategy and HR strategy are designed jointly, and HRM has a strong impact on the organization.

Golden and Ramanujam (1985) and Gratton *et al.* (1999a) both take a more extensive perspective on the link between strategy and HRM, focusing on process and content dimensions of strategic fit. Boon and colleagues (Boon *et al.*, 2007; Boon, 2008) build on the work of Golden and Ramanujam and Gratton *et al.* and propose an operationalization of strategic fit consisting of three elements: a content element, a process element, and an implementation element. The *content* element focuses on the alignment between elements of strategy and HRM, following Gratton *et al.* (1999a). This element covers the extent to which different HR practices aim at achieving business objectives, and the number of HR practices that are linked with strategy. The *process* element focuses on the role of HRM in strategy formulation, following Golden and Ramanujam (1985). The process element covers the extent to which HR is involved in strategy formulation and whether HR is a member of the management team on different levels in the organization. Achieving a strong fit would imply full integration of strategy and HR processes.

Besides the process and content approaches to strategic fit, the importance of (HRM) strategy *implementation* is also stressed in order to draw attention to the lack of attention to employee interests (Boxall and Purcell, 2003) of classic approaches to strategic fit. Gratton and Truss (2003) emphasize the difference between policy formulation and implementation. A strong linkage between strategy and HRM in theory, but not in implementation, will not have the desired positive effect on performance. Becker and Huselid (2006) also argue that strategy implementation should be given more attention in strategic HRM. Implementation is not any more seen as the process that automatically follows strategy formulation. Instead, strategy formulation and implementation are co-dependent (Grant, 2005). 'A strategy that is formulated without regard to its implementation is likely to be fatally flawed' (Grant, 2005: xii). Resource-based view researchers state that 'the ability to implement strategies is, by itself, a resource that can be a source of competitive advantage' (Barney, 2001: 54). Also, the degree to which employees participate in the objective setting process, in other words adding a bottom-up process to implementation, can foster desired employee behaviours (Gratton *et al.*, 1999a). Thus, strategy implementation is crucial, but often overlooked in research on strategic HRM. Consistent implementation of strategy through HR practices is also necessary for strategic fit to be effective. So we can conclude that in order to achieve strategic fit the following elements are crucial:

- *Content*: to what degree are HR practices really focussed on achieving business objectives as stated by the organization?
- *Process:* to what degree is the HR function involved in the process of strategy formulation?
- *Implementation:* to what degree and in which way (top-down/bottom-up) are employees involved in the implementation of strategy?

Dynamics and agility

Besides the three elements that make up fit, Boon *et al.* (Boon *et al.*, 2007; Boon, 2008) also propose to add a dynamic element to strategic fit, labelled *adaptation.* Adaptation focuses on how supportive of change and how proactive or reactive organizations and their HR systems are, which is important for maintaining strategic fit in changing environments. Dynamism has not received sufficient attention in strategic fit. Most organizations operate in dynamic environments, and have to cope with change by continually adapting their business strategy to the turbulent environment. Yet, most HR researchers take a static approach in measuring fit, and attention to dynamics has been limited (Boxall and Purcell, 2003: 55). Some researchers have studied the influence of dynamic environments on fit. For example, Wright and Snell (1998) and Boxall and Purcell (2008) draw attention to the importance of flexibility in strategic HRM, optimizing adaptability and efficiency simultaneously (Paauwe, 2004). Chakravarthy (1982) introduces 'adaptive fit', and distinguishes three types of adaptive fit: unstable fit, stable fit, and neutral fit. *Unstable fit* reflects a defensive interaction with the environment, *stable fit* reflects a reactive response to environmental changes, corresponding with Mirvis' (1997) 'fast follower'. *Neutral fit* is the strongest type of fit, and reflects a proactive approach although the name suggests otherwise. In case of neutral fit, organizations are proactive, and anticipate changes before they occur. 'They often create changes in their environment, to which their competitors must respond' (Chakravarthy, 1982: 36). Lengnick-Hall and Beck (2005: 742) stress that organizations do not move from one equilibrium to another and argue that organizations should have a close connection to the environment in order to achieve long term successfulness. Similarly, Miles and Snow (1994) see fit as a process of continuously adapting to changes in the environment and stress that 'unless a firm is alert and adept, today's fit becomes tomorrow's misfit'. While tight fit implies a close linkage between strategy and HRM, early fit is even more proactively oriented. Early fit is a tight fit that is achieved before competitors do, and aims at gaining a leading position.

The concept of *agility* even goes a step further than adaptation. An agile organization (Dyer and Shafer, 1999 in Boxall and Purcell, 2003; Paauwe, 2004) aims to develop a built-in capacity to shift, flex and adjust, either alone or with alliance partners, as circumstances change, and to do so as a matter of course. While adaptation focuses on strategic changes to cope with changing environments, agility implies that the whole firm should be flexible. Strategy as such is not important; instead all work processes should be organized such that they can move along with changes in the environment. In line with this, Paauwe (2004: 99) even goes one step further by suggesting 'agile' HR systems, which – once achieved – can act as an enabling device for a whole range of strategic alternatives. As the dynamics in the marketplace increase for a range of sectors, we should not be bothered anymore with trying to align HRM practices and policies with the business strategy, as the time lag between the two takes too long (see above, where we estimated that it takes at least 12–18 months development and implementation time, let alone the time before HR practices really start to take effect). The very moment the HR practices are finally in place, the business strategies from which they were derived are already outmoded, and replaced by new insights. So, in these circumstances it might be better to focus on creating a workforce characterized by agility, by which we mean the creation of a workforce which is eager to learn, able to handle changes as a normal way of life, and is able to work in both virtual configurations as well as in reconfigurable real life teams, which can easily be resolved and reformatted into another composition, dependent on the demands put forward by the market place. Of course this is an extreme position which is only relevant for organizations operating in highly dynamic markets. The truth is somewhere in between. On the one hand HRM is dependent on the strategic positioning of the firm as it attempts to fit with the market environment; on the other hand human resources can be cultivated and developed in order to form, to build strategic capability that will result in a competitive advantage. So the apparently conflicting perspectives of 'outside-in' and 'inside out' are in reality a paradox; a situation in which two seemingly contradictory, or even mutually exclusive, factors are both true at the same time. We will now reconcile the two perspectives in our search for a synthesis.

In search of a synthesis

In US-based models of strategic HRM the shareholder's perspective is often dominant, emphasizing that all HRM strategies, tactics, policies and practices serve only one goal, which is to increase shareholders' value. In European (especially mainland European) based models, however, more stakeholder-oriented approaches are used, balancing the needs, interests and aspirations of the various stakeholders both inside and outside the organization. These two different perspectives contrast profitability and responsibility. Paauwe and Boselie (2003, 2005), for example, draw attention to the importance of legitimacy and responsibility of organizations, which shows similarities with the systemic approach to strategy (Whittington, 1993). They apply institutional theory to strategic HRM to incorporate pressures of the institutional context on HRM.

Given the many different stakeholders that influence HRM, there is a need for a synthesis which brings all elements together. But how do we bring it all together? Paauwe (2004) presents a *contextually based human resource theory* which takes into account the importance of the internal and external context of organizations. The model incorporates inside-out and outside-in approaches, institutionalism, takes a stakeholder perspective, and includes both content and processes of HRM. In this model, two external dimensions influence the shaping of the HRM system by determining the room for manoeuvre for the organization: the Product/Market/Technology (PMT) dimension and the Social/Cultural/Legal (SCL) dimension.

The PMT dimension reflects the competitive mechanisms that the organization faces. The relevant product market combinations and the technology that is used influences the design of the organization and its HRM system. These demands from the competitive environment include efficiency, effectiveness, flexibility, quality, innovativeness, and speed. The organization has to meet these criteria in order to be competitive in the market.

The SCL dimension reflects the institutional mechanisms that have an impact on the organization. Social, cultural and legal forces influence the HRM system in the organization. Whereas the PMT dimension reflects the free market, the SCL dimension emphasizes the boundaries that are set by the institutional context of the organization. The rules, regulations and norms about the employment relationship dominate the shaping of the HRM system in an organization. The demands from the institutional environment imply meeting fairness and legitimacy criteria. Fairness refers to a fair relationship between the individual and the organization, and legitimacy is the 'acceptance of organizations in the wider society in which they operate' (Paauwe, 2004). Looking at these two external dimensions, the PMT dimension refers to the economic rationality of the competitive organization. The SCL dimension focuses on relational rationality by maintaining long-term relationships with important internal and external stakeholders.

Apart from the two external dimensions that shape HR policy, there is a third dominant influence: the organizational, administrative, and cultural heritage of the organization. The history that is unique to an organization results in a unique organizational configuration. The structure, culture, and systems in the organization have been developed over time because of decision making in the past and other changes inside and outside of the organization. This unique configuration also shapes the HRM system. The configurational approach of Delery and

Doty (1996) is applicable here. According to this approach, there is a unique organizational configuration within which all organizational systems and the HRM system fit together.

The three dominant factors (PMT dimension, SCL dimension, and configuration) influence the degree of leeway the dominant coalition has in making strategic choices. The dominant coalition consists of actors that represent the relevant stakeholders of the organization, for example the CEO, board of directors, works councils, and the HRM manager (Boselie and Paauwe, 2002). The nature of this dominant coalition is influenced by several internal and environmental factors, including organizational history, values, leadership, competition, market, rules and regulations, finance, marketing, and external stakeholders of the firm (Gratton *et al.,* 1999b).

Despite the different external and internal factors that dominate decisions with respect to the HRM system, the dominant coalition has a certain room for manoeuvre (Figure 3.4). How much leeway the dominant coalition has to shape the HRM system depends on the nature of the external and internal influences. For example, in case of a market monopoly, the room for manoeuvre is obviously much larger than in the case of fierce market competition. In this case, there will be little room for shaping the HRM system (Paauwe, 2004). The dominant coalition is challenged to enable HRM to make a genuine contribution to sustained competitive advantage

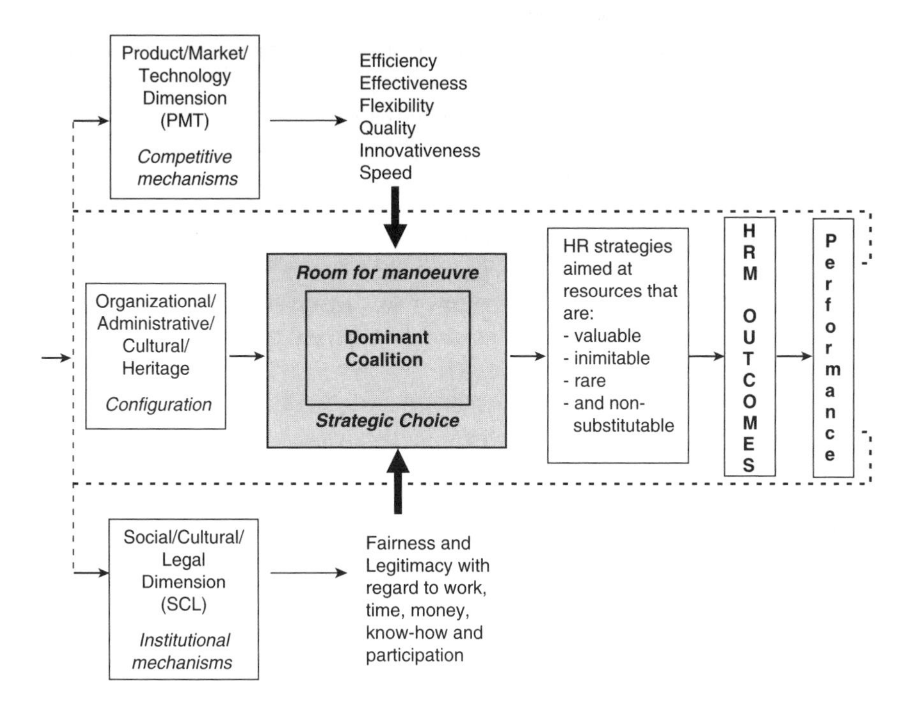

Figure 3.4 Contextually based human resource theory (*Source:* Paauwe, 2004: 91).

by selecting HR practices which are based on three firm-specific dimensions as outlined above, contribute to 'uniqueness' or, in the words of the RBV: 'heterogeneity' (Mahoney and Pandian, 1992). This uniqueness is valuable, scarce, virtually inimitable and difficult to replace in the short run (Barney, 1991). The resource-based view focuses on the key success factors of individual firm behaviour to achieve firm-specific advantages by means of a portfolio of differential core skills and routines, coherence across skills and unique proprietary know-how. Many of these core skills and routines are embedded in the attitudes and behaviours of the people employed or otherwise linked to the company. Linking the resource-based view to institutional theory can contribute to uniqueness by optimally blending environmental factors (which can be both an opportunity as well as a constraint) with internal resources and capabilities.

This way we have been able to align a variety of perspectives which are all important in strategic HRM: outside-in and inside-out approaches, strategic contingency theory, RBV and institutional theory, systems' approach and actors' approach by including the dominant coalition and the emphasis on achieving uniqueness in order to achieve a sustained competitive advantage and thus contributing to firm performance.

At the same time we need to be aware of the fact that, reflecting on reality, in many cases HRM is not strategic at all. The strategic role of HRM largely varies between companies and sectors and can depend on market conditions. Sometimes HRM is very reactive and short term oriented. For example in case of a sudden drop in sales – caused by an energy crisis – the HR function is involved in the termination of labour contracts, cutting the outsourcing of activities and stops making use of temporary work agencies, just in order to cut expenses and help to restore a proper balance between cash inflow and cash outflow. And sometimes in highly stable situations, HR is only concerned with the administration and control of regular inflow, throughout and outflow of people based on acceptable degrees of labour turnover. However, due to fierce and very often international competition and the introduction of market mechanisms in former public sectors (think of energy, water, health care, etc.) increasingly more companies are faced with competitive demands which necessitate a strategic approach to the management of people.

References

Atkinson, J. (1984). Manpower strategies for flexible organizations, *Personnel Management*, 66: 28–31.

Baden-Fuller, C. and Stopford, J. M. (1994). Creating corporate entrepreneurship, *Strategic Management Journal*, 15(7): 521–36.

Barney, J. B. (1991). Firm resources and sustained competitive advantage, *Journal of Management*, 17(1): 99–120.

Barney, J. B. (2001). Is the resource-based 'view' a useful perspective for strategic management research? Yes, *Academy of Management Review*, 26(1): 41–56.

Becker, B. and Huselid, M. A. (1998). High performance work systems and firm performance: a synthesis of research and managerial implications, *Research in Personnel and Human Resource Management*, 16: 53–101.

Becker, B. and Huselid, M. A. (2006). Strategic human resource management: where do we go from here? *Journal of Management*, 32(6): 898–925.

Beer, M., Spector, B., Lawrence, P., Quinn Mills, D. and Walton, R. (1984). *Human Resource Management: a General Manager's Perspective*. New York: Free Press.

Bennett, N., Ketchen, D. J. Jr. and Schultz, E. B. (1998). An examination of factors associated with the integration of human resource management and strategic decision making. *Human Resource Management*, 37(1): 3–16.

Boon, C. (2008). *HRM and Fit: Survival of the Fittest!* ERIM/ Erasmus University Rotterdam, Rotterdam.

Boon, C., Boselie, P., Paauwe, J. and Den Hartog, D. N. (2007). *Measuring strategic and internal fit in HRM: An alternative approach. Proceedings of The Academy of Management Annual Meeting*, Philadelphia, PA.

Boselie, P., Dietz, G. and Boon, C. (2005). Commonalities and contradictions in HRM and performance research, *Human Resource Management Journal*, 15(3): 67–94.

Boselie, P. and Paauwe, J. (2002). Het geheim ontrafeld? De bijdrage van strategisch human resource management aan prestatieverbetering, *Management en Organisatie*, 56(4): 5–24.

Boxall, P. and Purcell, J. (2003). *Strategy and Human Resource Management*. New York: Palgrave MacMillan.

Boxall, P. and Purcell, J. (2008). *Strategy and Human Resource Management* (2nd edn.). New York, NY: Palgrave MacMillan.

Chakravarthy, B. S. (1982). Adaptation: A promising metaphor for strategic management, *Academy of Management Review*, 7(1): 35–44.

De Wit, B. and Meyer, R. (1998). *Strategy: Process, Content, Context: An International Perspective* (2nd edn.). London: Thomson.

Delery, J. E. (1998). Issues of fit in strategic human resource management: Implications for research, *Human Resource Management Review*, 8(3): 289–309.

Delery, J. E. and Doty, D. H. (1996). Modes of theorizing in strategic human resource management: Tests of universalistic, contingency, and configurational performance predictions, *Academy of Management Journal*, 39(4): 802–35.

Dyer, L. and Shafer, R. A. (1999). From human resource strategy to organizational effectiveness: lessons from research on organizational agility, *Research in Personnel and Human Resource Management*, 4: 145–74.

Fombrun, C. J., Tichy, M. M. and Devanna, M.A. (1984). *Strategic human resource management*. New York: John Wiley.

Gerhart, B. (2004). Research on human resources and effectiveness: Selected methodological challenges, *HRM: What's Next?* Rotterdam, The Netherlands: Erasmus University.

Golden, K. A. and Ramanujam, V. (1985). Between a dream and a nightmare: On the integration of the human resource management and strategic business planning processes, *Human Resource Management*, 24(4): 429–52.

Grant, R. M. (2005). *Contemporary Strategy Analysis* (5th Rev Edn). Oxford, UK: Blackwell Publishing.

Gratton, L., Hope-Hailey, V., Stiles, P. and Truss, C. (1999a). Linking individual performance to business strategy: The people process model, *Human Resource Management*, 38(1): 17–31.

Gratton, L., Hope-Hailey, V., Stiles, P. and Truss, C. (1999b). *Strategic Human Resource Management: Corporate Rhetoric and Human Reality*. New York: Oxford University Press Inc.

Gratton, L. and Truss, C. (2003). The three-dimensional people strategy: Putting human resources policies into action, *Academy of Management Executive*, 17(3): 74–86.

Hendry, C. and Pettigrew, A. (1986). The practice of strategic human resource management, *Personnel Review*, 15(5): 3–8.

Huselid, M. A. (1995). The impact of human resource management practices on turnover, productivity, and corporate financial performance, *Academy of Management Journal*, 38(3): 635–72.

Koch, M. J. and McGrath, R.G. (1996). Improving labor productivity: human resource management policies do matter, *Strategic Management Journal*, 17(5): 335–54.

Lawrence, P. R. and Lorsch, J. (1967). *Organization and Environment*. Boston: Harvard School of Business Administration Press.

Lengnick-Hall, C. A. and Beck, T. E. (2005). Adaptive fit versus robust transformation: How organizations respond to environmental change, *Journal of Management*, 31(5): 738–57.

Mahoney, J. T. and Pandian, J. R. (1992). The resource based view within the conversation of strategic management, *Strategic Management Journal*, 13(5): 363–80.

Miles, R. E. and Snow, C. C. (1978). *Organizational Strategy, Structure, and Process*. New York: McGraw-Hill.

Miles, R. E. and Snow, C. C. (1994). *Fit, Failure, and the Hall of Fame: How Companies Succeed or Fail*. New York, NY: The Free Press.

Mintzberg, H. (1979). *The Structuring of Organizations,* London: Prentice Hall.

Mintzberg, H. (1987). Five p's for strategy. *California Management Review*, 30: 11–24.

Mintzberg, H. (1990). The design school: Reconsidering the basic premises of strategic management, *Strategic Management Journal*, 11: 171–195.

Mintzberg, H., Ahlstrand, B. and Lampel, J. (1998). *Strategy Safari: A Guided Tour Through the Wilds of Strategic Management*. New York: Free Press.

Mirvis, P. H. (1997). Human Resource Management: Leaders, Laggards, and Followers, *Academy of Management Executive*, 11(2): 43–56.

Montemayor, E. F. (1996). Congruence between pay policy and competitive strategy in high-performing firms, *Journal of Management*, 22(6): 889–908.

Paauwe, J. (2004). *HRM and Performance: Achieving Long-term Viability*. Oxford: Oxford University Press.

Paauwe, J. and Boselie, P. (2003). Challenging 'strategic HRM' and the relevance of the institutional setting, *Human Resource Management Journal*, 13(3): 56–70.

Paauwe, J. and Boselie, P. (2005). HRM and performance: What's next? *Human Resource Management Journal,* 15(4): 68–83.

Porter, M. E. (1985). *Competitive Advantage: Creating and Sustaining Superior Performance*. New York: Free Press.

Schuler, R. S. and Jackson, S. E. (1987). Linking competitive strategies with human resource management practices, *Academy of Management Executive*, 1(3): 207–19.

Vloeberghs, D. (1997). *Handbook human resource management*. Leuven: Acco.

Whittington, R. (1993). *What is Strategy, and Does It Matter?* London: Routledge.

Wright, P. M. and Haggerty, J. J. (2005). Missing Variables in Theories of Strategic Human Resource Management: Time, Cause, and Individuals: 17. Ithaca, NY: CAHRS at Cornell University.

Wright, P. M. and McMahan, G. C. (1992). Theoretical perspectives for strategic human resource management, *Journal of Management*, 18(2): 295–320.

Wright, P. M. and Snell, S. A. (1998). Toward a unifying framework for exploring fit and flexibility in strategic human resource management, *Academy of Management Review*, 23(4): 756–72.

Youndt, M. A., Snell, S. A., Dean, J. W. and Lepak, D. P. (1996). Human resource management, manufacturing strategy, and firm performance, *Academy of Management Journal*, 39(4): 836–66.

4 HRM and organizational performance

Stephen Wood

Introduction

Strategic human resource management (HRM), which came to the fore in the liberal market economies in the 1980s, places primacy on the impact of the human resource and its management on strategic outcomes. It reflects what Collings and Wood refer to in the opening chapter as the use of the term HRM to indicate a 'more strategic role' for people management than it had under a regime of personnel management; the fulfilment of which is oriented to 'the agenda of shareholder value'. Other stakeholders' interests, including employees, are at best secondary or are to be reconciled with those of the shareholders. A contrasting, stakeholder approach sees strategic HRM as more a process of managing human resources in the light of competing pressures and in which management reconciles competing tensions where possible or makes appropriate trade-offs where necessary.

At the extreme, the former, shareholder approach treats employees like any other commodity, as a resource to be used to maximize the profits of the firm, or in the case of other organizations, the key performance indictors, and to be discarded when of no further use. While the latter, stakeholder approach treats employees' humanity as distinguishing them from other resources and giving them a prominent position, even unique right, amongst stakeholders. The emphasis for HRM in the shareholder approach would be on its direct effect on the profitability and asset value of the organization, whilst in the stakeholder approach its impact directly on employees would be a priority. Indeed, the stakeholder approach probably has arisen partly as a conscious counteraction to the shareholder approach, as European writers in particular sought to rebalance priorities in HRM thinking.

Allied to the rise of strategic HRM was the development of new models of people management with an emphasis on employee involvement and development. It was argued that traditional methods of management often characterized as Taylorist after the founder of Scientific Management, with its focus on standardizing work and narrowly defined job specifications, was no longer appropriate in an increasingly dynamic and competitive economy. Such Taylorism led to an underutilization and development of human skills; but in the current context approaches that involve workers more or enhance their skills ought to yield competitive advantages for firms or increase the efficiency and quality of public service provision.

Given this expectation that innovative approaches that reverse certain features of Taylorism would guarantee higher levels of performance than would traditional systems, these in fact became known as high performance systems. Moreover, it was widely assumed that increased opportunities for involvement and development would be beneficial for workers and deemed desirable by them. High performance systems were thus portrayed as delivering the fulfilment of both employees' and employers' needs, offering mutual gains to both parties. An approach that satisfies stockholder's needs could yield employee satisfaction and well-being and hence a key tension that was thought to require managers to make trade-offs no longer existed, and the distinction between the stockholder and shareholder approaches becomes redundant.

In the wake of such claims a line of research developed in the early 1990s that examined whether particular HRM models are indeed associated with higher levels of organizational performance. This chapter introduces some of the key studies and assesses whether they support the claims made that HRM can be decisive for organizational performance, or more specifically that an HRM centred on employee involvement or development justifies the high performance tag.

The concepts underlying the HRM-performance studies

Human resource management increasingly replaced personnel management as a term to represent that part of an organization's activities concerned with the recruitment, development and management of its employees in organizations, professional circles and academia in order to convey a modernization of personnel management. At its simplest modernization entailed placing much more emphasis on the contribution of people to the key performance indicators, that is on treating employees on a par with technology as an asset of the organization, rather than a cost that should minimized.

Pfeffer (1998) indeed characterizes the high performance system as 'profits through people'. He saw this initially as involving 13 main practices: employment security, selectivity in recruiting, high wages, information sharing, teams and job redesign, training and skill development, symbolic egalitarianism, cross-utilization and cross-training, incentive pay, employee ownership, participation and empowerment, wage compression, promotion from within. But in a subsequent listing he reduced these to a core, the first seven in the list above (Pfeffer, 1998). These practices are contrasted with non-people-centred methods such as those associated with the control-centred Taylorist approach, the heavy use of contingent employment relations and piecework compensation systems.

The rationale underlying Pfeffer's listing (final or original) of practices appears to be that they represent sophisticated people management or HRM, much of which builds on behavioural science research, for example on selection. However, in keeping with the emphasis on strategic HRM fulfilling stakeholder's objectives,

Huselid *et al.* (1997) and others distinguish strategic practices from technical practices on the basis that the former contribute to profitability, innovation and the asset base of the organization. In contrast, technical ones played a maintenance role, ensuring that the correct human resources are in place. Most of the practices in Pfeffer's list are in Huselid *et al.*'s terms strategic, but selection methods is the most prominent practice in Pfeffer's list that is treated by them as technical, playing a maintenance role.

The implication of Huselid *et al.*'s definition is that strategic practices are concerned with the development and utilization of the people once they are in place in the organization. This has been the key focus of the high involvement modernization agenda. Here the emphasis is on the advantages of involving all employees through giving them more discretion over how they do their job and engaging them in broader modes of involvement entailing innovation and managerial decision-making. Capturing this vision, Lawler (1986), Walton (1985) and others in the 1980s portrayed the HRM required for the future as what they termed the high involvement or high commitment model. It covers both job and organizational involvement, to use Wall *et al.*'s (2004) terms, and includes job enrichment, teamwork, idea-capturing methods such as quality circles, functional flexibility, extensive training and development, as well as motivational methods to support these, such as internal promotion and contingent reward systems. The adoption of such practices involves the curtailment of certain Taylorist principles, which rested on a divorce of the conception of tasks from their execution, the former the prerogative of managers, the latter the role of workers.

It is claimed that increased uncertainty, competition, and technological development are demanding that all employees should be more engaged and proactive in their jobs than they were Taylorist mass production system – the car assembly line being the paradigm case of this – if organizations are to survive in an increasingly competitive context. The participative philosophy underlying high involvement management would demand and, by implication, successfully engender, a greater level of employee commitment and involvement. Its core, the increasing employee involvement, would chime with employees' motivational needs for satisfying and challenging jobs and to identify with the organizations for which they work, as well as enhance their job security and income growth. In so doing high involvement management would guarantee effective sustained organizational performance in an increasingly competitive, uncertain and rapidly internationalizing economy.

A final influence on the modernization agenda, particularly in the USA, was the perception that if employers were going to maximize their return on 'their' human resources, promotion and pay needed to be more strongly linked to performance than they had in the past. It was thought that in many organizations seniority rules and other bureaucratic practices, often thought to be associated with trade union influence, had led to a too loose connection between performance and key personnel decisions. As such, whilst employee voice is welcomed as an input to change programmes or organizational innovations, the kind of employee voice concerned with grievances and trade unions is less welcomed. In some circles it is seen as antithetical to successful high performance HRM as it is thought to have detrimental effects on performance, when in fact Walton was at pains to stress that unionism is not necessarily antithetical to high commitment or involvement management.

We can see that there are a number of overlapping currents influencing the development of the HRM-performance field and the concepts underlying it, which can be summarized thus:

1 The consolidation of developments in personnel management, some based on behavioural science methods, into a coherent sophisticated HRM approach to people management that signifies employees are valued, as opposed to a more *ad hoc* or neglectful approach.
2 The quest for a personal management that could visibly contribute to the key performance indicators of organizations.
3 The importance of human capital to the organization, focused on the investment in the human asset or employee development, and the involvement of employees in both their immediate job and the wider context in which it is embedded, reflecting the need for the organization to pro-actively respond to an increasingly dynamic environment.
4 A HRM centred on performance as the key criteria for selection, promotion, reward and evaluation, i.e. in which seniority and other status criteria are not significant.

While these concerns overlap, distinguishing them helps us to understand the different foci of the studies of HRM performance that we will review. They are in fact blended together in the Ability-Motivation-Opportunity (AMO) Framework (Boxall and Purcell, 2003; Gerhart, 2008: 318–22) that underpins some of the studies. This framework is a theory of individual performance that extends Vroom's (1964) earlier emphasis on ability and motivation by adding an 'opportunity to participate' in Appelbaum *et al.*'s terms, or 'opportunity to contribute to effectiveness' in Gerhart's terms (2008: 319). The trichotomy is reflected in a characterization of high performance systems as having three components, each of which correspond to the three elements of the AMO Framework, thus: (1) a work organization element which is about the opportunities for employee involvement and participation, (2) a training and development component which is concerned with human capital or skill and knowledge acquisition, and (3) a motivational-enhancement part concerned with incentives to perform in order to ensure that employees are motivated to use their discretion in line with the organization's objectives (Bailey, 1993; Appelbaum *et al.*, 2000; Kalleberg *et al.*, 2006).

Boxall and Purcell (2003) suggest that the Ability-Motivation-Opportunity Framework is increasingly the performance theory that underlies the stream of research which emerged in the 1990s that tests the link between human resource management and performance. This may mislead people into inferring that the studies are more homogeneous than they are. There are clear differences in the sets of practices used in the studies, as Boxall and Purcell (2003) note, yet the diversity within the studies reflects more than this, as their underlying foci are often quite dissimilar. I will now consider some studies to illustrate the diversity.

Key HRM performance studies

I present five studies, each of which illustrates one of the following concerns:

1 The profits (or performance) through people approach, through a coherent sophisticated approach that signifies employees are valued.
2 The quest for a personal management that could visibly contribute to the key performance indicators of organizations.
3 The importance of human capital to the organization, focused on the investment in the human asset.
4 The high involvement management approach that reverses Taylorism.
5 A HRM centered on perfomance.
6 The AMO Framework.

Consequently I will not present the studies in the oft-used chronological order.

The studies have been based on correlational analyses, in which HRM is measured through a method that captures the collective use of a set of human resource practices which is then correlated with measures of performance. This reflects an underlying current in the literature that human resource practices need to cohere if performance is to be optimized.

Performance through people: West, Guthrie, Dawson, Borrill and Carter's use of Pfeffer's practices in a hospital context

Our first study is in fact one of the most recent and is atypical in that it is not dealing with profit-making organizations, as West *et al.* (2006) investigated the link between the human resource system and performance in a sample of 52 hospitals in England. A high performance human resource system is taken to be one that uses the core practices in Pfeffer's framework and West *et al.* include six practices in their measure of it: training, performance management, participation, decentralization, teams, employment security. Each of these was measured using several items. For example, for performance management, respondents (a) rated the priority the hospital placed on conducting performance appraisals for all employees, (b) indicated the percentage of staff in each occupational group receiving an appraisal in the past twelve months and the frequency of these appraisals, (c) estimated the percentage of staff in each occupational group that received training in the conduct of performance appraisals and whether the appraisal system was subject to systematic evaluation. Through aggregating the answers to these dimensions a measure of what West *et al.* (2006) call 'the sophistication and extensiveness of the performance management system' was created. Their overall index of a high performance human management system was measured by standardizing and aggregating such measures. They also included in their index, somewhat oddly as it is not a practice, a measure of whether the hospital had Investors in People accreditation, a national accreditation that organizations in the UK can apply for that looks at, among other things, their training and development (http://www.investorsinpeople.co.uk). Health care was measured by the standardized mortality ratio, which indicates whether more or less patients have died than one would expect, taking in account a set of standardizing factors, or if in fact the amount is exactly as expected. The HRM system is found to be associated with mortality rate even controlling for prior mortality.

Strategic 'bottom-line' personal management: Huselid, Jackson and Schuler's study of strategic and technical HRM

Huselid *et al.*'s (1997) focus is on the differentiation between strategic and technical practices, as outlined earlier. The strategic, defined by their being connected directly with the achievement of business objectives, are associated with the kinds of practices that are prominent in the high involvement model, AMO or high performance work systems models – team-based job designs, flexible workforces, and employee empowerment. Huselid *et al.* also consider them to be 'relatively recent innovations' (p. 172). In contrast, they claim technical HRM activities are better established and it is precisely because they are institutionalized that they cannot give organizations a competitive advantage. They entail practices associated with recruiting, selection, performance measurement, training and the administration of compensation and benefits.

Using a sample of 293 US firms from ten different sectors, Huselid *et al.* (1997) studied the effectiveness of the HRM activities, and not just their use of practices, as the other studies we will consider do. The assessment of effectiveness was made by the respondents, senior managers (92 per cent of whom were in HRM positions) who answered a postal questionnaire. They were asked to rate their satisfaction with 'the results currently being achieved' (Huselid *et al.*, 1997: 175) for individual practices. Factor analysis of the ratings confirmed a separation between the activities that Huselid *et al.* designated as 'Strategic HRM Effectiveness' from the technical. The strategic activities included a number of practices associated with their definition that cohere to some extent: teamwork; subordinate participation and empowerment; employee–manager communications; workforce flexibility and deployment; and management development and succession planning. But it also included advanced issue identification and strategic needs analysis and work/family programmes. Compensation is mentioned as important to strategic HRM, which might be taken to mean incentive systems as these are prominent in the high performance literature, as Huselid *et al.* acknowledge. But these are identified along with items such as benefits and service, retirement strategies, recruiting and training (significantly treated together), and performance appraisal as technical practices.

Performance was measured by (a) productivity (sales per employee); and (b) two measures of profit, namely gross return on assets (GRATE) and a market value index (Tobin's q). Statistical analyses controlled for a large number of factors known to relate to performance, including firm size and industrial sector. The focus was on business performance subsequent to when the data on human resource practices was collected, in order to determine whether HRM practices in one year predicted performance in the following year, which strengthens the basis for causal inference.

The analyses revealed a positive relationship between strategic HRM effectiveness and gross return on assets and a marginal relationship ($p < 0.10$) for productivity and the Tobin's q measure of profit. For technical HRM effectiveness, however, there was no statistically significant relationship with any measure of performance, thus supporting Huselid *et al.*'s differentiation of types of HRM.

Human capital focus: Koch and McGrath's human resource management sophistication

Koch and McGrath (1996) define HRM in terms of the identification and development of human capital. These practices, it is argued, 'are associated with the creation and maintenance of human capital as a strategic resource' (p. 336), that is they may give the firm a competitive advantage. Three practices comprise sophisticated human resource management: investments in human resource planning, the accurate projection of human capital needs; investments in hiring, the identification of individuals that are best suited to meet organizational objectives; and investments in the development of employees. Using indices created from multiple measures of these, which were gained from questionnaires sent to executives in 319 US business units, Koch and McGrath found that hiring was strongly related to labour productivity and that planning and development related to it but not so strongly, i.e. was significant only at the 5 per cent level. However, the association of all three was stronger in units with high levels of capital intensity, measured by the log of the assets per employee, i.e. it was moderated by capital intensity. This moderation was greater for planning than for the others. An overall index of human resource sophistication, created by combining the three other indices, was also related to labour productivity and this relationship intensified as the capital of the firm increased. Nonetheless productivity gains from human resource management sophistication were apparent at all but the lowest levels of capital intensity.

High involvement management: Arthur's steel mill study

Arthur (1994) concentrates on employee involvement, using Walton's high commitment management as its organizing principle. This model, and its opposite, the control or Taylorist model, are seen as approaches to human resource management that have the effect of 'shaping . . . employee behaviour and attitudes at work'. The control approach is defined by its goals 'to reduce labor costs, or improve efficiency, by enforcing compliance with specified rules and procedures and basing employee rewards on some measurable output criteria'. In contrast the underlying orientation of the commitment approach is to develop committed employees who can be trusted to use their discretion to carry out their tasks in ways that are consistent with the organization's goals. It is clear that Arthur sees high commitment management as entailing organizational involvement, including employees thinking of better ways of doings their jobs, as the measure of it included high levels of employee involvement in managerial decisions, formal participation programmes, and training in group problem-solving.

Other practices included in the study, some of which were less obviously central measures of high commitment management, were general training, zero or low levels of incentive pay, formal grievance procedures, social gatherings, percentage of craft workers, supervisor/worker ratio, as well as wage and benefit measures such as the total employment cost per production and maintenance worker.

Arthur (1994) collected data on HRM practices and organizational performance by questionnaires completed by human resource managers in a sample of 30 small US steel mills. Using cluster analysis, he discriminated between those plants adopting high commitment management from those using the high control approach. For example, the commitment workplaces were characterized by employee involvement in managerial decisions, formal participation programmes, training in group problem-solving and an emphasis on skilled work. Fourteen of the mills fell into the commitment category, while the remaining 16 were of the control type.

The commitment plants were found, controlling for such factors as plant size and degree of trade union membership, to be associated with higher labour efficiency (average number of labour hours required to produce one ton of steel); lower scrap rates (tons of raw steel required to produce one ton of finished product) and lower labour turnover (number of shop floor workers who had left in the last year).

A performance-based HRM: Delery and Doty's study of market and internal systems

Delery and Doty (1996) focus is on differentiating a performance-based system – labelled the market-type of employment system – from one based on an internal labour market. The emphasis in the market system is on performance being gauged by results, whilst on the internal system perfomance is judged by behaviour. Employee development, the human capital focus, is limited to the internal system as in the ideal type of the market system no formal training and minimal induction is given. Practices associated with high involvement are, however, not consistently allocated to one of the systems: the key non-Taylorist practice of loose job definitions is associated with the market system, whilst jobs are very tightly defined in the internal system; but participation in decision making and employee voice are seen to be part of the internal system and employees are given little voice in the market system. In many respects the market system is the one that Pfeffer and others sees as antithetical to the high performance system.

In a study of 1050 US banks, Delery and Doty concentrated on the management of one occupation, the loan officer. They acquired information on the human resource practices and business strategy from the bank's senior human resource manager and further 'general information' (Delery and Doty, 1996: 814) about the bank and its strategy from the bank's president.

Delery and Doty tested effects of their seven individual practices on performance. The main finding was that results-oriented appraisal, profit-sharing and employment security were positively associated with the return on average assets, while profit-sharing, and, though only marginally, results-oriented appraisal, were associated with return on equity; but the relationship between the results-oriented appraisal and both measures of performance was found to vary depending on the degree to which the bank adopted an innovation-oriented strategy, though it still had a pay-off in all circumstances. This offers some support for the contingency argument that a third factor, e.g. whether the organization is following a particular business strategy, moderates the relationship between HRM and performance.

Examining the two systems of employment, the market and internal systems, Delery and Doty (1996) found that the more closely an organization's employment system resembled the market type the better its return on average assets and equity. In contrast the greater the proximity to the internal ideal type the lower the performance on these two measures. None of their tests for contingency theory showed that the association between the systems depended on the strategic fit.

While the research suggests that the market system is positively associated with performance, the problem is how the concept relates to the high-involvement or performance terminology, since, on the one hand, it contains the non-Taylorist job design but relies on an external labour market and is characterized by low degrees of training and participation.

Applying the Ability-Motivation-Opportunity framework: Huselid's study of private companies in the USA

Huselid (1995) studied a set of 968 organizations with over 100 employees by sampling firms from all major industries in the US private sector. He focuses on the three types of practices that make up the AMO framework, which he labels collectively a high performance work system. He argues that the use of such a system gives employees a high level of skill and motivation, and structures their jobs so that they have the opportunity to use these skill and abilities. Having obtained information on the firms' human resource management practices by a questionnaire mailed to the senior human resources professional in each company, Huselid used principle component analysis to investigate the relationship between the practices and found that they formed two identifiable factors. He labelled these in terms of the AMO vocabulary. The first, he termed 'Employee Motivation', the second he argued captured the other two dimensions, skills and work organization, together, and thus he termed this 'Employee Skills And Organizational Structure,'. The motivation factor covered such practices as performance appraisal, compensation based on appraisals, staff recruitment and promotion on merit (rather than on seniority). The second factor, skills and organization structure, included information sharing, formal job analysis, attitude surveys, training and selection testing, participation in quality circles or labour-management teams, and incentive payment schemes. The intelligibility of the factors is not perhaps as clear as Huselid takes them to be, particularly as one would expect incentive payment schemes to be under employee motivation, and there may be some overlap between it and appraisal being used to determine employee's compensation.

Huselid examined how each factor was related to labour turnover, productivity, measured by sales per employees, and two measures of corporate financial performance, a capital-market index of the value of the firm (Tobin's *q*, reflecting current and potential profitability) and gross rate of return on capital.

Neither factor was related to labour turnover, the human resource outcome. Employee Motivation, but not Employee Skills and Organizational Structures, was significantly positively associated with productivity. It was also related to Tobin's *q* measure of market value, but not to the gross rate of return on assets. In contrast the Employee Skills and Organizational Structures index was strongly related to the gross rate of return on assets but only weakly associated with Tobin's *q*.

Comparing the studies

The results of all the studies reviewed point in the direction of a link between HRM and performance. However, even in the same study the impact of HRM differs across performance outcomes. West *et al.* (2006) tested for one performance outcome and found a link between it and HRM. In those that tested for multiple outcomes Arthur's (1994) is the only study in which the measure of HRM is strongly related to all the (three) performance measures considered. Huselid *et al.* (1997) found that the strategic mode of HRM had an impact on performance, albeit weakly on one of their measures, but the technical mode did not, as they predicted. In Huselid's (1995) study, for example, the motivation factor was related to productivity but the skills and organization one was not, whilst the strength of the associations with the two profit measures varied between the two factors. Neither was related to labour turnover. Similarly, Delery and Doty (1996) identified seven aspects of HRM and two performance indicators. Only four of the 14 relationships were statistically significant. Moreover, their market system, which is related to performance, is almost antithetical to the high involvement system that to some extent the other studies are measuring. More generally Wall and Wood (2005) overviewed 25 studies from refereed journals and in only three of these were all the tested performance effects supported by the data.

Moreover, the studies are disparate in terms of the concepts and measures they use. Though in broad terms they cover similar practices, their emphasis and specific measures differ considerably. Huselid *et al.* (1997) is an exception to the others as it measured the effectiveness of practices in terms of respondents' satisfaction with the use of each practice, whereas the others record whether or not a practice is used but not its effectiveness. For example, Huselid (1995) measures whether appraisal is used to determine employees' pay, but did not assess how frequently or how well the appraisal was done. In West *et al.*'s study an index is used, whereas in Huselid's (1995) study two or more dimensions of HRM have been identified. One of the starkest contrasts is in the treatment of some practices and particularly performance-related pay, which for Arthur (1994) is associated with the control model, whereas for Huselid (1995) it is part of the high performance work system that entails employee involvement. It is especially significant that work enrichment or job empowerment is included in Arthur (1994) and Huselid *et al.* (1997) and omitted in Huselid (1995) and Koch and McGrath (1996), as this was a foundation of the original concept of high involvement or commitment management. Wood and Wall (2007) have indeed shown that there is an increasing tendency in the HRM-performance stream to omit work enrichment in their practices.

That there are differences is not a criticism of the individual studies, it is simply a statement about them as a whole. However, it makes it difficult to determine the nature and meaning of the overall pattern of results and implies that there are limits to what one can conclude from the studies. There is no clearly identifiable relationship between the types of practices included in the studies and the results. There is thus no stronger or weaker relationship between one set of practices than another. However, since the emphasis is on using indices or cluster analysis few studies have tested whether certain practices have stronger effects than others, as Delery and Doty (1996) did.

The studies we have reviewed, and others beside, have a number of other weaknesses. First, there are methodological problems, the most fundamental of which is that they are cross-sectional. They only test an association between HRM and performance at one point in time. This thus limits the extent to which one can make causal inferences about HRM affecting performance. It could be that high performing organizations are the ones that introduce certain types of HRM. Other methodological problems include the researchers' reliance on a single respondent in the organization for the measures of human resource practice and, in some cases, for performance measures. If the same person provides information on the practices and the performance this may result in common method bias as some respondents may over-estimate both their use of practices and their performance, while others may be systematically less optimistic in both respects. This may result in a positive relationship between the practices and performance being over-estimated.

Second, the studies have concentrated on human resource practices, which means that there is no control for other types of managerial practices. It could be that organizations that use sophisticated human resource practices tend also to use the most sophisticated practice in one or more areas of management and it is either these or the synergistic relationship between these and human resource management that is most telling for performance. Moreover, HRM practices, particularly ones associated with high involvement management, are widely associated with new operational management methods such as total quality management or lean production, which is an American expression for the use of Japanese management methods that aim to produce on a just-in-time basis using total quality management procedures (Womack *et al.*, 1990). In some accounts of these they are indeed assumed to be an integral part of them (e.g. Shah and Ward, 2003).

Third, few studies have evaluated competing hypotheses or models of performance. Typically a composite measure of HRM is used. Exceptions like Huselid's identification of two dimensions (motivation, and skill and organization factors), and tests of the interaction between these are rare. Even scarcer in these studies are tests of the association between performance and individual practices or adequate tests of synergies between practices (Wall and Wood, 2005)

The significance given to measuring the collective use of high involvement practices rests, so Appelbaum *et al.* (2000: 34) say, on the compelling 'argument that firms adopting a coherent set of workplace practices designed to maximize horizontal fit should have superior performance'. Yet there are three meanings of coherency referred to in the literature, namely: (a) the workplace practices are complementary, (b) synergies exist between the practices leading to positive interaction effects on performance, and (c) the practices form an integrated system. These are nonetheless often treated as if they are the same, when – as Wood and de Menezes (2008) show – they are not and entail discrete models of performance.

First, a complement of practices consists of all those practices that individually have a positive association with performance. As such, a complement of high performance practices would be made up of the practices that are best in each of the domains of HRM. Each would add something unique.

Second, synergistic practices are those that enhance the effect on performance of each other. A high performance synergistic set would be one in which all practices interact positively with each other so that the combined use of the practices has a greater effect than the sum of the effects of the individual practices.

Third, an integrated approach implies that the practices reflect an underlying orientation to HRM or distinctive approach, to use Arthur's term (1994), and it is this that is positively associated with performance. Orientations in general are organizing principles for guiding people's judgements and behaviour, so in the case of high involvement management such an orientation reflects an organization-wide concern for employee involvement. The core of this orientation is thus a philosophy, but it also entails the adoption of practices that are consistent with the high involvement concept. The practices can thus be treated as manifestations of the underlying philosophy or orientation.

The integration or orientations model should be tested by using scales that measure the underlying construct created from items – in this case practices – that are assumed to reflect or be caused by it. Such scales are sometimes called reflective indicators (Diamantopoulus and Siguaw, 2006) or effect indicators (Bollen, 1989: 64–5).The underlying assumption and essential requirement for creating scales is that the items are unidimensional, and hence that they are strongly associated with each other (Hattie, 1985). Reflective scales are contrasted with indices based on what are also known as formative indicators (Diamantopoulos and Siguaw, 2006) or cause indicators (Bollen, 1989: 64–5). DeVellis (1991: 204) gives the example of an index of socioeconomic status, which includes education that clearly influences rather than is caused by higher status. The assumption behind an index is that the items do not reflect or represent a single concept and that they are independent of each other. Aggregating the number of human resource practices used, as we have seen, is commonplace in the HRM area, assumes that each practice has an equal effect on organizational performance. They can thus be seen as tests of the complementary model, but only on the assumption that the beta coefficients in a performance equation for the variables in the index do not differ significantly.

However, most, if not all, of the researchers using indices refer to the synergistic nature of the relationship between the practices and performance. For example, Hoque (1999: 422) uses an index of practices to test what he refers to as 'the synergistic benefits resulting from the introduction of HRM as a . . . package of practices that cohere with and mutually reinforce each other'. This is not appropriate. The synergistic approach is best tested by inserting interaction terms involving two or more practices in performance equations. Cluster analysis, as used by Arthur and others, is also used on the assumption that testing the association between cluster membership and performance is a test of the synergistic model. But this is not an adequate test as it simply compares groupings of organizations on the basis of their having particular practices, not on the strength of the interaction effect.

Testing the orientations approach may entail an initial examination of the correlations between practices prior to determining whether an orientation underlies the data. Such assessments are rare. Equally, tests of the contingency argument that the strength of the relationship between HRM and performance is stronger or even only exists in certain circumstances, are uncommon; Delery and Doty's study is a rare exception. Finally there have been few attempts to examine the intermediate variables between HRM and performance, that is what might mediate any relationship that is found. Several factors have been mentioned as accounting for the relationship, including job satisfaction, organizational commitment, organization of work and methods of working, skill and knowledge levels, and proactive behaviours (Wood and Wall, 2007).

Though the three problems we have identified are widespread in the HRM-performance literature, there are, however, studies that have overcome one or more of these three problems. We will now introduce these studies.

Some other key HRM-performance studies

Capelli and Neumark: longitudinal analysis

Capelli and Neumark's (2001) study was the first that assessed the HRM-performance relationship using a longitudinal design. They use the high performance work practices nomenclature, but place 'employee involvement' at its centre. They particularly highlight teamwork as 'the typical mechanism through which employee involvement operates', but argue that other practices such as suggestion schemes and job rotation can create a sense of involvement as well. They also identify training in teamwork, pay-for skill and gain-sharing as important supporting practices.

Capelli and Neumark use a secondary data set, the National Employers Survey of the USA, which is administered by telephone interviews with the plant manager in the manufacturing sector or the local business manager in the service sector. The sample is of establishments in the private sector with 20 or more employees. Core work organization practices included in the study are team meetings (including quality circles), self-managed teams, and job rotation, whilst the other measures included are cross training, teamwork training, pay for skill, profit sharing and total quality management, which is treated as a form of employee involvement.

Productivity was measured by sales per worker, whilst labour costs per workers and unit labour costs were also estimated. Cappelli and Neumark test the complementary and synergistic models of performance.

None of the practices was significantly positively related to productivity, as expected. The one significant result was a negative association between job rotation and productivity. Nor was there any strong evidence of synergies between key practices, as measured by two-way interactions between practices. The interaction between profit-sharing and self-managed teams was significant in some specifications. Some of the practices were found to raise labour costs per worker – total quality management, team training and profit-sharing – but none of the key work organization ones did. This suggests that these practices raise wages or other benefits of workers, and hence compensation costs. Yet these costs are compensated for by some small increase in productivity so unit labour costs do not rise significantly. Overall the study found no strong support for a relationship between HRM and performance.

MacDuffie: Extending high involvement management to lean production

MacDuffie (1995) conducted a study of 62 car assembly plants, the majority of which were in the USA, Europe and Japan. This study was the first to include measures of lean production. The data was collected as part of a wider project, The MIT Future of the Automobile Project, from which the concept of Lean Production was developed.

MacDuffie separated three systems. First, a work system, which is centred on a high involvement management and is concerned with 'how work is organized, in terms of both formal work structures and the allocation of work responsibilities, and the participation of employees in production-related problem-solving activity' (p. 207). It was measured by an index (or formative scale) constituted by the percentage of the workforce involved in (a) teams, (b) employee involvement groups; the number of production-related suggestions received from employees; the percentage of suggestions implemented; the extent of job rotation; and the degree of production worker involvement in quality tasks.

The second system is the human resource system, which is concerned with the HRM practices that provide ways for workers to acquire skills and the incentives to boost their motivation (p. 200). It was measured by an index based on the following practices: staff selection was based on an openness to learning, rather than on previous relevant experience; minimal status barriers between managers and workers (i.e., harmonization across grades); training being provided for (a) new recruits and (b) experienced production staff and other staff; and pay levels were dependent on plant performance.

The third system is the lean production system, which measured the extent to which the system is buffer-less using an index of buffer-use based on three items: the average number of vehicles held in work-in-progress buffers as a percentage of output; the average level of components kept in stock; and the percentage of space dedicated to final repair. The lower the scores on each of these the more lean is the plant.

In MacDuffie's study plant performance was measured by labour productivity, defined as the labour hours to build a vehicle; and quality, the number of defects per vehicle. Labour productivity was made comparable across plants by adjustments to reflect differences due to the complexity of the product (e.g., number of components and welds).

MacDuffie found that the three indices were associated with productivity and moreover the three-way interaction was likewise related, indicating a synergistic relationship between them. MacDuffie called such a system the flexible production system. In the case of quality, the work system index and the human resource policies index were associated with superior quality, but the lean index was not significantly related to it, and there was not a synergistic relationship amongst the three sets of practices. The results offered considerable support for the hypothesis that both high involvement management and supporting motivational HRM practices are associated with superior performance or at least productivity and quality in manufacturing, and in the case of productivity that these have a synergistic relationship with lean production. We again though have a slight difference in results across performance measures.

Birdi, Clegg, Patterson, Robinson, Stride, Wall and Wood: Extending high involvement management to lean production with longitudinal analysis

Birdi *et al.* (2008) examined both the complementary and synergistic models of performance. They focused on the impact of three human resource practices central to either the high involvement or human capital perspective: empowerment, teamwork and extensive training. Each was measured by a single item – but the respondents were given a description of the practice by the interviewer. In the case of empowerment it was defined as 'passing considerable responsibility for operational management to individuals or teams (rather than keeping all decision-making at the managerial level)'. The measure thus captured both the job involvement associated with enriched jobs with high levels of discretion and the type of organizational involvement associated with problem-solving and idea generation, as in the high involvement model. Teams was defined separately from empowerment as placing operators into teams with their own responsibilities and given the freedom to allocate work between team members. Birdi *et al.* also included three operational management techniques associated with lean production – just-in-time, total quality management, supply-chain partnering, as well as advanced manufacturing technology.

Birdi *et al.*'s study involved analyzing the performance of 308 UK companies over 22 years. During the 22-year period the companies implemented some or all of these practices. The longitudinal research design enabled the researchers to assess the extent to which the introduction of a practice had some effect on their indicator of company performance, value-added, which is a key measure of productivity that they derived from the companies' profit and loss accounts.

Using multi-level regression analysis, with time embedded in company, Birdi *et al.* found that, of the seven practices, only empowerment and extensive training had a clear impact on value-added in the years following their introduction, an effect that did not differ across types of manufacturing firms. Extensive training had a significant effect on productivity following its introduction, but the size of its effect varied across firms.

Highly significantly, Birdi *et al.* also found that the performance of all practices was enhanced by teamwork. Empowerment and extensive training thus had even more effect when firms used teamwork. Moreover, all the operational practices, just-in-time, total quality management, supply-chain partnering, and advanced manufacturing technology, had a positive effect on performance if teamwork was being adopted, when they did not have an effect where work was not organized on a team basis. Empowerment and Extensive Training also enhanced the effect of TQM, while empowerment had a similar effect on the impact of supply-chain partnering, and extensive training on just-in-time.

Birdi *et al.*'s study thus showed that some but not all HRM practices have a unique association with productivity. Empowerment and, to a lesser extent, extensive training are crucial in their own right; while teamwork has a synergistic effect on all other practices, including the operational methods. As such the study shows that relative to operational practices, human resource factors are more significant than operational practices, or at least are vital ingredients for making lean production work. Without empowerment or teamwork the potential returns on investing in just-in-time, total quality management and supply-chain partnering will not be fully realized.

Wood and de Menezes: Testing competing hypotheses

Wood and de Menezes (2008) explicitly test the complementary, synergistic and integration perspectives, that is the associations between performance and (a) individual practices, (b) the joint use of individual practices, and (c) a high involvement orientation. They use data from the UK's Workplace Employee Relations Survey of 1998, which is a survey based on managerial respondents of 2,191 workplaces across the whole economy, private and public.

Because of their interest in the orientation perspective they first assessed whether an orientation underlaid the use of practices associated with high involvement management such as teamwork, quality circles, functional flexibility, suggestion schemes, and training geared to aiding these, and the motivational supports for these (reported in full by de Menezes and Wood, 2006). They first established that there was a strong correlation amongst all the practices, regardless of whether they were high involvement or motivational practices. They then showed that the correlation between the high involvement practices concerned with work organization and skill acquisition was explained by a common factor, and thus they tended to be used as a single coherent system, which reflected an underlying high involvement orientation. The motivational practices were neither part of the high involvement orientation nor formed a unified set. The work enrichment measures were also discrete from high involvement management or the individual motivational supports. This suggests that the use of high involvement management is not limited to contexts where jobs have high levels of autonomy or variety. Also the use of the motivational supports may be quite common without high involvement management. Wood and de Menezes also found a strong association between high involvement management and total quality management, which itself is an identifiable orientation.

Given this prior analysis, Wood and de Menezes (2008) assessed the association between high involvement management, enriched jobs, motivational supports and total quality management on performance discretely. High involvement management and total quality management were measured by a reflective scale, while enriched jobs and motivational supports were measured by individual practices.

Wood and De Menezes measured the workplaces' performance on four dimensions: productivity, the rate of change in productivity, labour turnover and absenteeism. The first two measures were based on an assessment by the managers responding to the question, the other two on their reporting of actual levels.

The tests of the complementary and synergistic perspective revealed that the individual practices that reflect the high involvement orientation or two-way interactions between them were not related to any performance measure.

However, there was some support for the orientations perspective, since the high involvement orientation was linked to both the level and rate of change in labour productivity. But it was not, however, a main effect, as its relationship with productivity was moderated by total quality management. Similarly, the high involvement orientation's association with the rate of change in productivity was moderated by a motivational support, variable pay.

Total quality management was a main effect in both the level and rate of change of productivity equations. While variable pay was a main effect in the productivity change model. Finally, and most significantly, the practices that were mostly strongly related to productivity were job variety and method control, both dimensions of enriched jobs.

The high involvement orientation was not related to labour turnover and its association with absenteeism was the opposite of that predicted: the greater the level of the orientation, the higher the absence. Job security guarantees, a motivational practice, was, however, related to labour turnover. But no motivational or work enrichment practice was associated with absence. The study shows the advantage of testing competing hypotheses and differentiating different aspects of HRM, as the links to performance vary across them and between performance measures.

Wood, van Veldhoven, Croon, and de Menezes (2008) assessing mediators of HRM-performance links

Wood *et al.* (2008) used the WERS survey of 2004, using data from the equivalent management survey to the 1998 one used by Wood and de Menezes and the employee survey that is conducted in the majority of those workplaces that responded to the management survey. First, they show that high involvement management, using the measure used in the above Wood and de Menezes (2008) study, was associated positively with productivity (also measured as in the 1998 survey) in the 2004 data. A measure of work enrichment was also associated positively with this; but in addition it was positively associated with quality and financial performance, both measured by an assessment by the managerial respondent, and negatively related to absenteeism.

Wood *et al.* (2008) examined the association between high involvement management and work enrichment on employees' well-being using multi-level regression analysis. Well-being was measured using data from the employee survey by a scale of job satisfaction (based on eight facets of job satisfaction) and Warr's (1990) measure of contentment–anxiety. High involvement management was found to be unrelated to job satisfaction, and negatively related to contentment–anxiety, which is not as predicted. High involvement management increased anxiety. In contrast, work enrichment, concerned with the extent of discretion and variety the employee had, was positively related to both well-being measures, job satisfaction and contentment–anxiety. Furthermore, Wood *et al.* (2008) showed that job satisfaction mediated the relationship between work enrichment and all four of the performance outcomes, and this mediation was particularly strong in the case of quality.

That job satisfaction is an intervening variable between work enrichment and performance offers support for the mutual gains model of HRM. However, in the case of high involvement management, the findings suggest that there may be a conflict between its effects on employers' outcomes and those on employees as their anxiety may increase with its use. Wood *et al.* suggest that this may arise if high involvement management entails labour intensification, i.e. people having to work harder. But it also may arise because the encouragement of workers to be proactive and flexible creates anxieties through the implied pressure to improve their overall contribution to the organization. These may, in turn, raise concerns in the worker's mind about both their competencies and their job security, since the high involvement management may be seen as threatening their jobs if they do not raise their performance.

Conclusions

This review of the research on the HRM-performance relationship has painted a mixed picture. The studies differ in their foci, coverage of practices and performance measures, as well as samples and methods of data collection. The results vary significantly even across performance measures in the individual studies. At best they show that it is a promising area of study. But it is premature to conclude that certain practices are superior to others or that a particularly HRM approach can be singled out as the high performance approach. We need to establish more clearly the nature of any links between practices or orientations and particular outcomes before we can be more decisive.

The way forward has been shown by the studies we reviewed in the latter half of the chapter. We need to clearly assess the relationship between practices prior to any attempt to develop composite measures. This will determine the nature of any integrated use of practice or managerial orientations. We need then to test the relationship between individual practices and performance, individually and jointly through interaction terms, and compare these with the relationship between orientations, where these are identified, and performance. Then tests involving mediators and moderators can be introduced. Given the negative results in the longitudinal study of Capelli and Neumark it clearly cannot be taken for granted that some links between certain practices or dimensions of HRM will be found. Nonetheless, theoretical analysis could usefully be focused more than it has on why we might find different relationships across performance measures.

It is also too early to make hard-and-fast decisions about the merits of the shareholder and stakeholder models or whether they are reconcilable. Not only is the evidence of performance effects not strong enough but more importantly there has been insufficient attention to the mediators of any HRM-performance or link and the association of HRM with worker outcomes. Nonetheless, the study by Wood *et al.* (2008) suggests that the conclusions may differ depending on the practice. In the case of work enrichment it appears from their study to benefit both shareholders and stakeholders. But in the case of high involvement management it appears to have benefits for shareholders but may have costs in the form of increased anxiety for workers. This may imply that managements might need in the long-run to make trade-offs between profits and workers' well-being or find ways of reducing the anxiety currently associated with high involvement management.

References

Appelbaum, E., Bailey, T., Berg, P. and Kalleberg, A. L. (2000). *Manufacturing Advantage: Why High Performance Work Systems Pay Off.* Ithaca, NY: Cornell University Press.

Arthur, J. B. (1994). Effects of human resource systems on manufacturing performance and turnover, *Academy of Management Journal*, 7: 670–87.

Bailey, T. (1993). Discretionary effort and the organization of work: employee participation and work reform since Hawthorne, *mimeo*, Teachers College, Columbia University.

Bollen, K. A. (1989). *Structural Equations with Latent Variables*. New York: Wiley.

Boxall, P. and Purcell, J. (2003). *Strategy and Human Resource Management.* Basingstoke: Palgrave MacMillan.

Cappelli, P. and Neumark, D. (2001). Do 'high performance' work practices improve establishment-level outcomes? *Industrial and Labor Relations Review*, 54: 737–75.

Delery, J. E. and Doty, D. H. (1996). Modes of theorizing in strategic human resource management: tests of universalistic, contingency, and configurational performance predictions, *Academy of Management Journal*, 39(4): 802–35.

de Menezes, L. M. and Wood, S. (2006). The reality of flexible work systems in Britain. *International Journal of Human Resource Management,* 17: 1–33.

DeVellis, R. F. (1991). *Scale Development: Theory and Applications*. Newbury Park, California: Sage.

Diamantopoulos, A. and Siguaw, J. (2006). 'Formative versus reflective indictors in organizational measure development: A comparison and empirical illustration', *British Journal of Management*, 117: 263–82.

Gerhart, B. (2008). Horizontal and vertical fit in human resource systems, in C. Otroff and T. A. Judge (Eds), *Perspectives on Fit*, pp. 317–48. New York: Lawrence and Erlbaum.

Hattie, J. (1985). Methodology review: Assessing unidimensionality of tests and items, *Applied Psychological Measurement*, 9: 139–64.

Hoque, K. (1999). Human resource management and performance in the UK hotel industry, *British Journal of Industrial Relations*, 37: 419–43.

Huselid, M. A. (1995). The impact of human resource management practices on turnover, productivity, and corporate financial performance, *Academy of Management Journal*, 38: 635–72.

Huselid, M. A., Jackson, S. E. and Schuler, R. S. (1997). Technical and strategic human resource management effectiveness as a determinant of firm performance. *Academy of Management Journal*, 40: 171–88.

Kalleberg, A. L., Marsden, P. V., Reynolds, J. and Knoke, D. (2006). 'Beyond Profit? Sectoral Differences in High-Performance Work Practices', *Work and Occupations*, 33: 271–302.

Koch, M. J. and McGrath, R. G. (1996). Improving labor productivity: Human resource management policies do matter, *Strategic Management Journal*, 17: 335–54.

Lawler, E. E. (1986). *High Involvement Management*. San Francisco: Jossey-Bass.

MacDuffie, J. P. (1995). Human resource bundles and manufacturing performance: organizational logic and flexible production systems in the world auto industry, *Industrial and Labor Relations Review*, 48: 197–21.

Pfeffer, J. (1998). *The Human Equation: Building Profits by Putting People First*. Boston, MA: Harvard Business School Press.

Shah, R. and Ward, P. T. (2003). Lean manufacturing: Context, practice bundles, and performance, *Journal of Operations Management*, 21: 129–49.

Vroom, V. H. (1964). *Work and Motivation*. New York: Wiley.

Wall, T. D. and Wood, S. (2005). The romance of human resource management and business performance and the case for big science, *Human Relations,* 58: 1–34. [Reprinted in Anderson, N. (Ed.) (2007). *Fundamentals in HRM: Sage's Major Works*, Volume 4 (pp. 71–95). London: Sage].

Wall, T. D., Wood, S. J. and Leach, D. J. (2004). Empowerment and performance, in C. L. Cooper and I. T. Robertson (Eds), *International Review of Industrial and Organizational Psychology*, Vol. 19, pp. 1–46. London: Wiley.

Walton, R. E. (1985). From 'control' to 'commitment' in the workplace, *Harvard Business Review*, 63: 77–84.

Warr, P. (1990). The measurement of well-being and other aspects of mental health, *Journal of Occupational Psychology*, 63: 193–210.

West, M. A., Guthrie, J. P., Dawson, J. F., Borrill, C. S. and Carter, M. (2006). Reducing patient mortality in hospitals: The role of human resource management, *Journal of Organizational Behaviour*, 27: 983–1002.

Womack, J., Jones, D. T. and Roos, D. (1990). *The Machine That Changed the World*. New York: Rawson.

Wood, S. and de Menezes, L. M. (2008). Comparing perspectives on high involvement management and organizational performance across the British economy, *International Journal of Human Resource Management*, 19: 639–83.

Wood, S., van Veldhoven, M., Croon, M. and de Menezes, L.M. (2008). High involvement management, work enrichment and well-being: Mutual gains or conflicting outcome?, paper presented at the IWP2008 conference, *mimeo*, Sheffield: Institute of Work Psychology, University of Sheffield.

Wood, S. J. and Wall, T. D. (2007). Human resource management and employee voice, *International Journal of Human Resource Management*, 18: 1335–72.

5 HRM

An ethical perspective

Mick Fryer

Introduction: questioning welfare humanism

Discussions about the relationship between HRM and ethics often make a *welfare humanist* presupposition. By this, I mean that they assume that the ethicality of HRM practice should be measured in relation to its responsiveness to the needs and aspirations of employees. An ethical premium is thus placed on those practices which promote the self-actualization and self-esteem of individuals, which safeguard their material interests and which facilitate their emotional well-being. This presupposition opposes what might be called an agenda of *managerialist performativity*. In other words, it is presented as standing against pressures to conform to the imperatives of commercial performance and to place the achievement of strategic success above other considerations. According to the welfare humanist presupposition, then, looking after people is an ethically sound basis for HRM practice. Conversely, looking after business, where this conflicts with looking after people, is seen as morally questionable.

Now, it is easy to sympathize with the welfare humanist agenda, for its intuitive moral allure is readily apparent. Welfare humanism radiates a comforting, moral glow while managerialist performativity reflects the steely glint of calculating instrumentalism. However, unquestioned allegiance to the welfare humanist moral agenda is problematic in at least two respects. The first problem is that welfare humanism must confront some persuasive, moral arguments in favour of prioritizing organizational success over and above employee well-being. For example, supporters of the managerialist performativity agenda might draw on the work of Adam Smith (1998 [1776]) to argue that if businesses focus purely on maximizing profit within free market conditions this will, ultimately, be in everyone's best interests. Alternatively, they may point to Milton Friedman's (1970) contention that the only moral responsibility that is apposite to the business context is managers' responsibility to maximize financial returns for shareholders. In order to challenge positions such as these we need to be armed with more than an emotivist commitment to the principles of welfare humanism. A sound basis of ethical rationale is called for if HRM is to be cast as anything more than the champion of employees' rights and interests against those of other stakeholders.

A second respect in which allegiance to the welfare humanist agenda may be problematic is that spelling out of that agenda is not a simple matter. The task of definition is complicated partly by the possibility that the perceived rights or interests of one group of employees may conflict with those of other groups (Stanworth, 2000). For example, tension between core employees and agency workers, between the local workforce and remote employees, or even between junior and 'managerial' employees may present dilemmas. Furthermore, it is not always easy to build a clear understanding of an organization's moral responsibilities even as they relate to one specific group of employees. For instance, should feelings of paternalistic care take precedence over libertarian principles of self determination; or does the apparent 'fairness' of performance-related pay justify a consequent intensification of risk for employees (Heery, 2000)?

Where should we turn for guidance, then, if they wish to move beyond unquestioning acceptance of welfare humanism? Fortunately, an abundant reservoir of moral theory is available to assist those who seek an ethical basis for HRM practice. Even if we confine ourselves to the Western philosophical tradition, we are able to draw upon the insights offered by more than two and a half millennia of enquiry into the nature of right and wrong, good and bad. Unfortunately, though, the extent and multifarious nature of moral philosophy also presents HRM practitioners with a difficulty. Despite the protracted history of ethical enquiry moral philosophers have yet to reach consensus. Their endeavours have resulted in a bewildering array of conclusions and perspectives, presenting diverse and often contrasting implications for workplace practice.

In response to this difficulty I will propose, in this chapter, an approach to mapping some of these theories and considering what they have to say for HRM. This approach consists of differentiating theories in relation to their *meta-ethical* presuppositions. In other words, it consists of grouping ethics theory according to different ways of *thinking about* ethics. I will refer to three meta-ethical perspectives, or three different ways of thinking about ethics, as *objectivist theory*, *relativist theory* and *intersubjectivist theory*.

In the following sections I will describe each of these three meta-ethical perspectives and outline some implications that each holds for HRM. I will begin by considering, in turn, objectivist theory and subjectivist theory. I will suggest that each offers valuable insights to the relationship between ethics and HRM. However, I will also suggest that each presents, at best, an ambivalent guide for HRM practitioners. In presenting the third perspective, intersubjectivist theory, I will suggest that, although its implementation presents a number of practical challenges, it nevertheless provides a magnetic pole towards which HRM practitioners might orientate their ethical compasses. I will go on to discuss some practical applications of intersubjectivist ethics in the realm of HRM. Specifically, I will reflect on its resonance with the notion of *employee voice*. I will also describe how the lens of intersubjectivist ethics might help us to evaluate the ethicality of contrasting applications of employee voice.

Objectivist theory

Objectivist ethical theory is characterized by a belief that moral rightness and wrongness can be assessed in accordance with standards that are valid for all people, at all times and in all places. Although these universally valid standards need to be interpreted and applied in a manner which responds to the uniqueness of each specific situation, objectivist theorists propose that the standards themselves remain the same. According to objectivist theory, then, finding a recipe for ethical HRM practice would comprise indentifying those universally valid standards and applying them to the work context.

In seeking to identify the absolute standards which should shape our moral evaluations, different objectivist theorists have arrived at different conclusions. I will discuss two particular paths that objectivist theorists have taken: *utilitarianism* and *deontological theory*. In focusing on these two approaches, I will omit discussion of some other prominent objectivist theories that readers may have encountered. However, I believe that the points that I will make about utilitarian and deontological theory also relate to other objectivist approaches.

Utilitarian theory proposes that the 'right' thing to do is to promote the greatest amount of good for the greatest number of people. When faced with a moral dilemma, utilitarians suggest that we should consider the likely consequences of the various choices open to us and select the option that will bring about the greatest good. Maximization of the good is therefore the objective standard that utilitarians apply to guide their moral deliberations.

There is some disagreement amongst utilitarians about quite what 'the good' consists of. Jeremy Bentham's (2000 [1789]) seminal elaboration of utilitarianism proposed that pleasure is the ultimate good; therefore maximization of pleasure and minimization of suffering should comprise the absolute standard of moral evaluation. Other utilitarians find Bentham's analysis too narrow, suggesting, for example, that it is also intrinsically good for people to achieve self-actualization and to satisfy so called 'higher order' needs. Despite these disagreements in defining 'the good', the implication of all of these variants of utilitarianism for HRM is that HRM practice is ethical insofar as it brings about the best possible consequences for the greatest number of people.

Whereas utilitarianism judges the moral probity of our actions in relation to the consequences that they bring about, deontological theory focuses on rights and duties. When considering an ethically-charged situation, deontologists propose that we should pay attention to the rights and duties that pertain to that situation. This accords with the way we often talk about ethics. For example, we often speak about 'human rights', 'citizenship rights' or 'employment rights'. The assumption underpinning such discourse is that people have certain rights, which carry intrinsic value, and that others have a duty to respect those rights. Within the business ethics context, deontological discourse sometimes revolves around discussion of the rights of *stakeholders*. The idea behind such discussion is that various stakeholders – such as employees, suppliers, customers and shareholders – have rights because of their relationship with the business (Donaldson and Preston, 1995). This entails that businesses have a duty to respect those rights.

The implication of both utilitarian and deontological theory for HRM is that, when confronted with a moral dilemma, practitioners should apply the universal principles upon which the respective theory is based in order to identify the morally correct course of action. Practitioners may find themselves confronted with an immediate difficulty though. This is that utilitarian and deontological principles often lead to contrasting practical prescriptions. This is hardly surprising given that utilitarianism focuses on maximizing beneficial consequences for all, whereas deontological theory emphasizes moral commitments that are enshrined in specific rights and duties. Very often, there is a conflict between consequential considerations of the greater good and our perceived duties towards specific individuals. Practitioners may therefore have to find some further basis upon which to choose which theory they should favour in concrete situations.

A further difficulty is that, even after we have made a choice between utilitarian and deontological theory, the pathway towards moral probity may remain unclear. Despite the apparent simplicity of the decision making principles proffered by objectivist theories, these still have to be interpreted and applied to specific situations. And in the act of interpretation and application there is ample scope for ambivalence. This soon becomes apparent when we consider how either a utilitarian or deontological rationale can be used to provide legitimacy for both the welfare humanist and managerial performativity agendas.

Let us begin by considering these respective agendas on utilitarian grounds. On the one hand, a supporter of managerial performativity might point out that many people benefit from the commercial prosperity of a business: its shareholders, its suppliers, its customers and the majority of its employees. Therefore, actions which cause a certain amount of moral disquiet in relation to particular groups of employees, such as imposing stressful working practices, are justified as long as they enhance commercial performance and thus benefit those wider groups. In such instances, HR managers' sense of responsibility to care for the interests of minority groups of employees takes second place to their responsibility to maximize the greater good.

On the other hand, a supporter of welfare humanism might call upon us to broaden the scope of consequential consideration beyond those who are most directly affected by a business's activities and take into account its wider impact on society. We might thus conclude that some actions which enhance commercial performance, and which thus maximize the good for those directly impacted by the business, undermine maximization of the good on a broader plane. For example, it could be argued that an overriding focus on competitiveness and commercial success, along with the psychological, emotional and physical pressures that this places on employees, generates all sorts of personal and family-related malaise, the consequences of which society has to bear. Therefore, a more responsive approach to employee well-being, one which sought to minimize such pressures, would, ultimately, be in everyone's interest.

Clearly then, utilitarian judgements are not always straightforward in HRM contexts. They depend upon a range of empirical and evaluative premises. They require complex predictions and comparisons of the likely consequences of contrasting courses of action. They also require us to decide how far we should extend the scope of our consequential calculations. Deontological evaluation is similarly fraught with ambivalence. This is partly because HRM-related moral dilemmas generally involve tension between competing rights or between conflicting duties to different people. The notion of stakeholding is particularly laden with such tension, since it entails ample scope for conflict between the rights of different stakeholder groups.

Although we sometimes talk of natural rights as if they are intuitively apparent, the occurrence of conflict between apparently intuitive rights has encouraged some philosophers to seek a rational basis upon which we can precisely define rights and duties and thus resolve such conflicts. However, contrasting rational accounts can still lead to contrasting practical prescriptions. Two such attempts, which have particular resonance within the business ethics context and which illustrate how different rationales can point towards contrasting conclusions, are those of Robert Nozick (1974) and John Rawls (1971).

Nozick (1974) places a great deal of emphasis on property rights. He suggests that the right to hold and transfer property is fundamental to Western culture and that it should be respected at all costs. *Shareholder theorists* carry this preoccupation with property rights into the arena of corporate governance. Milton Friedman (1970), for example, proposes that, since business managers are employed by shareholders to manage their property, those managers' overriding responsibility is to do what shareholders wish them to do with that property. According to Friedman, shareholders generally wish to make as much money as possible from their shares. Therefore, the overriding responsibility of business managers is to maximize profit. This prioritization of property rights clearly lends itself to the managerial performativity HRM agenda: if property rights are all important and business managers' paramount duty is to maximize shareholder returns, then it is morally legitimate to subordinate the interests of employees to that end.

An alternative approach to defining duty, which avoids an overriding emphasis on the property rights of shareholders, is offered by John Rawls (1971). Rawls offers a way of deriving a notion of fairness which can, in turn, be used to identify the nature of our duty. Rawls proposes that, in order to ascertain fairness in a particular situation, we should imaginatively project ourselves to an 'original position' in which we are ignorant of our actual status in our current situation. We should then ask ourselves to consider, from this hypothetical original position of impartiality, what would be a fair resolution to that current situation. Rawls suggests that a 'reasonable citizen', when adopting such a stance, would opt for resolutions which favour less advantaged groups. So, whereas Nozick's (1974) focus on property rights prioritizes business's duty to maximize shareholder wealth, Rawls' approach accentuates business's duty to other, less advantaged stakeholders such as employees and local communities. Whereas Nozick's theory is consistent with the managerial performativity agenda, Rawls's approach tends to be more sympathetic to a welfare humanist stance.

Despite the intuitive reasonableness of each objectivist theory, then, these theories do not provide the unequivocal guide to ethical HRM practice that, at first sight, they may promise. The moral conclusions to which objectivist theory leads will depend very much on the particular theory that is chosen and on the manner in which it is interpreted and applied. But this is not the only problem faced by objectivist theory. A further difficulty is articulated by John Kaler's (1999) suggestion that we do not tend to think about practical problems of business ethics in terms of principles such as 'maximization of the good' or by considering specific rights and duties. This, Kaler argues, assumes an overly methodical understanding of moral evaluation. Instead, he suggests that we tend to base our business ethics judgements on an overall apprehension of what is the morally correct thing to do in the circumstances. Indeed, Kaler notes that we tend to test our moral theories with reference to our common sense judgements of right and wrong, rather than the other way round: if a theoretical principle points in a direction with which we feel morally uncomfortable, Kaler suggests that we would be more inclined to ditch the theoretical principle than to act against our moral gut feel.

If we agree with Kaler, then there would seem to be little need for objectivist moral theories in the resolution of our HRM dilemmas: we should let intuitive moral judgement be our guide rather than going to the trouble of interpreting and applying theoretical principles. Combining Kaler's analysis with my observations about the ambivalence of objectivist theory, we might conclude that objectivist theory's prime purpose is a justificatory one: it can be used mainly to reassure ourselves and to persuade others of the ethical probity of the actions towards which our intuitive moral judgement has already pointed us.

Criticisms such as these might be used to point towards a relativistic meta-ethical perspective, which I will discuss shortly. Before doing so, though, I will just say a few words in defence of objectivist ethics. Even if we agree that objectivist theories do not provide unequivocal prescriptions for action, and even if we agree with Kaler that we do not make moral decisions with reference to ethical theories, we might nevertheless accede that different objectivist theories serve a useful purpose in drawing attention to relevant aspects of morally charged situations that we might not otherwise have considered. Thus, a utilitarian perspective invites us to think of the long-term consequences of our actions, particularly as they affect people who do not spring readily to our attention. Similarly, deontological theory might evoke sensitivity to the relationship that a business has with its less strident stakeholders. Even if we agree with Kaler that we make moral decisions by applying a sort of moral gut-feel, we might nevertheless argue that the quality of our decision-making will be enhanced if that gut feel is exposed to a degree of critical reflection. Furthermore, a useful way of carrying out that critical reflection is to consider a morally charged situation through the lenses of a range of objectivist theories.

Relativist theory

Whereas objectivist theory proposes that absolute standards of moral rightness exist which apply to all people in all places at all times, relativist theory challenges that notion. Relativist ethics accentuates the role of individual choice and cultural habituation in our moral evaluations. Relativist ethics therefore casts into doubt the idea that the moral rightness of workplace practice can be evaluated by the application of objective standards.

One of the most influential and energetic proponents of relativist theory is Friedrich Nietzsche. Nietzsche (2003 [1887]) proposes that the basis for any system of moral values lies in convention and has no claim to legitimacy outside of that convention. Furthermore, he suggests that those moral standards that gain conventional acceptance within any culture tend to be those which are consistent with the interests of that culture's dominant members. Later theorists, who are sometimes referred to as *postmodern*, echo aspects of Nietzschean thought in drawing attention to the culturally embedded dimension of value judgements. They emphasize the extent to which upbringing, prior social interactions, material circumstances and personal aspirations shape the way that we perceive, understand and evaluate our world. Michel Foucault (2002 [1954–1984]), for example, emphasizes the connection between power and our attributions of 'knowledge', thus alerting us to way in which some of the fundamental presuppositions of our value systems are shaped by power relationships.

The significance that these commentators place on cultural habituation tends to undermine any solid basis for judging right and wrong. They propose that criteria of evaluation, including moral evaluation, are no more than contingently accepted norms which lack legitimacy outside of the community of thought within which they prevail. The rug is thus pulled from beneath any supposedly objective, absolute standards of moral rightness.

Whereas postmodern theory emphasizes the extent to which moral sentiment is shaped by cultural habituation, *existentialism* stresses the autonomy of the individual as a moral author. Jean-Paul Sartre offers a personal account which expresses the existentialist approach to morality. Sartre relates how he is approached by a student for advice about an agonizing moral choice that the student faces. Confronted by two possible options, both of which have implications that are deeply troubling on a moral level, the student asks Sartre what he should do. Sartre's response is: 'you are free, therefore choose' (1973 [1946]: 38). The message entailed in Sartre's advice is that there are no absolute standards to which the student can refer in making his choice. The only legitimate criterion of moral choice, according to Sartre, is one's personal commitment to that choice. Presumably, if Sartre had been confronted by an HRM practitioner seeking advice on a particularly thorny work-related dilemma, his response would have been the same: he would have emphasized the practitioner's freedom to make their own moral choice and to act on that choice.

Despite differences in emphasis between various strands of postmodern and existentialist ethics, they hold similar implications as far as the relationship between morality and HRM is concerned. They suggest that there are no absolute standards by which HRM practice can be morally evaluated. The moral path that we choose to follow can be no more than an expression of cultural habituation or individual commitment. Such choices are deprived of objective legitimacy and there are no absolute standards by which their rightness or wrongness can be assessed. Observers who are inspired by postmodern thought might account for disagreements about ethical HRM practice as arising from contrasting backgrounds, divergent experiences and conflicting material aspirations.

Alternatively, they might consider such disagreements as the outcome of contrasting power-oriented agendas, with each side seeking to assert its own interests and aspirations over those its opponents. Meanwhile, existentialists would suggest that selecting between the moral claims of different HRM agendas is a matter of individual commitment that admits of no further appeal. Moral debate about HRM thus approximates to a shouting match, with each side upholding its own perspective and the side that is better placed to impose its agenda is most likely to end as the winner.

Postmodern and existentialist theorists offer persuasive philosophical rationales in support of their meta-ethical stance. However, despite the persuasiveness of these underpinning rationales, the relativist conclusions to which they lead seem, on the face of it, to offer little assistance to those seeking a guide to ethical HRM practice. To be told that moral judgement is no more than an expression of cultural habituation or that there is no basis, other than one's personal commitment, upon which moral choices can be made might seem a little frustrating. Intellectually stimulating though relativist ethics might be on a theoretical level, it seems to offer little in the way of practical guidance.

However, before we write-off the practical relevance of relativist theory, it is important to highlight some important insights that it offers to our practical deliberations about workplace ethics. First, by pointing to the significance of cultural habituation, postmodern theory reminds us of the extent to which our value judgements are influenced by our background and by the views of our social and professional peers. It therefore alerts us to the need to open the presuppositions upon which we base our moral evaluations to critical reflection. In pointing to the contingent element in our moral commitments, postmodern theory may thus encourage respect for diversity: appreciation of the extent to which our own value judgements may be restricted by our own context encourages us to give a more receptive hearing to discrepant perspectives which we might otherwise have dismissed. In particular, consideration of the relationship between power and conventional values alerts us to the extent to which accepted norms might be shaped by the interests of the status quo.

A second important message lies in the emphasis which existentialists place on moral autonomy. By drawing attention to the extent to which we are always free to make choices, existentialism leaves no hiding place from our moral responsibilities. We may feel constrained by peer pressure, by self-interest or by the expectations of influential parties to do things which make us feel morally uncomfortable. However, existentialism reminds us that we are always free to resist these constraints. Whether or not to act in what we consider to be a moral fashion is a choice that we are always free to make.

Intersubjectivist theory

Objectivist theory seeks to identify universally valid foundations of moral legitimacy while relativist theory draws attention to the role of cultural habituation and individual choice in moral evaluation. Intersubjectivist theory adopts neither an objectivist nor a relativist stance. Instead, it offers a process-based model of moral legitimation: it proposes that the moral desirability of states of affairs derives from the processes by which those states of affairs are brought about. To be more exact, it accords legitimacy to states of affairs insofar as they emanate from processes of discourse involving those people who are implicated in them. Therefore, according to the intersubjectivist meta-ethic, the ethicality of HRM practices is determined by the extent to which those practices promote and respond to discourse amongst the people who they affect.

In order to elaborate the intersubjectivist stance, I will begin by reflecting on how *virtue ethics* points us in the direction of intersubjectivist theory. I will then describe how Jürgen Habermas, in his discussion of communication (1979 [1976], 1984 [1981], 1987 [1981]) and *discourse ethics* (1990 [1983]), develops certain aspects of the virtue tradition in order to present some processual conditions to which discourse needs to conform in order to provide a source of moral legitimacy.

Virtue ethics theory proposes that the moral probity of a person's actions can be judged in relation to their conformity to the standards of virtuous conduct that prevail within a given community. Stated as simply as that, virtue theory seems to offer a relativist analysis of morality. If morality is to be judged purely in relation to the ethical norms that are accepted within a particular community, then surely this leaves us in the cultural relativist position that I have just discussed. However, virtue ethicists avoid the slide into cultural relativism by emphasizing certain aspects of the community whose value system is thus accorded moral legitimacy. Those conditions feature prominently in the descriptions of virtue offered by Aristotle (1999 [334–322 BC]), virtue theory's most prominent ancient proponent. As far as Aristotle was concerned, moral behaviour is behaviour which conforms to the virtuous standards of the community within which he taught philosophy. That community was the Ancient Greek city-state of Athens. And an important feature of Athens in the fourth century BC which, for Aristotle, lent moral legitimacy to its standards of virtue was the involvement of its citizens in the key decisions which affected them. For the Athenian political system comprised a type of direct democracy in which citizens regularly met to discuss and decide on how the city-state was to be run.

Aristotle considered our capacity to participate in direct democratic processes to be the defining characteristic of humanity. He believed that this capacity for political participation distinguishes us from other sentient creatures and thus offers a foundation for the attribution of moral probity. However, it is important to note that Aristotle does not attribute the morally legitimizing force of direct democracy to its efficacy in identifying moral outcomes. If this were his stance, he would be adopting an objectivist perspective: he would be assuming that there is an objectively 'right way' and that direct democracy is the most effective way of identifying that right way. But this is not Aristotle's position. For Aristotle, the fact that an issue has been decided upon by all those who it affects *confers* moral legitimacy on its outcome; direct democracy is not a means of *identifying* moral probity; it is a means of *conferring* moral probity.

More recently, Alasdair MacIntyre (1984, 1988), an influential contemporary advocate of virtue theory, has suggested that the standards of virtue that prevail within a community, or 'tradition', are partly legitimated by the extent to which that tradition is open to engagement with contrasting moral perspectives of other traditions. MacIntyre is particularly keen to emphasize the importance of *imaginative* engagement. He points out that merely listening to other people's views may not provide an adequate basis for understanding those views. In order to really understand other people, we need to try to 'get inside' their perspective; to make a proactive effort to see things on their terms rather than on our terms.

In the writing of Aristotle and MacIntyre, then, discourse is offered as a basis of moral legitimacy. Both writers propose that the moral legitimacy of the standards of virtue that prevail within a particular community of thought derives from the extent to which that community of thought is prepared to reflect on its moral agenda and to open its moral perspective to imaginative engagement with alternative, competing perspectives. Although not generally identified with virtue theory, Habermas (1979 [1976], 1984 [1981], 1987 [1981], 1990 [1983]) follows the Aristotelian lead, offering a systematic philosophical justification for intersubjectivist ethics and also spelling out some of the procedural conditions to which discourse needs to conform in order to confer moral legitimacy on its outcomes.

Habermas bases his moral philosophy on a social understanding of human beings. He thus adopts a different starting point from those philosophers who portray human beings as separate, self-contained entities and who present ethics as a set of laws designed to regulate relationships between those atomistic individuals. Like Aristotle, Habermas emphasizes that people live in social groups, they always have done and they probably always will do. Any plausible system of morality must acknowledge that social character. Habermas also points to the centrality of communication to the human condition. We communicate in order to reach the shared understandings upon which the coordination of our social relationships depends. For this reason, Habermas believes that, in order to analyze morality we must analyze communication. Since communication is fundamental to the human condition, and since morality is concerned with the normative regulation of that human condition, the roots of morality must lie in communication.

Habermas asks what conditions communication must conform to if it is to achieve its purpose of enabling shared understanding. He suggests that a self-evident starting point is that any person who is in any way implicated in a matter under consideration should be able to participate in communication about that matter. If our aim is to achieve full and comprehensive understanding through communication, it makes no sense to exclude from that communication any parties who may be involved in or affected by the topic that we seek to understand.

Furthermore, Habermas suggests that communication should be conducted in accordance with certain principles. He notes that the achievement of shared understanding demands that all parties be permitted to express their views and also to challenge the views expressed by other participants. These challenges should be permitted on three different levels. If participants in communication disagree with the factual content of a statement made by another participant, they should be able to challenge it. They should also be at liberty to pass comment on the extent to which the speaker is qualified to make a statement. Third, they should be able to question the intentions that a speaker has in making a statement. As Habermas puts it, they should thus be free to challenge the 'validity claims' (1984 [1981]), (1987 [1981]) raised by the speaker with respect to factual accuracy, normative rightness and sincerity.

If we apply this rationale to the HRM context, then the moral legitimacy of decisions taken within that context lies not only in the involvement of the full range of affected stakeholders; it also includes the manner of that involvement. It is important that every stakeholder is able to participate on an equal footing. Each must be able to introduce any assertion whatsoever into the discussion and each must feel at liberty to challenge the assertions made by other discussants.

Applying Habermas's model of discourse ethics to HRM practice clearly presents difficulties. The most evident is that many of the discussions which take place within a work environment are not conducted in the spirit of disinterested neutrality which Habermas envisages. It might therefore be suggested that, although his model of discourse is suitable for a philosophy seminar, it holds little relevance for practical HRM contexts. In anticipation of criticism such as this, Habermas acknowledges that 'ideal speech situations' (1984 [1981]), (1987 [1981]), aimed purely at achieving understanding, are comparatively rare. He accedes that we generally have some degree of emotional commitment or vested interest in the outcome of the discursive processes in which we engage. However, he proposes that this need not undermine the morally legitimating force of communication as long as all participants openly declare any affiliations, personal interests or emotional attachments that may introduce a note of partiality. If this condition is met, and as long as all parties are free to challenge the assertions made by their co-discussants on the dimensions of factual accuracy, normative rightness and sincerity, the quest for shared understanding can proceed unimpeded.

A further difficulty with Habermas's model is that it may sanction a particular form of rational articulation at the expense of alternative modes of expression (Young, 1996). If moral legitimacy is located in discourse, then those who are able to engage most effectively in discourse will be most influential in shaping that legitimacy. Moral legitimacy will not therefore derive from a representative and balanced synthesis of the perspectives of all those who are implicated in the matter under discussion; it will derive from the triumph of those perspectives that are delivered with the greatest rhetorical eloquence. In the work context, we may find that discursive contributions that are emotionally-controlled and logically-presented are accorded precedence, with the consequence that voices that do not conform so readily to this model of rational articulation are marginalized. Relevant perspectives may thus be excluded or downgraded, not because of the nature of their content but because of the manner of their expression; what is said becomes less important than how it is said.

Concerns about the hegemony of rational articulation can, however, be allayed if we introduce further criteria of intersubjectivist legitimisation. If discourse is not to be distorted in favour of the rationally articulate, diverse modes of expression should be accommodated. Furthermore, participants need to be sensitive to these diverse modes. Passive receptivity on the part of participants does not seem sufficient to ensure adequate representation and consideration of all relevant perspectives. An active effort of understanding is also required. Therefore, although a commitment to personal transparency and openness on the part of all participants is a necessary condition for morally legitimizing communication, this needs to be augmented by a willingness to imaginatively engage with whatever mode of expression may be favoured by fellow interlocutors.

To summarize the intersubjectivist stance with respect to HRM, the ethicality of HRM practice is not measured in relation to the conformity of its outcomes to some assumed absolute standard of moral rightness. Nor does the absence of such a standard entail that HRM ethics is no more than a matter of personal conviction or an expression of cultural habituation. Intersubjectivist ethics understands HRM to be ethical insofar as it facilitates and responds to discourse. More specifically, that discourse should embrace all those who may be affected by the situation under discussion. Each participant should be able to contribute without constraint. Each should be free to introduce any assertion into the discussion that they see fit. Furthermore, each should be able to challenge any aspect of the assertions made by fellow discussants in order to ensure a shared basis of understanding with regards to the factual accuracy of what is being said, the speaker's eligibility to make that assertion and the effect that the speaker seeks to bring about in making the assertion. All parties should also be committed to transparency with regard to any vested interests or emotional attachment that they may have to the outcomes of the discussion. All should also be sensitive to diverse modes of expression and should seek to imaginatively engage with perspectives that may differ from their own.

Although these procedural conditions of legitimation flow from intersubjectivist theory, they also chime with some of the morally significant insights afforded by objectivist and relativist theory. I suggested earlier, in discussing criticisms of objectivist ethics, that critical reflection on the nature of our moral sentiments seems desirable. Imaginative engagement with perspectives that contrast with our own can only enrich that reflective undertaking. Intersubjectively-enriched reflection also seems particularly apposite given the proclivity for culturally-embedded moral sentiment to which relativist theory alerts us. If our moral sentiments are partly shaped by our personal circumstances and cultural experiences, then it seems desirable to expose them to rigorous examination through imaginative engagement with alternative perspectives.

Intersubjectivist ethics and employee voice

Insofar as it validates actions and situations that are discursively agreed to, intersubjectivist theory presents a challenge to the moral legitimacy of unilateral management decision-making. In this respect, it stands in contrast to both objectivist and relativist theory. Objectivist theory offers a basis against which managers can unilaterally assess the moral rightness of their decisions. There is no need for managers to seek the views of others in order to know that they are behaving morally; they just have to apply the rules offered by their chosen objectivist theory. Meanwhile, relativist ethics legitimizes management decisions according to their congruence with those managers' heartfelt moral principles or their cultural habituation. Again, the assessment of moral legitimacy is a one-sided affair. In neither case is engagement with other parties a necessary ingredient to moral probity. For intersubjectivist ethics, on the other hand, engagement is fundamental to moral legitimation. Intersubjectivist theory in workplace context therefore resonates with the notion of *employee voice* that is increasingly prominent in practitioner and academic HRM literature (Dundon *et al.*, 2004).

Ian Beardwell defines employee voice as the 'expression of employee perspectives within [their] organization' (1998: 32). The term has been applied to a range of formal and informal mechanisms that enable such expression, either on a group or individual level and either directly or through representation. Employee voice might be viewed from within the pluralist industrial relations tradition (Ackers, 2007) as a mechanism for representing employees' interests, primarily their financial interests, and for ensuring that those interests are taken into account in management decision-making. Alternatively, at the other end of the spectrum of interpretations, the high involvement/high commitment literature understands employee voice as a means of building employee loyalty and driving improvements in commercial performance (Dundon *et al.*, 2004). While the former has traditionally been associated with collective bargaining, usually involving trade union representation, the latter is associated with direct communication through upward problem-solving mechanisms such as suggestion schemes, attitude surveys, project teams and electronic media (CIPD, 2007a).

As well as drawing attention to the relationship between employee voice and ethical HRM practice, intersubjectivist theory offers a framework for considering the ethicality of these diverse interpretations and applications of employee voice. I will consider shortly how some versions of employee voice might fall short in this respect. First, though, I will briefly mention some general criteria that employee voice practices ought to meet in order to offer a basis for intersubjectivist moral legitimation.

The first criterion relates to the attitude that various parties adopt towards employee voice practices. In particular, those who hold *de facto* power in organizations need to respect the outcomes of those practices. Superficial, 'stage managed' (Dundon *et al.*, 2004) practices which are aimed purely at engendering a sense of belonging amongst employees but which have no real impact on decision-making should be avoided. Tim Claydon (2000) suggests that upward problem solving mechanisms and other forms of direct participation may be particularly susceptible to this charge of 'pseudo–participation'.

It is also important that all parties approach employee voice forums in an open and transparent manner. It is perhaps inevitable that parties will be predisposed towards outcomes that further their own interests or the interests of those who they represent.

Intersubjective legitimacy is not thus precluded, but it does require the declaration of vested interest: it is essential that all discussants, both managerial and non-managerial, approach the table of intersubjective dialogue with openness of intent.

A third criterion that employee voice needs to satisfy concerns the breadth of its subject matter. To limit the intersubjective agenda either to employment conditions or to 'trivial' (Dundon *et al.*, 2004) housekeeping matters at the exclusion of broader operational and strategic issues would place an unwarranted restraint on its capacity to lend moral legitimacy to organizational outcomes. Important those such matters are, intersubjectivist ethics highlights the desirability of employees also contributing to the strategic context within which they are located.

Different participants in employee voice mechanisms may favour contrasting modes of communication. Therefore, the availability of a broad range of employee voice media is morally significant. To present traditional collective bargaining and direct communication mechanisms as mutually exclusive alternatives may unnecessarily restrict the breadth of available media. In this respect, Dundon *et al.* (ibid.) discuss various direct and indirect, individual and collective avenues, pointing to the desirability of a comprehensive and integrated approach. The growing ease noted by these writers on the part of line managers, union representatives and employees with employee voice practices that are 'inclusive (direct and indirect) rather than exclusive (direct versus indirect)' (ibid.: 1167) is good news.

Although a great deal of recent European and national legislation is driven by an agenda of economic liberalism, there has also been some regulative support for the extension of employee voice practices and thus for intersubjectivist legitimation of HRM. European Works Council regulations call upon transnational organizations to implement employee voice channels, while the Information and Consultation of Employees Regulations have extended this requirement to all organizations above a certain size. Notably, these regulations call upon organizations not only to implement employee voice practices but to involve employees in the design of those practices. The impact of these regulations has been sporadic, partly because of the relatively toothless nature of the legislation; partly because of caution on the part of employers and trade unions (Hall, 2005; CIPD, 2007b). Nevertheless, they offer at least a starting framework within which greater intersubjective legitimation might be created by HRM practitioners who seek to promote the social democratic ideals which inspire the regulations.

If this regulative framework is to work, and if employee voice is to achieve its intersubjectively legitimating potential, then the backing of key actors is necessary. Dundon *et al.* (2004) note that employee voice mechanisms need to become embedded in organizations if they are to be effective. These authors discuss a number of factors which may indicate and contribute towards such organizational embeddedness. Along with those already mentioned here, they draw attention to confidence on the part of management to organize direct exchanges of opinion with employees as well as an expectation on the part of union representatives and employees that managers do so. Such embeddedness requires more than managerial, union and employee support for a framework of consultation, however. If employee voice is to serve a morally legitimizing role in organizations, it needs to comprise more than a series of one-off events organized around a specific agenda. Intersubjective discourse needs to become embedded in organizational practice and the personal qualities that are supportive of imaginative engagement need to be encouraged.

HRM practice can play a part in creating this intersubjectively fertile terrain, using selection, development, reward and career planning processes to encourage appropriate attitudes and behaviours. In this respect, culture management need not imply alignment to a homogenous set of values that are unilaterally defined by senior management. Rather, culture management might be understood as an opportunity to encourage the expression of diverse attitudes and to create space for contrasting cultural commitments; to endorse heterogeneity rather than homogeneity. Respect for difference might thus replace conformity as a cultural lynchpin.

Concluding comments

I began this chapter by proposing that discussion about ethics and HRM should go beyond a simple association of moral probity with welfare humanism. I set out to describe how different ethical theories might be used to enhance our understanding of ethical HRM practice. I outlined objectivist, relativist and intersubjectivist theory as alternative ways of thinking about morality in relation to HRM, dwelling in particular on the practical application of intersubjectivist theory and particularly on its congruence with employee voice. I suggested that intersubjectivist ethics might also offer a lens through which different applications of employee voice might be assessed.

I will conclude with a brief reflection on the part that managers might play in promoting intersubjectively ethical HRM practice and the opportunities that this might present for HRM practitioners. Clearly, managers can be influential in facilitating employee voice, in ensuring that its outcomes contribute to organizational decision-making and thus in ensuring the intersubjectivist moral legitimacy of those decisions. Fulfilling this role may call for reappraisal of the prerogatives and responsibilities of management. Habermas (1984 [1981]), (1987 [1981]) notes that one of the greatest challenges to morally legitimizing discourse is that communication is prone to distortion by asymmetrical power relationships. In particular, some discussants may feel inhibited from expressing their views or from challenging the validity claims raised by other parties as a consequence of status differentials. In a work context, contributions from more senior employees may thus enjoy immunity from challenge, while their junior colleagues may feel inhibited from giving full expression to their own views. As a result, the perspectives of senior managers may assume unwarranted authority, leading to distortion of outcomes and thus undermining the morally legitimating force of discourse. But while status differentials may thus present a challenge to the realization of intersubjective ideals, they may also offer a focal point for HRM endeavours. In particular, HRM practices that foster sensitivity to status differentials may encourage managers to view them, not as advantages to be leveraged in order to assert their preferred agenda, but as barriers to be dismantled in order to facilitate intersubjectively legitimated organizational outcomes.

References

Ackers, P. (2007). Collective bargaining as industrial democracy: Hugh Clegg and the political foundations of British industrial relations pluralism, *British Journal of Industrial Relations*, 45–1, March: 77–101.

Aristotle (1999 [334–322 BC]). *Nicomachean Ethics*, T. Irwin (Transl.). Indianapolis: Hackett.

Beardwell, I. (1998). *Voices on*, People Management, 32–6, May.

Bentham, J. (2000 [1789]). *Principles of Morals and Legislation*, in T. Griffin (Ed.), *Selected Writings on Utilitarianism*. Ware: Wordsworth.

CIPD (2007a). *Employee Voice Factsheet*, http://www.cipd.co.uk/subjects/empreltns/comconslt/empvoice.htm

CIPD (2007b). *European Works Councils Factsheet*, http://www.cipd.co.uk/subjects/empreltns/wkcncls/eurwcon.htm

Claydon, T. (2000). Employee Participation and Involvement, in J. Woodall (ed.), *Ethical Issues in Contemporary Human Resource Management*. Macmillan, Basingstoke.

Donaldson, T. and Preston, L. (1995). The stakeholder theory of the corporation: concepts, evidence and implications, *Academy of Management Review*, 20(1): 65–91.

Dundon, T., Wilkinson, A., Marchington, M. and Ackers, P. (2004). The meanings and purpose of employee voice, *International Journal of Human Resource Management*, 15–6, September: 1149–70.

Foucault, M. (2002 [1954–1984]). *Power: Essential Works of Michel Foucault*, J. D. Faubian (Ed.). London: Penguin.

Friedman, M. (1970). The social responsibility of business is to increase its profits, *The New York Times Magazine*, September 13.

Habermas, J. (1979 [1976]). *Communication and the Evolution of Society*. London: Heinemann.

Habermas, J. (1984 [1981]). *The Theory of Communicative Action, Volume One: Reason and the Rationalisation of Society*. Boston: Beacon Press.

Habermas, J. (1987 [1981]) *The Theory of Communicative Action, Volume Two: Lifeworld and System: A Critique of Functionalist Reason*. Boston: Beacon Press.

Habermas, J. (1990 [1983]). *Moral Consciousness and Communicative Action*. Massachusetts: MIT Press.

Hall, M. (2005). How are employers and unions responding to the Information and Consultation of Employees Regulations? Warwick Papers in Industrial Relations, No. 77, Industrial Relations Research Unit, Warwick University.

Heery, E. (2000). The new pay: risk and representation at work, in D. Winstanley and J. Woodall (Eds.), *Ethical Issues in Contemporary Human Resource Management*. Basingstoke: Palgrave MacMillan.

Kaler, J. (1999). What's the good of ethical theory, *Business Ethics: a European Review*, 8(4): 206–13.

MacIntyre, A. (1984). *After Virtue*. London: Duckworth.

MacIntyre, A. (1988). *Whose Justice? Which Rationality?* London: Duckworth.

Nietzsche, F. (2003 [1887]). *The Genealogy of Morals*. New York: Dover.

Nozick, R. (1974). *Anarchy, State and Utopia*. New York: Basic Books.

Rawls, J. (1971). *A Theory of Justice*. Oxford: Oxford University Press.

Sartre, J. P. (1973 [1946]). *Existentialism and Humanism*. London: Methuen.

Smith, A. (1998 [1776]). *Wealth of Nations*, K. Sutherland (Ed.). Oxford: Oxford University Press.

Stanworth, C. (2000). Flexible working patterns, in D. Winstanley and J. Woodall (Eds.), *Ethical Issues in Contemporary Human Resource Management*. Basingstoke: Palgrave MacMillan.

Young, I. M. (1996). Communication and the other: beyond deliberative democracy, in S. Benhabib (Ed.), *Democracy and Difference: Contesting the Boundaries of the Political*. New Jersey: Princeton University Press.

6 Organizational outsourcing and the implications for HRM

Richard Haines

The nature and scope of outsourcing

This chapter provides an overview of the concept of outsourcing, and its implications for the HR function. The term and concept of 'outsourcing' became part of the business lexicon during the increased economic and corporate growth of the 1980s. Outsourcing is essentially the transfer by a firm of products or services to an outside vendor or supplier as opposed to sourcing the same work within the firm's own facilities. It is a strategic decision by the firm in question, and often taken in the interests of achieving cost efficiencies.

Outsourcing is a relatively new concept in lexicographic terms, entering into popular dictionary journal usage in the period 1979–82.[1] Significantly, the genesis of the term reflects in part the efforts of business at the time to reduce union influence in the workplace (Maynard, 2004). Since the early 1980s, the term outsourcing has expanded to include all parts of the enterprise, not just manufacturing.

While the term is relatively new the practice of outsourcing, however, has a longer history. When Adam Smith (1995) was describing the increasing division of labour in factory production of late eighteenth century Britain, he was commenting in part on sub-contracting and outsourcing arrangements. But it was developments during the twentieth century which enable us to understand the particular set of meanings and applications of outsourcing.

In the contemporary economy, outsourced work has expanded beyond manufacturing processes to include many business functions such as human resources, payroll, marketing, technical support, and customer service. In many ways, outsourcing is a synonym for sub-contracting. Virtually any activity that is performed by a company can be, and probably has been, outsourced (Mol, 2007: 1–2).

The emergence of the concept and more defined practice of outsourcing in the 1980s, is in turn the product of multiple causes. For one, as we will discuss in a subsequent chapter (see Chapter 17 of the current volume), outsourcing can be seen as one of the effects of the growing predominance of MNCs in global trade and production from the late 1950s onwards (e.g. Harvey, 1990; Hardt and Negri, 2000). Second, it can be seen as part of the increased prevalence of post-Fordist models of production from the 1980s onward. Thirdly, the growing recourse to outsourcing was shaped in part by the expansion of the US retail model which shifted from local to national and then international sourcing of suppliers. Fourth, it embodies a paradigm shift in corporate strategy. Before the mid-1980s, mergers and acquisitions of other companies and the diversification of business interests to reduce risks and widen exposure in the markets was the orthodoxy. As it became increasingly evident such a strategy often led to a lack of synergies between the (often) diverse set of business within a particular corporate fold. This realization contributed in turn to (i) a divestment of subsidiaries and (ii) an emerging concern with 'core business' and 'core competencies' (Mol, 2007: 11–12).

Outsourcing was also facilitated by the information technology (IT) revolution of the late twentieth century, characterized *inter alia* by the advent and growth of the internet, email and electronic communication, which in turn have fed into post-industrial production processes and the compression of time and space (Harvey, 1990; Hardt and Negri, 2000). Outsourcing as a business/production paradigm has expanded significantly since the early 1980s. Initially, large corporations of advanced economies sold of factories and/or offshored and outsourced manufacturing to cut costs, boost efficiency and focus their energies. Research and development operations remained essentially in-house. By the early 2000s the situation had changed. Particularly in the electronics sector, a host of large corporations in the US and EU countries bought complete designs for a range of digital devices/products from Asian companies, making small-scale additions to bring them up to their in-house specification, and then branding them (Engardio and Einhorn, 2005: 50–1).

Outsourcing is very much a growth industry in its own right, although the current levels are viewed by industry participants as a fraction of the potential for outsourcing.[2] And with the expansion of outsourcing in scale and complexity, the accompanying specialist definitions have expanded. Common examples of business functions outsourced include: the manufacture of components; computer programming services; transport and logistical services; tax and accountancy services; the management of facilities and real estate; human resources; and customer support and call centres. A further trend is that of employee leasing in which specialized producers recruit, train, remunerate clients' employees, as well as arrange health care and other benefits.

Outsourcing can be distinguished from subcontracting, in that the business function is provided for on a continuous basis, rather than for a specific project. There is also a common tendency to conflate outsourcing and offshoring with outsourcing. Offshoring is the transfer of a business function or process to a separate country, irrespective of whether the work is outsourced or stays within the same company. Offshoring generally involves exploiting the advantage of lower-cost labour in the country in question (Kalakota and Kalokota, 2004).

The increasing globalization of outsourcing models and approaches has seen a new body of terminology with terms such as 'nearshoring' and 'rightsourcing' reflecting the geo-spatial complexities of the processes (Trampel, 2004). In its most radical form, outsourcing would allow the creation of a large, virtual company with the entrepreneur as the only employee.

There is even a trend to outsourcing the outsourcing process, sometimes termed 'Integral Outsourcing', though this is seen as still a rather risky undertaking (Simchi-Levi, *et al.*, 2004: 146). To illustrate: In recent decades several non-core processes have been outsourced in many an organization. Company canteens, cleaning and security are common examples. A problem with such transfer of functions is that managers may well be required to ensure that outsourcing partners are performing diligently, and all outsourced processes are running well. This function – effectively the management of outsourcing – can be outsourced itself to specialized firms, sometimes called 'Integrated Facility Management' firms (Brachner *et al.*, 2002).

Outsourcing business models

Vendors undertaking outsourcing services are usually grouped into two models, the Business Process Outsourcing (BPO) and Application Service Provider (ASP). Under the BPO model substantial resources and assets are transferred from the firm to the vendor. Business process outsourcing (BPO) entails the transfer of substantive internal business processes or services internal resources and assets from the firm to the vendor. These include customer relationship management, finance and accounting, human resources and procurement. It is understood that the external service provider will improve these processes and administer these functions to an agreed service standard and usually with cost reductions (May, 1998: 136–7; Mol, 2007: 31–2).

As participating companies must in effect relinquish a considerable degree of control over an aspect of their business, BPO is mostly deployed for non-core and non-critical types of work. Though there is a blurring of categories, one can generally distinguish between offshore outsourcing and BPO: the former approach tends to focus on manufacturing, IT, and back-office services, while the latter focuses more on call centres, finance and accounting, human resources, and transaction processing. In the BPO model at least three outsourcing approaches can be identified: the shared service centre; a spin-off; and outsourcing to an external organization. In the ASP model, the vendors focus more on providing certain services for a variety of clients. However, it should be borne in mind that there are significant variations within each model (Currie, 2003: 207–8).

Outsourcing has stimulated a range of scholarly debate which we will discuss in more detail via select issues in the sections that follow. What we will do here is to consider briefly the potential advantages and disadvantages from an immediate business position.

Rationale for outsourcing

From the point of view of management and the outsourcing industry the following are the most commonly cited reasons for the decision to outsource:

Cost reductions

Savings on operational costs is often the prime reason for outsourcing. Outsourcing has traditionally been seen a mechanism for lowering the overall cost of the service or function to the business. Companies usually outsource to a vendor that specializes in a particular function and performs that function better through economies of scale/transaction volume (Embleton and Wright, 1998: 96, 98–9; Lankford and Parsa, 1999: 312; Heshmati, 2003; Levy, 2004: 20). This allows firms to get access to cheaper and relatively more efficient labour. Also, the agency handling the outsourced work often may have world-class capabilities and access to technology which might not be affordable for the outsourcing firm. *Inter alia* this can open access to lower cost economies through offshoring to take advantage of the wage differential between developed and developing economies. Also, there can be savings on labour training costs. And overall, outsourcing can help change favourably the ratio of fixed to variable costs for a company, and by making variable costs more stable and predictable (Lankford and Parsa, 1999).

Staffing dynamics

Another important reason for outsourcing is to cut the size of the workforce and/or to reduce and stabilize the fluctuations in staffing which may occur because of changing demand for a product or service. Firms may also outsource to reduce the workload on their employees and/or to help free them up for more productive and profit-making activities for the business (Lankford and Parsa, 1998: 312). In addition, there is the possibility of improved development paths for certain employees by reducing the volume of tedious day-to-day tasks they were allocated.

Some commentators argue that outsourcing can improve company morale by helping shift employees from non-core tasks performed without enthusiasm and much efficiency, and which often duplicate and overlap.

Organization focus/core competencies

A growing number of companies outsource in an attempt to streamline their organizational structure and to assist them in concentrating on core competencies. This can have a particular appeal for start-up companies (Embleton and Wright, 1998: 99; Lankford and Parsa, 1999: 312). Outsourcing can cut the time-consuming and tedious work, such as payroll management, and create opportunities for more strategic and productive efforts by the entrepreneur, including product design, marketing and sales activities. These activities in turn will enhance a company's longer-term growth prospects (Levy, 2004).

Competitiveness

An increasing number of companies view the outsourcing route as a means of keeping ahead or at least abreast with the competition. This continued race for competitive advantage helps explain the trend to outsourcing irrespective of a growing list of failures (Sharpe, 1998: 535–6).

Knowledge and technology access

Outsourcing of computer programming and other IT functions is championed as a means of accessing new technology and expertise outside of the company. Such a position may be of particular benefit to smaller businesses which may not be able to afford to have computer experts on their books and/or develop the requisite expertise in-house (Lankford and Parsa, 1998: 312; Levina and Ross, 2003). By outsourcing such functions the smaller companies may be able to leverage new technology to enable them to compete more effectively with larger companies.

Quality and accountability

The initiation of an outsourcing relationship assumes that such an arrangement demands a quality service from the vendor in return for payment. And given a contractual arrangement there is a related element of in-built accountability.

Disadvantages of outsourcing

There are a range of practical disadvantages to outsourcing for management of a firm or organization. There are also broader issues in regard to the relationship of outsourcing to the intensification of globalization, and the opposition of trade unions, and the individual employees' rights within workplace organization – debates which will be considered in more detail in later sections.

A chief criticism of outsourcing is that the business value promised the client does not materialize (Lankford and Parsa, 1998: 312–13; Levy, 2004: 23–4; Power *et al.*, 2004). Poor quality control, a decline in company morale and loyalty are other potential weaknesses. This is particularly the case of a service provider in a developing country who services many other companies. This increases the possibilities of the service provider being more partial to one client than the other because of factors such as disparity in payment. Also, service providers may employ less qualified staff than was the case with the client company. A further important factor is the negative public relations accruing to a particular company from the often vigorous public opinion on the subject, especially when outsourcing is combined with offshoring which affects jobs and livelihoods in a particular area (Kshetri, 2007).

Further problem areas include the following:

- Outsourcing can reduce direct contact between a company and its clients. This makes it difficult to create/maintain close and substantive relationships with customers.
- Outsourcing may lead to a loss of control of some or all aspects of the corporate function/s, and impaired communication and development in project implementation.

- With knowledge capital being of increased importance in business transactions in the twenty-first century outsourcing can be a high-risk option. For instance, there may be a loss of sensitive information and a company may become overly dependent on its outsourcing providers. Among other things, this could lead to problems should the client wish to exit the contract.
- When staff are no longer directly responsible or new staff are used by the service provider, loyalty may be diluted and security risks increased. The related likelihood of fraud is also a problem (Embleton and Wright, 1998: 99–100; Lankford and Parsa, 1998: 312–13; Power *et al.*, 2004).

Human resource outsourcing

Outsourcing what are sometimes considered non-core functions such as human resources has in recent decades come to be seen as smart management practice. While human resource (HR) activities have traditionally been performed internally, by the late 2000s outsourcing had come to be seen as one of the most significant trends in HR management (Belcourt, 2006; Ordanini and Silvestri, 2008). The increase in HR outsourcing also corresponds to a sweeping change in which non-transactional activities, such as recruitment, selection and training, are among the most outsourced HR practices (Ordanini and Silvestri, 2008). The rationale for outsourcing HR functions, as with outsourcing more generally, includes financial efficiencies, an increased focus on strategic issues, improved access to technology and specialized expertise, as well as recourse to measurable and improved levels of service.

The emergence of HR outsourcing and related approaches is indicative of a qualitative restructuring of the nature of production and work, in the increasing application of IT solutions to these environments. With the Fordist production models and practices of the 1950s and 1960s there was a tendency for employees to look to lifelong employment within an organization. With the growth of the IT and related high-tech industries in regions such as Silicon Valley in the 1970s and after, there was a growing realization that the finding and retaining of highly skilled workers had become far more problematic than in previous decades (Appelbaum and Batt, 1994). By the 1990s, the shift to more flexible and spatially fragmented forms of production, rapidly changing labour markets, especially in advanced economies, the burgeoning of the knowledge economy, as well as events such as the boom and subsequent decline of dot.com companies, meant that individuals might have several careers within their lifetimes.

Companies have indeed been outsourcing human resource functions on a modest scale for decades, with a selective use of outside vendors for items such as payroll management, training and development and selected recruitment (usually of a temporary or contingent nature, or executive head hunting). HR services most frequently outsourced include employee benefits administration and maintenance, payroll, recruitment and termination related processes and procedures, and employee training and development programmes.

Companies can also outsource HR services by the project. HR firms provide all kinds of specialized services, such as developing an employee handbook, set up compensation programmes, or establish performance management systems for the evaluation of a firm's employees. And, increasingly, companies and organizations are looking at more holistic HR outsourcing. This is especially the case for a large number of smaller businesses in dynamic and advanced economies that experience rapid growth, and consequently look to more inclusive HR outsourcing as a viable alternative to hiring internal staff to accomplish the tasks associated with the human resources needs of the business. HR outsourcing, as its advocates contend, can often help to fulfill the strategic goals of the business to reduce costs and allow for the current staff's skill sets, experience and energy to be strategically directed towards the aspects and functions of the business at which they are most effective (Hindle, 2005; Aberdeen Group, 2006).

The shift since the later 1990s to a more thorough approach to outsourcing in the HR fields is exemplified by the concept and associated discourse of HRO (Human Resource Outsourcing) and especially HR BPO (Business Process Outsourcing). In turn the key components of HRM which are amenable to outsourcing have also been outsourced in a more extensive and intensive manner, with matching terminology such as RPO (Recruitment Process Outsourcing) and PEO (People's Employment Outsourcing) coming into existence. The maturation of HRM as a discipline and discourse has also conditioned these developments.

Towards more comprehensive outsourcing? HRO and HR BPO

During its relatively short history HRO has shifted from being little more than a service bureau that provides a limited number of services, to widely used business methods, although it is not yet a fully mature industry.

By the mid-2000s HRO had expanded to encompass all HR functions, with providers becoming 'one-stop' agencies for organizations looking to outsource any and all of their company's HR responsibilities. HRO market size was still increasing at the end of the 2000s, but the growth rate had slowed (Fitzgerald, 2006). While companies and organizations were increasingly looking at HRO for multiple value creation opportunities, suppliers were looking to provide improved services at an optimal level to clients at a cost that would still allow a profit. Many proclaimed HRO vendors were often supplying components of an HR service rather than a full blown outsourcing solution and application. And companies were often wary at the thought of outsourcing functions that have been handled in-house since the start of their business (Aberdeen Group, 2006: 1–3).

Those businesses that outsource HR in a significant way still tend to be small to mid-sized firms, with a number of employees ranging from 10 to 1500, though this is a more distinct trend in the more advanced economies (TRG, 2004; Kakabadse and Kakabadse, 2005). For these small and mid-sized businesses, HR outsourcing is often deployed as a strategic approach to relieve internal staff of

HR-related responsibilities and allow them to focus more on the core operations of the business. In outsourcing the functions of the HR department, the firm can access the experience and knowledge of HR professionals to improve employee relations, ensure regulatory compliance, and help to manage and reduce operating costs.

While there is something of an increase in large-market outsourcing by corporations, the percentages remain small. A range of critics and commentators contend that HRO has been relatively sluggish in terms of corporate acceptance because HR departments have become firmly embedded over time, and because the larger and higher-revenue corporations do not generally feel obliged to outsource everything. And although the business case for HR outsourcing remains strong, there are concerns about the ability of any one supplier to manage big end-to-end HRO deals (*Workforce Management*, Feb. 27, 2008). But despite initial slow adoption of HRO, it has become an established and viable way to manage HR.

HR Outsourcing (HRO) is a generic term and covers a number of discrete and overlapping services that are typically provided by the HR department. HRO can be defined 'simply as a vendor providing HR services for an employer'. Most firms and organizations to date have not outsourced their so-called 'strategic HR function' which forms a core part of an organization. Organizations are still desirous of retaining control of the decision-making process regarding (i) the kinds of staff they wish to recruit, dismiss or retain; (ii) the remuneration of the staff and (iii) how careers should be developed for each employee. However, all other functions have proved quite amenable to outsourcing, in areas such as payroll processing, recruitment, training, benefits administration, help desk queries, staff relocation and pension administration.

For many CEOs the thought of outsourcing any organizational activity can be daunting, but particularly so when they are considering the HR activity. Whether companies are opting for select HR services and/or are moving to more inclusive forms of HR outsourcing, the arguments in favour include the following:

- HR outsourcing (in part or whole) will improve business focus.
- It will facilitate a more productive use of time and resources. When a firm's HR department or its management is swamped in daily personnel issues and is struggling to keep up with ever changing employment legislation it can be hard to find the time to focus on the business.
- HR outsourcing will provide organizations with guidance from experts from across the business spectrum.
- Business process outsourcing of certain functions can help improve basic services while allowing HR professionals time to play a more strategic role, and contribute to helping their organizations become and/or remain competitive.
- Outsourcing HR functions allows companies to shift internal resources and capital funds to profit-driven activities.

- Companies will be able to reduce expenditure on expensive software and IT systems.

HR suppliers generally argue that there is significant scope to streamline the HR function. One point in their favour is that HR in most organizations has often developed in a piecemeal and haphazard fashion over time (Hendry and Pettigrew, 1992: 138–9). Seldom has it been engineered from first principles and there has been a tendency for HR divisions to fight shy of extensive use of technology. This resulted in a raft of inefficiencies and duplications, with the consequence that suppliers have been able to find both cost savings and efficiencies. Many of the HR suppliers that have emerged in recent years, such as Exult, Accenture, E-Peopleserve, PwC, Unisys and EDS built their expertise as IT services suppliers.

HR outsourcing services can be divided into four categories: PEOs, BPOs, ASPs or e-services. These categories are not watertight. Also, it is worth bearing in mind that these terms are used somewhat loosely in the industry, so it is important for companies to be well informed when investigating and/or employing an outsourcing firm.

A Professional Employer Organization (PEO) recruits, hires, and employs on behalf of the client company. It becomes the employer of record for all or certain categories of the company's employees, whom it essentially leases back from the PEO. This process is often engineered via a co-employment contract which sees the company and vendor sharing and managing a range of employer-related liabilities and responsibilities (Tang, 2007). In this arrangement workers become in effect employees of two employers: the client retains supervision for production or delivery of service, and the PEO is responsible for human resources and personnel services.

Business Process Outsourcing (BPO) is a broad term referring to outsourcing in all fields, not just HR. A BPO differentiates itself by either putting in new technology or applying existing technology in a new way to improve a process. Specifically in HR, a BPO would make sure a company's HR system is supported by the latest technologies, such as self-access and HR data warehousing.

Application Service Providers (ASPs) host software on the Web and rent it to users – some ASPs host HR software. Some are well-known packaged applications (People Soft) while others are customized HR software developed by the vendor. These software programs can manage payroll, benefits and more.

E-services are those HR services that are web-based. Both BPOs and ASPs are often referred to as e-services.

In addition to these categories, one of the current trends is for companies to opt for a mix of outsourcing and technology to find a model suitable for their particular needs. With new dedicated software and IT systems vendors offer companies flexible, web-based offerings which allow outside assistance to manage certain tasks, combined with real-time access to your data for the companies, allowing them more visibility of and control over the work at hand.

In decisions to outsource HR functions, firms encounter providers who will only handle all the firm's HR functions or none at all. Other vendors offer either their services on an 'a la carte' basis – meaning you select a firm from a menu of services offered – or provide one or more speciality services in areas such as payroll and benefits administration, recruitment and employment, and risk management and compliance (Adler, 2003; Klaas, 2008). Some services are full-service and will provide these as well as additional services like on-call consultants, who will come in to undertake activities such as specific training or settling a dispute (Hayes, 2008).

Online services tend to be more limited in their offerings, but firms will have additional options such as web access, which will allow them to view information (like benefits packages) and even make changes to such information online.

By taking the HR outsourcing route as opposed to hiring or retaining a full-time, in-house HR department is not unproblematic. By not having a HR manager/staff in-house an organization can lose on a range of tangible and intangible benefits. For instance, an in-house HR person will provide 'soft services' and perks that are not necessarily provided by a HR vendor (e.g. exploring group offerings, designing employee incentive programmes). In addition, employees often appreciate having an impartial co-worker with whom they can build up a relationship of trust and consult on a regular basis, especially in dealing with work-related problems and disputes with other co-workers, and in advising on benefits. In-house HR staff is often in a better position to understand the employee perceptions and play a role in benefits advice and negotiation to reinforce employee retention. In-house HR staff may also be able to build up a bank of relevant knowledge over time – a form of social capital – which is valuable to the company and its management.

Also, in the case of companies using a PEO, giving up the right to hire and fire your employees may not be desirable for the particular business. Although companies may save on time by not having to deal with the stress of this process, they may wish to retain this right. And for firms opting to use an e-service, the potential problems remain. With data being stored and handled online, there will be concerns about both security as well as malfunctioning of the servers.

Common complaints about HR outsourcing range from payroll mix-ups to payroll not being deposited on time to denied medical claims.

Outsourcing decisions need of course not to be taken lightly, and the process of selecting and maintaining a relationship with a vendor, which we discussed earlier, applies in regard to HR outsourcing as well. The decision to outsource is determined in part by the nature and size of a company (Hansen, 2007). If a firm has less than 100 employees, there are certain advantages. Firms of this size often do not possess the resources for in-house HR staff, so outsourcing might be an option. For smaller firms a PEO could be an option. In the US, for instance, most PEOs only take on businesses with a minimum of 12 employees. For firms with less than this minimum number of employees, online services are generally preferable.

Outsourcing human relations functions

Payroll processing

Another key function many companies outsource is payroll processing. This presents to the business a particular challenge, as employee compensation requirements are often diverse and changing. There is a need for accuracy and ease of use in the process. There are a range of services on offer which allows clients access to, and control over, employee information, links with the internet, and interfacing with or deployment of popular HR software such as SAP and PeopleSoft.

Benefits management

Benefits administration services/management is a related process/function, with vendors promising to help in-house HR departments to focus on a strategic/'big picture' initiative, rather than being bogged down with repetitive and time-consuming benefits administration and compliance issues. Outsourced benefits services ideally will optimize an organization's benefits programmes, whether a stand-alone service or a completely integrated benefits solution is required. Some benefits administration outsourcing companies might use call centres, to reduce costs for the vendor and provide a relatively inexpensive option for the client. Other benefits administration outsourcing firms look to provide each client with a management team that will handle all of the benefits administration needs. Benefits management will include matters such as health care, retirement services, employee assistance, life insurance (group, term and dependent), disability assistance, credit assistance, and educational assistance (Schiff, 2006).

Recruitment and selection

Staffing for temporary and contingent positions, as well as executive search and placement were among the first wave of HR outsourcing. The processes relating to the ongoing management of the organization's core workforce have historically been less legitimate to outsource, and in general were less frequently outsourced than staffing and other administrative activities (Davis-Blake *et al.*, 2002: 1). Since the 1990s the outsourcing of recruitment and selection has been qualitatively transformed – re-engineered according to industry protagonists (Feinberg, 2004). The functions of temporary, contingency and executive selection and replacement have become more intensive and complex due to the changing and more heterogeneous nature of national and global markets, and the increased incidence of skills shortages, and the growing application of dedicated software packages and other IT applications to this field. For example, leading staffing agencies, in undertaking executive, permanent, contract, and temporary appointments, are able to offer a number of advantages such as:

- Up-to–date mastery of internet search techniques as well as traditional 'grass roots' sourcing methods
- Insights into industry developments and salary trends
- Streamlining internal processes
- Providing a powerful resumé collecting, sorting, tracking, and search capability.

But while there are a range of seeming advantages, there is still a marked tendency by many companies to look to substantive recruitment outsourcing. While they use recruiters to find suitable candidates, the majority of companies are inclined to retain control of staffing activities such as hiring and firing.

The operational nature of recruitment is well suited to outsourcing. Partnering with a recruitment provider allows a company to benefit from the vendor's technology and expertise, reduce costs, meet fluctuating demands while maintaining a viable/strategic headcount, as well as leveraging existing resources in a manner contributing significantly to organizational effectiveness and boosting company profits.

Companies looking to recruit talent nowadays are faced with a bewildering array of offerings from intermediary labour vendors, as well as differing partnerships. This situation reflects a shift from the traditional recruitment model, especially by larger and more profitable and/or dynamic companies. This is due in part to the evolution of services such as human resource business process outsourcing (HR BPO) and human resource outsourcing (HRO). These services have led to a 'parallel' staffing creation: recruitment process outsourcing (RPO) (Collings, 2006).

RPO is a term which is not precisely defined or applied within the HR outsourcing industry, but can be distinguished from more traditional forms of recruitment outsourcing by virtue of its emphasis on a more substantive transferring of processes and function (or the HR function) in its entirety to the recruitment vendor or vendors in question. One of the HRO industry insiders describes RPO as follows:

> RPO is a continuum of work-definition and job filling services that goes beyond the traditional filla-spec recruiting service. At the front end, it is helping define the work needs, translating those needs into requests for jobs, and designing a career path for each individual (a departure from the one-career-path-fits-all model). On the market side, RPO helps establish market rates for labor, market-by-market (a change from the employer-set wage rate model). In filling jobs, RPO goes beyond the traditional screen-and-pass-along model to psychological profiling and behavior-based interviewing methodologies. And in keeping jobs filled, RPO includes retention, reassignment,

and replacement – a step usually skipped by traditional recruiting firms (Feinberg, 2004).

Recruitment outsourcing has a range of options and applications, ranging from fully fledged RPO to a very selective approach such as:

- The firm can retain the direct hiring process in house while shifting 'ownership' of the contingent workforce to a staffing vendor.
- Submitting temporary and temporary-to-hire requests to the staffing partner on an 'as needed' basis.
- Using talent recruitment to expand, assist or wholly manage outreach projects such as college and other recruiting, job fairs, etc.

Outsourcing of recruitment appears to be a strengthening trend. With more than half of the HR budget typically accounted for by recruitment-associated costs, the potential savings for a company in reducing costs are pretty clear. In addition, the benefits of a properly conducted RPO solution have been touted as being relatively larger and quicker, and more readily implemented than any other element of HR BPO and HRO (e.g. Insearch, n.d.).

By outsourcing time-consuming recruitment processes, an organization can free its HR function and hiring managers to focus on core business. In addition, successful RPO can deliver higher quality of hires, reduce hiring times, decrease hiring costs, increase retention, produce higher user satisfaction, improve metrics, enhance internal and external reputation of HR, increase referrals rates, and improve internal and external recruitment branding.

The advent of RPO and other more intensive forms of recruitment outsourcing has been accompanied and partly prefigured by the growing complexity of client-agency organizational structures. Temporary staffing agencies have become more sophisticated and extended their range of services. Such developments have been supplemented by the emergence of PEOs, which on paper at least offer a much broader range of services than temporary employment agencies. In addition to the PEOs and temporary staffing agencies, one finds also hybrid organizations in the labour intermediary field, which undertake discrete functions related to recruitment and selection, as well as other related aspects. PEOs are also proliferating more rapidly than temporary employment agencies, and were seen by the *Harvard Business Review* as constituting the fastest growing industry during the 1990s (cited in Adams, 2007: 2).

Ideally, a PEO can undertake RPO as well as other HR outsourced functions. However, there are confusions in the market both in the OECD countries and globally as to the nature and extent of RPO and the nature of its applications. PEO and other RPO solution providers 'seem to have done a spectacular job of muddying the waters with inconsistent and changing definitions' (Collings, 2006: 1).

Industry commentators point out that RPO and other recruitment and selection vendors need to take more cognizance of the difference in organizations, and to offer more bespoke solutions. More fundamentally, certain critical academic studies are underlining more structural flaws in the RPO and PEO phenomena (Davis-Blake *et al.*, 2002; Young, 2007).

A 2002 US study focusing on temporary staffing agencies and PEOs, suggests that the proliferation of labour market intermediaries, in particular full-service intermediaries, may well be part of a process of legitimating and institutionalizing new forms of work which may not be in the interests of companies, and even more so in the interests of their employees (Davis-Blake *et al.*, 2002). These and related issues are discussed in more detail later in the chapter.

Training and development

The benefits of outsourcing training make it well worth considering. 'The fact is, training is critical to business, but it's not the business most companies are in' (Miller, 2003).

While companies have been sub-contracting and/or outsourcing modest components of their training and development for decades, they have increassingly begun to look to outside vendors to provide their training and learning and development (L & D) functions (Gainey and Klaas, 2003). A 2006 Accenture comparative study of outsourcing businesses in six countries found training technologies, training delivery and training content development were among the most heavily outsourced HR and learning activities (Accenture, 2006).

The breadth of outsourcing varies by company, as well as industry sector, and ranges from the entire function to selected projects. Companies historically outsourced a few specific tasks, and once trust and competency had been tested and proven, they began to look to outsourcing more cumbersome projects – even entire training initiatives. Among the most common aspects topics that companies hand off are health and safety training, executive coaching and programme management (Simba Information, 2005: 21–30).

The pressure is on businesses to increase the outsourced component in a more substantive manner including the aspect of training administration. This more inclusive and extensive form of outsourcing is at times termed a managed learning service or training and learning BPO (see Miller, 2003). Currently, a small percentage of companies outsource their entire L & D function. For example, a 2005 UK survey found only 3 per cent of companies outsourcing this function. (PCG, 2005), and the percentage of firms using a managed service is still modest. For instance, around 5 per cent of UK large firms in 2008 were using such a service according to one survey (Wigham, 2008).

The outsourcing drive in the training and development field is conditioned by demands for a more dynamic and flexible workforce, the growth of e-learning, and the increased recognition of the relationship between learning and company productivity and morale. Industry protagonists argue that outsourcing will enable in-house L & D practitioners to focus on more strategic tasks, and to overcome a lack of internal resources, particularly in regard to IT solutions and web-based technology. Outsourcing also enabled firms to widen the range of teaching and learning options, and gave them more scope to improve the scope and efficacy of learning, as well as providing access to best practice. Overall, by outsourcing companies would be able to improve the performance of their learning and related HR functions, and boost the performance and business contribution of their overall workforce.

However, the strategic importance of many training programmes often introduces unique challenges for organizations outsourcing this function. Gainey and Klaas (2003) suggest that socially-oriented trust and contractual specificity mediate the relationship between client satisfaction and a number of vendor, relationship, training, and firm characteristics. In this and other forms of outsourcing it is important to bear in mind change management (e.g. Miller, 2003). With due investment in strategy and tactics in this area outsourcing may well usher in a significant change to the organization. Employee responsibilities will change, with some of the firm's employees even possibly working for the service provider. It is thus important that both parties consider the impact on employees before proceeding with the implementation of the contract.

Regulatory compliance

The field of regulatory compliance is a further field where there is significant/increasing degree of HR outsourcing. Relevant service providers in this area often emphasize their experience, mastery of IT/web-based solutions, and also their emphasis on preventive and proactive HR in the field of regulatory compliance. Vendors offer to help companies reduce their HR related expenses by designing policies and procedures and auditing the firms' current policies and procedure, as well as helping clients resolve issues in-house without incurring exposure and liability before third parties (Little and Day, 2007). Also, vendors provide services oriented towards the more traditional areas of labour and employee relations that often prove costly for firms, such as unemployment compensation, in-house dispute resolution and investigations, or representation before government agencies or in court (ibid.).

The specific services offered by relevant vendors can be divided into three broad categories. First, with regard to employment, services include: policies and procedures – drafting and review; investigations, e.g. harassment, discrimination, misconduct and performance; employment agreements and negotiations, e.g. hiring, separation and severance; maternity and paternal leave; representation before governmental, industry and other regulatory agencies, alternative dispute resolution, e.g. mediation and arbitration; and litigation. Second, in regard to labour, services may include: union relations; union avoidance; collective bargaining; negotiations; investigations; litigation; representation before labour relations agencies; and alternative dispute resolution, e.g. arbitration and mediation. Third, in the realm of compliance, services encompass policy and procedure development, implementation and audit.

The arguments for regulation outsourcing are that it allows the key people to focus on their core business activities safe in the knowledge that the business is conforming to good employment practices and is meeting employment legislation requirements. Furthermore, it is put forward as a cost effective alternative to undertaking regulation compliance in-house. However, it can mean that firms can absolve themselves of any more than a minimalist approach to compliance, rather than proactively engaging with the challenges of present regulations and likely future trends.

Further HR outsourcing activities

In addition to the areas discussed above there is also an increase in outsourcing of certain strategic HR functions, and at a micro level, certain more specialist functions which become seemingly more important with the deepening of new production forms and the continued globalization of business. In terms of the former there is a small but growing market dealing with the interface between high-end HR functions and the company's overall business strategies and plans (Klaas, 2008). Such potentially outsourced functions may include assessment and refining the organizational climate and culture of a firm, and even advising on what HR and other business functions to outsource. Another niche area is that of merger-outplacement-downsizing (Angione, 2003; Meyer, 2004; Kaplan 2006: 1–2). Among the niche areas at micro levels are the design of performance appraisal systems and/or the utilization of performance appraisal and assessment centres.

Shortcomings of HR outsourcing

In this section we will consider several actual and/or potential problem areas with HR outsourcing. Key reasons for outsourcing are primarily those of cost reductions and improved efficiencies, as well as providing for more scope for internal HR staff to focus on strategic issues. However, international research (Downey, 1995; Brachner *et al.*, 2002; Dasborough and Sue-Chan, 2002; Adler, 2003; Galanaki and Papalexandris, 2005) suggests that the main reason traditionally for HR outsourcing is to reduce costs. Such activities, while improving the balance sheet in the short term, will not necessarily lead to longer term productivity, efficiencies and company stability. Transferring HR service to a vendor may have a serious impact on employee morale, and expose the firm to the risk of transferring expertise and insider knowledge to outsourcing providers. This dimension should be accorded careful consideration by the company in question.

If a company intends to proceed with an HR outsourcing it needs to ensure that the process is informed by substantive prior strategic exercise with due diligence applied at all stages, in regard to what functions are/should be outsourced, the choice of vendor, the formalization of the contractual side of the relations, and continuous monitoring of the relationship with the vendor/s. As Belcourt (2006) stresses, managing the outsourcing arrangement is critical. Taking due cognizance of employee uncertainties in the process is vital.

One area relates to the shortcomings of HR outsourcing agencies. A study (Davis-Blake *et al.*, 2002) of PEOs and temporary staffing agencies in the US labour market, argues that the increasing prevalence of labour market intermediaries facilitates the unbundling of various aspects of employment and allows one or more of the central aspects of production to be offered outside the perimeters of the company. This process has three dimensions. First, the expansion of outsourcing institutions in labour markets seem less the result of established firms to achieve economies of scale and scope, than an attempt to attract new business to relatively fragile firms. A related point is that services directly linked to the companies' productivity and commitment being outsourced to more fragile service providers. This could contribute to instability in unbundling differing aspects of the employment relationship. Second, institutional dynamics associated with labour market intermediaries suggest that various kinds of organizations in the field will in effect work together to create a discourse of legitimation for the unbundling of various aspects of employment. In the third place, the proliferation of PEOs could potentially affect the institutional underpinnings of the organization of work. The emergence of full-scale service intermediaries, with a related set of emerging industry practices and regulations, might be viewed as a vehicle for rationalizing the institutionalization of new forms of work.

In addition, there have been a number of cases in the late 2000s which reveal some distinct shortcomings, especially in terms of HRO provider capacity, for large market HR outsourcing ventures (Hansen, 2007; Wentworth, 2008). For instance, Starbucks, after signing a large deal ($350–400 m) for HRO with Convergys in 2007, was obliged to end the contract less than a year later in order to focus on a restructuring of the company to deal with a downturn in its trading and market circumstances (*Workforce Management*, 19 March 2008). In the terms of the original deal, the Cincinnati-based HRO provider was to handle HR administration and payroll for all of Starbucks' employees in Canada and the US and take over benefits administration for the company's Canadian workforce (*Workforce Management*, 19 March 2008).

A similar case is that of Wachovia's recall during 2008 of a number of HR processes previously outsourced to Hewitt Associates, a large HRO provider. Wachovia is taking back a number of HR processes it had outsourced to Hewitt Associates, a potential blow for the Lincolnshire, Illinois-based HRO provider. In 2005, the two firms signed a seven year $450 million deal, wherein Hewitt would oversee payroll, call centre, benefits administration and various learning processes for Wachovia's 90,000 employees. Wachovia opted for a move to a 'blend of in-house and outsourced solutions (*Workforce Management*, 27 February 2008).

In a further illustrative case, American Airlines, after looking for a macro HRO outsource vendor, found that there was no agency sufficiently capable of dealing with HR functions in its entirety (Wentworth, 2008). It was obliged to take a consortium approach where IBM and Mercer shared a range of outsourced HR processes. Other Fortune 500 companies and large firms more generally are finding it difficult to find established market HRO vendors able to cope sufficiently with the full spectrum of HR outsourcing.

Conclusion

Large scale outsourcing of both line and supporting HR functions has accelerated over the past two decades. The advantages it imparts include flexibility in allowing firms to adjust their workforce sizes at short notice, to reduce the resources devoted to recruitment, supervision, appraisal, rewards, training and planning, and to reduce the upfront cost for capital equipment previously required to support functions now outsourced. However, outsourcing is not without costs. It takes a narrow resource based view of people as simply a commodity that should be sourced in the cheapest manner possible; one person may be easily substituted with another. However, this discounts the value that may accrue to the firm through accumulated organization, specific knowledge and wisdom, and the greater productivity that may be reaped through committed employees that are committed to the firm itself.

Notes

1 For instance, the 1976 version of the Pocket Oxford Dictionary of 1976 carries no such listing. The *Pocket Oxford Dictionary of Current English*, compiled by F. G. Fowler and H. W. Fowler. Fifth edition, 12 impression. Oxford: Claredon. 1976. The *Merriam-Webster Online Dictionary* dates the term from 1979 (Merriam-Webster Online Dictionary. 2008. http:/www.merriam-webster.com/dictionary/outsourcing. (Accessed 20 September 2008). Maynard (2004) sees it being institutionalized around 1982.

2 For example, NWU's McKinsey Global Institute estimates that the amount of the IT and business-process services shifted abroad constitutes about one-tenth of the potential market. *BusinessWeek*, 30 January 2005, Special Report.

References

Aberdeen Group (2006). *The HRO Benchmark Report*. Boston: Aberdeen Group.

Adams, R. G. (2007). Professional employer organizations: lightening the HR load. *Financial Executive*, June 2007. http://www.napeo.org/e-news/financial_exec_06-2007.pdf. (Accessed 23 September 2008).

Adler, P. S. (2003). Making the HR outsourcing decision, *Sloan Management Review*, 45(1): 53–60.

Angione, J. (2003). Outplacement's role in outsourcing: semantics clouds the issue. *HRO Today*: July 2003/August. http://www.hrtoday.com/Magazine.asp?artID=636 (Accessed 22 September 2008).

Appelbaum, E. and Batt, R. (1994). *The New American Workplace: Transforming Work Systems in the United States*. Ithaca, NY: ILR Press.

Belcourt, M. (2006). Outsourcing – The benefits and the risks, *Human Resource Management Review*, 16: 269–79.

Brachner, J., Adolfsson, P. and Marcus, J. (2002). Outsourcing facilities management in the process industry: A comparison of Swedish and UK patterns, *Journal of Facilities Management*, 1(3): 265–71.

Collings, J. (2006). Defining RPO in the European Market, *HRO Europe*. December 2005/March 2006.

Currie, W. L. (2003). A knowledge-based risk assessment framework for evaluating web-enabled application outsourcing projects, *International Journal of Project Management*, 21: 207–17.

Dasborough, M. and Sue-Chan, C. (2002). The role of transaction costs and institutional forces in the outsourcing of recruitment, *Asia Pacific Journal of Human Resources*, 40: 306–32.

Davis-Blake, A., Broschak, J. P., Wang, L. and Chng, D. (2002). Organizing contingent work: the role of temporary employment agencies and professional employer organizations, paper presented at the *2002 Annual Meeting of the Academy of Management*.

Downey, J. M. (1995). Risk of outsourcing – applying risk management techniques to staffing methods, *Facilities*, 13(9/10): 38–44.

Embleton, P. R. and Wright, P. C. (1998). A practical guide to successful outsourcing, *Empowerment in Organizations*, 6(3): 94–106.

Engardio, P. and Einghorn, B. (2005). Outsourcing: a special report, *BusinessWeek*, 21 March.

Feinberg, H. (2004). Human Resource Outsourcing – A New Term You Need To Know. August 11. http://netassets.net/templates/template.asp?articleid=412&zoneid=16 (Accessed 6 June 2008).

Fitzgerald, J. (2006). Time to Tidy the Market Now that Growth Is Showing Signs of Slowing HRO Europe. August 2006/September 2006. http://www.europre.com/Magazine.asp?artID=1409 (Accessed 30 August 2008).

Gainey, T. W. and Klass, B. S. (2003). The outsourcing of training and development: factors impacting client satisfaction, *Journal of Management,* 29: 207–29.

Hansen, F. (2007). Midsize employers in sweet spot for end-to-end HR outsourcing. *Workforce Management*, February 12, pp. 23–6.

Hardt, M. and Negri, M. (2000). *Empire*. Cambridge: Harvard University Press.

Harvey, D. (1990). *The Condition of Postmodernity: An Enquiry into the Origins of Cultural Change*. Cambridge, MA: Blackwell.

Hayes, A. (2008). HR Outsourcing: Friend or Foe? H. R. Zone. http://www. hrzone.co.uk/cgi-bin/item.cgi?id (Accessed 23 October 2008).

Hendry, C. and Pettigrew, A. (1992). Patterns of strategic change in the development of human resource management, *British Journal of Management*, 3(3): 137–56.

Heshmati, A. (2003). Productivity growth, efficiency and outsourcing in manufacturing and service industries, *Journal of Economic Surveys*, 17: 79–112.

Hindle, J. (2005). HR outsourcing in operation: critical success factors, *Human Resource Management International Digest*, 13(3): 39–41.

Kakabadse, A. and Kakabadse, N. (2005). Outsourcing: current and future trends, *Thunderbird International Business Review*, 47(2): 183–204.

Kalakota, M. and Kalakota, R. (2004). *Offshore Outsourcing: Business Models, ROI and Best Practice*, 2nd edn. Atlanta: Mivar Press.

Kaplan, J. (2006). Downsizing outsourcing. *Network World*, 13 February. http://www.networkworld.com/columnists/2006/021306.kaplan.html (Accessed 31 October 2008).

Kshetri, N. (2007). Institutional factors affecting offshore business process and information technology outsourcing, *Journal of International Management*, 13(1): 38–56.

Lankford, W. M. and Parsa, F. (1999). Outsourcing: a primer, *Management Decision*, 37: 310–16.

Levina, N. and Ross, J. W. (2003). From the vendor's perspective: exploring the value proposition in IT outsourcing, *MIS Quarterly*, 27: 331–64.

Levy, B. (2004). Outsourcing strategies: opportunities and risks. *Strategy and Leadership*, 32(6): 20–5.

Little, J. and Day, J. (2007). Outsourcing Leadership News. 2007. http://www. outs ourcingleadership.com/outsourcing.contracts.shtml. (Accessed 31 October 2008).

May, A. S. (1998). Business Process Outsourcing: A New Test of Management Competence, *Career Development International*, 3(4): 136–41.

Maynard, A. B. (2004). *Outsourcing 101 – A Primer*. http://www.reliability.web.com/ outsourcing (Accessed 28 March 2008).

Meyer, K. (2004). Banking mergers boost outsourcing activity, *Outsourcing Journal*, April, http:www.outsourcing-journal.com/apr2004b-everest.html. (Accessed 22 September 2008).

Miller, D. (2003). The advantages of outsourcing training. http://www.gpworldwide. com/pdf/bpo/TBPOWhitePaper.pdf. (Accessed 23 May 2008).

Mol, M. J. (2007) *Outsourcing: Design, Process, and Peformance*. Cambridge: Cambridge University Press.

Ordanini, G. and Silvestri, G. (2008). Recruitment and selection services: efficiency and competitive reasons in the outsourcing of HR practices, *The International Journal of Human Resource Management*, 19: 372–91.

PCG (Professional Contractor's Group) (2005). Training administration outsourcing to increase,http://www.pcg.org.uk/cms/index.php?option=com_content&task=view&i d=2729&Itemid=592 (Accessed 30 October 2008).

Power, M. J., Bonifazi, C. and Desouza, K. C. (2004). Ten Outsourcing Traps to Avoid, *Journal of Business Strategy,* 25(2): 37–42.

Schiff, J. (2006). Outsourcing HR reaps benefits for small business. http://www. smallbusinesscomputing.com/news/article/php/396341 (Accessed 6 June 2008).

Sharma, C. K. (2005). The political economy of global outsourcing. *South Asian Journal of Socio-Political Studies*, 5(2): 76–82.

Sharpe, M. (1998). Outsourcing, organizational competitiveness, and work, *Journal of Labor Research*, 18: 535–49.

Simba Information (2005). *Corporate Training Market 2005: Forecast and Analysis.* www.simbainformation.com/pub/1078909.html (Accessed 30 October 2008).

Simchi-Levi, D., Kaminsky, P. and Simchi-Levi, E. (2004). *Managing the Supply Chain: The Definitive Guide for The Bussiness Professional.* New York: McGraw-Hill.

Smith, A. (1995). *An Inquiry into the Nature and Causes of the Wealth of Nations*. Online Edition@1995–2005 Adam Smith Institute. http://www.adamsmith.org/smith/won/ won-index/html. (Accessed 15 July 2008).

Tang, A. (2007). PEOs back with a vengeance. *HRO Today*, May. http://www.hrotoday. com/magazine.asp?artID=1694 (Accessed 23September 2008).

The Pocket Oxford Dictionary of Current English (1976). Compiled by F. G. Fowler and H. W. Fowler. 5th edition, 12 impression. Oxford: Claredon.

Trampel, J. (2004). To offshore or nearshore IT services? – an investigation using transaction cost theory. http://129129.3.20.41/econ (Accessed 21 September 2008).

Trestle Group Research (TRG) (2004). Small to medium enterprise outsourcing guide. http://nuw.amcham.de/fileadmin/user_upload/Business_services/Trestle_Group_SMEs _Outsourcing_Guide.pdf (Accessed 22 September 2008).

Wentworth, D. (2008). TrendWatcher: Backsourcing – Bringing HR processes back in-house, *HR World*, 3 November. http://www.hrworld/features/treandwatcher-back sourcing-072508. (Accessed 3 November 2008).

Wigham, R. (2008). Outsourcing: off-loading the burden, *Personnel Today*, Com. 4 March. http://www.personneltoday.com/articles/2008/03/04/44396/outsourcing-off-loading-the-burden.html (Accessed 31 October 2008).

Young, S. (2007). Outsourcing: uncovering the complexity of the decision, *International Public Management Journal*, 10: 307–25.

7 The socio-cultural aspects of knowledge management and the links to HRM

A critical perspective

Donald Hislop

Introduction

Despite the fact that interest in the topic of knowledge management only began to take off noticeably in the mid-1990s a massive amount of writing and analysis has now been produced on the topic. This literature is highly diverse (covering technological, psychological and sociological issues addressed via a wide range of theoretical lenses), covers a wide range of topics (from the role of IT systems in knowledge management to how retaining key workers helps organizations retain tacit knowledge), and is riven with debate and disagreement (including on questions as fundamental as the nature of knowledge and whether it is manageable). Thus, in the space of one book chapter it is impossible to provide a comprehensive review of all topics, debates and perspectives.

In this chapter the primary aim is to utilize a critical perspective to examine the role of socio-cultural factors in knowledge management. More specifically, the chapter adopts what Schultze and Stabell (2004), mirroring Burrell and Morgan, label a dissensus-based perspective on social order, which represents a relatively marginal perspective within the literature on knowledge management, with the mainstream perspective in this literature adopting a consensus-based perspective on social order. Another way of narrowing the focus of the chapter is by examining knowledge management initiatives within the context of private business organizations only.

The chapter is structured around three key topics. The first topic unpacks the question of what knowledge management is and gives a brief overview of the diverse perspectives on the topic. The second and largest section highlights why socio-cultural issues are central to the topic of knowledge management and examines some of the key factors which shape the willingness of workers to participate in organizational knowledge management processes. This extends from the nature of the employment relationship, to the role of inter-personal trust and the extent to which people identify with colleagues and the teams or groups they work with. The third and final section then takes a critical look at how HRM and culture management practices can be used to facilitate knowledge management initiatives. One issue that is not touched on here, due to constraints of space, but which arguably represents an important way in which HRM practices can underpin knowledge management initiative, is how the development of workers' loyalty and commitment can be used to prevent the loss of crucial knowledge from an organization that can occur when key people leave.

What is knowledge management?

As the central focus of the chapter is on socio-cultural 'people-related' aspects of knowledge management, and the role of the HRM function and HR practices on knowledge management processes, it is not the intention to take up a lot of space defining key terms. However, it is necessary to devote some space to such issues, as there is much disagreement in the knowledge management literature regarding what constitutes 'knowledge', and 'management'. Further, how people define these terms shape how they conceptualize the nature of knowledge management processes, and the role of the HRM function in shaping them.

What is knowledge?

In addressing this question, the focus is purely on how the contemporary knowledge management literature defines knowledge. There is broad agreement that there are two quite different and distinctive epistemological perspectives that exist (see Table 7.1), with the objectivist epistemology representing the mainstream perspective (Cook and Brown, 1999; Empson, 2001; Schultze and Stabell, 2004; Hislop, 2005). An enormous amount of space could be devoted to describing, comparing and contrasting these perspectives, however here it is only possible to provide the briefest of descriptions and comparisons.

First, while the objectivist epistemology assumes that knowledge can exist in the form of an object or entity, separate from people (codified knowledge) the practice-based epistemology suggests that knowledge is deeply personal and

Table 7.1 Key characteristics of two epistemologies in the knowledge management literature

Objectivist epistemology	*Practice-based epistemology*
Knowledge can exist as a disembodied entity	Knowledge/knowing embodied in people and embedded in work practices
Tacit and explicit knowledge represent separate and distinctive types of knowledge	Tacit and explicit knowledge are inseparable
Codified knowledge regarded as objective	Knowledge is socially constructed, culturally embedded
Privileging of explicit, objective knowledge over tacit knowledge	No privileging of explicit knowledge
Examples of work adopting this perspective: Voelpel *et al.* (2005), Haas and Hansen (2007)	Examples of work adopting this perspective: Gherardi (2000), Orlikowski (2002), Strati (2007)

embodied in people, as well as being embedded in and inseparable from their work practices. From this perspective people develop and use their knowledge through carrying out their work, with it only ever being possible to partially codify such knowledge. Second, the objectivist perspective assumes that tacit knowledge (knowledge that is personal, partially conscious and which cannot be articulated explicitly) and explicit knowledge (knowledge that can be codified and written down) are separate and distinctive types of knowledge. In contrast, those adopting a practice-based epistemology regard tacit and explicit knowledge as intimately inter-linked and inseparable (Tsoukas, 1996). In conceptualizing this difference Schultze and Stabell (2004) talk of the objectivist epistemology having an either/or logic to tacit and explicit knowledge, while the practice-based epistemology has a both/and logic. Third, while the objectivist perspective assumes that explicit or codified knowledge represents an objective form of knowledge, the practice-based epistemology emphasizes the socially constructed and cultural embeddedness of all forms of knowledge. Finally, while the objectivist epistemology typically privileges and prioritizes explicit/codified knowledge over tacit and contextual knowledge, there is no such hierarchical privileging of knowledge types in the practice-based epistemology. These assumptions about knowledge are reflected in the type of research and writing used by writers adopting these perspectives – see examples in Table 7.1. Those utilizing the objectivist epistemology typically adopt a positivistic approach to research, testing hypotheses via the statistical analysis of quantitative data. By contrast, those adopting a practice-based epistemology typically utilize a social constructivist perspective and examine knowledge processes through case study analyses and the use of qualitative data.

Unsurprisingly, the way knowledge management processes are conceptualized by these epistemologies is quite different. Knowledge management from an objectivist epistemology often has a strong IT emphasis, with it being assumed that much important knowledge can be codified and then stored in databases that others can have access to. In contrast, knowledge management from a practice-base perspective emphasizes the role of people-to-people communication and interaction. Thus, the existence of these two distinctive epistemologies represents one of the key reasons why, as will be seen later, there is a diversity of perspectives on how knowledge in organizations can be managed.

What is management?

While there is an enormous amount written in the knowledge management literature on epistemology, it is virtually silent on the equally fundamental issue of the character of management. Alvesson and Kärreman (2001), in one of the only pieces of writing in the area to engage with this question, suggest that this is because its meaning is largely considered to be self-evident, which is an assumption they regard as problematic.

In addressing this question they develop a two-dimensional matrix which contains four generic styles of management. Their first dimension, which they label the 'domain of intervention' differentiates between management styles focussed either with directly controlling and monitoring worker behaviour versus those concerned with controlling and shaping workers' attitudes. Behavioural focussed management styles are synonymous with Taylorism, where management control how tasks are carried out and workers have little autonomy or discretion to deviate from such procedures, while attitudinal focussed management styles are synonymous with normative or culture based control systems, where management efforts are focussed on shaping workers' attitudes and values (Ogbonna and Harris, 2002). The other dimension in Alvesson and Kärreman (2001) typology of management styles, which they label the 'mode of intervention', characterizes the strength of managerial interventions. Strong management styles are characterized by the use of specific, detailed targets for worker performance, whereas weak forms of management play more of a co-ordinating role with the use of direct control being minimal.

The relevance of this framework to the topic of knowledge management is that Alvesson and Kärreman (2001) suggest that the particular approach to management used in organizations will shape the way they attempt to manage knowledge. Thus, from their framework of four distinctive management styles they develop a typology of four different approaches to knowledge management, which is examined in the following section.

What is knowledge management?

In considering the question of how knowledge in organizations can be managed, there is a related debate on the more fundamental question of whether knowledge is manageable at all. There are three broad perspectives on this question, with the mainstream knowledge management literature assuming that through the use of appropriate means that knowledge in organizations can be managed. At the other extreme are those, such as Fuller (2002), who believe that the concept of knowledge management is an oxymoron. Finally there are those who take a more intermediate position (such as von Krogh *et al.*, 2000; Alvesson and Kärreman, 2001) who suggest that while the characteristics of knowledge (such as its tacit, subjective, ambiguous and contextual qualities) make it a resource which cannot be directly managed, that organizational management do have some powers to manage knowledge more indirectly, via shaping the way staff use, create, and share knowledge.

Of those who assume that knowledge is manageable, either directly or indirectly, there is no agreement on exactly how this can or should be done, which is witnessed by the fact that a number of typologies of distinctive knowledge management strategies have been developed (Hansen *et al.*, 1999; Earl, 2001; Hunter *et al.*, 2002). For example, Earl outlines seven different approaches to managing knowledge from a 'spatial' approach, where office layout and architecture are used to facilitate inter-personal interaction and knowledge sharing to a 'systems' approach, where knowledge is managed by codifying it into IT systems which can be accessed by all.

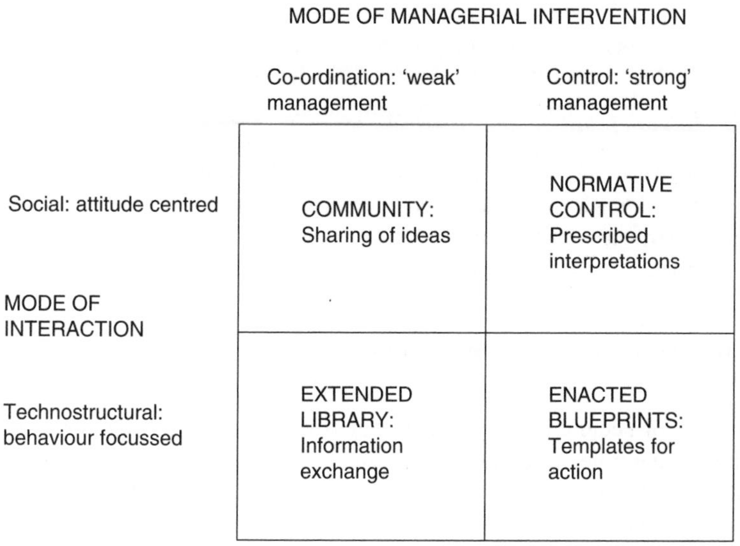

MODE OF MANAGERIAL INTERVENTION

MODE OF INTERACTION	Co-ordination: 'weak' management	Control: 'strong' management
Social: attitude centred	COMMUNITY: Sharing of ideas	NORMATIVE CONTROL: Prescribed interpretations
Technostructural: behaviour focussed	EXTENDED LIBRARY: Information exchange	ENACTED BLUEPRINTS: Templates for action

Figure 7.1 Alvesson and Kärreman's knowledge management approaches (adapted from Figure 2, Alvesson and Kärreman, 2001).

Alvesson and Kärreman (2001) used their framework of four management styles outlined earlier as the basis for developing four specific approaches to knowledge management (see Figure 7.1). Alvesson and Kärreman make clear that the distinction between the four different approaches to knowledge management they make are analytical rather than empirical and that organizations are unlikely to exclusively use one approach to knowledge management.

The Extended Library approach to knowledge management combines behavioural focussed controls with a relatively weak form of co-ordinated management and represents a relatively bureaucratic, centrally controlled, and top down form of knowledge management in which IT systems (such as knowledge databases) play an important role. The Community approach to knowledge management combines culture based socially focussed controls with a weak form of management. This approach to knowledge management gives a very limited role to IT systems, focussing instead around encouraging the direct sharing of knowledge between people. Management efforts with this approach are focussed on creating a climate, culture and context likely to induce such behaviours. The Normative Control approach to knowledge management combines socially focussed controls with a relatively strong form of managerial intervention. This is knowledge management via culture management, whereby management attempt to create a culture that encourages employees to embrace a value system which regards knowledge sharing as a norm. The fourth approach to knowledge management articulated by Alvesson and Kärreman is the Enacted Blueprints approach, which combines a strong form of managerial intervention with behavioural controls. This involves managerial efforts being concerned with creating codified databases of knowledge focussed around particular roles and tasks that provide a mechanism for giving employees access to what are considered a set of 'best practices'.

In conclusion, due to the diversity of ways that knowledge and management are conceptualized, the knowledge management literature suggests there are a heterogeneous range of ways via which organizations can attempt to manage the knowledge of their workforce.

What shapes employees' attitudes to knowledge management?

The importance of socio-cultural, people related issues to knowledge management is the crucial role they play in shaping whether people are willing to participate in such initiatives (Empson, 2001; Cabrera and Cabrera, 2002; Hislop, 2003; KPMG, 2003; Lam, 2005). This part of the chapter examines the range of factors which shape whether employees are willing or not to participate in knowledge management initiatives.

Knowledge as a 'public good' and workers' share/hoard dilemma

A number of writers characterize the decisions workers face regarding whether to participate in knowledge-related activities as comparable to a classical public good dilemma, with the knowledge workers have access to in their organizations being considered a public good (Dyer and Nobeoka, 2000; Cabrera and Cabrera, 2002; Fahey *et al.*, 2007; Renzl, 2008). A public good is a shared resource which members of a community, or network can benefit from, regardless of whether they contributed to it or not, and whose value does not diminish through such usage. Collective knowledge resources that workers have access to are thus a public good as anyone can utilize them whether they have contributed to their development or not. In such situations there is thus the potential for people to 'free-ride', by utilizing such resources but never contributing to them. The paradox of such situations at the group level is that the optimal behaviour for the individual (free-riding) will have negative consequences at the group level if everyone attempts to free-ride. In the case of collective organizational knowledge resources, if everyone acted as a free-rider there is the likelihood that such resources would lose their relevance and usefulness through never being refined, developed or changed. Effectively the knowledge base would stagnate.

However, the dilemma at the individual level is real. First, workers may feel a need to contribute something to the public good, the organizational knowledge base, due to an awareness that if everyone acted as a free-rider the resource would diminish. However the dilemma is that such feelings are tempered by concerns regarding potential negative personal consequences from sharing their knowledge and contributing to the public good. Thus, in deciding how to act in such situations workers are likely to attempt to evaluate the potential positive and negative individual consequences of sharing knowledge or hoarding knowledge (free-riding).

There is some evidence in the knowledge management literature that people consider such issues and that their knowledge behaviours are shaped by perceptions regarding their potential individual consequences. This research shows that people's fear of negative consequences from knowledge sharing can actively inhibit participating in knowledge management initiatives (Empson, 2001; Ardichvili, *et al.,* 2003; Lam, 2005; Martin, 2006; Mooradian *et al.*, 2006; Renzl, 2008). The potential benefits of knowledge sharing are that doing so may be intrinsically rewarding, that there may be benefits at the group level, that there is some material reward, or that a person's status as an expert is enhanced. However the negative aspect of contributing knowledge is that doing so may be time consuming and that workers have two fears about potential negative consequences: the fear of 'giving away' a source individual power and status, and the fear of ridicule (through revealing that the knowledge possessed may have limitations or be misguided).

Finally, there are the rewards/benefits of hoarding to also be accounted for. While the benefit of hoarding knowledge (free-riding) is that the worker avoids the risk of giving away knowledge, a potential negative consequence is that by doing so they never receive full recognition for what they do know.

Overall therefore, workers decisions on whether to participate in organizational knowledge management initiatives depend to some extent on their perception of the rewards and costs of doing so. Other research shows that workers' decisions on whether to participate in organizational knowledge management initiatives are shaped by factors such as the nature of their social relationship with peers and colleagues, and the extent to which they feel a member of and a commitment to a work group. However, before these issues are examined, the context in which a worker's act is examined, as this itself can impact on whether workers are willing to participate in organizational knowledge management initiatives.

The context of the employment relationship: employer–employee relations

The neglect in the vast majority of the knowledge management literature to explicitly take account of the fact that knowledge management initiatives occur in the context of business organizations operating in capitalist economies represents a significant weakness in this literature (Hislop, 2005). This is not only because this shapes managerial motivations and objectives in implementing knowledge management initiatives, but also that it shapes the nature of the relationship between employer and employee and can significantly affect the extent to which employees may be willing to participate in knowledge management initiatives. To understand why this is the case it is necessary to begin by articulating the basic characteristics of the employment relationship.

First, the employment relationship, which involves organizational management acting as the mediating agents of shareholders, typically places workers in a subordinate position, having no ability to shape corporate objectives and with one of management's key roles being to achieve their shareholders' objectives (for profit, market share, etc.) through controlling and directing workers' efforts (Coopey, 1998; Tsoukas, 2000; Contu and Willmott, 2003). Second, embedded in the employment relationship is the potential for conflict between the interests of managers and shareholders, and workers. In the context of workers' knowledge this may create tensions between management and workers over not only who 'owns' an employee's knowledge, but how such knowledge is used. For example, while management may perceive that it is the interests of the organization to encourage workers to codify their knowledge, workers may be reluctant to do so if they feel that such efforts will negatively affect them through diminishing their power and/or status. For example, such concerns were expressed by one worker interviewed by McKinlay (2002), who articulated their reluctance to codify their knowledge by saying, '*I'm being asked to give myself away*' (p. 81). Further, such concerns also explain the reluctance of some managers in the UK based pharmaceutical company studied by Currie and Kerrin (2004) to participate in their organization's knowledge management efforts. In this case attempts to manage knowledge took place in the context of a downsizing initiative, which created concerns that the codification and sharing of knowledge would make it easier for their employer to get rid of them and replace them with younger, less experienced staff.

Finally, it is useful to acknowledge that factors other than the employment relationship affect a worker's relationship with their employer and can shape knowledge sharing attitudes. First, Kim and Mauborgne (1998) found that the extent to which workers perceived organizational decision-making processes to be fair (what they termed 'procedural justice') had a positive relationship to knowledge sharing attitudes, a conclusion supported by Cabrera and Cabrera (2005).

The context of business organizations: the scope for inter-personal conflict

While the knowledge management literature contains numerous examples of how conflict has significantly shaped the dynamics of organizational knowledge processes (Newell *et al.*, 2000; Empson, 2001; Hislop, 2003; Currie and Kerrin, 2004), it is still true that a general weakness of the mainstream knowledge management literature is that issues of conflict, power and politics are generally neglected (exceptions being Storey and Barnett, 2000; Contu and Willmott, 2003; Currie and Kerrin, 2004; Marshall and Rollinson, 2004; Yanow, 2004; Willem and Scarbrough, 2006).

The neglect of such issues in the mainstream knowledge management literature is due to the assumptions of consensus and goal congruence in organizations that exist in the majority of the knowledge management literature. For example, Schultze and Stabell (2004), borrowing from Burrell and Morgan's paradigms of social science framework, suggest that one dimension against which the knowledge management literature can be characterized is the extent to which consensus in society and organizations predominates, with their analysis suggesting that the consensus perspective represents the mainstream perspective in the knowledge management literature. This perspective has echoes of Fox's (1974) Unitarist framework on organizations.

However, the dissensus perspective suggests that such a perspective on organizations is arguably naïve and unrealistic. The importance of taking account of how conflict shapes attitudes to knowledge management initiatives is that it is arguably a structurally unavoidable feature of business organizations, with scope for such conflict existing in a wide range of areas from personality differences, competition between people/groups/departments for scarce resources, over (limited) promotion opportunities, and in competing interpretations of events. Such a perspective is reinforced by research which suggests that politics is a normal and common feature in business organizations (Buchanan, 2008).

Inter-personal trust and attitudes to knowledge sharing

A significant amount of research suggests that the level of trust a worker has in other people can have a significant influence on their willingness to share knowledge with others (Andrews and Delahaye, 2000; Roberts, 2000; Mooradian *et al.*, 2006; Wang *et al.*, 2006). Trust can be defined as, 'the willingness of a party to be vulnerable to the actions of another party based on the expectation that the other will perform a particular action important to the trustor' (Mooradian *et al.*, 2006: p. 524). If trust exists a person is likely to act on faith by the unilateral provision of resources, information, etc. (in this context giving knowledge), with the expectation that this action will be reciprocated at some point in the future. In the previous section it was acknowledged that knowledge sharing had risks, due to potential negative consequences. The existence of trust in a person increases the likelihood of knowledge sharing occurring as it helps mediate and reduce the perception of risk people experience.

A specific example of the role that trust plays in shaping knowledge sharing decisions is provided by Andrews and Delahaye (2000), who examined cross-organizational collaboration between some bio-medial scientists. They found that all the scientists studied carried out a process of conscious reflection prior to sharing knowledge with people and that without trust existing they were unlikely to share knowledge. The risks that concerned the scientists related to credibility (where the misuse of their knowledge by others may have negatively affected their credibility), and visibility and ownership (where the misuse of their knowledge created the risk that they would lose visibility and ownership if someone claimed the knowledge as their own). Trust in colleagues mediated such concerns through creating a confidence that they would not act in such ways.

However, it is important to acknowledge that developing and sustaining trust-based relations with business colleagues is often not easy. One factor shaping levels of inter-personal trust is the extent to which people have common knowledge and values, shared interests, and some sense of shared identity.

The less of these elements that people have in common, the weaker is the foundation on which trust can be developed. However, work in business organizations often requires people to collaborate with others they, initially, have little in common with, such as in inter-organization, cross-disciplinary, or multi-occupational collaborations. Further, the ability to develop trust can be inhibited when opportunities to meet and interact face-to-face are limited and where interaction is predominantly by phone or email (Jarvenpaa and Leidner, 1999; Roberts, 2000). However, the increasing use of remote, virtual and dispersed forms of working means that workers increasingly have to work in such circumstances. Finally, the existence of conflict and differences of opinion, which the previous section suggests is an inherent feature of the dynamics of business organizations, represents another factor which can inhibit the development of strong levels of inter-personal trust between colleagues.

Overall, therefore, while the existence of trust increases the likelihood that people will share knowledge, as its existence mediates their concerns about the potential negative consequences of doing so, the nature of work in business organizations has a number of features which make developing and sustaining high levels of interpersonal trust difficult.

Identification with and trust in groups

In relation to workers' identification with and trust in work groups, the extensive literature on communities of practice (Roberts, 2006) suggests that when people feel a sense of identity with a community this facilitates the development of trust with other community members and is likely to create a positive attitude towards sharing knowledge with other community members. For example, Usoro *et al.* (2007), who examined a virtual, IT-mediated community of practice in what they describe as a Fortune 500 global IT company, found that the people's level of community trust was positively related to knowledge sharing. Further, Cabrera *et al.*'s (2006) findings of a study into the factors shaping the attitudes of workers to knowledge sharing in a single Spanish company also reinforce these conclusions. Of all the variables they examined, one of the three that had the strongest relationship with knowledge sharing was the level of knowledge management support. Specifically they found that people are more likely to share knowledge when they perceive that there is a high level of support for knowledge sharing among colleagues.

However, the existence of strongly individualistic cultures and values in organizations, where relations among colleagues can be highly competitive, can inhibit the development of strong forms of group identity and knowledge sharing, and may even have the effect of encouraging knowledge hoarding through the individualized career benefits people perceive they can derive from doing so (Lam, 2005; Oltra, 2005; Roberts, 2006). Thus, the development of communities of practice, a sense of collegiality and strong group-based identities typically requires a particular type of organizational culture to exist.

Finally, the community of practice literature can be criticized for exaggerating the extent to which consensus exists and to which community members have shared values and simultaneously neglecting to account for the extent to which conflict, politics and power differentials exist in communities (Contu and Willmott, 2003; Roberts, 2006). Thus, due to such factors, communities of practice may not be the idealistic knowledge sharing forums that much of the literature suggests.

HRM policies/practices for managing KM related people issuses

This section provides a critical review of the research on the role that particular HRM policies can have on knowledge management initiatives. However, before doing so it is necessary to discuss a more general issue: how the extent to which the HRM function has a role in strategic decision making processes affects how people management issues are taken account of in knowledge management initiatives.

While a common theme in the literature on knowledge management strategy is that HR practices should be designed to align with the specific type of approach to knowledge management adopted in organizations (Hansen *et al.*, 1999; Haseli and Boxall, 2005), little research has actually looked at whether this happens in practice, and what shapes the extent to which HRM factors are accounted for in the design and implementation of knowledge management initiatives. Two studies which examined and touched on such issues (Currie and Kerrin, 2003; Oltra, 2005) came to quite negative conclusions, although both are based on case studies whose findings may not be generalizable. Currie and Kerrin (2003) analyze a failed knowledge management initiative in the sales and marketing business of a UK based global pharmaceutical business. One of the findings of this study was that because HRM staff and the HRM function in general weren't strategically involved in the design and implementation of this initiative, people management issues were inadequately taken account of. This resonates with the finding that in many organizations, despite the rhetoric of 'strategic human resource management', the HRM function does not have a high level of involvement in strategic decision making (Caldwell, 2004). A similar conclusion was reached by Oltra (2005), based on the examination of three Spanish case studies. He found that the status and credibility of knowledge management initiatives in some of the organizations examined was compromised because they were led by staff from the HRM function when historically the HRM function had had a non-strategic role. In these organizations, the fact that HR staff were leading these knowledge management initiatives meant they were regarded as relatively non-strategic and somewhat unimportant.

The remainder of this section has a narrower focus, critically examining the way research suggests specific HRM policies and practices can be used to motivate workers to participate in organizational knowledge management initiatives.

Recruitment and selection

The key way in which recruitment and selection processes can facilitate knowledge management initiatives is to help organizations find people whose values and attitudes fit those of an organization's existing culture and norms. Thus, in organizations where this has been done and where organizational knowledge management efforts have been successful, effective recruitment has been key to their success (Swart and Kinnie, 2003; Robertson and Swan, 2003). For example, Robertson and Swan (2003) examined a consultancy company which had a culture where there was little hierarchy, where individualism was encouraged and where knowledge sharing was the norm, with consultants being happy to share relevant knowledge and experiences with each other. In its extensive and extended selection procedures, one of the key objectives was identifying people who embodied these values.

Creating/sustaining appropriate cultures

One of the most common ways the literature suggests that HRM practices can be used to support knowledge management initiatives is through facilitating a culture where knowledge sharing is valued and rewarded (Pan and Scarbrough, 1999; Robertson and O'Malley Hammersley, 2000; Cabrera *et al.*, 2006). This literature generally suggests that some of the key feature of such a culture are that knowledge sharing is regarded as a norm, that staff have a strong sense of collective identity, that colleagues have a high level of trust in and respect for each other, that organizational processes are regarded as fair and, finally, that staff have high levels of trust in and commitment to management. However, this literature can be criticized for providing little analysis of either what organizations require to do to achieve such cultures, or what barriers may exist to their development.

A more critical perspective, which mirrors one of the themes in the broader culture literature (Ogbonna and Harris, 2002), is that organizational cultures can be extremely difficult to change and transform, and that as a consequence it may be difficult to implement a culture where knowledge sharing is valued if this challenges historical cultural norms. Thus some suggest that the resilience of organizational culture means that knowledge management initiatives should be designed to reflect rather than transform an organization's existing culture (McDermott and O'Dell, 2001).

Finally, again reflecting a theme in the wider culture management literature, some analyses acknowledge that organizations may not have coherent and unitary cultures, and that distinctive sub-cultures may exist which shape the characteristics and dynamics of organizational knowledge sharing processes. For example, Currie and Kerrin's (2003) study referred to above found that the existence of strong sub-cultures within the sales and marketing divisions inhibited the sharing of knowledge between staff in them, despite a number of management initiatives aimed at changing this knowledge sharing/hoarding pattern. Further, Alavi *et al.* (2005–06), who examined how organizational culture shaped knowledge management practices in an American based global IT company, found that the existence of sub-cultures significantly shaped the way some of the standard knowledge management tools implemented by the company were used.

Job design

In the area of job design, there is widespread agreement in the knowledge management literature about the best way to structure jobs to facilitate appropriate knowledge sharing attitudes. Fundamentally, work should be challenging and fulfilling, providing opportunities for workers both to utilize existing skills and knowledge, but also to be able to continuously develop their knowledge and skills (Robertson and O'Malley Hammersley, 2000; Swart and Kinnie, 2003). Knowledge workers also typically regard having high levels of autonomy at work as important.

Cabrera and Cabrera (2005), based on the idea that the possession of social capital by workers (networks of relations with people which can provide access to resources such as skills and knowledge) facilitates inter-personal knowledge sharing, suggest that work processes should be designed to facilitate the development of social capital. Two ways they suggest that this can be done is through the development of communities of practice and the adoption of team based working (particularly multi-disciplinary, or cross-functional teams).

Training

Providing opportunities for self-development in work can be achieved as much through training, as through the way jobs are organized and designed. A significant amount of knowledge management research suggests that knowledge workers regard the provision of such opportunities by their employers to be a crucially important way to help both motivate them to share and create knowledge as well as to encourage them to remain loyal to their employer (Robertson and O'Malley Hammersley, 2000; Hunter *et al.*, 2002; Pérez López *et al.*, 2004). Finally, Garvey and Williamson (2002) suggest that the most useful sort of training to support and encourage a culture of learning and knowledge development is not investing in 'narrow' skills based training, but training with a broader purpose to encourage reflexivity, learning through experimentation, and how to conduct critical dialogues with others.

Reward

While there is general agreement in the knowledge management literature that rewarding people for appropriate knowledge related behaviours represents a potentially important way to use HRM practices to underpin organizational knowledge management efforts (Cabrera and Cabrera, 2005; Oltra, 2005), at a more detailed level there is disagreement on exactly how reward systems can and should be used to underpin knowledge management initiatives.

Thus, some research finds that individually focussed financial rewards can play a positive role. For example, Horowitz *et al.*'s (2003) survey of Singaporean knowledge workers found that providing a 'highly competitive pay package' (p. 32) was ranked as the second most effective way to help retain knowledge workers, with the lack of one being cited as the primary reason underlying the turnover of knowledge workers. Such findings reinforce Scarborough's (1999) assertion that knowledge workers are relatively instrumental in their outlook, with issues of pay being one of their primary concerns. However, these findings are contradicted by Pérez López *et al.*'s (2004) study of a small but representative sample of medium and large Spanish companies which found no relationship between the use of rewards systems and learning in organizations. National cultural issues may play a role in shaping worker behaviour and attitudes in these studies, however the nature of the role, if any, they play is uncertain as the role of national culture remains a relatively neglected topic in the knowledge management literature.

Further, there is disagreement on whether rewards should be given to individuals or teams. Thus some suggest that individually focussed rewards can inhibit knowledge sharing through creating an instrumental attitude to knowledge sharing. Further, such reward mechanisms may undermine people's sense of team or community spirit and reduce the likelihood that people will share knowledge where the primary benefits of doing so are to the community or group (Fahey *et al.*, 2007). Such writers thus suggest that the best way to develop group focussed knowledge sharing is through making a knowledge related rewards group, rather than individually focussed (Cabrera and Cabrera, 2005; Lam, 2005).

Conclusion

One of the key objectives of this chapter has been to illustrate how and why taking account of socio-cultural factors is key to understanding the character and dynamics of organizational knowledge management processes. This is to a large extent because, as has been illustrated, such factors play a crucial role in shaping workers' willingness to participate in organizational knowledge management initiatives. In taking a critical perspective to these issues the chapter has also highlighted the role of socio-cultural factors that the mainstream knowledge management literature typically neglects, marginalizes or excludes, such as how the potential for conflict between employers and employees embedded in the employment relationship can shape workers' willingness to participate in knowledge management processes. Further, conceptualizing the decisions workers face over whether to participate in knowledge management initiatives as being comparable to a public good dilemma allows acknowledgement of not only the potential benefits and rewards workers may experience from participating in such initiatives, but also the real and perceived negative effects workers may experience. Further, such a conceptualization of their knowledge related decision-making processes highlights how their attempts to evaluate such factors can play an important role in shaping how they act. Finally, while it has been suggested that there is scope for HRM practices to be used to encourage and reward workers for participating in knowledge management initiatives, it has also been shown that many of the features of contemporary business organizations make it difficult to create the sort of socio-cultural conditions that allow effective knowledge management.

References

Alavi, M., Kayworth, T. and Leidner, D. (2005-06). An Empirical Examination of the Influence of Organizational Culture on Knowledge Management Practices. *Journal of Management Information Systems*, 22/3: 191–224.

Alvesson, M. and Kärreman, D. (2001). Odd couple: making sense of the curious concept of knowledge management, *Journal of Management Studies*, 38(7): 995–1018.

Andrews, K. and Delahaye, B. (2000). Influences on knowledge processes in organizational learning: the psychosocial filter, *Journal of Management Studies*, 37(6): 797–810.

Ardichvili, A., Page, V. and Wentling, T. (2003). Motivation and barriers to participation in virtual knowledge-sharing communities of practice, *Journal of Knowledge Management*, 7(1): 64–77.

Buchanan, D. (2008). You stab my back, I'll stab yours: management experience and perceptions of organization political behaviour, *British Journal of Management*, 19(1): 49–64.

Cabrera, A. and Cabrera, E. (2002). Knowledge sharing dilemmas, *Organization Studies*, 23(5): 687–710.

Cabrera, E. and Cabrera, A. (2005). Fostering knowledge sharing through people management practices, *International Journal of Human Resource Management*, 16(5): 720–35.

Cabrera, A., Collins, B. and Salgado, J. (2006). Determinants of individual engagement in knowledge sharing, *International Journal of Human Resource Management*, 17(2): 245–64.

Caldwell, R. (2004). Rhetoric, facts and self-fulfilling prophesies: exploring practitioners' perceptions of progress in implementing HRM, *Industrial Relations Journal*, 25(3): 196–15.

Contu, A. and Willmott, H. (2003). Re-embedding situatedness: the importance of power relations in learning theory, *Organization Science*, 14(3): 283–96.

Cook, S. and Brown, J. (1999). Bridging epistemologies: the generative dance between organizational knowledge and organizational knowing, *Organization Science*, 10(4): 381–400.

Coopey, J. (1998). Learning the trust and trusting to learn: a role for radical theatre, *Management Learning*, 29(3): 365–82.

Currie, G. and Kerrin, M. (2003). Human resource management and knowledge management: enhancing knowledge sharing in a pharmaceutical company, *International Journal of Human Resource Management*, 14(6): 1027–45.

Currie, G. and Kerrin, M. (2004). The limits of a technological fix to knowledge management, *Management Learning*, 35(1): 9–29.

Dyer, J. and Nobeoka, K. (2000). Creating and managing a high-performance knowledge-sharing network: the Toyota case, *Strategic Management Journal*, 21: 345–67.

Earl, M. (2001). Knowledge management strategies: towards a taxonomy, *Journal of Management Information Systems*, 18(1): 215–33.

Empson, L. (2001). Fear of exploitation and fear of contamination: impediments to knowledge transfer in mergers between professional service firms, *Human Relations*, 54(7): 839–62.

Fahey, R., Vasconcelos, A. and Ellis, D. (2007). The impact of rewards within communities of practice: a study of the SAP online global community,' *Knowledge Management Research and Practice*, 5: 186–98.

Fox, A. (1974). *Beyond Contract: Work, Power and Trust Relations*. London: Faber.

Fuller, S. (2002). *Knowledge Management Foundations*. Oxford: Butterworth-Heinemann.

Garvey, B. and Williamson, B. (2002). *Beyond Knowledge Management: dialogue, creativity and the corporate curriculum*. Hemel Hempsted: Prentice Hall.

Gherardi, S. (2000). Practice based theorizing on learning and knowing in organizations, *Organization*, 7(2): 211–33.

Haas, M. and Hansen, M. (2007). Different knowledge, different benefits: toward a productivity perspective on knowledge sharing in organizations, *Strategic Management Journal*, 28(11): 1133.

Haesli, A. and Boxall, P. (2005). When Knowledge Management Meets HR Strategy: an Exploration of Personalization-Retention and codification-recruitment Configurations. *International Journal of Human Resource Management,* 16/11: 1955–75.

Hansen, M., Nohria, N. and Tierney, T. (1999). What's your strategy for managing knowledge?' *Harvard Business Review*, 77(2): 106.

Hislop, D. (2003). The complex relationship between communities of practice and the implementation of technological innovations, *International Journal of Innovation Management*, 7(2): 163–88.

Hislop, D. (2005). *Knowledge Management: A Critical Introduction*. Oxford: Oxford University Press.

Horowitz, F., Heng, C. and Quazi, H. (2003). Finders Keepers? Attracting, Motivating and Retaining Knowledge Workers, *Human Resource Management Journal*, 13/4: 23–44.

Hunter, L., Beaumont, P. and Lee, M. (2002). Knowledge management practice in Scottish law firms, *Human Resource Management Journal*, 12(2): 4–21.

Jarvenpaa, S. and Leidner, D. (1999). Communication and trust in global virtual teams, *Organization Science*, 10(6): 791–815.

Kim, W. and Mauborgne, R. (1998). Procedural justice, strategic decision making, and the knowledge economy, *Strategic Management Journal*, 19: 323–38.

KPMG (2003). *Insights from KPMG's European Knowledge Management Survey 2002, 2003.* KPMG Knowledge Advisory Services, Netherlands.

Lam, W. (2005). 'Successful knowledge management requires a knowledge culture: a case study, *Knowledge Management Research and Practice*, 3: 206–17.

Marshall, N. and Rollinson, J. (2004). Maybe Bacon had a point: the politics of collective sensemaking, *British Journal of Management*, 15, Special Issue, 71–86.

Martin, J. (2006). Multiple intelligence theory, knowledge identification and trust, *Knowledge Management Research and Practice*, 4: 207–15.

McDermott, R. and O'Dell, C. (2001). Overcoming Cultural Barriers to Knowledge Sharing. *Journal of Knowledge Management*, 5/1: 76–85.

McKinlay, A. (2002). The limits of knowledge management, *New Technology, Work and Employment*, 17(2): 76–88.

Mooradian, T., Renzl, B. and Matzler, K. (2006). 'Who trusts? personality trust and knowledge sharing, *Management Learning*, 37(4): 523–40.

Newell, S., Scarbrough, H., Swan, J. and Hislop, D. (2000). Intranets and knowledge management: de-centred technologies and the limits of technological discourse, in C. Prichard, R. Hull, M. Chumer, and H. Willmott (Eds), *Managing Knowledge: Critical Investigations of Work and Learning*, pp. 88–106. London: MacMillan.

Ogbonna, L. and Harris, E. (2002). Managing organisational culture: insights from the hospitality industry, *Human Resource Management Journal*, 12(1): 33–53.

Oltra, V. (2005). 'Knowledge management effectiveness factors: the role of HRM, *Journal of Knowledge Management*, 9(4): 70–86.

Orlikowski, W. (2002). Knowing in practice: enacting a collective capability in distributed organizing, *Organization Science*, 13(3): 249–73.

Pan, S. and Scarbrough, H. (1999). Knowledge Management in Practice: An Exploratory Case Study, *Technology Analysis and Strategic Management*, 11/3: 359–74.

Pérez López, S., Peón, J. and Ordás, C. (2004). Managing Knowledge: the Link Between Culture and Organizational Learning, *Journal of Knowledge Management*, 8/6: 93–104.

Renzl, B. (2008). Trust in management and knowledge sharing: the mediating effects of fear and knowledge documentation, *Omega*, 36: 206–20.

Roberts, J. (2000). From know-how to show-how? Questioning the role of information and communication technologies in knowledge transfer, *Technology Analysis and Strategic Management*, 12(4): 429–43.

Roberts, J. (2006). Limits to communities of practice, *Journal of Management Studies*, 43(3): 623–39.

Robertson, M. and O'Malley Hammersley, G. (2000). Knowledge Management Practices within a Knowledge-Intensive Firm: The significance of the People Management dimension. *Journal of European Industrial Training*, 24/2-4: 241–53.

Robertson, M. and Swan, J. (2003). Control – What Control? Culture and Ambiguity Within a Knowledge Intensive Firm. *Journal of Management Studies*, 40/4: 831–58.

Scarbrough, H. (1999). Knowledge as Work: Conflicts in the Management of Knowledge Workers, *Technology Analysis and Strategic Management*, 11/1: 5–16.

Schultze, U. and Stabell, C. (2004). Knowing what you don't know: discourse and contradictions in knowledge management research, *Journal of Management Studies*, 41(4): 549–73.

Storey, J. and Barnett, E. (2000). Knowledge management initiatives: learning from failure, *Journal of Knowledge Management*, 4(2): 145–56.

Strati, A. (2007). Sensible knowledge and practice-based learning, *Management Learning*, 38(1): 61–77.

Swart, J. and Kinnie, N. (2003). Sharing Knowledge in Knowledge-Intensive Firms. *Human Resource Management Journal*, 13/2: 60–75.

Tsoukas, H. (1996). The firm as a distributed knowledge system: a constructionist approach, *Strategic Management Journal*, 17: Winter Special Issue, 11–25.

Tsoukas, H. (2000). What is management? An outline of a metatheory, in S. Ackroyd and S. Fleetwood (Eds), *Realist Perspectives on Management and Organizations*, pp. 26–44. London: Routledge.

Usoro, A., Sharratt, M., Tsui, E. and Shekar, S. (2007). Trust as an antecedent to knowledge sharing in virtual communities of practice, *Knowledge Management Research and Practice*, 5: 199–212.

Von Krogh, G., Ichijo, K. and Nonaka, I. (2000). *Enabling Knowledge Creation: How to Unlock the Mystery of Tacit Knowledge and Release the Power of Innovation*. Oxford: Oxford University Press.

Voelpel, S., Dous, M. and Davenport, T. (2005). Five Steps to Creating a Global Knowledge-Sharing System: Siemens' ShareNet. *Academy of Management Executive*, 19/2: 9–23.

Wang, J. K., Ashleigh, M. and Meyer, E. (2006). Knowledge sharing and team trustworthiness, *Knowledge Management Research and Practice*, 4: 175–86.

Willem, A. and Scarbrough, H. (2006). Social capital and political bias in knowledge sharing: an exploratory study, *Human Relations*, 59(10): 1343–70.

Yanow, D. (2004). Translating local knowledge at organizational peripheries, *British Journal of Management*, 15: Special Issue, 71–86.

8 HRM in small and medium-sized enterprises (SMEs)

Tony Dundon and Adrian Wilkinson

Introduction

Small and medium-sized enterprises (SMEs) are often deemed critical to the economy of many countries. The reasons for this are twofold: first, there are so many smaller firms that they make up a large proportion of employment; second, because the way people are managed is regarded as central to the competitive standing of firms and industries (Boxall and Purcell, 2003). Such a recognition has provoked debate about the role of human resource management (HRM) as a means to enhance organizational effectiveness (Den Hartog and Verburg, 2004). What is problematic, however, is that much of the literature that espouses the virtues of HRM is almost exclusively derived from larger firms (Dundon and Wilkinson, 2004).

Evidence shows that the bulk of SMEs operate in the local rather than global market, with around 6 per cent of all UK-based SMEs trading in either European or other international markets (BERR, 2008). At the same time however, globalization has important implications for SMEs. Many well-known multinational firms started as small local enterprises, such as the UK-owned fish and chip chain *Harry Ramsden's*. Even more noteworthy is that many small firms control a significant proportion of global market share. For example, the German-owned coffee bean manufacturer *G. W. Barth*, with 65 employees, controls around 70 per cent of the world's market share for cocoa roasting machines (Briscoe and Schuler, 2005). In the authors' own research, a North West SME specializing in software and IT consultancy, employing 150 people, responded to globalization by establishing international networks and small subsidiary offices in Dublin and Dallas (Grugulis *et al.*, 2000). Clearly SMEs are important in terms of the engines of growth, international trade and numbers employed. However, much of the HRM literature worldwide looks at mainstream (i.e. large) firms. It is often assumed that the lessons from these larger organizations can be applied to people management practices of SMEs. As Edwards and Ram (2009) note, large firms are very much shaped by their national environments. Here consultation arrangements may be regulated by law whereas, in small firms, such formal institutional effects are weaker, and 'informality' is much more common. Many SMEs tend to have a very particularistic approach to HRM, with authoritarian management styles instilled by founding-owners with a tendency to avoid commercial alliances in favour of their own in-house strengths and expertise (Briscoe and Schuler, 2005).

The purpose of this chapter is to assess the nature and extent of HRM among SMEs. We adopt a generalist approach to HRM, which includes employment relations broadly defined. In this way the chapter can report on various practices while providing an analysis about the meanings and interpretations of management action in the context of a smaller rather than larger firm, mostly from a UK perspective. The chapter starts by asking what an SME is, commenting on the importance of SMEs for the economy as a whole and for human resource management specifically. Traditional approaches to HRM are then considered, assessing how they have been applied to smaller businesses. From this it is suggested that much theorizing about HRM in SMEs is limited in that analysis often gravitates around one of two polarized perspectives: the 'small is beautiful' versus 'bleak house' scenario (Wilkinson, 1999). The remainder of the chapter then reviews current research evidence concerning the core dimensions of HRM among SMEs (e.g. informality, recruitment, training, employee involvement/voice and related management practices).

What is an SME?

Storey notes 'there is no single or acceptable definition of a small firm' (1994: 8). The American Small Business Administration once defined as a small to medium-sized firm if it employed fewer than 1,500 people! Earlier definitions in Britain defined a small manufacturing firm as one that employed fewer than 200 workers (Bolton Commission, 1971). These definitions have been frequently criticized given their lack of context. The European Commission (DTI, 2001) has a single SME definition that includes *micro* firms (less than 10 employees), *small* businesses (10–49 employees) and *medium*-sized enterprises (50–249 employees). However, as a definition for SMEs, such conceptual distinctions can be problematic (Dundon and Wilkinson, 2004). First, small firms differ in terms of what they do and who they employ: a hairdressing shop employing 10 or 12 people would be quite large for this segment of the retail market. Second, the nature of each firm differs with a vast array of market conditions. Some firms are dependent on larger organizations for their survival through outsourcing and contract services, while others operate in discrete and niche markets, such as hi-tech or business consultancy (Goss, 1991). As Edwards *et al.* (2006) remind us, many studies fail to capture the specific economic position and social norms that govern management actions in each firm. Third, the use of alternative (and mostly normative) models of HRM tend to be applied to smaller firms as though they are the same as larger organizations (Harney and Dundon, 2006). In short, SMEs are not homogenous but differ in terms of context, family and kinship along with variable labour and product markets (Edwards and Ram, 2009). These conditions need to be recognized more fully in much of the mainstream literature surrounding HRM and SMEs.

The importance of SMEs for employment and economic growth cannot be overstated. In most westernized economies smaller firms account for a significant proportion of economic activity. In Britain, SMEs represent over 90 per cent of all establishments, accounting for around 47 per cent of financial turnover and over 40 per cent of non-government employment (DTI, 2000). However there are dangers in using such figures in a general or deterministic way. For example, around 70 per cent of all smaller firms are not actually 'companies' but rather 'sole proprietorships' with no other employees (Wiseman *et al.*, 2006). Many small firms are also more prominent in key sectors of the economy. Of those that have employees, the key sectors include retail, hotels and restaurants, transport and communications, financial services and business services (Wiseman *et al.*, 2006). Many SMEs are also family-owned (71 per cent), with the majority managed by first or second generation family members (Wiseman *et al.*, 2006: 198). Indeed, the role of familial relations has been noted as one of the more important set of factors that can influence how a small firm manages its human resource (Ram, 1994). In particular, the prevalence of dominant family values is crucial in order to understand HRM at the workplace level, including the ideas of a founding owner or the ethnicity of family-run businesses on its people management practices (Edwards and Ram, 2009).

Yet the role of SMEs stands in stark contrast to our limited understanding of HRM activity within them (Arthur and Hendry, 1992: 246). Efforts to explain this deficiency typically point to definitional complexities, access difficulties or resource constraints inherent within SMEs (Wilkinson, 1999). Much of this neglect can be traced back to an implicit assumption that findings concerning HRM in large organizations have a universal relevance (Cassell *et al.*, 2002). HRM prescriptions assume a ready-made, large scale, bureaucratic corporation and in so doing suffer from what has been labelled 'little big business syndrome' (Welsh and White, 1981). The implications for both theory and practice are of particular relevance, with concerns that research about HRM in smaller firms is dislocated from its environmental context (Barrett and Rainnie, 2002).

Theorizing HRM in SMEs: from 'bleak-house' to 'small is beautiful'

Some of the earlier studies about employment and HRM among SMEs tended to conflate the characteristics of smaller firms along opposite ends of a continuum (see Table 8.1). At one end the 'small is beautiful' view argues that informal communication flows between employees and owner-manager helps to generate commitment and loyalty. This perspective was epitomized in the findings of the Bolton Commission (1971), suggesting that SMEs provide a better (*sic*) employee relations environment than that found in larger firms. SMEs were believed to have a more committed and motivated workforce accompanied by lower levels of conflict.

The opposite end of this continuum paints a Dickensian picture of employment conditions in many SMEs (Sisson, 1993). According to this view employees suffer poor working conditions, inadequate health and safety and have less access

Table 8.1 From small is beautiful to bleak house

Small is beautiful perspective	*Bleak house perspective*
Positive HR	Negative HR
Harmonious	Hidden conflict
Good HR	Hostile IR
Little bureaucracy	Instability
Family style	Authoritarianism

Adapted from Wilkinson (1999: 207).

to union representation than employees in larger establishments. Conflict is not so much lacking but rather expressed through higher levels of absenteeism and labour turnover (Rainnie, 1989). The argument posits that the 'happy family' image of many SMEs hides a form of authoritarian management, with few employees capable of challenging management decisions without reprisals or that workers become bound by a network of family and kinship ties that govern employment relations (Ram, 1994).

As might be expected these polarized perspectives are the subject of much debate and criticism. While there is the possibility of some truth to each extreme, in reality SMEs are best characterized by a complex web of social and familial norms, economic conditions and sector variability (Edwards *et al.*, 2003). Informality, for example, cannot be automatically associated with harmonious work relations (Ram *et al.*, 2001: 846); nor should the formalization of management techniques indicate a measure of the substance of HRM within the smaller enterprise (Gunnigle and Brady, 1984).

Theorizing about HRM in SMEs in these 'either/or' terms can simplify practices that are much more complicated in reality (Wilkinson, 1999). Studies show that employees who work in smaller firms display a high degree of satisfaction in relation to their counterparts in larger establishments (Forth *et al.*, 2006). However, what is more difficult to explain is whether such satisfaction is attributable to the size of the firm or because of other contributory factors such as the role of management, leadership style, or familial culture (Tsai *et al.*, 2007). The work of Rainnie (1989) and Goss (1991) addressed the issue of variability in the types of SMEs. *Dependent* and *dominated* small firms are those that rely on large firms for their main customer base, responding to market pressures with low cost-differentiation strategies. As such employees tend to experience low wages and generally poor conditions, although there can be variation between these types of firms. Examples are often found in sub-contacting or retail outlets competing with larger firms (Scase, 2003). In contrast, *isolated* and *innovative* small firms tend to operate in markets that large firms avoid due to limited or minimal financial returns. *Isolated* SMEs often have to compete on the basis of low costs, whereas *innovative* SMEs may be competing in high risk markets that require specialist expertise or high employee skills.

While these typologies offer a greater degree of specificity about the wide range of SMEs that exist, they have been criticized for being too deterministic by reducing factors to external market influences and neglecting internal social relations at enterprise level. It is certainly evident that many smaller firms are dependent upon larger organizations for their economic survival, with the larger firm often holding a degree of market power over the actions and decisions of managers (Bacon and Hoque, 2005). However, many smaller firms do operate in niche markets characterized by innovation and employee creativity, such as high-tech and business services (Harney and Dundon, 2006). These sorts of debates have led to some rich and varied studies concerning SMEs. One school of thought suggests that it is not size *per se* which best explains HRM in SMEs but rather the type of sector and market economy in which smaller firms have to operate (Curran and Stanworth, 1981). In contrast, other commentators argue that it is the type of management style and the associated informal and family cultures that shape the employees' experience of work in many SMEs (Ram, 1991, 1994). Recent evidence also indicates that despite a lack of formal HR policy among SMEs, many employees are highly satisfied with their working experience (Forth *et al.*, 2006). Tsai *et al.* (2007: 1780) go further and explain job satisfaction in SMEs to be related to a 'commonality' of personal relationships that exist 'across different sectors of the economy' that indicates a relationship between size of firm and HR outcomes.

Given that many workers in SMEs appear satisfied while others face exploitative practices, both the 'small is beautiful' and 'bleak-house' perspectives are likely to be too polarized to reveal the complexity and unevenness of people management practices among the diverse range of SMEs. Therefore, in the following section we examine some of the main trends and developments in HR practice among SMEs to provide a more holistic overview. While this can never be exhaustive in a single chapter, we paint a broad picture of the central components of HRM and comment on the meanings and interpretations of these practices for smaller firms. These include: the prevalence of informality; recruitment practices and training policy; union membership and employee involvement and voice and the emergence of so-called 'newer' management techniques.

HRM in practice in SMEs

Informality and people management

It is generally accepted that an informal rather than bureaucratized relationship is one of the key defining characteristics of HRM in SMEs. Small firms rarely consider formalizing their working practices and rely on an emergent approach with an absence of structured or professional HR management (Marlow, 2005). This is partly the result of a lack of resources, with 'informal routinization' playing a large part in the day-to-day running of the firm. Informality, however, does not imply a particular view of the substance of work relations: it could be associated with an autocratic as much as a harmonious enterprise. This results in a situation where management policy and practice is 'unpredictable' and at times 'indifferent' to the human resource needs of a firm (Ritchie, 1993: 20).

The significance of informality on any subsequent HR approach cannot be overstated. One implication is that personalized and family ties can overlap and shape the nature of employment contracts and management actions in very informal ways.

In terms of HRM, informal interactions offer the owner-manager a range of advantages, such as speed of decision-making, clarity of instruction and unclogged communication channels. However it is also apparent that these informal benefits become constrained as a firm grows in size. One study found that an informal people management approach is more problematic when a firm employs more than 20 or more workers (Roberts *et al.*, 1992: 255). This fits with the view that once the organization grows above a certain size, management needs to become more professional and structured (Loan-Clarke *et al.*, 1999). In many smaller firms during a growth stage, the owner-manager simply becomes 'harassed' with the day-to-day work pressures of customer demands and finds little 'spare time' to handle the varied and emerging range of people management issues (Roberts *et al.*, 1992: 242). In such situations, HRM is often accorded a low priority over meeting targets and production schedules.

Evidence shows that few SMEs have a strategic plan concerning HRM: 40 per cent of smaller firms compared to almost 90 per cent of large organizations (Forth *et al.*, 2006). The latest WERS[1] data used four indicators to assess the extent of formalized strategic planning among SMEs (see Table 8.2). As might be expected, there is a greater tendency to have a strategic plan as the size of a firm grows. Owner-manger firms were less likely to have specific HR strategies (30 per cent) than family-run businesses (38 per cent).

Table 8.2 People management strategies in large and SME firms (per cent)

		All private sector	*Size of firm*			
			All SMEs	*Small firms*	*Medium firms*	*Large firms*
Strategy covering employment relations		52	34	30	54	77
Strategy, does not cover employment relations		8	6	6	10	11
No. strategy		40	59	65	35	12
Investors in People (IiP) accredited		31	15	12	25	57
Strategic HR Index	0	40	59	63	39	11
	1	13	8	8	8	20
	2	29	23	21	31	40
	3	18	10	8	21	29

Forth *et al.* (2006: 26).

The latest WERS data created a 'strategic index' to reflect the extent to which SMEs have a strategy towards employment and HR-related matters (see bottom half of Table 8.2). The scale, running from zero to three, shows that 59 per cent of all SMEs scored zero, with just 10 per cent attaining the highest ranking of three (Forth *et al.*, 2006: 26). The summary of this data suggests that while SMEs are less likely to have a formalized approach to HR than larger organizations, there does appear to be a degree of diversity between small and medium-sized enterprises, and between family-run and non-family-owned businesses. At one level it is evident the absence of HR specialists or fomalized strategies is because many owner-managers see such policies as burdensome. The owners' particular sensitivity to market pressures and the need for speedy operational decisions has been employed as an argument against formalized procedures, often couched in the view from the Institute of Directors that small businesses were perennially 'drowning in a sea of paperwork' (Thatcher, 1996). At another level, however, it also seems probable that many managers in SMEs recognize the need for policy to control employees, but these are often used in tandem with informal relations. Therefore, procedures need to be understood alongside owner-manager preferences for informality.

Recruitment and training in SMEs

Smaller firms are less likely to use personality tests when recruiting new staff and place a lower priority on off-the-job training than larger firms. Arguably, difficulties of labour supply can be magnified for smaller firms compared to the experiences of many larger organizations, given the lack of available recourses and the absence of HR specialists (Marlow, 2005). While there is a preference for informality, recruitment methods have also been shown to vary between industries and sectors. What is almost self-evident for SMEs is that because they have fewer employees to begin with, it is extremely difficult to maintain or develop an internal labour market based on recruitment and career development (Taylor, 2005). For most SMEs, recruitment of new staff is via *closed* and *responsive* methods that rely on informal networks (Carrol *et al.*, 1999).

The implications of how SMEs recruit people can lead to potential problems of discrimination. In a survey by Scott *et al.* (1989), almost all owner-managers were 'ignorant of sex discrimination legislation', and few had knowledge of their responsibilities or obligations in the area of equal opportunities. Similarly, according to the latest WERS findings, very few SMEs monitor their recruitment methods with regard to equal opportunities (Forth *et al.*, 2006). Further problems can arise with an *ad hoc* and informal approach to recruitment. For example, 'indirect' discrimination can be evident when workers are recruited from the same ethic group or from within a particular familial and social milieu (Ram, 1991; Ram and Holliday, 1993: 640). Indeed, the use of family and ethnic labour can be extremely gendered with women occupying positions of subordination in smaller (ethnic and family-run) firms: 'roles are rewarded accordingly, influenced by the "male-breadwinner" and female "actual or potential wife and mother" ideology'

(Ram and Holliday, 1993: 644). In pragmatic terms many owner-mangers find word-of-mouth recruitment to be a simple and cost effective method, with virtually no or little consideration given to equal opportunities implications. According to Holliday (1995), what is important for owner-managers is whether new recruits can 'fit-in' to the existing culture of a small firm. To this end Carrol *et al.* (1999: 24) concluded that:

> [W]ord-of-mouth recruitment methods are potentially discriminatory. On the other hand, given the lack of in-house expertise in human resource management techniques and the nature of the labour market, it could be argued that these methods are the most appropriate. Hiring 'known quantities' could be seen as a very effective way of reducing uncertainty in recruitment decisions.

The recruitment of new employees also has the potential to inject new skills and experiences into the organization. Thus recruitment can to some extent substitute for training, which tends to be less among SMEs. However, there is also the argument that training could be based on informal learning and the development of tacit skills. Therefore the lower incidence of formal off-the-job training among SMEs may not be the same as a lack of learning and skill development found in larger organizations (Kitching and Blackburn, 2002). This debate aside, it seems that many owner-managers are either 'ignorant' of the softer people skills such as training, or they are too busy and pre-occupied with 'getting the products out the door' that they have little time to consider training needs in a coherent manner (Westhead and Storey, 1997). A further explanation for the lack of formal training in SMEs is that managers simply fear they will lose newly trained employees to competitors. Wynarczyk *et al.* (1993), for example, found that many small business owners expected line managers to leave the company if they wanted to advance their career.

In summary, SMEs have a different approach to recruitment and training than larger organizations. It is an approach that is less formal and based on owner-manager views about what is appropriate for the business at a particular time (Taylor, 2005). Smaller firms have little internal labour market movement through promotion or career development, and recruitment can be one way to inject new skills into the organization. Yet such recruitment methods raise a number of concerns about the potential discrimination surrounding informal and *ad hoc* processes.

Trade union membership and employee participation in SMEs

The available data on union membership in SMEs is patchy and disjointed. The Labour Force Survey is a household dataset and cannot pinpoint union membership by firm size. Nonetheless, it is generally accepted that union membership and employer recognition of trade unions is less common in small firms (Millward *et al.*, 1992; Kersley *et al.*, 2006). In the private sector union membership correlates with firm size: 7 per cent of employees in small firms are union members; 10 per cent in medium-sized enterprises, compared with around 28 per cent in larger organizations (Forth *et al.*, 2006: 47). Further to this is that a greater proportion of employees in SMEs have never been a trade union member: 71 per cent compared to 55 per cent in larger firms (Forth *et al.*, 2006: 47).

As might be expected, owner-managers are less likely to recognize a union for bargaining purposes than is the situation for larger companies. Compared to 31 per cent of large firms, only 3 per cent of SMEs recognize a union (Forth *et al.*, 2006: 48). There is only a modest variation between sectors: 5 per cent for manufacturing firms and 3 per cent for service sector establishments. Given the absence of collective representation for workers employed in SMEs, it is perhaps not surprising that most owner-managers prefer to communicate with employees directly. For example, 86 per cent of managers said they would rather consult with employees than deal with a trade union (Forth *et al.*, 2006: 45). While most managers (72 per cent) say they have a 'neutral' attitude towards unions at their establishment, a growing proportion indicate they either 'actively discourage' union membership or are 'not in favour' of unions (see Table 8.3).

Table 8.3 Employee communication channels in SMEs (per cent)

	All private sector	*Size of firm*			
		All SMEs	*Small firms*	*Medium firms*	*Large firms*
Face-to-face meetings:					
Meetings between senior managers and the whole workforce	74	68	67	77	81
Team briefings	58	50	45	73	68
Any face-to-face meeting	85	80	78	88	93
Written two-way communications:					
Employee surveys	32	16	14	23	56
Regular use of e-mail	34	25	22	39	47
Suggestion schemes	25	13	11	20	43
Any written two-way communication	57	40	35	58	81
Downward communications:					
Notice boards	64	49	44	70	85
Systematic use of management chain	52	40	38	51	68
Regular newsletters	38	16	11	41	69
Intranet	27	8	6	16	54
Any downward communication	72	57	51	81	93

Forth *et al.* (2006: 52).

Despite the informal nature of communication flows noted earlier as a characteristic feature of smaller organizations, many report a range of communication and consultation methods (see Table 8.3). Over two-thirds have formal meetings with employees and half have team briefings. For most SMEs, face-to-face meetings are the dominant mode of communication (80 per cent among all SMEs: 93 per cent in large firms) while written communications are less common. In addition to the reported existence of such communication and involvement methods, the WERS survey asked employees in SMEs about the quality of management information. In this regard the utility of information-sharing from management was more favourable among employees in small firms compared to those employed in medium-sized and large organizations. One particular feature seems to be that among those SMEs without an owner-manager on site, employees were more positively disposed toward management communications than in those firms that are run by the owner (Forth *et al.*, 2006: 55). This may suggest that owner-managers have a tendency to guard company information as privy to them or their immediate family rather than sharing this or consulting with employees (Wilkinson *et al.*, 2007).

As insightful as the WERS studies have been for exploring HRM in SMEs, it is also known that large scale surveys cannot capture the complexity and unevenness associated HRM. And when these practices are determined by an owner-manager or an owner who may also be the head of a family unit, then the outcomes can be very different for workers. For example, a paternalistic or friendly managerial approach does not negate the fact that owner-managers discriminate workers and devise soft HR strategies to ensure the firm remains union-free (Dundon and Rollinson, 2004). In one study concerned with the extent to which SMEs are prepared for European employee information and consultation regulations, most owner-managers inform staff but fall short of the consultative requirements (Wilkinson *et al.*, 2007). Added to the complexity is what Ram (1994) describes as a 'negotiated order' between owner and employee which serves to constrain the power of owner-mangers, especially when influenced by family and kinship links that override the formalized structures of an employment contract. It is these sort of qualitative studies that suggest the meanings ascribed to specific HR practices may not be the same as the picture derived from large scale surveys (Dundon *et al.*, 2004). For example, the enlargement of work tasks is more likely in an SME given the lack of job hierarchies and absence of formalized structures. In other words, it would be typical for an employee in a small firm to complete multiple work tasks as an organic part of their everyday work (Edwards and Ram, 2009). Likewise, reporting the existence of teamworking in a smaller firm is not the same as a team-based structure in a large organization. In SMEs employees tend to work together by definition of the smaller work environment: this is not a team as conventionally understood in much of the mainstream literature on HRM (Edwards and Ram, 2009).

Pay among small firms

As already noted, pay tends to be lower among SMEs than in larger firms. Research commissioned by the Low Pay Commission in the UK found that, overall, small businesses had adapted well to the introduction of the National Minimum Wage (NMW), although with some sector variation. In the sectors of 'security and cleaning', the introduction of the NMW had actually improved competitiveness and protected employment: '[T]he National Minimum Wage has protected employment and encouraged companies to tender for contracts on the basis of the service they can provide rather than how little they pay their staff' (LPC, 2000: 49). A security firm employer commented that: 'With a level playing field, clients will opt for the best standards available for the money they pay . . . We welcome the sympathetic and supportive response from private sector clients which helped us manage the introduction of the minimum wage' (LPC, 2000: 51).

In SMEs only a small proportion of employees (5 per cent) have their pay determined by collective negotiation (Forth *et al.*, 2006). Around 20 per cent of SMEs utilize a performance or incentive-based system for employee remuneration (Forth *et al.*, 2006: 61). However, these have also proved to be difficult for SMEs, with a desire for more informal approaches overriding formalized variable pay schemes (Cox, 2005). Much more common are *ad hoc* wage payment systems which lack transparency about what other employees earn, even in the same firm (Gilman *et al.*, 2002). Arguably, pay determination in the context of an SME is often based on managerial 'gut instinct', 'prejudice' by owner-managers or 'market pressures' at a given moment in time. In our own research (Dundon *et al.*, 1999), one garage mechanic explained the procedure for a pay increase:

> I know when we get a rise. It's each Christmas. It's not automatic though, you only get a rise if they think you should have a pay rise [and] . . . that's based on not dropping a bollock in the year . . . It's a letter in the Christmas card saying we're getting a rise . . . it really pisses the lads off. I mean a little card, 'all the best and all that', but nought about your money and so and so next to you gets something.

Overall, pay remains lower for workers in smaller firms, even though many report higher rate of satisfaction than their counterparts in larger organizations (Forth *et al.*, 2006). It is also important to be critical of wide-sweeping generalizations, as a great deal can depend on the precise occupational category or sector in which employees work. For some owner-managers, statutory instruments such as the NMW have limited their freedom to impose unilateral decisions. In other SMEs, variable pay schemes have been implemented, although they are not without difficulties when they formalize an established informal routine (Cox, 2005). Moreover, many variable pay schemes in smaller firms seem to be based on managerial 'gut instinct' rather than clear systematic and objective performance criteria (Gilman *et al.*, 2002).

New management techniques in SMEs

One of the more contradictory images of HRM in smaller firms is the apparent coexistence of 'informality' with a new wave of 'professionalized' management strategies. What has been labelled 'new management techniques' (NMT) cover a range of practices that are similar to the 'high performance workplace' of larger organizations (Duberley and Whalley, 1995). Examples include devolved managerial responsibilities, cultural change programmes, team working and a range of employee involvement initiatives (Dundon *et al.*, 2001). According to Bacon *et al.* (1996), the use of 'new' management techniques among many SMEs is not necessarily 'new'. Initiatives such as quality and cultural change programmes may have been present for as long if not longer than those in larger organizations. Downing-Burn and Cox (1999) report on small engineering firms using various high commitment practices such as quality audits, team working, job rotation and communication techniques. Wilkinson *et al.* (1996) show how a small firm had a range of innovative practices with employee voice and reward systems supported by culture.WERS found that around one-fifth of SMEs use five or more new management practices such as those described in Table 8.4, with some increase in practices over time (Cully *et al.*, 1999; Forth *et al.*, 2006). Other studies show the degree to which innovative HR strategies and cultural change programmes can become embedded in particular small firms (Grugulis *et al.*, 2000). Bacon *et al.* (1996) argue that owner-mangers are not merely picking-up NMT as 'flavours of the month'. They suggest that 'the new management agenda has penetrated deep into the UK economy and that innovative and progressive employee relations practices are no longer restricted to large mainstream companies' (Bacon *et al.*, 1996: 87).

Table 8.4 Examples of new management techniques in SMEs (1998–2004)

	% of workplaces	
	1998 [1]	*2004* [2]
Joint consultative committee	17	10
Equal treatment/equal opportunity practices	24	36
Union representatives	n/a	1
Union recognition	12	3
Arrangements for worker/employee representation	10	17
Flexibility working arrangements	48	n/a
Any merit or payment-by-results payment scheme	n/a	34
Employment tribunal complaints/ claim (rate per employee)	2.4	2.6

[1] Calculated from WERS data 1998 (Cully *et al.*, 1998).
[2] Calculated from WERS data 2004 (Forth *et al.*, 2006).

These figures are broadly indicative and should be treated with caution as some questions and scales were not identical between the two WERS surveys. Cully *et al.* (1998) are based on responses from stand-alone private sector workplaces with 10–99 employees; Forth *et al.* (2006) included workplaces with five or more employees.

However, as noted earlier in the chapter, how these practices actually translate to a smaller firm is debatable (Dundon *et al.*, 2001). First, as is often the case in larger organizations, it is unclear why these managerial techniques should be viewed as positive. Many of these so-called new managerial practices can implicitly and explicitly rely on more traditional 'harder' employment conditions of work intensification which ensures a degree of managerial control over employee effort (Keenoy, 1997). Second, it is often 'assumed' that communication flows in small firms are automatically good because of the flexibility and close proximity between employee and owner-manager. However, this may be 'one-way' communication and based upon a 'need to know' approach defined by the owner-manager. There is always a danger that samples reporting such change are self-selecting, and therefore give a misleading impression of what is going on among SMEs as a whole (Curran *et al.*, 1997). A third concern, already noted, is that many SMEs can be dependent on larger organizations for business survival. In these situations owner-managers may feel obliged to conform to certain (new) managerial practices deemed desirable by the larger firm and adopted in name only in order to pacify (large firm) customer relations (Kinnie *et al.*, 1999). For example, MacMahon (1996) found that sub-contracting translated to little more than a shift in 'risk' by providing the products and services deemed non-essential by many larger organizations. Examples include catering, cleaning, security and transport in which a significant proportion of the employees work part-time, experience casual and temporary contracts and are low paid women workers.

Yet the exploitative bleak-house perspective can be equally misleading. Reports from workers employed in smaller establishments have been surprisingly positive (Guest and Conway, 1999; Forth *et al.*, 2006). Tsai *et al.* (2007) argue that satisfaction among employees is best understood in the light of the personal relationships between employee and owner-manager: a factor evident across different economic sectors. One possible explanation is the way in which employees in smaller organizations experience and perceive their psychological contract (Cullinane and Dundon, 2006). Employee perceptions of trust and mutual obligations can have a greater resonance in a small social setting where friendly relations can develop over time (Guest and Conway, 1999).

Notwithstanding the utility of a social and psychological contract explanation, there remains a contradictory image of how employees experience their work environment in SMEs. Of course this is also evident in larger firms. The idea that workers are satisfied in smaller firms and that relationships are friendlier is not always just a matter of size. HRM is often mediated on systems of 'unbridled individualism' with informality the central *modus operandi* in the day-to-day management of people. Many employees in smaller firms experience work-related illness, face dismissal and have less access to union representation than their counterparts in larger organizations: the fact they also seem highly satisfied is what challenges the discipline in seeking meaningful explanations that transcend polarized perspectives or static typologies of managerial action.

Conclusion

The numerical significance of SMEs to the economy, both nationally and internationally, means they warrant serious study and analysis. As Storey (1994: 160) has argued: 'any consideration of the small firm sector which overlooked employment issues would be like *Hamlet* without the prince'. This importance has begun to be addressed by a range of studies, of which the inclusion of SMEs in the WERS data is particularly insightful (Cully *et al.*, 1999; Forth *et al.*, 2006; Kersley *et al.*, 2006). However, it still remains debatable about the extent to which the size of a firm is more or less important than other contextual factors such as labour and product markets, ownership, familial features, management ideology or industrial sub-culture; or the combinations thereof. Given that we do understand that in large firms HRM is not simply a function of them being large, the task of unravelling the relationship between factors in small firms should not be beyond us. If what constitutes 'smallness' is contextual and possibly subjective and interpretational, then we need to examine what factors come together to explain patterns of employment relations rather than assume one particular type, be it either small is beautiful, sweatshop or the innovative high-tech SME.

Given the general overview of this chapter, there are a number of concluding comments to the issues and debates raised thus far. To begin with, much of the extant literature on HRM in SMEs tends to be characterized by size determinism. Arguably this represents a simplistic labelling of HRM that has been perpetuated by the absence of a theoretical framework to understand and prioritize particular contextual influences (Harney and Dundon, 2006). Smaller firms may manage their human resources differently than larger organizations, although in itself size by the numbers employed is not a very good predictor as to 'why' they are different. In this chapter attention has been given to charting the extent of various HR and newer type managerial practices. By combining evidence from large scale surveys and case study analysis, it is argued here that size is best viewed as a variable that mediates various priorities such as labour and product market pressures, supply chain relationships or inter-firm networks, along with the political and familial environment for SMEs. In short, the context in which SMEs operate remains a crucial factor in explaining people management outcomes, be they employee job satisfaction or more hostile managerial attitudes towards collective representation. Issues concerning gender, industrial sector, occupational class and family ideologies are important explanatory factors that help unravel the nature and logic of management actions among a diverse range of small social settings. Which of these factors are more or less important is likely to vary over time and space. It is this dynamic that represents a key challenge for HRM.

Note

[1] WERS is the Workplace Employment Relations Survey series: a structured sample of organizations and employee views in Britain. It started in 1980 and the most recent survey was conducted in 2004.

References

Arthur, M. and Hendry, C. (1992). HRM and the emergent strategy of small to medium sized business units, *International Journal of Human Resource Management*, 3(3): 233–50.

Barrett, R. and Rainnie, A. (2002). What's so special about small firms? Developing an integrated approach to analysing small firm industrial relations, *Work, Employment and Society*, 16(3): 415–32.

Bacon, N., Ackers, P., Storey, J. and Coates, D. (1996). It's a small world: managing human resources in small businesses, *International Journal of Human Resource Management*, 7(1): 83–100.

Bacon, N. and Hoque, K. (2005). HRM in the SME sector: valuable employees and coercive networks, *International Journal of Human Resource Management*, 16(11): 1976–99.

BERR (2008). *BERR's Role in Raising Productivity: New Evidence*. BERR Economic Paper No. 1. London: Department for Business Enterprise and Regularity Reform.

Bolton Report (1971). *Report of the Commission of Inquiry on Small Firms*. chaired by J. E. Bolton, Cmnd 4811. London: HMSO.

Boxall, P. and Purcell, J. (2003). *Strategy and Human Resource Management*. London: Palgrave.

Briscoe, D. R. and Schuler, R. S. (2005). *International Human Resource Management*, 2nd Edition. London: Routledge.

Carrol, M., Marchington, M., Earnshaw, J. and Taylor, S. (1999). Recruitment in small firms: processes, methods, and problems, *Employee Relations*, 21(3): 236–50.

Cassell, C., Nadin, S., Gray, M. and Clegg, C. (2002). Exploring human resource management practices in small and medium sized enterprises, *Personnel Review*, 31(5/6): 671–92.

Child, J. (1972). Organisational structure, environment and performance: the role of strategic choice, *Sociology*, 6(1): 1–22.

Cox, A. (2005). Managing variable pay in smaller workplaces, in S. Marlow, D. Patton and M. Ram (Eds), *Labour Management in Small Firms*. London: Routledge.

Cullinane, N. and Dundon, T. (2006). The psychological contract: a critical review, *International Journal of Management Reviews*, 8(2): 113–29.

Cully, M., Woodland, S., O'Reilly, A., Dix, G., Millward, N., Bryson, A. and Forth, J. (1998). *The 1998 Workplace Employee Relations Survey: First Findings*. London: Department of Trade and Industry.

Cully, M., O'Reilly, A., Millward, N., Forth, J., Woodland, S., Dix, G. and Bryson, A. (1999). *Britain at Work: As Depicted by the 1998 Workplace Employee Relations Survey*. London: Routledge.

Curran, J. and Stanworth, J. (1981). A new look at job satisfaction in the small firm, *Human Relations*, 34(5): 343–65.

Curran, J., Blackburn, R., Kitching, J. and North, J. (1997). Small firms and workforce training: some results, analysis and policy implications from a national survey, in M. Ram, D. Deakins and D. Smallbone (Eds), *Small Firms: Enterprising Futures*. London: Paul Chapman Press.

Den Hartog, D. N. and Verburg, R. (2004). High performance work systems, organisational culture and firm effectiveness, *Human Resource Management Journal*, 14(1): 59–79.

DTI (2000). *Small to Medium Sized Enterprise: Statistics for the UK*. London: Department of Trade and Industry, Small Business Service.

DTI (2001). *Small to Medium Sized Enterprise (SME) – Definitions*. London: Department of Trade and Industry, Small Business Service (www.sbs.gov.uk/statistics/smedefs.asp).

Downing-Burn, V. and Cox, A. (1999). Does size make a difference?, *People Management*, 5(2): 50–3.

Duberley, J. and Whalley, P. (1995). Adoption of HRM by small and medium sized manufacturing organisations, *International Journal of Human Resource Management*, 6(4): 891–909.

Dundon, T. and Rollinson, D. (2004). *Employment Relations in Non-Union Firms*. London: Routledge.

Dundon, T. and Wilkinson, A. (2004). Employment Relations in Small and Medium Sized Enterprises, in *Handbook of Employment Relations and Employment Law*, B. Towers (Ed.). London: Kogan Press.

Dundon, T., Grugulis, I. and Wilkinson, A. (1999). Looking out of the black hole: non–union relations in an SME, *Employee Relations*, 21(3): 251–66.

Dundon, T., Grugulis, I. and Wilkinson, A. (2001). New management techniques in small and medium enterprises, in T. Redman and A. Wilkinson (Eds), *Contemporary Human Resource Management: Text and Cases*. London: Prentice Hall.

Dundon, T., Wilkinson, A., Marchington, M. and Ackers, P. (2004). The meanings and purpose of employee voice, *International Journal of Human Resource Management*, 15(6): 1150–71.

Edwards, P. and Ram, M. (2009). HRM in small firms: respecting and regulating informality, *Sage Handbook of Human Resource Management*. London: Sage.

Edwards, P., Gilman, P., Ram, M. and Arrowsmith, J. (2003). Public policy, the performance of firms and the 'missing middle': the case of employment regulation and the role of local business networks, *Policy Studies*, 23(1): 5–20.

Edwards, P., Ram, M., SenGupta, S. and Tsai, C. (2006). The structuring of working relationships in small firms: towards a formal framework, *Organization*, 13(5): 701–24.

Forth, J., Bewley, H. and Bryson, A. (2006). *Small and Medium-Sized Enterprises: Findings from the 2004 Workplace Employment Relations Survey*. London: Routledge.

Gilman, M., Edwards, P., Ram, M. and Arrowsmith, J. (2002). Pay determination in small firms in the UK: contours of constrained choice, *Industrial Relations Journal*, 33(1): 52–67.

Goss, D. (1991). *Small Business and Society*. London: Routledge.

Grugulis, I., Dundon, T. and Wilkinson, A. (2000). Cultural control and the 'culture manager': employment practices in a consultancy, *Work, Employment & Society*, 14(1): 97–116.

Guest, D. and Conway, N. (1999). Peering into the black hole: the downside of the new employment relations in the UK, *British Journal of Industrial Relations*, 37(3): 367–89.

Gunnigle, P. and Brady, T. (1984). Industrial relations in small firms, *Employee Relations*, 6(5): 21–5.

Harney, B. and Dundon, T. (2006). Capturing complexity: developing an integrated approach to analysing HRM in SMEs, *Human Resource Management Journal*, 16(1): 48–73.

Holliday, R. (1995). *Investigating Small Firms: Nice Work?*. London: Routledge.

Keenoy, T. (1997). Review article: HRMism and the language of re-presentation, *Journal of Management Studies*, 34(5): 825–41.

Kersley, B., Alpin, C., Forth, J., Bryson, A., Bewley, H., Dix, J. and Oxenbridge, S. (2006). *Inside the Workplace: Findings from the 2004 Workplace Employment Relations Survey*. London: Routledge.

Kinnie, N., Purcell, J., Hutchinson, S., Terry, M., Collinson, M. and Scarborough, H. (1999). Employment relations in SMEs: market-driven or customer shaped?, *Employee Relations*, 21(3): 218–35.

Kitching, J. and Blackburn, R. (2002). The nature of training and motivation to train in small firms, *Department for Education and Skills Research Report 330*. London: DES.

Loan-Clarke, J., Boocock, G., Smith, A. and Whittaker, J. (1999). Investment in management training and development by small businesses, *Employee Relations*, 21(3): 296–311.

Low Pay Commission (2000). *The National Minimum Wage: The Story So Far* (second report of the Low Pay Commission), Cm 4571. London: HMSO.

MacMahon, J. (1996). Employee relations in small firms in Ireland: an exploratory study of small manufacturing firms, *Employee Relations*, 18(5): 66–80.

Marlow, S. (2005), Introduction, in S. Marlow, D. Patton and M. Ram (Eds), *Labour Management in Small Firms*. London: Routledge.

Millward, N., Stevens, M., Smart, D. and Hawes, W. R. (1992). *Workplace Industrial Relations in Transition. The ED/ESRC/PSI/ACAS Surveys*. Aldershot: Dartmouth.

Rainnie, A. (1989). *Industrial Relations in Small Firms*. London: Routledge.

Ram, M. (1991). Control and autonomy in small firms: the case of the West Midlands clothing industry, *Work, Employment and Society*, 5(4): 601–19.

Ram, M. and Holliday, R. (1993). Relative merits: family culture and kinship in small firms, *Sociology*, 27(4): 629–48.

Ram, M. (1994). *Managing to Survive: Working Lives in Small Firms*. Oxford: Blackwell.

Ram, M., Edwards, P., Gilman, M. and Arrowsmith, J. (2001). The dynamics of informality: employment relations in small firms and the effects of regulatory change, *Work, Employment and Society*, 15(4): 845–61.

Ritchie, J. (1993). Strategies for human resource management: challenges in smaller and entrepreneurial organisations, in R. Harrison (Ed.), *Human Resource Management*, pp. 111–35. Addison-Wesley.

Roberts, I., Sawbridge, D. and Bamber, G. (1992). Employee relations in smaller enterprises, in B. Towers (Ed.), *Handbook of Industrial Relations Practice*. London: Kogan Press.

Scase, R. (2003). Employment relations in small firms, in P. Edwards (Ed.), *Industrial Relations: Theory and Practice,* 2nd Edition. Oxford: Blackwell.

Scott, M., Roberts, I., Holroyd, G. and Sawbridge, D. (1989). *Management and Industrial Relations in Small Firms*. London: Department of Employment Research Paper, No. 70.

Sisson, K. (1993). In search of human resource management, *British Journal of Industrial Relations*, 31(2): 201–10.

Storey, D. (1994). *Understanding the Small Business Sector*. London: Routledge.

Taylor, S. (2005). The Hunting of the Snark, in S. Marlow, D. Patton and M. Ram (Eds), *Labour Management in Small Firms*. London: Routledge.

Thatcher, M. (1996). The big challenge facing small firms, *People Management*, 25 July, pp. 20–25.

Tsai, C., SenGupta, S. and Edwards, P. (2007). When and why is small beautiful? The experience of work in the small firm, *Human Relations*, 60(12): 1779–807.

Welsh, J. and White, J. (1981). A small business is not a little big business, *Harvard Business Review,* July/August, pp. 18–32.

Westhead, P. and Storey, D. (1997). *Training Provision and the Development of Small and Medium Sized Enterprises*, Department for Education and Employment, Research Report No 65. London: DfEE/HMSO.

Wilkinson, A. (1999). Employment relations in SMEs, *Employee Relations*, 22(3): 206–17.

Wilkinson, A., Redman, T. and Snape, E. (1996). Richer sounds: payment for customer service?, in J. Storey (Ed.), *Blackwell Cases in Human Resource and Change Management,* 266–74. Oxford: Blackwell.

Wilkinson, A., Dundon, T. and Grugulis, I. (2007). Information but not consultation: exploring employee involvement in SMEs, *International Journal of Human Resource Management*, 18(7): 1279–97.

Wiseman, J., Roe, P. and Elliott, J. (2006). *Annual Survey of Small Businesses: UK 2005–2005*, Department of Trade and Industry Research Report, March, London.

Wynarczyk, P., Watson, R., Storey, D., Short, H. and Keasey, K. (1993). *The Managerial Labour Market in Small and Medium Sized Enterprises*. London: Routledge.

Section II

The practice of HRM

9 Recruitment and selection

Rosalind Searle

Introduction

This chapter focuses on recruitment and selection processes. These systems may be the first formal interaction which candidates have with the organization. Their impact may extend across a range of stages in the pre-employment relationship with the organization, not only during the initial attraction, the selection process and the offer of employment, but also in the subsequent attrition, and decision by existing staff to leave. The two processes are discussed and distinct tools and instruments are explored. Three distinct paradigms for examining these initial Human Resources (HR) processes are outlined, with an exploration of how these perspectives have shaped both research and practice. The subsequent discussion of the recruitment and selection tools notes the influences of these approaches. Finally, emergent concerns are identified, including demographic changes, global recruitment and selection, and the role of trust in shaping perceptions and behaviours of selectors and applicants.

What is selection and recruitment?

There are many definitions of recruitment and selection. However, all contain common elements: the focus on the attraction, identification and retention of staff. The two terms are often treated as one term, but there are differences. For some recruitment focuses on the identification and selection of individuals from a pool of applicants external to the organization, whilst selection is focused on internal applicants (e.g. Searle, 2003). For others recruitment is about the identification and attraction of competent applicants and ends when an application is made. For the purposes of this chapter recruitment is taken to mean the attraction of capable candidates to a vacancy, whilst selection concerns the assessment and identification of the suitability of such applicants from this pool.

Recruitment and selection offer key opportunities for an organization to alter the type of staff it employs, but such changes may need to be considered in the context of attrition levels and an investigation of precisely who is leaving and why (Schneider, 1987). So whilst an organization might identify the need for distinct and different profiles in its new recruits, such as where technology has advanced and a skill shortage has been identified, the organization also needs to be aware that inducting and retaining their new employees might require attention too. In addition the attraction, selection and attrition of new staff can create *restrictions of range*. This is a reduction in the variance of individual differences in a context that is greater than that which would be expected by chance. Thus, paradoxically, an organization, although seeking to broaden the range of potential applicants from which to select new staff, may actually have a reduced pool of applicants who are attracted to *that* type of job role within *this* type of organization. The range of employee diversity can be further restricted through the selection of successful applicants and any resulting turnover amongst existing staff. Thus the homogeneity of their employees can increase, potentially reducing the organization's flexibility and long term viability.

Recruitment and selection might be just one stage in the HR cycle for a firm, but it can have a very significant impact on its future effectiveness, productivity and viability. Whilst it is central to the onset of employment it can also have wide ranging implications for other HR processes, such as organizational development and change. Evaluating the effectiveness of recruitment and selection involves assessing not only the quality of the new recruit but also their effective integration and retention, and their impact on existing employees and on the organization's performance.

Three paradigams for selection and recruitment

Organizational and occupational psychology has much to say about the effective enactment of different selection activities, but first we will step back and look briefly at three distinct paradigms that determine the focus and the questions researchers use.

Through understanding these distinct perspectives we can begin to respond more meaningfully to questions, such as, why is there a gap between research and practice?

Psychometric paradigm

The most well-established approach to recruitment and selection is the *psychometric or predictivist paradigm* (Schmitt and Chan, 1998). Implicit in this approach is the dominance of the organization, and who is regarded as able to identify, measure and select the applicant with the best knowledge, skills and abilities (KSA) for the job.

Central to this paradigm are three key factors: *individual difference,* in which applicants are regarded as having discernable and stable differences; job roles which can be performed only one way and can be objectively captured and quantified to create a criterion space; and finally, that there is rationality in the decision-making of organizations and their agents. Despite much being known about the cognitive limitations of individuals and the bounded rationality of human decisions (Simon, 1960), especially in a selection context (Zedeck, 1986), the impartiality of organizations remains unchallenged by this approach.

In this paradigm the applicant has an essentially passive role by providing data, by means of undertaking the tests and tools designated to assess their KSA, and thus their suitability. Much of the research undertaken here is from large volume multiple vacancy positions, such as government agencies, armed forces or accountancy. In such situations recruitment involves large scale processing with multiple applicants. Such volume processes are increasingly being outsourced to external recruiters. This high volume process requires a large pool of qualified applicants from which to choose, and assumes that every job can be reduced to a set of KSA to which applicants can be compared. Indeed because recruitment becomes a routine process such selection systems require the ongoing availability of large candidate pools (LaHuis *et al.*, 2007). Initially rejected candidates may reapply and have developed sufficiently to pass later tests (Lievens *et al.*, 2005). Thus, the ongoing attractiveness of both employer and job can become a significant concern.

A central critique of the effectiveness and validity of this paradigm is the stability of the job role criterion. Such stability, however, is increasingly being challenged, due to organizations' speed of change, in both their structures and more global locations, their flexibility of organizing, especially through team-based working, and a reduction in predictability concerning the future (Howard, 1995). The stability of the *criterion space* used to identify applicants has been undermined (Anderson *et al.*, 2004). As a result recruiters must first predict the most likely components of the job role to change *before* job criteria can be identified with any accuracy. Thus the predictive validity of this approach has been further compromised.

Social process paradigm

An alternative is the *social process approach* (Herriot, 1987) which holds increasing importance in a rapidly-changing, more global context, where labour scarcity is also emerging for certain roles. This paradigm seeks to re-balance by focusing attention on the social interaction between the two central parties; the applicant and the recruiting organization. Thus, the applicant becomes an active negotiator and co-constructer of any recruitment or selection activity, and is no longer positioned as having just one set of KSA, but having multiple facets and skills they can bring to the job role, potentially changing how their role is undertaken. Attention centres on the development of a relationship between applicant and the organization, fostered in a conducive environment in which mutual trust is enhanced.

This approach is most effective in relation to specific, one-off vacancies, such as those found in senior professional roles where the organization is seeking an applicant with specific skills, abilities and approaches that will, at best, mesh and potentially enhance the delivery of the job. Therefore, during the process of recruitment both the applicant and the organization are continually assessing, and adjusting, their views of each other.

This paradigm does not purport to provide an alternative as to how employees might be selected, but it does challenge us to look afresh at the pre-entry process

(Ryan *et al.*, 2000), and begin to regard applicants as *already* having perceptions of the organization (Herriot, 2004; Searle, 2006b), rather than these being formed soley by the selection process. These perceptions may often be informed by the choices of selection tool (Reeve and Schultz, 2004).

Person Organization (PO) Fit

More recently a third paradigm has emerged which highlights the multidimensionality of these processes – Person Organization (PO) Fit (Bowen *et al.*, 1991; Levesque, 2005). It focuses on the interaction between an individual and their surroundings, arguing that the environment in which people find themselves is related to their behaviour (Mischel, 1968). Research suggests that the interaction of person and situation factors is approximately twice as powerful a predictor of behaviour than either person or situation factors (Bowers, 1973). This view is in direct contrast with the psychometric paradigm which contends that individual traits shape behaviour and that inconsistencies in behaviour are an error in the measurement.

Like the social interaction perspective, this approach highlights the balance between the individual and the organization, with a unique emphasis on achieving a mutually beneficial goodness of fit. Employees are regarded as whole people with external lives that may impact on the organization and who may change the organization through their presence and interaction with the context and other employees. The approach tried to focus on the continual evolution of organizations, and the complexity involved in the identification and isolation of individual factors which contribute to the prediction, with any degree of success, of prolonged high performance.

Attraction and selection

In the next two sections the key processes common attraction and selection will be discussed. Due to space constraints the focus here must be limited, but see Hough and Oswald (2000) or Searle (2003) for a more comprehensive and in-depth review of the plethora of tools available. It should also be noted that all of these processes are constrained by external factors, such as national laws. In the UK applicants are protected from discrimination on the grounds of gender, race, disability, sexual orientation, religion and belief and age (see UK government website for more details, http://www.direct.gov.uk/en/Employment/Employees/DiscriminationAtWork/).

Attraction

A two tier job market has emerged over the last few years with increased competition amongst employers to attract the most qualified applicants (Micheals *et al.*, 2001). As a result, attracting the best candidates is more critical to organizational success (Chapman *et al.*, 2005), whilst those without qualifications find it increasingly difficult to become shortlisted. A recent survey from the CIPD (2007) suggested that 84 per cent of organizations experienced difficulty in recruiting suitably qualified staff. This has reinvigorated interest in understanding the reasons behind job seekers' attraction to firms (Barber and Roehling, 1993; Imus and Ryan, 2005).

Organizations have to attract a pool of potential applicants for their vacancies. In most countries there are legal frameworks governing the processes for advertising new positions and to ensure fair and due process. A central issue can be the interface and engagement with the external world as a main source of generating applicants. There are a number of tools organizations utilize to attract applicants. We focus on the most common: job advertisements, paper-based and internet and word-of mouth recruitment.

Media and internet

In the last ten years the internet has radically shifted the process of attracting applicants. Its use has increased 60 per cent through the application of corporate web sites for recruitment purposes, with 91 per cent of Global 500 firms web sites featuring vacancies. It provides organizations with a highly cost effective and efficient means of reaching applicants on a global basis, reducing traditional job adverts cost of $3,295 to $377 for their web-based counterparts (Harris and De War, 2001). In addition, it offers a more consistent portal for organizations to publicize relevant and dynamic job information (Lievens and Harris, 2003), as well as showcasing their achievements and credentials. These web sites can enable jobs to be more effectively previewed and deter unsuitable applicants early on in the process (Dineen *et al.*, 2002). Whilst this early deterring offers a significant cost saving for recruitment, it also enables the relationship with would-be applicants to be sustained and even enhanced, with deterred applicants feeling that the organization has saved them time, effort and face.

Technology development allows companies to create an additional presence on other sites, such as Second Life, YouTube, MySpace and Vivo, extending their appeal and raising their profile to a computer literate youth market. At the same time these sites provide additional access to information about applicants through their personal postings. This new application and its impact remains under research.

Applicants have never had such an immediate availability of sites (such as monster.co.uk) to assist them in their job search. This has changed the way job search information is used, with more attention being given to independent non-company sites (Cable and Turban, 2001). The digitization of job search has potentially removed geographical barriers to applicant attraction. However, it has also provided new means of identifying desirable candidates through both legitimate 'spiders' or 'bots' to search for candidates, or more covert and surveillance-based processes, such as 'flipping' and 'peeling' (Searle, 2006a).

Word of mouth

One of the most enduring sources of job seekers' information is word of mouth. It remains a highly credible and important source, especially when it is focused on the organization (Van Hoye and Lievens, 2007). It is not merely supplying independently credible information about the potential employer, dependent on the reliability of the source (Fisher *et al.*, 1979), but providing a means of discerning organizational attractiveness and enabling insight into person-organization-fit.

The internet has evolved new ways of communicating in a more personal way. Organizations are now attempting to mimic this process through posting employee testimonials on their web sites (Fisher *et al.*, 1979; Van Hoye and Lievens, 2007). Its role, however, as a source of real information remains under-researched.

Selection

The psychometric paradigm has long dominated research into the selection process, focusing on the effectiveness of distinct selection tools. The most prized evidence comes from job performance validity studies, which are increasingly being collected and utilized in meta analytic papers, perpetuating this debate. Amongst such research is the central role of intelligence testing as the best predictor of job performance, above personality or value fit (Schmidt and Hunter, 1998). What is more striking for the HR community is the significant gap between research evidence and HR practice regarding selection tools: senior HR professionals appear to either ignore or remain unaware of clear scientific findings (Rynes *et al.*, 2007). Let us explore some potential reasons for this divergence by focusing on the most commonly used tools in selection processes, including: interviews, ability testing, personality assessment, work sample tests or situational judgement tests, and integrity tests (for information on complete range of tools see Searle, 2003).

Interviews

Interviews remain the most common method of selection. Their criterion related validity co-efficient, a measure of the relationship between this assessment and subsequent job performance, varies from $r = 0.19$ (Schmidt and Radar, 1999) to $r = 0.62$ (Wiesner and Cronshaw, 1988). A number of biases have been identified including: race, gender, appearance, age, attitude, non-verbal behaviour, physical setting and job-market situation (Avery and Campion, 1982). On average, white applicants perform better than those from ethnic minority groups, although the magnitude of difference can be reduced through the use of structured formats with recruiters asking pre-defined questions and assessing responses against pre-defined response categories (Huffcutt and Roth, 1998). This type of structured approach can, however, place interviewing on a par with cognitive tests alone ($r = 0.51$; Robertson and Smith, 2001), reducing the quality of the interaction to that of a verbally administered ability test (Kohn and Dipboye, 1998).

Herriot (1993) identified the interview as the most important social process tool in assessment, representing an opportunity for both parties to meet and formally assess each other. Further corroboration of this perspective has highlighted the role of recruiters in influencing the decision making of applicants (Carless, 2003; Wang and Ellingson, 2004). Interviewer behaviour has been found to significantly influence the attractiveness of the organization and the acceptance of job offers (Carless and Imber, 2007; Goltz and Giannantonio, 1995).

There are major cultural differences in the use of interviews, with French recruiters favouring them as a means whereby everyone who would work with the applicant becomes involved, versus a more Anglo-American approach of typically one or two interviews (Shackleton and Newell, 1994). However changes are occurring with some Anglo-American organizations, such as Google, favouring a multiple interview format with interviews ascending to director level for even fairly low level vacancies. This reflects their focus, as with the French, on organizational and employee fit. These preferences around the interview highlight fundamentally different approaches to selection, but also reflect how too candidates' expectations of the process might vary.

Cognitive ability tests

Cognitive ability testing is arguably one of the most effective means of selecting to enhance job performance (e.g. Robertson and Smith, 2001). The job performance validity for cognitive ability tests alone is around $r = 0.51$, but taken together with structured interviews, in which the format of the interview is focused onto the job criterion, it increases to $r = 0.63$. Ability tests are designed to assess the maximum performance a candidate can currently achieve. These tests are timed and comprise multiple choice items based on numerical and comprehension skills. There is an array of instruments designed for distinct job levels, such as graduate and managerial, clerical or craft roles. Whilst evidence shows these tests can differentiate between individuals, concern remains as to the lower performance of ethnic minority groups (Bobko *et al.*, 1999; Schmitt and Mills, 2001) and which remains when shifting onto internet delivery platforms. Internet-based tests favour those who are more familiar with new technology, such as young, more highly educated, white males (Czaja and Sharit, 1998; McManus and Ferguson, 2003). As selection processes become more global, care must be taken to ensure that the best candidate is identified and previous biases are not perpetuated, resulting in the false rejection of otherwise effective candidates.

The link between assessment and job performance is complex, but given the more dynamic nature of job roles and the aforementioned compromised criterion space, how certain can we be that the ability tools used can discriminate effectively and identify the best candidate? An underlying factor concerns what ability tests actually measure. Cognitive ability can be categorized into *fluid intelligence*, involving the application of reasoning skills into novel problem-solving situations; and *crystallized intelligence*, which focuses on more culturally-developed and education-derived reasoning skills. An instrument may purport to measure one dimension, but may be assessing both. Much has been written about how tests are constructed and the problems associated with different development techniques (Searle, 2003). Kline (1993) has highlighted the role of 'statistical convenience' rather than the underlying theoretical rationale behind inclusion of items in a test. Frequently tests are validated against other general intelligence instruments rather than against external work-related outcomes, such as on-the job performance. The resultant scores represent only part of the picture, because they need to be compared against a relevant norm group in order to interpret their meaning. Test manuals contain these norm groups, which ideally should reflect the applicant population in terms of ethnicity, age, gender, and job role. However, this is not always possible, particularly where selection is being used to increase employee diversity, thus norms with similar composition, or job perfor-mance do not exist.

Three important factors may influence the effective measurement of ability to some degree. One may be the failure of tests to actually measure fluid intelligence and instead concentrate on more culturally-specific crystallized knowledge. Thus minority ethnic groups' true ability remains un-assessed. This view is supported by a significant body of research (Chan and Schmitt, 1997; Chan *et al.*, 1997; Ryan, 2001). In addition, demographic studies suggest differences may be exacerbated by age, with older people more likely to use culturally specific crystallized skills in problem-solving (Horn and Noll, 1994). Whilst having a good brain does permit intelligent performance, it does not dictate it (Hunt, 1999) and motivation to perform to one's maximum remains subsumed in any assessment (Goff and Ackerman, 1992). It has been suggested that the impact of motivational differences is so significant that its elimination could reduce race-related cognitive ability test difference (Ployhart and Ehrhart, 2002). Motivation remains an important but under-researched component to understanding the effectiveness and fairness of assessment.

The social process paradigm has shifted attention onto the perception of the organization. The inclusion of information, such as the use of ability tests within selection procedures, has been found to reduce organizational attractiveness for some applicants, regardless of their personal experience of these tools (Reeve and Schultz, 2004). Whilst the inclusion of test validity data can positively enhance such perceptions (Holtz *et al.*, 2005), evidence shows that accumulated historical experiences of certain groups, such as black applicants, may significantly reduce their efforts for selection and recruitment because they do not believe they will be offered a job even if they score well (Sanchez *et al.*, 2000). The complexity of these different group differences remains a significant and important research topic if we are to improve the effectiveness and ultimately the fairness and veracity of these tools.

Personality tests

Personality testing is a common technique used to discern candidates' behavioural style and disposition. Its predictive validity varies considerably (Barrick and Mount, 1991) with job performance validity quite low, between $r = 0.21$ (Schmidt *et al.*, 1984) to $r = 0.40$ (Robertson and Smith, 2001). There has been ongoing debate concerning the breadth of factors, or bandwidth, to which personality can be meaningfully reduced. Some favour a multiple factorial design of tools going into thirty or so factors (although there can be limited agreement as to their labelling) whilst others support a 'big five' model, featuring: openness, conscientiousness, extroversion, agreeableness and neuroticism (Costa and McCrea, 1985). Validity evidence suggests that conscientiousness is the main predictor of job performance ($r = 0.22$; Robertson and Smith, 2001). The increasing use of meta-analytic ensures this debate will continue.

Popular personality tests have begun to divert into novel fields. This includes assessment of factors such as candidates' derailment potential with Hogan's 'dark side' inventory (Hogan, 1992) or differentiating between behavioural styles and motivation to deploy them (MacIver *et al.*, 2006). As with other psychometric tools they do discriminate unfavourably for ethnic minorities (Chan, 1997). However, through contextualizing the items to a work-context, some of these differences can be reduced (Holtz *et al.*, 2005).

Work sample

Tools which appear to reduce the negative impact for ethnic minority groups, and show higher face validity, are work sample or situational judgement tests (Lievens and Klimosky, 2001; Schmitt and Mills, 2001). These focus on applicants' work-based judgements, abilities and behaviours and used alone show consistently high job performance validity ($r = 0.56$), increasing to $r = 0.60$ when coupled with ability tests (Robertson and Smith, 2001).

One of the central ways these tests differ from ability tools is through the contextualization of the content into a specific work situation. These tools can therefore provide data on the applicants' specific skills, but also assess cultural fit. This is an important development, shifting the emphasis away from *what* is done, i.e. skill and ability assessment, towards *how* tasks are performed. Together with the incremental validity these instruments provide, above that of cognitive and personality testing (Chan and Schmitt, 2002; Clevenger *et al.*, 2001), and their ease and cost effective delivery through the internet, they are rapidly replacing multiple-assessor, multiple-test approaches, or are being used in pre-screening. They have a strong fidelity, or relationship with the assessment and the actual work, which appeals to both applicant and recruiter (Kanning *et al.*, 2006).

Work sampling is, however, not without its drawbacks: They require more in-depth job knowledge than with generic ability tests and so can be time consuming and costly to produce, and can offer limited transportability to different jobs or contexts. Due to their contextualized skill assessment, they are difficult to use with applicants of limited work experience, such as graduates. Of more concern, however, is their openness to faking or response bias. Although faking can be reduced through altering instruction from behavioural-tendency (e.g. 'what are you most likely to do?') to knowledge-based formats (e.g. 'what is the best answer?') it may adversely affect bias and potential for more culturally-based discrimination (Nguyen *et al.*, 2005). Finally, the durability of these results is lower than for more generic ability tools (Siegel and Bergman, 1975). These tools achieve a number of functions, assessing how and what a candidate can perform, but also providing applicants with job preview information, enabling them to make more informed decisions.

Integrity tests

Integrity tests are a more recent addition to the suite of tools available to recruiters. Together with ability testing they show high job performance validity ($r = 0.65$) (Robertson and Smith, 2001). Integrity tests predict undesirable work behaviours, such as theft, absence or other behaviour which takes advantage of the employer without discriminating against ethnic minority groups (Ones and Viswesvaran, 1998). They are included here to typify the gap between theory and practice, namely because of their limited adoption in selection despite strong research support.

Integrity tests make faking more likely due to the clear social cues about the preferred response, especially within a hiring context. As a result their value is reduced, both as an accurate tool but also because their inclusion may raise questions for candidates about the organization and its ethos. Implicitly they raise interesting questions about the perceived trustworthiness of new staff. As a result they are more likely to be found in situations where their inclusion acts as a legal safety net for employers should a violation occur.

Emergent issues and concerns

In this final section we reflect on some overarching concerns which have emerged from exploring recruitment and selection tools.

Faking and cheating

The use of the internet as a medium for delivering tests has enabled a most cost-effective high volume administration across wider geographical areas. The widening of applicant pools has also seen an escalation in concerns about cheating and faking (Bartram, 2000). In high stakes environments, selectors are aware that the temptation and reward for cheats are high. For example, salary details on CVs have long been finessed and job responsibilities expanded. The proliferation of non-supervised testing, however, has focused recruiters' and test developers' attention on how to identify and reduce the impact (Lievens and Harris, 2003). Solutions include (Searle, 2006): increasingly sophisticated candidate verification, from photographic verification systems through to iris recognition; two tier systems in which the same forms of tests are administered later in a controlled setting and the results compared; the use of sophisticated item response and item generation systems which ensure that whilst the content of the test is the same, the items are not; and additional in-test measurements, such as the applicants' latency of response, which increases with faking. All of these techniques maximize the benefits of large scale unsupervised testing and reduce the damage of fraud.

There is, however, another sensitive issue that remains more limited in its discussion: cultural difference. The increasing globalization of some applicant pools means that the stakes in some contexts are far higher. Indeed, in some contexts, selection is viewed as a game in which the applicant uses every resource to acquire a job (Searle, 2003). In these contexts behaviour such as using others to take tests, or taking the credit for others' work, especially if they work for you, might be perceived as expected, even acceptable forms of behaviour. The intention behind this behaviour might not be to deceive *per se*, but to maximize one's own chances. We know job applicants are more likely to favourably manage impressions on tests than non-applicants (Birkeland *et al.*, 2006). From this perspective faking and cheating behaviour can be viewed as an adaptive behaviour; a complex culturally-determined function of the capacity, willingness, and opportunity to fake. For example, a commonly used fake-checking item in personality tests is 'I'm always willing to admit when I make mistakes', with this item eliciting different responses in Japan or Greece in a high stakes selection context from that in the UK, where a more socially conditioned response is expected. Until we have more insight into how cultural factors might impact on perceptions of honesty and integrity within selection contexts we should be cautious of the acceptance of global behavioural dimensions.

Global systems?

A consequence and tension produced by the increasing internationalization of recruitment and selection is the need to balance systems that can be used across multiple countries with recognition of local particularities (Schuler *et al.*, 1993). These tensions include not only the aforementioned tensions pertinent to assessment centres, but wider issues such as the differences in cultural values, power distance and uncertainty avoidance (Ryan *et al.*, 1999), and the value and acceptance of distinct characteristics and criteria. For example, explicit proven job experience is deemed important in Australia, Canada, Germany and the US, whilst innate potential and team working is preferred in South Korea, Taiwan and Japan (Huo *et al.*, 2002; Von Glinow *et al.*, 2002).

In addition, the acceptance and value of multiple tool selection processes varies across different cultures. Whilst no studies have examined the generalizability of the criteria used in selection procedure on a global basis, evidence for the universality of selection exercises is limited (Lievens and Chapman, forthcoming).

Older workers

Demographic changes in many countries have altered employment patterns with a large number of older workers, from choice or economic necessity continuing or re-entering the labour market. The whole issue of older worker attraction and selection have remained under-researched (Warr, 2001). It is likely to lead to work shifting more to a part-time occupation, thus becoming part of how older adults spend their time. In addition its influence might alter the criterion space, forcing more organization-person-fit dimensions to the fore as older workers tend to have distinct needs, focusing on the social and esteem requirements of work (Hedge *et al.*, 2006).

Limited attention has considered the validity of the assessment and measurement of older workers. Older workers are more conscientious than their younger counterparts (Warr, 2001). They have a wider breadth of knowledge and experiences. Paradoxically, studies find fluid intelligence a less effective predictor of knowledge than crystallized intelligence (Beier and Ackerman, 2001). In addition, older workers may actively compensate for any potential decline in their performance by adopting new strategies which optimize their existing skills and abilities. Thus older workers may in fact be adapting and doing things more effectively than their younger colleagues, but current selection processes may not be effective in assessing their skills.

Technology

Technological innovation is influencing the design and delivery of many psychometric tools. It is also shifting the way other selection tools, such as role play and interviews, can be delivered. One of the key controversies within this area concerns the removal of people from the recruitment and selection process. Through the increased deployment of technology to collect, shift and identify applicants the process by default becomes predictivist. Whilst this might reduce some bias and subjectivism, it can also significantly alter the process away from the relational and towards the comodification of people as human resources and human capital. The lack of stability and predictability for jobs has compromised the criterion space on which such technology based systems are premised, and so caution is required.

The increased use of technology in the deployment of ability and other selection test far earlier in the selection process has given recruiters and test developers access to a much wider range of candidate data. These new data have provided novel opportunities for the 'forensic' analysis of data streams (Bartram, 2008). Technology presents unique opportunities to extend the boundaries of recruitment and selection processes, to truly open access to new applicants wherever they are. However, we must be vigilant to ensure that previous biases and discrimination against minority groups are not perpetuated through a new medium. Test development is based on individual differences and we need to ensure that we are identifying real job performance differences, not creating new barriers to entry.

Trust

The emphasis of both the social process and the organizational-person fit is on the quality of relationship between the organization and the candidate. Researchers in organizational behaviour and HR have become increasingly interested in employer trust: such trust is also an issue at this pre-entry stage, yet it remains under-researched. Inherent in trust is the decision to rely on another party (i.e. person, or organization) under a condition of relational risk with the expectation of at the least benign, if not positive outcome (Rousseau *et al.*, 1998). This reliance results in a willingness to be vulnerable (Mayer *et al.*, 1995). In recruitment and selection this vulnerability stems from the risk that the candidate will be discriminated against, and not offered the job, and thus not attain the expected positive outcomes due to the untrustworthiness of the recruiter or the organization. Expectations of the intentions and behaviour of the trusted party, i.e. the perceived trustworthiness of the trustee, are pivotal to enable the trustor to take the necessary leap of faith for the decision to trust (Lewis and Weingert, 2006). Thus trust is required at the onset of the recruitment process in order for an applicant to transform their intention to apply into the submission of their application (Searle, 2006b). Arguably, candidates require trust at three distinct stages in the recruitment and selection process: at the onset trust is required in the decision to to submit their application; in attending any subsequent selection and assessment, trust is needed for a candidate to participate fully and to the best of their ability (indeed any perception that the assessment or the assessor is biased may significantly reduced performance); finally, trust is necessary in order for any resultant job offers to be accepted.

The inclusion of trust within the recruitment and selection process extends the analysis of applicant reactions, and gives new insight into perceptions of testing and assessment, applicant and assessor interactions and to the ongoing relational dynamic. It may reveal whether minority ethnic group applicants are different in their perceptions of trust and whether this has a role in their motivation and behaviour during selection.

Conclusions

Recruitment and selection are the key processes at the onset of the HR cycle. Their impact is wider, with the potential to alter the composition and culture of the organization. Yet what is striking is the limited attention HR practitioners appear to give empirical evidence regarding effective processes. Perhaps this lack of synergy reflects inadequate training, but maybe it suggests a lack of understanding between recruiters and researchers and a subsequent failure to tap into and inform the central concerns of organizations. Indeed, much of the research evidence in this field is garnered from undergraduate student populations whose insights, attitudes and behaviours may be very different from experienced professional applicants.

Recruitment and selection are distinct processes, focusing attention both externally and within the organization. Distinctions however can, and should, be drawn between volume processes and those concerned with the attraction and selection of individual job vacancies. The importance of the social process and resultant fit may be enhanced in the case of one-off jobs, which may involve key positions such as the chief executive; however, they should not be overlooked in large volume situations. The increased levels of competition within the labour market and a shift in recent years of research away from the organization onto the applicant and their reactions and attitudes has revealed the importance of the quality of the interaction between organization and applicant: rejected applicants may also be current and future customers and consumers of the organization, performing an ambassadorial function for an organization.

Emerging from this chapter are some overarching concerns which have highlighted significant shifts in applicant populations. One change is the increased globalization of applicant pools, in which further complexity has emerged with challenges to the fairness and discrimination of the testing processes, attitudes towards cheating and faking of results, and the familiarity with technology. A second challenge is through an ageing population, which may alter the emphasis onto the social and esteem components of work, challenge job criteria and their assessment. All of these issues reflect the ongoing changes to the structure and location of work, the predictability and stability of job roles. Thus finding and identifying new employees remains a complex balance between data gathering and relationship building.

References

Anderson, N., Lievens, F. and van Dam, K. (2004). Future perspectives on employee selection: key directions for future research and practice, *Applied Psychology: An International Review*, 53(4): 487–501.

Avery, R. D. and Campion, J. E. (1982). The employment interview: a summary and review of research, *Personnel Psychology*, 35: 281–322.

Barber, A. E. and Roehling, M. V. (1993). Job postings and the decision to interview: a verbal protocol analysis, *Journal of Applied Psychology*, 78: 845–56.

Barrick, M. R. and Mount, M. K. (1991). The Big Five personality dimensions and job performance: a meta-analysis, *Personnel Psychology*, 44: 1–26.

Bartram, D. (2000). Internet recruitment and selection: kissing frogs to find princes. *International Journal of Selection and Assessment*, 8(4): 261–74.

Bartram, D. (2008). Technology and its impact on changing recruitment and selection practices. Paper presented in Symposium *Current Controversies In Recruitment And Selection* at British Academy of Management, Harrogate, Sept. 2008.

Beier, M. E. and Ackerman, P. L. (2001). Current-events knowledge in adults: an investigation of age, intelligence, and nonability determinants, *Psychol Aging*, 16(4): 615–28.

Birkeland, S. A., Manson, T. M., Kisamore, J. L., Brannick, M. T. and Smith, M. A. (2006). A meta-analytic investigation of job applicant faking on personality measures, *International Journal of Selection and Assessment*, 14(4): 317–35.

Bobko, P., Roth, P. L. and Potosky, D. (1999). Derivation and implications of a meta-analytic matrix incorporating cognitive ability, alternative predictors, and job performance, *Personnel Psychology*, 52(3): 561–90.

Bowen, D. E., Ledford, G. E. and Nathan, B. R. (1991). Hiring for the organization, not the job, *Academy of Management Executive*, 5(4): 35–51.

Bowers, K. S. (1973). Situationism in psychology: An analysis and critique. *Psychological Review*, 80: 307–36.

Cable, D. M. and Turban, D. B. (2001). Establishing the dimensions, sources and value of job seekers' employer knowledge during recruitment, in G. R. Ferris (Ed.), *Research in Personnel and Human Resources Management*, Vol. 2. New York: Elsevier Science.

Carless, S. A. (2003). A longitudinal study of applicant reactions to selection procedures and job and organisational characteristics, *International Journal of Selection and Assessment*, 11: 345–51.

Carless, S. A. and Imber, A. (2007). The Influence of Perceived Interviewer and Job and Organizational Characteristics on Applicant Attraction and Job Choice Intentions: The role of applicant anxiety, *International Journal of Selection and Assessment*, 15: 359–71.

Chan, D. and Schmitt, N. (1997). Video-based versus paper-and-pencil method of assessment in situational judgement tests: subgroup differences in test performance and face validity perceptions, *Journal of Applied Psychology*, 82: 143–59.

Chan, D. and Schmitt, N. (2002). Situational judgment and job performance, *Human Performance,* 15: 233–54.

Chan, D. (1997). Racial subgroup differences in predictive validity perceptions on personality and cognitive ability tests, *Journal of Applied Psychology*, 82(2): 311–20.

Chan, D., Schmitt, N., de Shin, R. P., Clause, C. S. and Delbridge, K. (1997). Can racial difference in cognitive test performance be reduced by presenting problems in a social context?, *Journal of Applied Psychology*, 82(2): 300–10.

Chapman, D. S., Uggerslev, K. L., Carroll, S. A., Piasentin, K. A. and Jones, D. A. (2005). Applicant attraction to organizations and job choice: a meta-analytic review of the correlates of recruiting outcomes, *Journal of Applied Psychology*, 90(5): 928–44.

CIPD (2007). *Recruitment, Retention and Turnover Survey.* Online available http://www.cipd.co.uk/NR/rdonlyres/746F1183-3941-4E6A-9EF6-135C29AE22C9/0/recruitretntsurv07.pdf.

Clevenger, J., Pereira, G. M., Wiechmann, D., Schmitt, N., and Harvey, V. S. (2001). Incremental validity of situational judgment tests, *Journal of Applied Psychology,* 86: 410–17.

Costa, P. T. and McCrea, R. R. (1985). *The NEO Personality Inventory Manual.* Odessa, FL, Psychological Assessment Resources.

Czaja, S. and Sharit, J. (1998). Age differences in attitudes toward computers, *Journals of Gerontology: Series B: Psychological Sciences and Social Sciences*, 53: 329–40.

Dineen, B. R., Ash, S. R. and Noe, R. A. (2002). A Web of applicant attraction: person-organization fit in the context of Web-based recruitment, *Journal of Applied Psychology,* 87: 723–34.

Fisher, C. D., Ilgen, D. R. and Hoyer, W. D. (1979). Source credibility, information favorability, and job offer acceptance, *Academy of Management Journal*, 22: 94–103.

Goff, M. and Ackerman, P. L. (1992). Typical intellectual engagement. *Journal of Educational Psychology*, 84(4): 537–52.

Goltz, S. M. and Giannantonio, C. M. (1995). Recruiter friendliness and attraction to the job: the mediating role of inferences about the organization, *Journal of Vocational Behavior*, 46: 109–18.

Harris, M. M. and De War, K. (2001). Understanding and using web-based recruiting and screening tools: key criteria, current trends, and future directions, workshop presented at the *Annual Conference of the Society for Industrial and Organizational Psychology*, San Diego, CA, May 2001.

Hedge, J. W., Borman, W. C. and Lammlein, S. E. (Eds). (2006). *The Aging Workforce.* Washington, DC: American Psychological Association.

Herriot, P. (1987). The selection interview, in P. Warr (Ed.), *Psychology at Work*. London: Penguin.

Herriot, P. (1993). A paradigm bursting at the seams. *Journal of Organizational Behavior*, 14: 371–75.

Herriot, P. (2004). Social identities and applicant reactions, *International Journal of Selection and Assessment*, 12(1/2): 75–83.

Hogan, R. (1992) *Hogan Personality Inventory Manual.* Hogan Assessment Systems.

Holtz, B. C., Ployhart, R. E. and Dominguez, A. (2005). Testing the rules of justice: The effects of frame-of-reference and pre-test validity information on personality test responses and test perceptions, *International Journal of Selection and Assessment,* 13(1): 75–86.

Horn, J. L. and Noll, J. (1994). A system for understanding cognitive capabilities: a theory and the evidence on which it is based, in D. Detterman (Ed.), *Current Topics in Human Intelligence,* vol. 4, *Theories in Intelligence*. Norwood, NJ: Ablex.

Hough, L. M. and Oswald, F. L. (2000). Personnel selection: looking toward the future – remembering the past, *Annual Review of Psychology,* 51*:* 631–64.

Howard, A. (Ed.) (1995). *The Changing Nature of Work.* San Francisco: Jossey-Bass.

Huffcutt, A. I. and Roth, P. L. (1998). Racial group differences in employment interview evaluations, *Journal of Applied Psychology*, 83(2): 179–89.

Hunt, E. (1999). Intelligence and human resources: past, present and future, in P. L. Ackerman, P. C. Kyllonen and R. D. Roberts (Eds.), *Learning and Individual Difference: Process, Trait and Content Determinants*. Washington: American Psychological Association.

Huo, Y. P., Huang, H. J. and Napier, N. K. (2002). Divergence or convergence: a cross national comparison of personnel selection practices, *Human Resource Management*, 41: 31–44.

Imus, A. and Ryan, A. M. (2005). The rigor and relevance of the applicant reactions literature, in N. Anderson, D. S. Ones, H. K. Sinangil and C. Viswesvaran (Eds), *Handbook of Industrial, Work, and Organizational Psychology*. London: Sage.

Kanning, U. P., Grewe, K., Hollenberg, S. and Hadouch, M. (2006). From the subjects' point of view – Reactions to different types of situational judgment items, *European Journal of Psychological Assessment*, 22*:* 168–76.

Kline, P. (1993). *The Handbook of Psychological Testing*. London, Routledge.

Kohn, L. S. and Dipboye, R. L. (1998). The effects of interview structure on recruiting outcomes, *Journal of Applied Social Psychology,* 28: 821–43.

LaHuis, D. M., MacLane, C. N. and Schlessman, B. R. (2007). Do applicants' perceptions matter? Investigating reapplication behavior using fairness theory. *International Journal of Selection and Assessment*, 15(4): 383–93.

Levesque, L. L. (2005). Opportunistic hiring and employee fit. *Human Resource Management*, 44(3): 301–17.

Lewis, J. D. and Weigert, A. (2006). Trust as a social reality, *Social Forces,* 63(4): 967–85.

Lievens, F. and Chapman, D. S. (forthcoming). Recruitment and selection, in A. Wilkinson, T. Redman, S. Snell and N. Bacon (Eds), *Handbook of Human Resource Management*. London: Sage.

Lievens, F. and Harris, M. M. (2003). Research on internet recruiting and testing: current status and future directions, in C. L. Cooper, and I. T. Robertson (Eds), *International Review of Industrial and Organizational Psychology*, Vol. 18. Chichester, UK: John Wiley.

Lievens, F. and Klimoski, R. J. (2001). Understanding the assessment centre process: where are we now?, in C. L. Cooper and I. T. Robertson (Eds), *International Review of Industrial and Organisational Psychology*, Vol. 16. Wiley: Chichester.

Lievens, F., Buyse, T. and Sackett, P. R. (2005). Retest effects in operational selection settings: development and test of a framework, *Personnel Psychology*, 58: 981–1007.

MacIver, R., Saville, P., Kurz, R., Mitchener, A., Mariscal, K., Parry, G., Becker, S., Saville, W., O'Connor, K., Patterson, R. and Oxley, H. (2006). Making waves – Saville consulting wave styles questionnaires, *Selection Development Review*, 22(2): 17–23.

Mayer, R. C., Davis, J. H. and Schoorman, F. D. (1995). An integrative model of organizational trust, *Academy of Management Review,* 20 (3): 709–34.

McManus, M. A. and Ferguson, M. W. (2003). Biodata, personality and demographic differences of recruits from three sources, *International Journal of Selection and Assessment*, 11(2–3): 175–83.

Micheals, E., Handfield-Jones, H. and Axelrod, B. (2001). *The War for Talent*. Cambridge, MA: Harvard Business School Press.

Mischel W. (1968). *Personality and Assessment*. New York: Wiley. Republished 1996. Mahwah, NJ: Erlbaum.

Nguyen, N. T., Biderman, M. D. and McDaniel, M. D. (2005). Effects of response instructions on faking a situational judgment test, *International Journal of Selection and Assessment,* 13(4): 250–60.

Ones, D. S. and Viswesvaran, C. (1998). Gender, age, and race differences on overt integrity tests: Results across four large-scale job applicant data sets, *Journal of Applied Psychology,* 83: 34–42.

Ployhart, R. E. and Ehrhart, M. G. (2002). Modeling the practical effects of applicant reactions: subgroup differences in test-taking motivation, test performance, and selection rates, *International Journal of Selection and Assessment*, 10(4): 258–70.

Reeve, C. L. and Schultz, L. (2004). Job-seeker reactions to selection process information in job ads, *International Journal of Selection and Assessment,* 12(4): 343–55.

Robertson, I. T. and Smith, M. (2001). Personnel selection, *Journal of Occupational and Organizational Psychology*, 74: 441–72.

Rousseau, D. M., Sitkin, S. B., Burt, R. S. and Camerer, C. F. (1998). Introduction to special topic forum: not so different after all: a cross-discipline view of trust, *Academy of Management Review*, 23(3): 393–404.

Ryan, A. M. (2001). Explaining the black-white test score gap: the role of test perceptions, *Human Performance*, 14(1): 45–75.

Ryan, A. M., McFarland, L., Baron, H. and Page, R. (1999). An international look at selection practices: Nation and culture as explanations for variability in practice, *Personnel Psychology*, 52: 359–91.

Ryan, A. M., Sacco, J. M., McFarland, L. A. and Kriska, S. D. (2000). Applicant self-selection: Correlates of withdrawal from a multiple hurdle process, *Journal of Applied Psychology*, 85: 163–79.

Rynes, S. L., Giluk, T. L. and Brown, K. G. (2007). The very separate worlds of academic and practitioner periodicals in human resource management: implications for evidence-based management, *Academy of Management Journal,* 50(5): 987–1008.

Sanchez, R. J., Truxillo, D. M. and Bauer, T. N. (2000). Development and examination of an expectancy-based measure of test-taking motivation, *Journal of Applied Psychology*, 85(5): 739–50.

Schmidt, F. L. and Radar, M. (1999). Exploring the boundary conditions for interview validity: meta-analytic validity findings for a new interview type, *Personnel Psychology*, 52: 445–64.

Schmidt, F. L. and Hunter, J. E. (1998). The validity and utility of selection methods in personnel psychology: practical and theoretical implications of 85 years of research findings. *Psychological Bulletin*, 124: 262–74.

Schmidt, N., Godding, R. Z., Noe, R. A. and Kirsch, M. (1984). Meta-analyses of validity studies published between 1964 and 1982 and the investigation of study characteristics. *Personnel Psychology*, 37: 407–22.

Schmitt, N. and Chan, D. (1998). *Personnel Selection: a Theoretical Approach*. Thousand Oaks, CA; Sage Publications.

Schmitt, N. and Mills, A. E. (2001). Traditional tests and job simulations: minority and majority performance and test validities. *Journal of Applied Psychology*, 86(3): 451–8.

Schneider, B. (1987). The people make the place, *Personnel Psychology*, 40: 437–53.

Schuler, R., Dowling, P. and DeCieri, H. (1993). An integrative framework of strategic international human resource management, *Journal of Management*, 19: 419–59.

Searle, R. H. (2003). *Selection and Recruitment: A Critical Text*. Milton Keynes: Open University/Palgrave McMillian.

Searle, R. H. (2006a). New technology: The potential impact of surveillance techniques in recruitment practices, *Personnel Review*, 35(3): 336–51.

Searle, R. H. (2006b). Crossing the organisation boundary: the role of trust in the application decision, Paper presented at the *European Group of Organization Studies*, Bergen, Norway, July 2006.

Shackleton, V. and Newell, S. (1994). European management selection methods: A comparison of five countries, *International Journal of Selection and Assessment*. 2: 91–102.

Siegel, A. I. and Bergman, B. A. (1975). A job learning approach to performance prediction, *Personnel Psychology*, 28: 325–39.

Simon, H. A. (1960). The new science of management decisions. New York: Harper and Row.

Van Hoye, G. and Lievens, F. (2007). Recruitment-related information sources and organizational attractiveness: can something be done about negative publicity?, *International Journal of Selection and Assessment*, 13(3): 179–87.

Von Glinow, M. A., Drost, E. A. and Teagarden, M. B. (2002). Converging on IHRM best practices: lessons learned from a globally distributed consortium on theory and practice, *Human Resource Management*, 41: 123–40.

Wang, C. and Ellingson, J. E. (2004). Building relationships through trust: a new perspective on the psychological process of recruitment, *19th Annual Conference of the Society of Industrial/Organizational Psychology*, Chicago.

Warr, P. (2001). Age and work behaviour: Physical attributes, cognitive abilities, knowledge, personality traits and motives, in C. L. Cooper and I. T. Robertson (Eds), *International Review of Industrial and Organizational Psychology*. London: Wiley.

Wiesner, W. H. and Cronshaw, S. F. (1988). The employment interview: A critical review, *Personnel Psychology*, 2: 17–46.

Zedeck, S. (1986). A process analysis of the assessment centre method, in N. B. Staw and L. L. Cummings (Eds), *Research in Organisational Behavior*, 8: 259–96.

10 HR planning

Institutions, strategy, tools and techniques

Zsuzsa Kispal-Vitai and Geoffrey Wood

Introduction

Human resource (HR) planning represents the range of philosophies, tools and techniques organizations may deploy to monitor and actively mould the ebb and flow of an organization's people, both in terms of numbers and attributes. As such, it encompasses broad approaches to recruitment, development, advancement reward, and termination. This may imply that HR planning represents the entirety of HRM, but in practice HR planning has taken to mean the usage of predetermined models, tools and techniques to predict, plan and adjust broad staffing, rather than the day to day implementation of the employment contract, and the nature and extent of the employee's involvement and participation in the organization of work (Gold, 2001).

As is the case with HRM more generally, HR planning may assume a strategic dimension, aligned with broad organization-wide strategies, or remain a basic administrative tool. It also may be used as a way of deepening implicit contracts, promoting longer term organizational commitment, or as a way of recasting them, and providing *post-hoc* 'scientific' justification for predetermined strategic choices.

This chapter is divided into two parts. In the first, we unpack what is meant by HR planning, and how organizations are likely to use HR planning in different contexts and locales. In the second, we provided a broad overview of the different applied tools and techniques of HR planning, their underlying assumptions and their purported benefits and limitations. Here a caveat is in order. Tools and techniques of HR planning tend to be highly structured and often quantitative: in practice, their effects will reflect not just the nature of the model itself, but the information inputted, and the manner in which the firm will choose to interpret and disseminate the results.

Philosophies towards and usages of HR planning in comparative context

HRM, HR planning, strategy and the firm

Human resource planning may be seen as simply a variation of the traditional practice of manpower planning, that is monitoring and management of the ebb and flow of people within a firm. In more quantitative approaches to manpower planning, the supply of people was managed to meet set targets on the basis on analyzing demand, predicting supply and designing interventions to solve any potential mismatches (Iles, 2001: 139). The latter could be done through drawing on the tools and techniques of operations management, using statistical formula to analyze turnover, service length, etc. (ibid.: 140).

However, more ambitious strategic accounts of HRM have cast it as the crucial linkage between strategic business planning and strategic HRM, whereby the recruitment and selection of key types of employers, job specification, training and retention policies are aligned to overall strategic vision (Iles, 2001: 139). However, as Gold (2001: 192) cautions, such approaches incorporate an inherent contradiction. Given that overall organizational strategies are likely to be geared towards specific numerical targets, HR planning will inevitably treat people as a factor in production, with the use of numerical models discounting the complexities of the human condition (Gold, 2001: 192).

As with HR more generally, there are hard and soft interpretations of HR planning, with the former founded on an instrumental philosophy regarding the utilization of people and the latter on an emphasis on issues such as commitment and culture (Gold, 2001: 192; Iles, 2001: 129). Whilst the tendency towards more hardline employer policies in liberal market economies may have encouraged the utilization of ever more sophisticated quantitative HR planning systems, the credibility of the latter was at the same time undermined both by a lack of evidence as to whether they actually worked, and by many organizations prioritizing numerical flexibility (Gold, 2001: 193). Quite simply, many organizations opt for short termist downsizing strategies, making a nonsense of sophisticated HR planning systems, many of which represent incremental developments of traditional personnel/manpower approaches to planning.

This tension reflects the central challenges and contradictions of HRM. The rise of contemporary HRM mirrored the rise of the shareholder dominant model that eclipsed the traditional Fordist model of the firm. The latter was about both struggles for control between managers and employees, but also about bargained compromises, permitting both the intensification of production and the deployment of new technologies (Jessop, 2001). During the 1950s and 1960s, the stability of this model allowed for longer term contracting, both regarding the usage of labour, and in relations with customers and suppliers, imparting a predictability to organizational life that had beneficial effects for all parties, with firms enjoying high returns, and employees enhancements in wages and general standards of living (Jessop, 2001). In contrast, the contemporary shareholder-orientated model represents a more experimental approach, aimed at restructuring firms to release resources, often entailing short term costs to employees and other stakeholders in the interests of owners (Wright and Wood, 2008).

The relatively longer time horizons that characterized traditional Fordism, and the use of technologies as a means of refining a particular production paradigm, rather than recasting it, fitted well with the manpower planning tradition. On the one hand, much of contemporary people management is still about the administration of existing systems, drawing on whatever proven tools and techniques are available (Storey, 2001: 11). On the other hand, contemporary strategic approaches to HR planning stress issues such as flexibility, which necessitate a radical recasting or at least rethink of ways of doing things (Storey, 2001: 14).

From an employee rights perspective, HR planning is similarly beset with contradictions. Manpower planning – and other consistent long term models to monitor and adjust the ebb and flow of an organization's people – imparted a greater predictability to the employment contract and lowering transaction costs (c.f. Marsden, 1999). The implicit duration and trajectory of a job formed part and parcel of a wider implicit contract, that allowed for both more harmonious employment relations within the firm, and less opportunistic approaches to the external labour market by both employers and employees (c.f. Marsden, 1999; Jessop, 2001). This is not to suggest that manpower planning was unequivocally good for employees: in the end, the choice of which model to opt for generally rested with managers, whilst the abstract and impersonal nature of such models coincided with the formalized and hierarchical nature of the classic Fordist production paradigm (Jessop, 2001).

The shareholder dominant model challenges such 'predictable' implicit contracts, holding that shorter term instrumentalism is more conducive to the bottom line. Whilst managers have an interest in predictability, and in co-opting employees in the interest of their personal empire building, proponents of the shareholder dominant model have charged that this is at the expense of their principles, the owners of the firm (Roe, 2003). Does this mean that HR planning is incompatible with the strategic shareholder orientated approach to HRM? In practice, HR planning may be still desirable for a number of reasons. The first is that both manpower and HR planning represent a technical system, that is in some manner removed from bargained terms and conditions of service: whilst employees may expect that a specific approach to manpower planning may make for stability and predictability, its implicit nature gives a greater flexibility to management than an explicitly bargained employment contract, even if embodied in the latter may be some assumptions regarding the former.

This flexibility gives management some room to manouevre: they may, for example, decide to cut back on skills development, decide to view a particular job as an end, rather than a stepping stone, and/or cut back recruitment as part and parcel of a drive to intensify work among existing staff. In short, whilst management may desire flexibility, they may also have an interest in a planned approach to long term resourcing, retention and development, in order to gradually recast the worth of a job, its trajectory, and task intensity.

A second benefit for managers is that HR planning, by its technical and structured nature, may impart legitimacy to what is being done. From a postmodernist perspective, it allows for managers to dominate the knowledge regarding the usage of such systems, deploying abstract statistical models that will be unintelligible to the average worker, yet providing a scientific authority to potentially unpalatable decisions (c.f. Foucault, 1988; Toms, 2008). The authors of this chapter remain sceptical as to the overall worth of postmodernism to studying organizations: the latter discounts the material bases of power imbalances within the firm, and the open ended labour commitment that is exchanged for wages in the employment contract (Kelly, 1988). At the same time, postmodern accounts do help shed some light on why HR planning remains so attractive to managers in contexts characterized by extreme short-termism in hiring and deploying labour. Specific knowledge sets may be harnessed as *post hoc* justification, rather than determining outcomes in itself (Foucault, 1988): hence, firms may use HR planning in such a way as to support what has already been decided, choosing between applied models and/or adjusting them, in order to support a specific agenda.

Country, sector, organization type, and HR planning

Before we turn to specific approaches to HR planning, it is worth giving some attention to what broad underlying philosophies regarding HR planning are likely to be encountered in different contexts. For what objectives are HR planning models likely to be deployed? In other words, where are organizations likely to take a longer term approach to staffing, and where a shorter term? Where is tenure likely to be more secure? Where are firms more likely to invest in their people? And, where less so? Or, to put it another way, for what objective are firms likely to use HR planning? Whilst HR planning may presume a longer term 'scientific' way of managing people, as we have seen, it may be used to support an essentially short-termist way of doing things.

The Varieties of Capitalism (VOC) literature has pointed to the persistence of differences in corporate governance, and internal firm level strategies and policies (Dore, 2000; Hall and Soskice, 2001). Central to the VOC literature is the assumption that the shareholder dominated model is not the only variation of capitalism in the post-1970s era. Whilst liberal market economies (LMEs) are characterized by the hegemony of the shareholder dominant paradigm, collaborative markets (CMEs) are defined by a more stakeholder orientated approach (Dore, 2000). Within the former, employee rights are likely to be weaker, with firms basing their competitiveness on high tech innovation ('Silicon Valley') or low value added cost-cutting production ('MacDonald's') paradigms (Brewster *et al.*, 2006; Wright and Dwyer, 2006). Meanwhile, in the latter, stronger employee – and other stakeholder – rights impart a more long term approach to the employment contract, with firms and employees giving more attention to the development of organization specific skills as a means of underpinning high value added incremental innovation in manufacturing and services (Thelen, 2001; Brewster *et al.*, 2006).

Underlying approaches to recruitment may also reflect the wider variety of capitalism. Within LMEs, good supplies both of cheap unskilled and generic tertiary level skilled labour are conducive to supporting low cost and 'blue skies' innovation respectively. Using the external labour market to meet broadly defined needs makes internal labour more dispensable, weakening the bargaining position of existing staff (Thelen, 2001). In contrast, in CMEs, firms rely on labour with strong vocational industry-specific skills: through long term contracting, employees have an incentive to develop and/or supplement these with organization specific skills (Thelen, 2001; Harcourt and Wood, 2007).

Within CMEs, firms are thus likely to have an internal orientation, aiming to develop existing staff, rather than plug skills gaps externally (Gold, 2001: 208). Employees are likely to enjoy a high degree of task discretion and stable earnings, allowing for a more satisfying work experience, deepening organizational commitment (ibid.). In contrast, in LMEs, a focus on generic skills and/or low skills, both of which may be readily obtained on the external labour market, lower degrees of task discretion, unstable earnings result in lower organizational commitment, more rapid adjustments to organizational size, and a prioritization of cost-cutting rather than the engendering of organization-specific knowledge and wisdom (Gold, 2001: 208).

In a recent article, Harcourt and Wood (2007: 141) shed further light on the relationship between career trajectories, development and varieties of capitalism. They note that:

> During the heyday of neo-liberalism, employment protection was widely believed to be one of the main causes of Europe's poor performance. Yet, the high value-added production paradigms that have sustained the export competitiveness of a number of leading coordinated market economies like Germany remain dependent on high levels of firm-specific human capital made possible by extensive job protection.

In turn, job protection is conducive for human capital development. Employees have more incentives to develop skills specific to their employer, as it is more certain they will be able to use them over the medium and longer terms (rather than face ejection into the external labour market) and will be able to advance their careers by developing them (as adverse to seeking promotion by job hopping) (Harcourt and Wood, 2007). However, a caveat is in order here. Any accommodation between employers and employees will invariably be contested, whilst national economies evolve in a dynamic and non-linear fashion (ibid.; Boyer, 2006; Deeg and Jackson, 2006). This means that, in addition to pressures to deepen, refine and strengthen existing collaborative national models, there will be countervailing pressures to greater short-termism, towards more instrumental approaches to HR planning (Harcourt and Wood, 2007). In contrast, within LMEs, excessive short-termism has proved deleterious to many sectors, leading to minorities of firms experimenting with alternatives (Boyer, 2006).

Recent research has also highlighted the nature of internal diversity within specific varieties of capitalism (Streeck and Thelen, 2005; Boyer, 2006; Brewster *et al.*, 2006). Such diversity may be on regional or sectoral grounds, reflecting the uneven nature of systemic change, regional production systems, and variations in technology (Lane and Wood, 2008). We have already seen that common in liberal markets are both 'high tech' and low value added production paradigms; within collaborative markets, incrementally innovative production coexists with lower value added strategies (Brewster and Wood, 2006). Even within sectors, individual firms may experiment with alternatives: whilst some of the latter may prove unsuccessful, others may throw up unexpected serendipidous complementarities that will be reinforced. In turn, this means that there will be variations in the manner in which firms use HR planning, not only between, but also within national contexts.

It will be apparent from the above that not only does the extent and nature of HR planning illuminate broader national, regional, sectoral and organizational philosophies and approaches to people management, but that certain types of organization are likely to make use of HR planning systems in particular ways. Organizations may use HR planning as a means of imparting greater stability and predictability into the employment contract and organizational life more generally. Alternatively, they may use HR planning as a means of bringing about and/or justifying more instrumental approaches to recruitment, job tenure and skills development. In the following sections, we review specific tools and techniques of HR planning, with the caveat that each individual technique has more than one application; each may be used in the pursuit of a number of alternative strategies to people management.

Tools and techniques for HR planning

Strategic human resource planning methods – listing and evaluation

Human resource planning is both a dynamic process and combines a number of possible ways forward (Ivanchevich, 2007). The first stage is simply that of stocktaking. It must identify how many people are needed at every level of the organization to achieve business objectives – in line with overall strategic plans – and what kind of knowledge, skills, abilities and other characteristics (KSAOs) these people need.

If the first phase is stocktaking, the second phase is forecasting (Gallagher, 2000). Armstrong (2006) breaks this into two sub-phases, forecasting future people needs (demand forecasting), and forecasting the future availability of people (supply forecasting). The third and final phase is assessing the gap between demand and supply in respect of present capacity, and present and future needs (ibid.). In other words, it is about distinguishing among existing capabilities what is missing in terms of people skills and capacities, and devising strategies to deal with them (Ward, 1996a, b). The decline of security of tenure has made this task more difficult: we have to identify carefully what we mean by 'employees', or 'workforce' of the organization. Can temporary employees be counted on? How does once count outsourced or subcontracted labour? Their relationship to the organization may be temporary, but, such people still have to be included in planning, but with perforce more attention being given to succession planning.

Human resource planning has, as we have seen, links to all of the HR functions of an organization (Macaleer and Shannon, 2003). If we simply think of strategy, the linking of HR plans to the organization's strategy is merely the baseline, since no strategy can be accomplished without people. A common theme through much of the mainstream HR literature is that it would be ideal were the HR department to be included in comprehensive planning for the whole organization, since this would guard against top management making major mistakes in HR decisions which could cost serious financial losses. It is commonly acknowledged that this is often not the case: too often HRM is only taken seriously when the organization is in crisis.

Setting priorities in human resource planning

There are many alternative methods for planning and forecasting; the choice management may make is invariably moulded by the wider institutional context, and the relationship between management and other stakeholders, including employees. More subjective judgemental models tend to be used more in an uncertain environment, although the accuracy of 'soft methods' is questioned by researchers. Judgment-focused firms can be found in any industry and the size of the company is not an affecting variable. Researchers claim that alternative, more quantitative-focused approaches have lower error rates and more accurate forecasting (Sanders and Manrodt, 2003). However, it can be argued that quantitative methods have their own limitations; they involve managerial judgement on issues such as accountability, the future suitability of a selected employee or the consequences of a layoff. If uncertainty is perceived to be rising, then sophisticated techniques will not be used since they have less value; likewise, if uncertainty decreases to a large extent, than forecasting will no longer be needed at all (Stone and Fiorito, 1986).

Specific approaches to planning

Workforce demand forecasting techniques – judgemental methods

Direct managerial input or unit forecasting: Each unit or each manager forecasts the future needs for employees. This could be done by both 'bottom-up' planning, that is, by unit forecasting, or by 'top-down' planning, where each unit is allocated a certain budget for employee payroll expenditure and this budget is then divided by management to serve the desired business need. Direct managerial input is based on 'hard' data, that is, on cash flow, rate of return, return on capital employed and on discounted cash flow on investment. Although a mathematical method and based only on financial data, this works well if the company wishes to concentrate on decreasing staff numbers. However, since it does not involve investigating either the skills which the company needs or the jobs which they cut, it may be mechanical and not have the desired effect. If a company reduces staff numbers with the simple aim of reducing the payroll, then it may be counterproductive by inadvertently discarding people they need most (Ward, 1996a; Mello, 2005)

Unit forecasting: This can be used to estimate future employee needs in a positive manner when managers at all levels decide how many employees they need for future improvements and new contracts – a 'bottom-up' approach. This technique can be most responsive to the needs of the market (Mello, 2005) since the responsibility for the decision lies where the decisions on production and services are made. However, it does have the disadvantage of tempting managers to 'hoard' employees for later needs and not to allocate them to those parts of the organization which could use them better (Mello, 2005).

Both bottom-up and top-down approaches show their own efficiency: the top-down variety is efficient from the perspective of resource allocation whilst the bottom-up variety addresses the requirements of the marketplace. Ideally, an organization would use both approaches in order to serve the market (and its own managers) well and also to nurture the efficiency of organizational resource allocation (Ward, 1996a; Mello, 2005).

'Best guess' formalized managerial judgement: According to Ward (1996a, b), was developed by a few companies and is essentially similar to unit forecasting, but with the difference that the forecast contains:

- current headcount requirements
- a 'best-guess' estimate of the impact of expected productivity and technology changes
- the managers' best guess of headcount changes due to expected business changes.

The future employee need is the sum of the 'best guesses'. It is a guessing method, which may or may not be accurate, and assumes that managers correctly forecast the future impact of technology and of the marketplace and that they can translate these to HR needs in terms of numbers and skills. It also assumes that managers have adequate time to use this method.

Ivanchevich (2007) identifies *trend projection* as finding a relationship between a factor related to business and a desired number of employees. Sales levels are usually related to employment trends, and in trend projection the planner relates employment to one single factor.

Historical ratios: Ward (1996a, b) argues that historical ratios can be good predictors if there is a significant correlation with headcount and certain business factors, such as the number of customers served and the number of units manufactured. This method provides a general estimate of all workers, but it cannot differentiate between temporary and permanent workers and cannot handle outsourcing requirements. Skills and other 'soft' issues cannot be taken into consideration here, although it is easy to administer and can be used with Lotus or Excel spreadsheets.

These two methods can also be termed *rule of thumb* as in Meehan and Basheer's (1990) example: 'one new production worker for every 1,000 additional items produced'.

The hypothetical approach based on process analysis (Business Process Re-engineering): This is mentioned in Ward, although he asserts that it has never actually been used! The concept is sound, since it says that, in process analysis a detailed analysis of process components of work activities should be developed and human resource needs could be quantified based on each unit. This concept has never been translated to an operational model, although it could have definite advantages in that qualitative thinking could be incorporated and since the analysis could involve aspects of skills and competencies.

The Delphi technique: This technique was originally developed by the RAND Corporation and is characterized by trying to bring experts to a consensus whilst eliciting as many different opinions as possible (Durnham, 1996). An important factor of the technique, however, is that it must be used anonymously. The target is problem-solving, planning and decision-making, and the method involves a facilitator who coordinates the process. The physical presence of the participants is not required – and, in fact, a lack of physical presence makes for greater effectiveness. In the first round the facilitator sends a questionnaire to the participating specialists and collects the answers. For the second round all of these ideas are incorporated in a new questionnaire. This iteration process continues until no new ideas emerge. This procedure gives specialists the chance to change and improve ideas, and, since it is anonymous, there are no personality, or other constraints on participants.

The nominal group technique: Also called 'the alternative way of brainstorming' (Ivanchevich, 2007) it involves a facilitator inviting group members to write down their ideas privately and then, one by one, each member of the group presents the ideas, one at a time. These are recorded on a flipchart but with no discussion. Each member can opt out of a round and the ideas need not be from the list written by a member; they could be invented when requested. After all ideas have been listed, the group discusses the ideas for a set period of time. Each member then, privately, ranks all of the ideas, and the resulting overall ranking will be their aggregate ranking (Nicholson, 1995). In human resource forecasting it can be a powerful tool, as this method can incorporate a number of qualitative factors which others cannot. Moreover, it is sufficiently comprehensive and can successfully eliminate group decision-making problems (such as 'group-think', or a dominating group member). It can, however, preserve the idea-generating effect which physical presence can have on people (further developing others' ideas). It may also be inaccurate, especially in a fast-changing environment, when unexpected occurrences simply cannot be taken into account by specialists in the specific setting.

Scenario analysis: A method very similar to the other two 'brainstorming' methods, but with the difference that ideas are then built into workforce scenarios of the future (Ward, 1996a,b). Managers then work backwards in order to identify important turning-points. The discussions can be wide-ranging and participants can identify more crucial factors than otherwise. Scenario-building is commonly used in strategic management. The creation of imaginary future event sequences leads to attempts to determine the places in the sequences where managerial intervention is needed and where such intervention might change an unwanted future.

Both positive and negative possibilities are weighed. One problem, however, is that this method cannot provide accurate, quantifiable data; it can merely encourage flexibility and adaptability – which is no novelty to any HR professional.

All of these methods can also be termed judgemental, since they all involve managerial judgement and decision-making and since they are based rather on a subjective evaluation of facts rather than on quantifiable statistical methods. Accuracy is most certainly an issue in forecasting, but subjective judgement (the 'gut feeling') can sometimes be more accurate than any statistical method, since they can take into account non-quantifiable factors, such as sudden changes in technology and political events (e.g. the transition in Central-Eastern Europe).

New approaches

There are approaches to HR planning which are based, not on the classical steps, but on new approaches to business, such as the Balanced Scorecard Approach which is the basis of the *HR Workforce Scorecard Approach* (Mello, 2005). This model focuses on the 'human resources deliverables' – that is, those factors which are critical to business success and lie within the human resources range. There are four components:

Workforce Success – goal accomplishment
Workforce Behaviour – what are the actions which are necessary for employees and leaders to take to achieve business objectives
Workforce Competencies – skills which belong to critical high performers to achieve success
Workforce Mindset/Culture – how employees understand organizational goals (Sanders and Manrodt, 2003; Mello, 2005).

An alternative contemporary approach is the new literature on talent management. The literature on talent management often emphasize the need for speed in filling gaps, through a close linkage between all the different aspects of the HR function (ibid.: 140). It also emphasizes the differences in individual talents, and the need to take account of this. But, is this really anything more than HR practice? Whilst, as Lewis and Heckman (2006: 140) note, this term is often used interchangeably with talent management, the contemporary understanding argues for something more: linking talent to the overall make-up, and hence to strategy. This can be done through either a resource based view, that links talent to overall results, or through an approach that calls for talent to be approached in a similarly quantitative way to financial resources, allowing the latter to be linked to wider organizational decision making in a scientific fashion (ibid.: 146). In the latter regard, the HC BRidge® Decision Framework developed by Ramstad and Boudreau focuses on critical competencies and key performers who have these competencies and on the practices which enable these people to achieve maximum performance. The key elements here are: impact, effectiveness and efficiency (Lewis and Heckman, 2006).

Assessing demand – statistical methods

Time series analysis: This method examines historical employment patterns and trends in the environment; from these two it attempts to extrapolate the future employment need. It is effective in a stable environment when the user can reasonably expect that trends can be extrapolated and that the employment pattern will remain the same. It is useful in industries where cyclical peaks and downturns are common (e.g., in services such as the leisure industry). It is relatively simple, but in large organizations where several job groups are in evidence the planner has to use more than one time series, since the trends can reflect only one job group. It is not useful in small organizations, when there are no historical data, or in a dynamic business environment.

The method projects past trends into the future, using time as the independent variable. This analysis can identify long-term trends, seasonal effects, cyclical effects and the residual effects which emerge from unpredictability in the environment and from the randomness of human action. It is especially good in predicting seasonal effects, recurring fluctuations, such as the effects of holidays, or other seasonal variations. Since the model uses time, it cannot cope with organizational circumstances and cannot be used for scenario analysis; it can, however, be used effectively to identify turning points (Gallagher, 2000).

Work-study: In the absence of historical data present but with a requirement to identify future needs, work-study is an alternative approach. This method is, for example, useful in new businesses. The actual work process is studied, together with the individual activities of the worker. This approach has a long history going back to F. W. Taylor. He monitored how long it took to perform the individual activities that make up a job with a view to closer and better time management, linking pay with output, and its track record in terms of production work is controversial: close monitoring and control of output may make it even more unpleasant. Where work is non-standard, such as some forms of white collar work, it is not a suitable method. Work-study engineers study the work process and assess rates of employee activity. This is known as 'effort rating'. From this a formula is created which defines 'standard performance' and, based on this formula, effort can be rated and the appropriate number of employees calculated.

Time series analysis coupled with productivity trends: This method is best suited to industries where long-term planning is possible. There is no assumption that productivity trends will remain the same and improvements in productivity are factored into the calculations and projected. It does, however, assume positive changes in staff productivity ratios.

Regression analysis models: Their usefulness is partly due to the fact that one can evaluate the required mix of employee categories. One can estimate the number of employees required in one category based on the level required in another. For example, how many more checkout staff would be needed if the number of items in a department store were increased? In multiple regression techniques the variables used in the historical ratio are used as independent variables. Regression models incorporate the rate of change based on historical productivity improvement trends. Regression analysis is a powerful statistical tool in that it can handle a number of variables and is relatively easy to administer. On the other hand, it has several disadvantages such as the fact that they cannot work without historical data. If relationships between the variables change, then the predictive accuracy is weakened. There are, nevertheless, a number of sophisticated computer packages for regression analysis (Ward, 1996a,b) which are widely used.

Additional combined statistical and judgmental models: Integrating models try to take into account a number of factors which influence the organization. They attempt to simulate the organization, the environment, through efforts to build in the effects of the environment, and they also attempt to simulate the movements of individuals into and out of the organization, skill requirements and HR activities.

Balancing equations: These are similar to regression models and include variables which are determinants of staffing requirements. Subjective weights are assigned to the determinants based, not on statistical relationships, but, rather, on expert judgement.

Combination technique – forecasting demand: This model incorporates both managerial judgement and statistical accuracy (Gallagher, 2000):

$$E = \frac{(L + G) \times 1/x}{Y}$$

Where E is the number of staff needed at a specific future date, L is the current turnover (financial), G is the expected growth in turnover, X is the productivity improvement expected during the period, and Y is the turnover divided by the number of staff.

Assessing supply – supply analysis methods

Internal supply: In this case the planner needs to know not simply the gross number of people, but also how many are needed for a specific job, at group or organizational level. Turnover, according to Gallagher (2000), is not a good indicator, since it provides only gross numbers, whilst specific turnover data would be more helpful if broken down into categories (job, age, skill-set). Internal supply is influenced by other HR processes within the organization such as training and development programmes, transfer and promotion policies, retirement, career planning and others (Mathis and Jackson, 2006).

Before any modelling can occur, the HR planner and the organization's management have to have a clear picture of the knowledge, skill and abilities of the members of the organization in order to be able to plan for the future. There are several expressions used for storing these types of data relating to the workforce. One such is *skills inventory*, whilst in some organizations the type and quantity of data to store. In addition to basic demographics, highly sophisticated data can also be useful. Into this category would fall participation in continuing education, supervisory ranking of employee capabilities, hobbies, personal career goals and objectives, geographical preferences and an indication of the time for retirement (Ivanchevich, 2007). With today's very advanced computerized data-handling methods, virtually all forms of data can be stored and also easily accessed when necessary. HRIS systems can be a powerful aid in planning and in implementing HR-related action.

Stock and flow models are used for forecasting supply. These models follow the employee's path through the organization over time and attempt to predict how many employees will be needed and in which part of the organization. According to Gallagher (2000) these are not sufficiently useful in forecasting the number of employees at various organizational activity levels.

Wastage analysis:

$$\frac{\text{The number of people leaving in a specific period}}{\text{The average number employed in the same period}} \times 100$$

It is a general rule that figure variances may be great within different categories of staff (such as men and women), age groups (wastage declines with age) or unemployment rates (wastage is low) (Gallagher, 2000).

Stability analysis: This concentrates on people who remain rather than examines any loss of personnel:

$$\frac{\text{Number of employees with} \times \text{years' service at a given date}}{\text{Number of employed} \times \text{years ago}} \times 100$$

Replacement charts: These charts list both jobs and individuals and show how key individuals move round the organization. They list the number of employees and also the skills which they have, their level of readiness, together with their willingness to move into a new job. These charts are then displayed on the organization chart and offer the possibility of promotion. The time when any selected employee will be ready for promotion is also indicated and is based upon the opinions and recommendations of higher ranking people (Mello, 2005). Some replacement charts are more systematic, showing skills, abilities, competencies and experiences. They are, therefore, more objective and help to overcome personal bias and succession-related problems. Replacement charts can be profitably used as a planning tool and could also be used as a component of the whole succession-planning effort (Mello, 2005).

Markov modelling: This model belongs to the stochastic process model sector which assigns probabilities to future events and tries to incorporate future possible occurrences into models (Parker and Caine, 1996). Examples of this might include the likelihood of securing a contract or of starting or finishing a project on time. The model is named after the Russian mathematician said to have developed the model in 1907. The Markov analysis is a derivative of probability theory and so is highly mathematical by nature. In a Markov analysis the planner attempts to describe the movement of personnel as stochastic possibilities, a series of stocks and flows where each event is decided by a preceding event. In a simple case the system is closed, but, in reality, in human resource planning the system has an incoming and also an outgoing component. This model is also called a transitional matrix, as it examines the overall pattern of movement of people between jobs inside the organization and at outward movement from the organization. When both incoming and outgoing personnel are featured, Markov modelling is easier to handle by computer. The underlying logic is simple: when employees move from one position to another they have to be replaced and this replacement usually comes from a position below the incumbent who is moving on. At the top of the matrix employees may also leave and disappear from the system.

The value of the approach depends on the mathematical ability of the user, although there are several computer programs by which these planning issues can be resolved (Parker and Caine, 1996).

There are other approaches to describe and predict people-movement in an organization such as the 'systems approach', also known as *holonic modelling* (Parker and Caine, 1996). It is easier to use, is based on system theory and dynamics and can be handled by less mathematically-oriented planners. It is also said to be more flexible and more helpful in the intuitive process of planning.

Succession planning: This is deemed to be a most important function in the organization as it deals with key management positions which the organization has to fill. If the organization has a clear idea of people who are able to fill important positions, it cannot fall into the unpleasant trap of suddenly finding an empty seat replacing a member. Although succession planning is considered to be a key activity in HR planning, it is not utilized as heavily as it should be. Wells (2003) writes that, in 2003, only 29 per cent of 428 HR professionals polled said they had succession planning or used replacement charts. Companies are not well-prepared for the coming mass retirement of 'baby boomers' in the US and they do not have appropriate strategies to deal with the approaching labour shortage. In a recent issue of *HR Magazine* (2008) a rather astonishing report appeared concerning the number of employers who have strategies to deal with 'baby-boomer' retirement. The numbers are rather more frightening than enlightening. Almost half of the organizations researched – 44 per cent – have no knowledge-transfer strategies whatsoever, and only 4 per cent have formalized methods of transmitting knowledge from the 'boomer' generation to other employees. It is common knowledge that Europe and the US are aging, and, according to statistical forecasts (Lanzieri, 2007) even though this generation is not known in Europe as the 'baby-boomer generation', the post-war generation has arrived at the point when it is starting to age. The overall population will not decline, according to statistics, but the number of people above the age of 65 will definitely increase. Old age dependency ratios will, in fact, grow according to other statistics. It is projected that the old-age dependency ratio will rise substantially from 2005 until 2050. In fact, an increase of 41 per cent is expected (from 39 per cent to 80 per cent) by 2050. (Population

Statistics, 2006) In the light of this knowledge, the naivety of companies without appropriate planning (especially at higher managerial levels) is astonishing: it reflects the fact, that, in LME contexts at least, HR planning remains confined by excessive short-termism. Companies that fail to account for long term demographic trends will potentially find themselves in a most difficult position when they suddenly lose more than one important employee or several higher level managers at the same time, and they will have little or no idea of the mechanisms to use or whom to use to replace the lost workforce.

Succession planning might help to identify talent and to plan training and development needs. As Mello (2005) says, it involves an investment-oriented approach toward employees. If there is a detailed mechanism in place which clearly shows where talent is, then it also clearly shows what kind of investment needs we have regarding that talent. The return on this investment is more significant if there is a mechanism and available information than if we are forced into a haphazard choice of someone, simply because we are in need. Wells (2003) provides statistics that prove that most high-performing companies have succession planning mechanisms in place, whereas these are missing in less well-performing firms

External supply: The planner at the company has to use outside information, such as statistics concerning the labour market and from the organization – in other words, external and internal statistics.

Examples of statistics which may be used would include

External statistics
Unemployment rates
Population density
Number of school-leavers
Proportion with (or in) higher education
Skill levels
Age profile
Number of competitors (Armstrong, 2006).

Internal statistics
Company growth
Age distribution of employees
Skill levels
Turnover ratios,
Overall profile/distribution of employment across job categories (Zeffane and Mayo, 1994).

Temporary workforce planning techniques

The demand for efficiency has raised an issue which earlier was not truly valid: a temporary or permanent workforce? Should firms use people who work exclusively and full-time for our organization, or use temporaries who only need to be hired in the event of more labour being justified? This is an especially pressing issue in industries where work demand fluctuates, where there is a good deal of seasonality (such as in the hospitality industry) or in agriculture (at harvest-time). However, this is not only a problem relating to blue-collar employees, since, in today's economy, the 'contingent-knowledge worker' is a factor which cannot be ignored (Redpath *et al.*, 2007). Here we encounter a further issue of significance – that of outsourcing. If outsourcing takes place, what are the guidelines and how should the firm plan it? These questions are even more difficult to answer than those dealing with a permanent workforce. The unpredictability and volatility of historical data could be high, and unexpected changes in the business environment could immediately damage well-developed plans.

Herer and Harel (1998) classifies *temporary workers* as:

Temporary employees
Contract employees
Subcontractors
Consultants
Leased employees.

In today's work environment we could add outsourcing as a temporary worker problem. Herer and Harel (1998) developed several mathematical formulae concerning the design and size of the temporary workforce as an inventory problem. Although the approach sounds mathematical, it is based on costs and benefits and cannot really take into account 'soft' factors (such as the capabilities and attitudes of the temporary staff, or the wider organizational consequences of using them), it does at least provide a reasonable estimate of the number of such workers needed.

Khanna and New (1996) created a model for planning *outsourcing* requirements in which the steps are Analysis and Evaluation. In the first they examine the real need for outsourcing, since major business problems can arise from rash decisions (the baggage handlers' strike at London Heathrow is quoted). There are also alternatives to outsourcing such as float-workers, temporary workers, part-time workers, pay-rolling, employee leasing or using independent contractors. Large consulting organizations may even provide short-term help in providing some of their employees to help the client firm. They also mention several other approaches which are beyond the scope of this chapter (Khanna and New, 1996).

In the next phase of the model, the contract negotiation phase, the outsourcing organization will evaluate the vendor and design the mechanisms inside to manage the vendor. If the basic plan was to economize on work via outsourcing, this cannot be achieved at this stage. It should be clear that, simply to manage what is outsourced, there must be several in-house groups with the expertise to do so. If there are no such people, then the organization has to train them. A phased transition is necessary to achieve this goal since a precipitate transfer of work to a third party is simply not possible. After these goals have been achieved, they

Table 10.1 Strategies for managing shortages of surpluses in the workforce

Strategies for managing shortages	*Strategies for managing surpluses*
Recruit new permanent employees	Apply a freeze on hiring
Offer incentives to postpone retirement	Do not replace those who leave
Rehire retirees on a part-time basis	Offer incentives for early retirement
Attempt to reduce staff turnover	Reduce working hours
Work current staff overtime	Leave of absence for voluntary service
Subcontract work out	Across-the-board pay cuts
Hire temporary employees	Lay workers off
Redesign job processes so that fewer employees are needed	Reduce outsourced work
	Increase employee training
	Switch to variable pay plan
	Expand operations

Adapted from Mello (2005).

need to maintain flexibility and build in continuous improvements to the system. Inevitably, perhaps, serious consideration of all of these processes might lead to the question: What is the point of outsourcing if we duplicate rather than save work? There are, of course, examples of outsourcing contracts which failed, such as that of Wachovia, who took their outsourced HR activities back from Hewitt or transferred them to other vendors (with the exception of benefits administration and customer services) (Khanna and New, 1996).

Action plans regarding supply and demand

After general planning is completed, there needs to be specific action in terms of what is to be done with supply and demand figures. Mello (2005) has drawn up a table relating to strategies for managing shortages or surpluses in the workforce (see Table 10.1).

Various other options are available, but a detailed analysis is beyond the scope of this work.

Conclusion

The more critical literature on work and employment relations has tended to neglect HR planning; often the latter has been dismissed as technicist, inflexible, and in some manner old-fashioned (Gold, 2001: 193; Iles, 2001: 140). Yet, HR planning tools and techniques remain in widespread use, with a trend being towards more flexible approaches to problem diagnosis and 'action planning' (Iles, 2001: 140). On the one hand, any planning process that incorporates an element of long-termism, and is based on consistent and predictable assumptions will constrain arbitrary managerial (and, indeed, owner) power, and, indeed, the ability of the firm to rapidly respond to challenges in the pursuit of maximizing shareholder value. For employees, this may make for more predictable rights, and encourage longer term approaches to the organization by themselves. On the other hand, HR planning may legitimize managerial actions, and may help redefine implicit contracts. Hence, the manner in which HR planning is used can be seen to be a contested domain. The choice of which set of tools and techniques individual firms use may be less important than the underlying philosophy guiding their usage, and the manner in which they are deployed in practice.

References

Armstrong, M. (2006). *Handbook of Human Resource Management.* Kogan Page, electronic book accessed at Ohio University Ebrary, Ebrary.com, 03. 03. 2008. 15:07 p.m. pp. 363–88.

Boyer, R. (2006). How do institutions cohere and change, in G. Wood and P. James, (Eds), *Institutions and Working Life*. Oxford: Oxford University Press.

Brewster, C., Brookes, M. and Wood, G. (2006). Varieties of capitalism and varieties of firm, in G. Wood and P. James (Eds), *Institutions, Production and Working Life*. Oxford: Oxford University Press.

Business Reference: Encyclopedia of Management: Str-Ti, Succession planning, downloaded from: http://www.referenceforbusiness.com/management/Str-Ti/Succession-Planning.html 04.03. 2008.15:05 p.m

Deeg, R. and Jackson, G. (2006). Towards a more dynamic theory of capitalist variety, *Kings College London Department of Management Research Paper 40*, London.

Dore, R. (2000). *Stock Market Capitalism: Welfare Capitalism*. Cambridge: Cambridge University Press.

Durnham, R. (1996). The Delphi Technique. Downloaded from http://www.medsch.wisc.edu/adminmed/2002/orgbehav/delphi.pdf 1. 03. 2008. 17:15 p.m.

Foucault, M. (1988). On Power, in L. Kritzman (Ed.), *Foucault: Politics, Philosophy, Culture*. New York: Routledge.

Gallagher, P. (2000). *Human resource planning*. Scitech Educational, electronic book accessed at Ohio University Ebrary, Ebrary.com, 03. 03. 2008. 12:15 p.m. pp. 23–31.

Gold, J. (2001). Human resource planning, in J. Bratton and J. Gold (Eds.), *Human Resource Management*. London: Palgrave.

Hall, P. and Soskice, D. (2001). An introduction to the varieties of capitalism, in P. Hall, and D. Soskice (Eds.), *Varieties of Capitalism: The Institutional Basis of Competitive Advantage*. Oxford: Oxford University Press.

Harcourt, M. and Wood, G. (2007). The importance of employment protection for skill development in coordinated market economies, *European Journal of Industrial Relations*, 13(2): 141–59.

Herer, Y. T. and Harel, G. H. (1998). Determining the size of the temporary workforce, an inventory modeling approach, *Human Resource Planning*, 21(2): 20–33.

HR Library downloaded from: http://hrlibrary.bna.com/hrlw/2000/split_display.adp?fedfid=3002853&vname=hregcdconcat&fn=3002864&jd=a0b1m4v5v6&split=0

Iles, P. (2001). Employee resourcing, in J. Storey (Ed.), *Human Resource Management*. London: Thomson Learning.

Ivanchevich, J. M. (2007). *Human Resource Management,* 10th Edition. New York: McGraw-Hill Irwin.

Jessop, B. (2001). Series preface, in B. Jessop (Ed.), *Regulation Theory and the Crisis of Capitalism Volume 4 – Developments and Extensions*. London: Edward Elgar.

Kelly, J. (1988). *Rethinking Industrial Relations: Mobilization, Collectivism and Long Waves*. London: Routledge.

Khanna, R. and New, J. R. (1996). An HR planning model for outsourcing, *Human Resource Planning*, 28(4): 37–43.

Lane, C. and Wood, G. (2009). Introducing Diversity in Capitalism and Capitalist Diversity, *Economy and Society,* 38, 3.

Lanzieri, G. (2007). *Statistics in Focus, Population and Social Conditions*, Eurostat, European Community, Brussels.

Lewis, R. E. and Heckman, R. J. (2006). Talent management: A critical review, *Human Resource Management Review*, 16: 139–54.

Macaleer, B. and Shannon, J. (2003). Does HR planning improve business performance? *Industrial Management*, 45(1): 14–21.

Marsden, D. (1999). *A Theory of Employment Systems*. Oxford: Oxford University Press.

Mathis, R. L. and Jackson, J. H. (2006). *Human Resource Management,* 11th edition. London: Thomson South-Western.

Meehan, R. H. and Basheer, A. S. (1990). Forecasting human resources requirements: A demand model, *Human Resource Planning*, 13(4): 297–307.

Mello, J. A. (2005). *Strategic Human Resource Management*. London: Thomson South Western.

Nicholson, N. (1995). *Blackwell Encyclopedic Dictionary of Organizational Behavior*. Oxford: Blackwell.

Parker, B. and Caine, D. (1996). Holonic modelling: human resource planning and the two faces of Janus, *International Journal of Manpower*, 17(8): 30–45.

Population Statistics (2006). Luxembourg: European Communities, Luxembourg Office for Official Publications of the European Communities.

Redpath, L., Hurst, D. and Devine, K. (2007). Contingent knowledge worker challenges, *Human Resource Planning*, 30(3): 33–8.

Roe, M. (2003). *Political Determinants of Corporate Governance*, Oxford: Oxford University Press.

Sanders, N. R. and Manrodt, K. B. (2003). The efficacy of using judgmental versus quantitative forecasting methods in practice, *Omega*, 31(6): 511–22.

Stone, T. H. and Fiorito, J. (1986). A perceived uncertainty model of human resource forecasting technique use, *Academy of Mangement Review*, 11(3): 635–42.

Storey, M. (2001). Human resource management today: an assessment, in M. Storey (Ed.), *Human Resource Management: A Critical Text*. London: Thomson Learning.

Streeck, W. and Thelen, K. (2005). Introduction: institutional change in advanced political economies, in W. Streeck, and K. Thelen (Eds.), *Beyond Continuity. Institutional change in advanced political economies.* Oxford: Oxford University Press.

Thelen, K. (2001). Varieties of labor politics in the developed democracies, in P. Hall and D. Soskice (Eds.), *Varieties of Capitalism: The Institutional Basis of Competitive Advantage.* Oxford: Oxford University Press.

Toms, S. (2008). 'Immeasurability': a critique of Hardt and Negri. Paper presented at the *Conference of Practical Criticism in the Managerial Social Science*, Leicester, January 2008.

Ward, D. (1996a). Workforce demand forecasting techniques, *Human Resource Planning*, 19(1): 54–5.

Ward, D. (1996b). Workforce demand forecasting techniques, downloaded from: http://www.allbusiness.com/human-resources/568478-1.html 2.03. 2008. 12:50

Wells, S. (2003). Who's next?, *HR Magazine*, 48(11): 44–50.

Wright, E. O. and Dwyer, R. (2006). The American jobs machine, in G. Wood and P. James (Eds), *Institutions and Working Life*. Oxford: Oxford University Press.
Wright, M. and Wood, G. (2008). *Financialization and Private Equity*, Working Paper, University of Sheffield.
Zeffane, R. and Mayo, G. (1994). Planning for human resources in the 1990s: development of an operational model, *International Journal of Manpower*, 15(6): 36–56.

11 Performance management

Anthony McDonnell and Patrick Gunnigle

> They [managers] had to identify the people in their organization that they consider in the top 20 per cent, the vital middle 70, and finally the bottom 10 per cent. The underperformers generally had to go. Making these judgements is not easy, and they are not always precise. Yes, you'll miss a few starts – but your chances of building an all-star team are improved dramatically. This is how great organizations are built. Year after year, differentiation raises the bar higher and higher and increases the overall calibre of the organization.
>
> Jack Welch, former CEO of General Electric (2001: 158)

Introduction

In recent times, the interaction between corporate governance and human resource management has become a topic of widespread interest. Particular concern has been expressed as to the extent organizations are solely focusing on maximizing shareholder value to the potential detriment of other stakeholders (Gospel and Pendleton, 2005). For example, there has been a purported decrease in job security for employees as well as increasing pay inequality, where senior executive pay levels are increasing much more than that of employees (Gospel and Pendleton, 2005). Many organizations are now operating in pressurized competitive environments than heretofore. This is largely the result of increased international trade and price competition, re- and de-regulation of product, capital and labour markets, and changes in technology and communications. As a consequence, many firms are reviewing their structures and operations, which often result in employment cuts while attempting to secure enhanced performance from the residual workforce. In other words, they are attempting to get more for less. Tied in with this has been the relatively recent emergence of performance management as an integral process in organizational management. The message portrayed above by Jack Welch, much vaunted for his management and leadership of General Electric (GE), encapsulates a particular, if perhaps extreme, view regarding how organizations should manage performance. He believed in and used forced rankings during his time at GE, working on the premise that 'managing out' the bottom ten per cent of employees could substantially enhance performance. But does this approach stand up to scrutiny in practical terms? By definition there will always be a bottom 10 per cent, no matter how well people perform. Indeed this percentile of staff may actually be performing at an acceptable level and 'managing out' may not necessarily be in a company's best interests.

Performance management has developed from a very operational focus to a more strategically oriented concept, i.e. where it plays an integral role in the formulation and implementation of strategy (Scott-Lennon, 1995). It is this strategic impetus which differentiates it from performance appraisal. Performance management seeks to align a number of processes (e.g. performance related pay systems) with corporate objectives (McKenna and Beech, 2008). Theoretically it involves a shared process between managers, individuals and teams where goals are agreed and jointly reviewed. Further, corporate, divisional, departmental, team and individual objectives should all be integrated. Performance appraisal is a crucial element of the performance management process, involving a formal review of individual performance. It is suggested that performance management represents possibly the greatest opportunity for a human resource (HR) system to make a telling contribution to organizational performance (Sparrow and Hiltrop, 1994). It represents a system that can inform how the firm's human resources contribute to the organization's strategic objectives. Unfortunately the extent to which it is an effective and useful system in practice remains open to question. For example, the high use of various facets of performance management does not always correlate with high results regarding perceived effectiveness (CIPD, 2005).

This chapter provides a contemporary review of performance management which is now believed to be used in some form or other in most organizations (Lawler, 2003; CIPD, 2005). We begin by defining performance management and reviewing its evolution. We then consider the performance management process by applying a critical lens to some of the main approaches set out thus far. Following this, we consider the primary tool used in performance management systems, namely performance appraisal. We then discuss some of the more contemporary developments, including the use of 360-degree feedback and forced distribution, before concluding.

Performance management: definition and evolution

Performance management represents a relatively new management concept with its roots traceable to Anglo-Saxon management (Sparrow and Hiltrop, 1994). It was not until the 1980s that it truly emerged as a standalone concept. In simple terms, performance management is a process that enables employees to perform their roles to the best of their abilities with the aim of achieving or exceeding established targets and standards that are directly linked with the organization's objectives. Performance management is posited as a strategic management technique that supports the overall business goals of the firm through linking each individual's work goals to the overall mission of the firm (Costello, 1994; Sparrow and Hiltrop, 1994). It is further hypothesized as an integrated system where management and employees work together in setting objectives, assessing and reviewing how these are being met and rewarding good performance. This requires 'the ability to interpret the more abstract goals and objectives at board level into more practical operational goals and objectives at employee level to meet them' (Chase and Fuchs, 2008: 226).

Performance management evolved from the *management by objectives* (MBO) approach, first popularized by Peter Drucker (1954). MBO was a scientific type approach with an emphasis on achieving results that were linked to established targets. It involved management focusing on achievable objectives to produce the best possible results using available resources. Both MBO and performance management hold a number of similarities, including the requirement for distinguishable job based goals and development objectives to be achieved (Fowler, 1990). However performance management has evolved considerably in the interim. MBO tended to be only applied to management whereas performance management is applied to all staff – it seeks to integrate all organizational actors in the pursuit of improved performance. MBO utilized quantitative performance measures, whereas performance management is more likely to include both quantitative and qualitative measures. This moved organizations away from solely focusing on financial performance and in parallel, to ensure its employees were being developed.

There are four principal normative concerns of performance management (Armstrong, 1999). First, is that it aims to improve performance. Second, it endeavours to develop employees. Third, it seeks to satisfy the expectations of the various organizational stakeholders. Finally, communication and involvement is imperative due to the ideology of arriving at jointly agreed goals and objectives. In other words performance management seeks management by agreement rather than dictation. However one must question whether such lofty expectations play out in practice? It is logical that top management may unilaterally agree the strategic objectives and then attempt to cascade these down the line and translate them into individual performance targets.

The performance management process

Many of the pertinent models on performance management involve a simple four or five step process (see Figure 11.1 for an example). These models tend to be based on the assertion that all work performance stems from and is driven by the corporate objectives. These are then broken into functional/departmental objectives. Individual objectives shoot out from these and all are monitored and reviewed on an ongoing basis with a formal review or appraisal conducted at least annually. The results of this may or may not be linked to pay. A body of work has taken place arguing for and against linking appraisals to pay. The main argument for this is that all parties take the process more seriously, while the main argument against is that pay becomes the central issue to the detriment of the developmental aspect of performance management (cf. Armstrong, 1999). Linking performance to pay is a market-based approach to gaining employee commitment, whilst

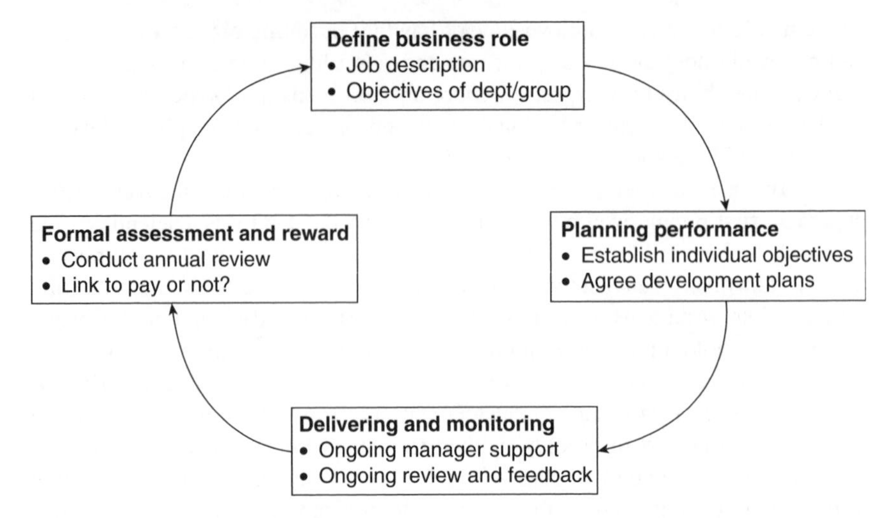

Figure 11.1. Stages of a typical performance management system. Adapted from Torrington *et al.* (2008: 299).

simultaneously helping 'to align managerial interests with shareholder value and shift downside risk' to the employees (Gospel and Pendleton, 2005: 17).

These models fail to adequately capture the intricacies of applying performance management in practice, or – more pragmatically – how performance management might be utilized as an effective means of managing and improving employee and organizational performance. In its current guise, performance management can be criticized for being overly normative. This is largely due to its apparently unitarist underpinning ideology. Indeed it has been proposed that the unitarist perspective 'may represent one of the threats to performance management as it fails to recognize the plurality of interests that are so much a part of organizational reality' (Williams, 2002: 252). For example, little consideration is given to the effect different markets play on employment relations systems. Gospel and Pendleton (2005: 10) note that Anglo-Saxon countries (e.g. US and UK) are characterized by 'labour management systems which are essentially based on market signals'. Depending on the conditions of the day, organizations in these countries will adjust recruitment levels and redundancies, pay tends to have a performance element, job tenures will vary and so forth. On the other hand, systems in other countries (e.g. Germany) are influenced less by market conditions. Jobs tend to be of longer tenure, organizations are more likely to invest in its workforce and pay tends to be based more on seniority than performance based.

No one best, universally agreed performance management model exists and – as already highlighted – those being used tend to be quite basic in their orientation. Buchner (2007) suggests there has been a failure to utilize sufficient theory to support performance management. More specifically he argues that existent models fail to make explicit linkages between the various elements of the process.

Similarly, Bevan and Thompson (1992) suggest a major issue is the lack of integration of activities and that some activities are utilized while others are not. This phenomenon is described by Torrington *et al.* (2008: 307) as 'unfortunate' since one of the primary espoused advantages of performance management is the integration of activities for managing performance: performance appraisal is integrated with performance planning where individual objectives are linked to the overall organizational objectives. The success of these objectives is supported through ongoing feedback and personal development plans and assessed in order to reward superior performance (Torrington *et al.*, 2008). Yet a key concern is that many organizations are purported as failing to know whether practices are actually aligned or pulling in different directions.

Den Hartog *et al.* (2004) have attempted to redress some criticizms of existing performance management models by setting out a conceptual model that gives greater prominence to the role of the line manager. Much research contends that for performance management to be effective and beneficial it needs to be owned and driven by line management (cf. Sparrow and Hiltrop, 1994; Williams, 2002; Torrington *et al.*, 2008). Simultaneously, top management must support and be committed to the system (Sparrow and Hiltrop, 1994). As with any system, if there is insufficient support from the top how can one expect that personnel further down the organizational hierarchy take the system seriously? Line management have a major mediating influence in the implementation of HR practices (Den Hartog *et al.*, 2004). Employee perceptions will be crucial. Consequently if there is perceived inequality over pay it may be difficult to achieve the espoused benefits of performance management (Gospel and Pendleton, 2005). For example, if a practice is perceived as being manipulative it may have a negative impact. This can be witnessed through both overt and covert outcomes through decreased motivation which may result in worse performance and increased labour turnover (Dobbins *et al.*, 1990). They also take account of possible reverse causalities and the contingencies that may evolve from these. The commonly held view is that human resource management is a possible cause of improved organizational performance. However the likelihood of a reversed link also exists. Organizations with improved financial performance may have greater scope for investing in human resource management.

Critiquing performance management

Classically, the starting point of a performance management system should be setting out the organization's mission, aims and values. Following this the organization's objectives are identified, and these need to be intrinsically linked to, and support, the firm's mission. These objectives should be cascaded down the organization with strong links to the objectives of the various managers and individual employees. The end result should be integrated objectives across all organizational levels and personnel (Fowler, 1990).

In practice though, converting the business strategy into clear performance objectives is often problematic for a variety of reasons. Business strategies do not always result from a rational plan but may – sometimes serendipitously – evolve over time. Mintzberg (1978, 1987) distinguished between 'realized' and 'unrealized' strategies and also between 'intended' and 'emergent' strategies. Deliberate organizational strategies refer to those that are intended and realized. However there are also 'unrealized' strategies, which for one reason or other are never implemented. In addition, 'realized' strategies may 'emerge' over time without the conscious intervention of strategists. Hence strategies may emerge that do not follow the traditional planned view but may develop in a more incremental fashion. There may be great difficulty in setting measurable objectives unless the firm operates in a relatively stable environment, which is often not the case in modern business. By means of emphasis, Mabey *et al.* (1998: 133) remark that 'it is possible that objectives and hence performance dimensions targeted today may be inapplicable tomorrow'. As such firms need to set out appropriate time intervals within which objectives apply and must be reviewed on an ongoing basis to establish if changes are required.

Furthermore, organizational objectives can conflict with one another. Corporate governance needs to be taken into account as managers do not make decisions in a vacuum. For example, if considerable emphasis is placed on shareholder value (Gospel and Pendleton, 2005), management will need to consider the effect any decision they make will have on this. A firm that is downsizing but maintains its commitment to investing in its workforce by not reducing headcount or cutting 'training spend' represents such a scenario. In this instance, commitment towards its employees may conflict with a corporate strategy of cost containment. Likewise adopting a total quality management (TQM) system sets out to do things right first time, whereas a learning organization orientation suggests that it is alright to make mistakes as long as one learns from them – two conflicting perspectives (Torrington *et al.*, 2008). The individual versus team dynamic represents another dilemma in performance management, which to date has not received sufficient attention. For example, there is a danger that individual objectives could be detrimental to the achievement of team based objectives and vice versa (Torrington *et al.*, 2008). Van Vijfeijken *et al.* (2006) illustrate this potential conflict through an interesting example regarding management teams. An employee may have individual objectives in relation to achieving their department's objectives. Simultaneously they may be part of the firm's management team which will have its own set of objectives. Conflict may arise, where for example, the management team have an objective of undertaking a major marketing campaign to increase the profile of a particular product or service. At the same time the head of marketing has an objective of reducing costs in his/her department. This clearly conflicts with the management team's objectives of which s/he is a part. Unfortunately these factors are sometimes not addressed when setting performance objectives and targets.

Performance measurement is a further area of contention. For effective performance management clearly the organization needs to know what performance it seeks (Torrington *et al.*, 2008). Fowler (1990) makes an interesting point in suggesting that particular performance dimensions are chosen by organizations, not because they are the most important but because they are the most straightforward to measure. This links into the much debated issue of demonstrating a link between human resource management practices and organizational performance (cf. Huselid, 1995; Guest *et al.*, 2003). To date there remains a lack of conclusive evidence on the existence of such a link, including research specifically on performance management and organizational performance (Bevan and Thompson, 1992; Armstrong and Baron, 1998). Furthermore, it is commonly assumed that improved individual performance will lead to better organizational performance. However, in reality it is much more complex. Improvements at lower individual levels may be insufficient in improving organizational performance (DeNisi, 2000). For example, improvements at an individual level may not result in improved organizational performance if their objectives are not intrinsically linked with team, departmental and organizational objectives.

The extent to which performance can be solely measured through quantitative measures is open to question (Fowler, 1990). Arriving at crude, quantitative measures (e.g. number of sales in a week or number of products produced) may mean a firm is not gaining a true picture of overall performance. An interesting example is provided by Chase and Fuchs (2008) regarding a teacher who tries exceptionally hard to improve his/her students learning but the final marks turn out similar to those of students whose teacher does not make half the effort. Which teacher is doing the most to improve performance? If rewards were based on student performance, it may serve to de-motivate the hard-working teacher. There is also the phenomenon of unanticipated side effects (see Figure 11.2).

A computer salesperson is primarily assessed on his quarterly sales. While he is aware that a current laptop range is being phased out, he focuses his efforts on maximizing sales of this line over the current quarter. He is successful in this regard and receives a substantial bonus for his sales effort. However, he also leaves many dissatisfied customers who soon realize the laptop they purchased has been replaced by a superior version at a similar price. The company goal of sales maximization is achieved but to the detriment of arguably more important goals of enhancing customer satisfaction and loyalty.

Figure 11.2. Unanticipated side effects to performance measures.

Qualitative measures, such as customer attitude surveys, can also yield vital information. Criticizms of the use of qualitative measures largely relate to their particularly subjective nature. Due to this, appraiser training provides an important tool in reducing subjectivity. Mabey *et al.* (1998) contend the greatest challenge faced regarding performance management is to ensure that the procedures incorporated in the system can be audited. This helps ensure a fair and effective system is being used. Regular appraisals are often utilized to bring a degree of formalization to the process of performance management. The most important characteristics of performance measures are their validity and reliability (Mabey *et al.*, 1998). Reliability simply refers to whether the same decision reached would be reached if other individuals made it. Validity refers to the extent to which the method used measures actually what it is supposed to measure. Thus it is imperative that sufficient time is given to deriving the performance indicators and ensuring they accurately depict the performance the organization wants to measure.

The provision of feedback is a major component of effective performance management. Buchner (2007) points to control theory as a basis for critically assessing feedback provided through performance management. Ongoing feedback and support is an absolute necessity, though the extent to which this takes place in practice is questionable (Coens and Jenkins, 2000; Fletcher, 2001). The performance of timely, ongoing feedback is highlighted by the very fact that unforeseen events occur. This may require a reappraisal of objectives. Having ongoing reviews allows the employee to provide detail on how they are progressing and the manager can provide detail on any organizational changes that may impact on the achievement of these objectives. It also allows one to see how their performance to date is being viewed and what might be required to engender improved performance (Williams, 2002). The annual appraisal remains the dominant mechanism whereby objectives are set and feedback is provided (in theory at least). Such a scenario is largely insufficient (Williams, 2002) because an annual appraisal cannot be construed as ongoing feedback.

Performance management: a beneficial management system?

From a normative perspective, the effective and strategic use of performance management provides a means for recognizing good performance, as well as clarifying tasks and providing support in achieving these. It carries the potential to provide a structured means of directing and guiding individual employees, teams, and departments towards the pursuit and achievement of corporate objectives. This can result in a greater level of decentralization with each organizational actor taking added responsibility for improving business performance, resulting in 'a cultural change centred around continuous performance improvement' (Sparrow and Hiltrop, 1994: 567). It can also be useful in identifying 'high potentials' thus helping succession planning and management development. Furthermore, it can aid the HR planning process through the identification of training and skills gaps. Through holding review sessions with employees the opportunity is afforded to set out action plans as well as discussing personal and career development. This can be extremely beneficial as it may be construed as showing how valued an employee is to the firm. In addition, it allows the identification of sub par performers. Firms may adopt the 'Jack Welch approach' and attempt to get rid of these poor performers or to bring their performance in line to what is expected.

However, the extent to which these benefits are actually realized remains open to question. This is largely due to an underlying dissatisfaction with performance management (Ellis and Saunier, 2004). It is viewed by some as representing another administration exercise for line managers in order to allow HR rate and reward employees (Armstrong, 1999; Ellis and Saunier, 2004). For many organizations performance management is about working out a rating for employees and making pay decisions based on this rating (Ellis and Saunier, 2004), rather than a concerted attempt to improve the organization's performance and develop employees. Others have suggested that there is often a failure to align performance management with other crucial organizational processes such as strategic planning (Ellis and Saunier, 2004; Torrington *et al.*, 2008). A study by Fletcher and Williams (1992) on 26 private and public UK organizations concluded that performance management tended to be a reactive process dealing with external pressures rather than a conscious strategic effort. Further they found that the development of employees, viewed (theoretically) as a major aspect of performance management, tends to be a decidedly secondary concern relative to the bottom line. There also appears to be a feeling among some organizations and managers that performance management brings a low return of investment in terms of the bottom line (Chase and Fuchs, 2008). Performance management is also posited on the assumption that individual employees take responsibility for improving their own performance. This assumes that every individual wants this increased responsibility, which may not necessarily be the case.

Performance appraisal

The performance appraisal is essentially a formal mechanism of reviewing individual employee performance. Fletcher (2001: 473) defines it as the 'activities through which organizations seek to assess employees and develop their competence, enhance performance and distribute rewards'. It generally involves line managers appraising their subordinate's performance, often on an annual basis. In terms of the content of appraisals, there is no definite 'one best' prescribed approach. For example, job performance will nearly always be reviewed, whilst personality and behaviour may or may not. Performance management is often conflated with performance appraisal and vice versa. Performance appraisals are concerned with individual performance, whereas performance management looks at individual, team, and organizational performance. The appraisal may be just another HR technique used by an organization, while performance management attempts to link the appraisal process to the wider values and objectives of the firm (Foot and Hook, 2008). However, appraisals constitute an integral part of the performance management process.

Traditionally, appraisals concentrated on aspects of personality that were believed to be integral to carrying out the role, e.g. being an extroverted person for a sales job. However such an approach is blighted by problems. People may define personality traits differently (Torrington *et al.*, 2008). This may cause problems if ratings are being used because appraisers may have different views on what the traits mean. Thus considerable potential for bias exists. Further, many organizations tend to have common appraisals across staff, meaning that some employees may be appraised on traits that are irrelevant to their role (Torrington *et al.*, 2008). Clearly appraisals carry a high potential for subjectivity, bias and prejudice. Consequently there have been developments to make the process more objective. Typically these involve establishing measurable objectives which are formally reviewed, normally on an annual basis, to establish whether they have been met or not. Survey data showed 89 per cent of respondent firms measured performance against objectives, 56 per cent measured against competencies and 53 per cent appraised against pre-set performance standards (IRS, 2005). Each employee may have a say in setting their objectives but the extent of this involvement varies greatly between firms. If objectives are not jointly agreed and/or there is no shared understanding and acceptance of them, the normative ideals of performance management are questionable. Furthermore, it is vital that the organization's own circumstances and what they are trying to achieve in appraising various employees are taken into account, rather than adopting the approach used in another organization, i.e. using an off-the-shelf appraisal may not be wise.

The effectiveness of appraisals

Appraisals are believed to enhance managerial and organizational performance as well as positively contributing to employee motivation (Randell, 1989). Conducted effectively, they are credited with a number of positive benefits (cf. Longenecker, 1997):

1 Performance planning and goal setting
2 Providing feedback and coaching
3 Employee development
4 Linking employee performance to compensation and promotion decisions.

However, Mabey *et al.* (1998) identify two schools of thought regarding problems with the effectiveness of performance appraisals in evaluating employee performance. The first school focus on performance appraisal as a social process. Since appraisal generally involves one person rating another's performance 'it is impossible to disentangle the social influences which are present' (Mabey *et al.*, 1998: 136). Second, performance appraisal has a political dimension (cf. Barlow, 1989). Rather than being an objective, neutral process, the performance appraisal represents a political process whereby those involved may pursue personal agendas and strategies (Mabey *et al.*, 1998). For example, there may be a poor working relationship between employee and appraiser. This may result in appraisees perceiving the appraisal as unfair. This may de-motivate employees, possibly resulting in overt and covert outcomes, including poor performance and higher labour turnover. In addition, the appraiser may not possess enough information to effectively review the employee's performance. This may lead to a situation whereby the appraisee receives incomplete and inaccurate information on their performance. Some firms have tried to negate such issues by having more than one appraiser, with the objective of reducing the potential for bias.

The use of inappropriate rating instruments is another source of criticism and a potential weakness in performance appraisal. Table 11.1 summarizes the main characteristics and some of the primary strengths and weaknesses of the most commonly utilized performance appraisal techniques. Many are criticized for failing to accurately capture what is involved in different jobs. Often managers

Table 11.1 Performance appraisal techniques.

Method	*Characteristics*	*Strengths*	*Weaknesses*
Rating	Appraiser specifies on a scale to what degree relevant (job, behaviour or personality) characteristics are possessed by appraisee	Ease of comparison; can range in complexity from very simple to very involved, using descriptions of behaviouror performance	Subjective; personality or behavioural traits difficult to measure; may ignore variables that impact on work performance; may suffer from 'central tendency'
Ranking	Appraiser ranks appraisees from best to worst, based on specific characteristics or overall job performance	Simple to use; facilitates comparisons	Limited basis for making decisions; degrees of difference not specified, subjective; may suffer from 'central tendency'
Performance or objective-oriented systems	Appraiser evaluates degree to which specific job targets or standards have been achieved	Job-related; objective; participative	Needs measurable targets, strong quantitative focus may overshadow more qualitative measures; danger of collusion
Critical incident	Appraiser observes incidence of good and bad performance. These are used as a basis for judging and assessing or discussing performance	Job-related; more objective; useful when jobs difficult to quantify in measurable terms	Needs good observational skills; time-consuming
Self-assessment	Appraisees evaluate themselves using a particular format or structure	Participative, facilitates discussion; promotes self-analysis	Danger of lenient tendency; potential sources of conflict between appraiser and appraisee

Adapted from Gunnigle *et al.* (2006: 193).

may have an overall opinion on how well a person has been performing but there is a lack of specifics on the employee's actual performance. For example, the 'recency effect' is a common error in the appraisal process. This refers to where the appraiser fails to keep a formal record of performance since the last appraisal. Consequently, at appraisal time the appraiser realizes s/he can only remember specific examples of performance within the most recent period.

The appraisal may suffer from trying to achieve too much (IRS, 2001). For example, performance appraisals may be used to identify poor, good and exceptional performers, spot high potentials, discover training and development needs, and decide on appropriate rewards. The most recent Cranet-E survey (2003) shows appraisals are most commonly used to identify training and development needs (Chase and Fuchs, 2008). Links to rewards are also strong but there are notable variations in how extensive this is across countries. For example, the link to rewards is far stronger in Germany and Sweden than in the United Kingdom. This is quite interesting given that Germany and Sweden are characterized by high levels of unionization and the conventional wisdom is that unions may often be averse to systems where pay increases are partially and wholly dependent on performance appraisals (cf. Gunnigle *et al.*, 1998). Utilizing appraisals for both developmental needs and for ascribing rewards is particularly interesting because – to all intents and purposes – they are two conflicting approaches. The appraisee might be loathe to identify training or developmental needs for fear of it being construed as a sign of weakness which may negatively impact rewards to be received.

Longenecker (1997) found that often it is the basic fundamentals of the appraisal process that reduce its effectiveness. For example, over eight in ten respondents in his study suggested that the failure to have clear performance criteria negated the potential benefits of conducting an appraisal. The conventional performance management literature is premised on the view that having clear and explicit goals is imperative in eliciting improved employee performance. Whilst ability and motivation are important ingredients they are not the sole determinant of improved performance (Torrington *et al.*, 2008). It draws from expectancy theory which basically sets out that employees will be motivated to perform as long as they believe their goals are achievable and that they will lead to valuable rewards (Vroom, 1964). Hence, if objectives are unclear the appraisal may do more harm than good. This can include both individual and organizational level outcomes. For example, individual level outcomes may include de-motivation amongst employees and increased tension in the manager-appraisee relationship. Organizational level outcomes may incorporate a loss of credibility for the HR department and a loss of managerial focus.

A key related question is what type of individual objectives should be set. Should only tightly defined results oriented objectives be set? This often seems to be the case, probably because they provide an easier benchmark against which to measure performance. It is argued that such objectives should follow the SMART (specific, measurable, appropriate, relevant, timed) rules (Torrington *et al.*, 2008). However setting SMART goals can be problematic if they are not continually reviewed and updated. The business environment is subject to rapid change, possibly rendering pre-set goals a constraint on the firm. Is setting results oriented objectives sufficient? People are not always necessarily in control of whether they can meet their goals or not. External influences can constrain the achievement of performance. Consequently it has been suggested that behavioural targets should also be set (Williams, 2002). Almond and Ferner (2006), in their research on US multinational companies in Europe, found that the nature of objectives were changing whereby objective criteria based on job performance were increasingly supplemented with softer, more difficult to quantify objectives such as 'cooperation' within the team.

Contemporary developments

Recent decades have witnessed considerable evolution in the spheres of performance appraisal and performance management.

Forced distribution

One such change has been the use of systems of forced distribution. Forced distribution forces the appraiser to rate a certain proportion of employees in different categories. Thus, a certain number of employees must be in the top grade, and further specific proportions must also be in the various lower grades. As mentioned earlier GE, under the leadership of Jack Welch, made this concept famous whereby on an annual basis they 'culled' the worst performers, termed the 'vitality curve' (Welch, 2001). He argued it was a good system because it continually raised the performance bar in the organization. He also contentiously argued it was 'good' for those employees who were 'culled' since it took them out of scenarios that were not good for them (Lawler, 2003). In the GE system, managers ('business leaders') were forced to identify the top 20 per cent of performers, the middle 70 per cent and finally the bottom 10 per cent. The primary aim was to avoid 'central tendency', i.e. clumping all employees in the middle performance categories in an attempt to avoid extremes. This system of identifying those poor performers and outstanding performers has seemingly increased in popularity in recent years (Lawler, 2003; Almond and Ferner, 2006; Gunnigle *et al.*, 2007). Whilst one may ascertain logic in this, such a system fails to take into account that competent performers may be sufficient in certain roles (Boudreau and Ramstad, 2005). In any workforce there will inevitably be differences in performance – even the best performing team will have its best and worst performers. However the 'worst' may be performing to a very satisfactory level. This system raises a number of questions. Can it be sustainable long term? If the firm operates in a tight labour market could it prove a detriment to organizational performance and success? Does it proffer the possibility of detrimental competition within an organization? And, more generally, has it the potential for placing undue stress on workers, leading to 'burn-out', work family balance, and so on?

360-degree feedback

A 360-degree feedback is credited with providing a more holistic and effective source of feedback on individual performance. Essentially it involves getting feedback from multiple sources, including peers, supervisors, colleagues and so on. We earlier noted that appraisals typically involve a manager giving feedback on their subordinate's performance – a very one-dimensional view. 360-degree feedback 'can provide a unique opportunity for individuals to make an objective comparison of their self-assessment with the assessments of their peers, managers and customers and other interested parties involved in the process' (Chase and Fuchs, 2008: 237). This is normally achieved through the use of questionnaires rather than face-to-face appraisals (Ward, 1995). Clearly this brings other potential difficulties since questionnaires may be overly long or complex (Fisher, 2005). A 360-degree feedback seems to be predominantly used as a development mechanism insofar as it provides a more rounded insight into how various stakeholders view performance. However, were it to be used as a basis for decisions regarding performance, promotion or pay, it is likely there would be greater issues (Fisher, 2005). Managers may view the multi-faceted feedback as an excellent exercise concerning their development but would be uncomfortable if their staff were influencing decisions regarding pay or promotion. This method is very time-consuming given the various sources of feedback that need to be collated and it requires skilled interpretation of results. Although it has been the subject of much research and interest Chase and Fuchs (2008) note that the most recent Cranet survey (2003) suggests it still remains a relatively uncommon mechanism utilized in European countries. Gunnigle and colleagues (2007) found that half of all multinational companies in Ireland utilize peer or 360-degree feedback for their managers.

Balanced scorecard

Another important development in performance management is the application of the 'balanced scorecard' (Kaplan and Norton, 1992, 1996a,b). The balanced scorecard is a strategic planning and management system used to align business activities to the organization's vision and strategy, improve internal and external communications, as well as monitor organizational performance against strategic goals. It seeks to integrate the various functions and translate corporate goals into short-term measurable objectives which are linked to the achievement of the firm's long term objectives. By integrating financial and non-financial data, managers are provided with a more rounded perspective to make better strategic decisions (Kaplan and Norton, 1992). Specifically three areas of measurement are identified in addition to financial measures: customer measures, internal business process measures and learning and growth measures (see Figure 11.3). This approach advocates the establishment of clear specific measures across each of these areas. Internal business measures should involve metrics which allow managers to know how well their business is running. Learning and growth measures are linked to individual and company self-improvement through incorporating employee training and development and changes in organizational culture. The customer perspective includes the need to incorporate indicators of customer satisfaction. The balanced scorecard approach claims to represent the first attempt to develop performance management in an 'integrated causal, and most importantly systematic way' (Voelpel *et al.*, 2006: 44). This should, they argued, lead to improved efficiency and effectiveness of communication priorities within firms, and increased individual and organizational performance (Kaplan and Norton, 1992).

Despite its fairly widespread acceptance, others have been slower to praise its usefulness and indeed some contend it is neither an overtly positive nor useful

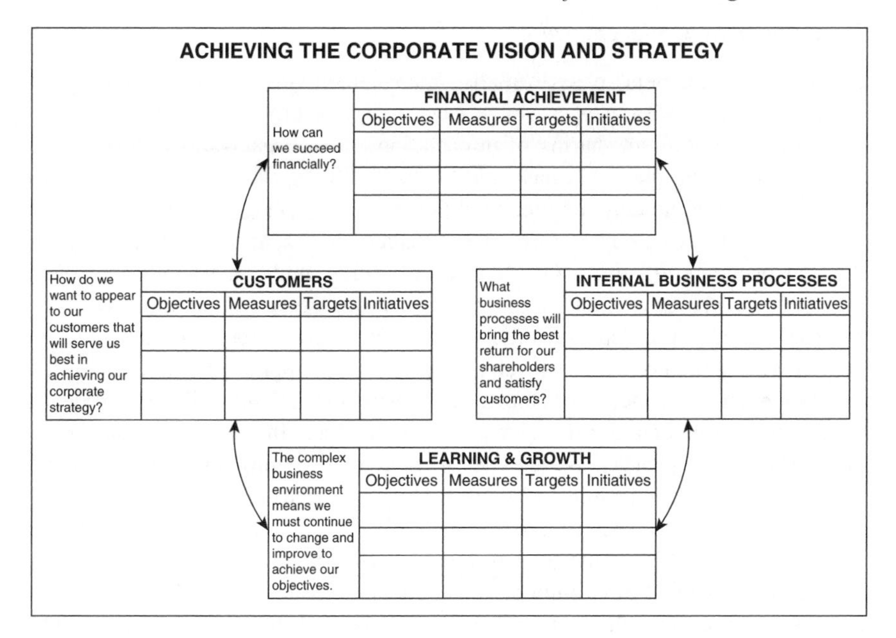

Figure 11.3. The balanced scorecard. Adapted from Kaplan (1996a: 54).

system in today's business environment. Voelpel and colleagues (2006: 49) go as far as to suggest it 'exerts a tyrannical impact and influence on the firm and its stakeholders'. They point to the rigidity of the measurement tool in limiting the number of perspectives that can be used. They argue that it fails to integrate additional perspectives which may be required. They also criticize the uniformity that the scorecard inevitably brings. The overall strategy is translated into particular measures that align the firms' objectives. This increases the orientation and uniformity towards the overall goal but it may neglect further possible goals and activities. For example, employees may have a number of set objectives which they will work towards achieving but outside of these they may do little else. In essence, they argue it may cause 'static-ism' that ensures maximum focus on a number of prescribed goals but may limit the opportunity to go beyond these (Voelpel *et al.*, 2006: 51). A third main criticism is that it fails to account for the external environment. Essentially it focuses on improving performance and realizing the achievement of strategy within the organization and ignores external factors that need to be integrated into the system: 'Today's business reality involves non-linear and interactive activities that consider the entire system, not only the direct and visible factors, but also those that reside unseen within the environment in which they take place' (Voelpel *et al.*, 2006: 54). Despite such criticism, the balanced scorecard continues to make beneficial contributions to organizations due in no small part to its continual development and refinement.

Increasing managerial control

A further development in performance management stems from technological advancements. These advances can be ascribed as a positive development through allowing more efficient sharing of information across organizational levels (e.g. local, regional and global) (Chase and Fuchs, 2008). However, it has also led to critical comment, notably the view that performance management represents the 'new Taylorism', whereby performance management is centre stage in controlling the performance of the workforce (Winstanley and Stuart-Smith, 1996). Performance management may or may not afford greater autonomy over how work is carried out. It depends largely on how it is administered and the underlying management ethos. At one level, the idea of being appraised can be construed as 'akin to a police state, where the control occurs through the collection of documentation and evidence, a dossier on the individual. Instead of standing over ones' shoulder, supervision becomes a matter of spying through keyholes' (Winstanley and Stuart-Smith, 1996: 69). This is an accusation that is particularly noteworthy in certain sectors, such as the call centre industry. This industry has been characterized by some as a re-creation of the sweat shops, 'dark satanic mills', and the ideal environment for exercising 'panoptican' control over all aspects of employee behaviour (cf. Taylor and Bain, 1999; Kinnie *et al.*, 2000). Call centre agents are often subject to the most in-depth monitoring of their performance through collecting 'hard' quantitative performance measures, including time to answer a call, call length, abandoned call rate, accuracy and adherence to script and wrap-up time. These scenarios can be categorized as a particularly illustrative controlling form of performance management. However it is not a unique scenario, what may be distinctive is the 'overt and pervasive nature' of this management approach (Holman, 2005: 115).

Conclusion

Stereotypically, performance management seeks to manage human resources through the establishment of specific objectives for individuals, teams, departments and divisions that tie in with achieving the overall strategic objectives of the firm. It draws together HR policies and practices to form an overall coordinated system in which to manage performance. Performance management draws, in particular, on two theories, namely, expectancy theory and goal-setting theory. Although this integration of theory is welcomed and indeed the case for more can be argued, these theories also point towards problems that as of yet remain unresolved. These include issues regarding setting feasible goals, how performance is measured, should there be a link to rewards and – if so – what type of rewards should be provided, and how does feedback work in the system.

Mabey *et al.* (1998: 149) note that performance management can be 'criticized for relying on a model of management which is more rational than is achievable in practice'. More specific criticisms include the universalistic form it tends to follow. By this we mean that performance management is often applied, with little consideration given to contextual factors such as the differences between organizational roles, cultures and national institutional environments. Performance management systems invariably incorporate multiple objectives and content including linking objectives to organizational strategy and developing employee skills. As a result, many practices and tools will have to be incorporated, rendering performance management systems quite complex. In turn, such complexity clearly poses considerable challenges to organizations regarding the design and implementation of performance management systems. Nor is this complexity likely to diminish anytime soon due to pressures for improved performance, technological advances, and cultural issues in implementing performance management across borders (cf. Fletcher, 2001; Almond and Ferner, 2006).

In conclusion, whilst performance management has come a long way and may be working effectively in many organizations there is a need for a more nuanced research agenda regarding the innermost workings of performance management. To date, many of the extant models are too simplistic. Not enough credence has been placed on the inherent complexities and potential for contradictions that exist in making performance management an effective system in organizations.

References

Almond, P. and Ferner, A. (2006). *American Multinationals in Europe: Managing Employment Relations Across National Borders.* Oxford: Oxford University Press.

Armstrong, M. (1999). *A Handbook of Human Resource Management.* London: Kogan Page Limited.

Armstrong, M. and Baron, A. (1998). *Performance Management: The New Realities.* London: Institute of Personnel and Development.

Barlow, G. (1989). Deficiencies and the perpetuation of power: latent functions in managerial appraisal, *Journal of Management Studies*, 26(5): 499–517.

Bevan, S. and Thompson, M. (1992). *Personnel Management in the UK: an Analysis of the Issues.* London: IPM.

Boudreau, J. W. and Ramstad, P. M. (2005). Talentship, talent segmentation, and sustainability: A new HR decision science paradigm for a new strategy definition', *Human Resource Management*, 44(2): 129–36.

Buchner, T. W. (2007). Performance Management Theory: A Look from the Performer's Perspective with Implications for HRD, *Human Resource Development International*, 10(1): 59–73.

Chase, P. and Fuchs, S. (2008). Performance management and appraisal, in M. Muller-Camen, R. Croucher and S. Leigh (Eds), *Human Resource Management: A Case Study Approach.* London: CIPD.

CIPD (2005). *Performance Management.* London: CIPD.

Coens, T. and Jenkins, M. (2000). *Abolishing Performance Appraisals.* San Francisco: Berrett-Koehler.

Costello, S. J. (1994). *Effective Performance Management.* New York: Irwin.

Den Hartog, D. N., Boselie, P. and Paauwe, J. (2004). Performance management: a model and research agenda, *Applied Psychology: An International Review*, 53(4): 556–69.

DeNisi, A. S. (2000). Performance appraisal and performance management, in K. J. Klein and S. Kozlowski (Eds), *Multilevel Theory, Research and Methods in Organizations.* San Francisco: Jossey-Bass.

Dobbins, G. H., Cardy, R. L. and Platz-Vieno, S. J. (1990). A contingency approach to appraisal satisfaction: An initial investigation of the joint effects of organizational variables and appraisal characteristics, *Journal of Management*, 16(3): 619–32.

Drucker, P. (1954). *The Practice of Management.* New York, Harper.

Ellis, C. M. and Saunier, A. M. (2004). Performance appraisal: myth and reality, in L. A. Berger and D. R. Berger (Eds), *The Talent Management Handbook: Creating Organizational Excellence by Identifying, Developing and Promoting Your Best People.* New York: McGraw-Hill.

Fisher, C. (2005). Performance management and performing management, in J. Leopold, L. Harris, and T. Watson (Eds), *The Strategic Managing of Human Resources.* Essex: Pearson Education Limited.

Fletcher, C. (2001). Performance appraisal and management: the developing research agenda, *Journal of Occupational and Organizational Psychology*, 74(4): 473–87.

Fletcher, C. and Williams, R. (1992). The route to performance management, *Personnel Management*, 24(10): 42–7.

Foot, M. and Hook, C. (2008). *Introducing Human Resource Management,* 5th Edition. Essex: Prentice Hall.

Fowler, A. (1990). Performance management: the MBO of the 90s, *Personnel Management*, 22(7): 47–51.

Gospel, H. and Pendelton, A. (2005). *Corporate Governance and Labour Management,* New York: Oxford University Press.

Guest, D. E., Michie, J., Conway, N. and Sheehan, M. (2003). Human resource management and corporate performance in the UK, *British Journal of Industrial Relations*, 41(2): 291–314.

Gunnigle, P., Heraty, N. and Morley, M. J. (2006). *Human Resource Management in Ireland,* 3rd edition. Dublin: Gill and Macmillan.

Gunnigle, P., Lavelle, J. and McDonnell, A. (2007). Human Resource Practices in Multinational Companies in Ireland: A Large-Scale Survey. Limerick: University of Limerick. Available [online] from: http://ssrn.com/abstract=1077266.

Gunnigle, P., Turner, T. and D'Art, D. (1998). Counterpoising collectivism, performance-related pay and industrial relations in Greenfield sites, *British Journal of Industrial Relations*, 36(4): 565–79.

Holman, D. (2005). Call centres, in D. Holman, T. D. Wall, C. W. Clegg, P. Sparrow and A. Howard (Eds), *The Essentials of the New Workplace. A Guide to the Human Impact of Modern Working Practices*. Chichester: John Wiley and Sons Ltd.

Huselid, M. A. (1995). The Impact of Human Resource Management Practices on Turnover, Productivity, and Corporate Financial Performance, *Academy of Management Journal*, 38(3): 635–72.

IRS (2001). Performance appraisal must try harder, *IRS Employment Trends*, 724, March, 2–3.

IRS (2005). Appraisals (2): learning from practice and experience, *IRS Employment Review*, 829, 12 August, 13–17.

Kaplan, R. S. and Norton, D. P. (1992). The balanced scorecard – measures that drive performance, *Harvard Business Review*, 70(1): 71–9.

Kaplan, R. S. and Norton, D. P. (1996a). Linking the balanced scorecard to strategy, *California Management Review*, 39(1): 53–79.

Kaplan, R. S. and Norton, D. P. (1996b). Using the balanced scorecard as a strategic management system, *Harvard Business Review*, 85(7/8): 62–77.

Kinnie, N., Hutchinson, S. and Purcell, J. (2000). 'Fun and surveillance': the paradox of high commitment management in call centres, *International Journal of Human Resource Management*, 11(5): 967–85.

Lawler, E. E. (2003). Reward practices and performance management system effectiveness, *Organizational Dynamics*, 32(4): 396–404.

Longenecker, C. O. (1997). Why managerial performance appraisals are ineffective: causes and lessons, *Career Development International*, 2(5): 212–18.

Mabey, C., Salaman, G. and Storey, J. (1998). *Human Resource Management: A Strategic Introduction.* Oxford: Blackwell.

McKenna, E. and Beech, N. (2008). *Human Resource Management: A Concise Analysis,* 2nd edition. Essex: Prentice Hall.

Mintzberg, H. (1978). Patterns in strategy formulation, *Management Science*, 24, May, 934–48.

Mintzberg, H. (1987). The strategy concept I: five Ps for strategy, *California Management Review*, 30(1): 11–24.

Randell, G. (1989). Employee appraisal, in K. Sisson (Ed.), *Personnel Management.* Oxford: Blackwell.

Scott-Lennon, F. (1995). *The Appraisals Pocketbook.* Alresford: Management Pocketbooks Limited.

Sparrow, P. and Hiltrop, J.-M. (1994). *European Human Resource Management in Transition.* Hertfordshire: Prentice Hall.

Taylor, P. and Bain, P. (1999). An assembly line in the head: work and employee relations in the call centre, *Industrial Relations Journal*, 30(2): 101–17.

Torrington, D., Hall, L. and Taylor, S. (2008). *Human Resource Management,* 7th edition. Essex: Pearson Education Limited.

Van Vijfeijken, H., Kleingeld, A., van Tuijl, H. and Algera, J. (2006). Interdependence and fit in team performance management, *Personnel Review*, 35(1): 98–117.

Voelpel, S. C., Leibold, M. and Eckhoff, R. A. (2006). The tyranny of the Balanced Scorecard in the innovation economy, *Journal of Intellectual Capital*, 7(1): 43–60.

Vroom, V. (1964). *Work and Motivation.* Chichester: John Wiley.

Ward, P. (1995). A 360° turn for the better, *People Management*, 1(3): 20–2.

Welch, J. (2001). *Jack: What I've Learned Leading a Great Company and Great People.* London: Headline.

Williams, R. S. (2002). *Managing Employee Performance: Design and Implementation in Organizations.* London: Thomson.

Winstanley, D. and Stuart-Smith, K. (1996). Policing performance: the ethics of performance management, *Personnel Review*, 25(6): 66–84.

12 Reward management

Suzanne Richbell and Geoffrey Wood

Introduction

> Reward management is concerned with the formulation and implementation of strategies and policies, the purposes of which are to reward people fairly, equitably and consistently in accordance with their value to the organisation and to help the organisation achieve its strategic goals.
>
> (Armstrong and Stephens, 2005).

The employment contract is an indeterminate exchange, whereby a labour power (in one form or another) is exchanged for a cash wage (Hyman, 1989). In other words, one of the key sources of disputes and conflicts in the employment relationship is the difficulty in quantifying what is a fair day's work for a specific pay rate; engaging with this is at the heart of reward systems. The latter is easy to quantify, the former less so. Not only does this make for an inherent tension in any employment relationship, but also places pressure on both the firm and the individual employee to quantify the former. Organizations may adopt a very simple approach to pay – for example, paying the bulk of frontline employees as little as the external labour market will bear, or in line with the minimum wage, or adopt a more sophisticated approach. The latter could entail negotiating wage rates with employees on a collective basis, or adjusting pay rates to the perceived contribution of individual employees. Looking back to the industrial revolution, pay systems were generally tied to output, which in most cases was easily measurable. As workers grouped together to fight the worst excesses of low rates and high quotas, there was a subsequent change in the power relationship between employer and employee. In Britain, this resulted in a shift towards agreed rates for a job, where collectively all performing a particular job would be paid according to the same scale. However, since 1979, there has been an ongoing and cumulatively dramatic decline in unionization and, at the same time, a growing popularity in a return to an emphasis on payment for output or results, this time in the shape of performance related pay, often on an individual basis.

This chapter is organized as follows. First, we introduce the concepts of motivation and reward, and the possible forms the employment contract can assume.

Second, we focus on strategy and reward, and the different approaches that may be taken to managing reward systems in a real world organizational context.

Thinking about reward systems

The key to an effective reward system is an understanding of what it is that employees need and expect from the work situation. Traditionally, employers have taken the rational economic man approach, resting on assumptions that labour is exchanged for financial gain, usually in the form of wages or salary. This was an exchange or transactional relationship in which labour was exchanged for payment, a reward extrinsic or independent to the actual work.

But money is not the only incentive and modern employment contracts spell out the details not only of wages but other benefits, an important one being job security. While many employees regard wages as an essential, they also regard it as equally important that these wages are secured on a regular basis. In times of economic uncertainty, the protection afforded by job security becomes highly valued. This means that, in times of recession, job seekers will tend to opt for securer jobs, even if this means foregoing some pay; this will make public sector jobs more sought after at such a time. Ironically, employees' quest for job security may work against the need for organizations to be quick to react to fluctuations in demand, limiting their capacity to be flexible. The financial responsibilities of modern living mean that most employees will deem it necessary that there is a long term basis to their ability to provide family support and meeting financial commitments.

A further issue is the prospects for upward promotion and pay dispersion. As Cappelli (1999) notes, a tendency towards flatter organizations or new organizational forms such as network organizations, makes it harder to provide internal careers: this may make mobility more attractive. Another tendency has been the divergence of pay rates between those in senior positions and the rank and file. Toynbee and Walker (2008) note that, some 20 years ago, CEOs in FTSE 100 companies on average earned 17 times the pay awarded to the average employee, whereas today it is approximately 75 times. Given that there seems no evidence that UK chief executives are any more competent than there were 20 years ago, and that manifest incompetence appears to often be associated with record pay awards, there is little doubt that such gross imbalances are likely to continue to erode employee morale and organizational commitment. Claims that the organization cannot 'afford' to keep pay in line with inflation, whilst senior managers help themselves to disproportionate amounts of organizational resources, will simply lack legitimacy to most employees.

Collective and individual contracts, pay and reward

In understanding pay and reward, a key distinction is whether pay rates are decided on a collective or individual basis: in other words, do people receive similar pay rates within the same job grade, or is pay varied according to perceived ability.

In unionized workplaces – where the union is recognized by the employer – collective contracts may be in place. Here, through (commonly) annual collective bargaining, the firm and the union's representatives, agreements are reached to set the pay scales (or, simply, a standard pay rate) to cover particular job grades. This means that all employees can expect the same basic terms and conditions of employeement, although employees may, of course, be advanced on a particular pay scale on the basis of seniority and/or, perhaps at the discretion of the employer (for example, an employee may be advanced on the pay scale on evidence of an exceptional contribution). Collective contracts have advantages and disadvantages for employers and employees. From an employee perspective, collective representation means that employers will have to take employee demands more seriously; it is a lot harder to ignore the collective voice of a workforce, than a request for more pay by a single individual. Moreover, as it recognizes that all employees (within a particular job grade) are worth roughly the same (with some variation according to the breadth of the pay scale agreed on), more vulnerable employees are protected. Employees that are in a stronger bargaining position may still pursue their individual interests through seeking promotion, whilst they have the protection of the collective contract to fall back on should they lose their comparative advantage through no fault of their own. From an employer perspective, an effective union negotiating employee interests may mean that you are forced to pay more than you may wish to (even if negotiations break down, employees still have legal rights, including, possibly, the right to strike), and makes things less flexible (it is hard to renegotiate an agreement should external circumstances change). However, it also means that the reward system in place has legitimacy (employees cannot easily complain about something their own representatives have agreed to, other than to the union involved). It is also administratively much simpler to administer one collective contract rather than many individual ones.

The 1980s marked a watershed in the nature of British employee/employer relations, although similar trends were also apparent in many other liberal market economies, ranging from New Zealand to the United States. This was the advent of Thatcherism, running in tandem with the steady and on-going decline of the stronghold of union power. Previous to this era, British organizations had tended to adopt a bureaucratic approach to their payment systems. Typically, rates for jobs were negotiated at a national level between employers' associations and trade unions and, at least in theory, were applied as standard throughout an industry. However, almost two decades earlier, the Donovan Commission (1968) had exposed the reality that the formal system of national negotiated rates had, for many employers, become a floor or minimum over which plant negotiations boosted pay and made for differences within an industry. Nevertheless, within an organization, the trend would be that, in accordance with collective agreements, pay scales were established and individuals would occupy positions on the scale depending on the nature of the work and seniority. Actual performance was not the measure for pay. Such a system provided a common understanding of the pay range, a legitimacy in that it was borne out of collective bargaining and an ease of administration. Hence, as noted above, the focus was on what the job was worth rather than on actual performance.

An individual contract is one where the employee has her/his own contract with the employer. In other words s/he may not necessarily have the same rewards or terms of conditions of service as others, as there is no obligation on the employer to harmonize pay, other than where inequalities are obviously discriminatory. The simplest form of individual contract is where the employer pays the bare minimum possible: either as little as possible to secure the services of a suitable job seeker or in line with a national minimum wage, where one is in force. However, this minimalist approach always opens the firm to poaching of staff (other than when unemployment is very high), as competitors have to offer very little more to attract experienced staff from it. Alternatively, it is possible to seek to link pay with skills, capacities, and/or physical output; this can range from a crude piece work (where a production worker is simply paid in accordance with output) to more sophisticated systems for analyzing the worth of an incumbent. What such approaches have in common is a belief that *rewarding* an employee for her/his contribution should be done on individual lines, taking account of her/his capacities, potential and underlying motivators. It also is an essentially unitarist approach, based on the assumption that it is up to management, and management alone, to dictate the basis under which pay is calculated (Heery, 1996).

Extrinsic and intrinsic rewards

Distinctions can be made between these forms of 'outside the job' or *extrinsic rewards* and other aspects of reward which stem from the actual content rather than the surrounding context of the work; such rewards constitute *intrinsic rewards.* A brief review of classic motivation theories provides an understanding of the range of human need and hence of desired rewards. Key issues include the extent to which people are likely to be motivated by money alone, or by other issues such as the intrinsic rewards of the job itself, or even by belonging to the social community that constitutes the workplace. While much criticism has been levelled at early content theories in terms of methodology (or lack of it) and the universalist nature of the findings, they do provide an insight into the complex nature of matching rewards to individual employee needs. The early work of Maslow (1954) suggests a hierarchy of needs which the individual will aim to satisfy in ascending order, from basic physiological needs, through safety and security needs, social or love needs, needs for esteem, both from others and from self and finally self fulfilment or the realization of one's own true potential. While this widens the range of potentially motivating rewards, it is very general and it is Herzberg (1966) who provides a more work specific theory of motivation.

Herzberg not only makes the distinction between extrinsic (hygiene factors) and intrinsic (motivators) rewards but he takes this further by suggesting that the traditional approach of rewarding labour with wages or salary does not result in positive job satisfaction for the individual employee. According to Herzberg, pay, along with other extrinsic factors such as job security and relationships with superiors, peers and subordinates are the factors that may cause discontent but, if improved or maintained well, will at best keep job dissatisfaction at bay but will not lead to job satisfaction. Such findings have massive implications for economies like the British, which have traditionally used financial incentives as a means to motivate workers. While there is much debate over the effectiveness of financial incentives, such findings do hold warnings for over reliance on financial rewards and point to a need to design a reward system which accommodates the other needs experienced by employees.

The motivators or intrinsic factors leading to job satisfaction are identified by Herzberg as achievement, recognition, interest in the work itself, responsibility, advancement and growth. The argument is that by building the possibility for such intrinsic rewards into employees' work, the level of job satisfaction will be increased.

Process theories break through the universalist approach and, in so doing, further emphasize the highly complex nature of motivating employees. Vroom's (1964) expectancy theory is helpful in emphasizing the complexity of individual thought processes which may or may not lead to action. It is suggested that assessments, firstly of whether effort is likely to result in achievement of a specific task and, most importantly from the point of view of the current discussion, whether success in the task will lead to the individual's desired personal reward precede any possible action. It is this calculative thought process and the fact that the individual's desired reward may not be money that emphasizes the complex nature of an effective reward system.

Another process theory relevant to the design and operation of a reward system is Adam's (1965) equity theory, which centres on the importance of feelings of fair treatment and the possible behavioural manifestations which may result from perceived inequity. This theory highlights the fact that individuals make comparisons and that feelings of unjust treatment in comparison with fellow employees may result in withholding effort, restricting output, reducing cooperation and even withdrawal.

Motivation theories argue that money is not the only motivator, that intrinsic rewards are important to individuals and should be built into any rewards system, but arguably overplay the importance of the latter (which organizations may find more attractive to focus on as they may appear superficially cheaper) at the expense of the former. Motivation theories suggest use of employment contracts, with their emphasis on the economic and the legal, might be argued as a form of deflection from a more holistic understanding of the expectations and aspirations embedded in the employment relationship. Much attention has focused in recent years on the notion of a psychological contract which basically incorporates the expectations and assumptions, many unwritten, subjective and changing over time, that both employee and employer bring to the relationship (Rousseau, 1998; Rousseau, 2001). If this more embracing view of the employment relationship is adopted, then the implications, for the motivation of employees, permeate all aspects of the work situation. The need for an integrated system of reward building motivational factors into all aspects or the management of employees becomes apparent. The approach of line management, and indeed the consistency of this approach, the recognition of achievements and the provision of interesting work, where possible become important aspects of securing motivation. For those core workers whom the organization is keen to retain, skills development and careers management are essential while, for the unskilled and semi-skilled or peripheral workers, the need for training to enhance future employability may be highly regarded.

Two possible critiques of psychological theories of motivation may be advanced. The first is that they make something very simple, rather complicated. The employment contract is about exchanging wages for labour power, and in the modern economy, wages are what really matters; employees are unlikely to be committed to a job that is superficially pleasant if wages are the bare minimum needed for survival (Hyman, 1989). And, no matter how much window dressing is provided by management, some jobs are intrinsically less pleasant than others: this may be through specific policy choices by management (e.g. rigid supervision and control) or simply represent the product of the dominant technology and/or the specific nature of the industry. Organizations such as Wall Mart and McDonald's that have controversial reputations for union busting and for low pay devote considerable resources to promoting the appearance (if not the substance) of team spirit amongst employees, yet high staff turnover rates underscore the extent to which it is difficult to secure commitment where wages are minimal (see, for example, Royle, 2000).

The second limitation is psychological theories of motivation tend to downplay the subjective effects of social context: 'social and structural factors . . . are generally reduced to the status of intervening variables' (Thompson and McHugh, 1999: 280). Motivational theories often assume that workers can be simply led or enticed, downplaying the importance of cooperation between workers themselves, and with management (ibid.: 279). In practice, work environments incorporate complex social dynamics: workers may adjust their output to 'fit in', to improve their standing in the eyes of co-workers (which may involve making short bursts of intense activity to impress others), for altruistic reasons (to protect weaker or less effective colleagues), or adjust output to lengthen breaks or to 'reward' or 'punish' supervisors (that are subject to performance linked pay themselves) (see Burawoy, 1979).

Employee commitment

Because of the global, highly competitive nature of business today, organizations cannot afford to disregard the likely consequences of ignoring the challenge of establishing an effective reward system. To remain competitive in a dynamic environment, organizations need to be flexible, with employees who are not only adaptable but also creative and proactive. The old bureaucratic management approach of rules and regulations to control inevitably makes firms less flexible. However, a strong focus on the bottom line may result in the organization being excessively short termist with regard to its HRM policy, with returns to shareholders being prioritized over reinvestment, sustainability, or genuinely investing in people (Dore, 2000).

What organizations seek now is a change in the fundamental nature of the employment relationship; the aim is to generate a high degree of employee commitment to organizational strategy. Clearly articulated mission statements and the involvement of employees in the generation and development of the organization's aims and objectives are recognized as appropriate paths to securing commitment: yet, how much commitment can there be in the absence of decent pay and job security? Schemes to further employee involvement and participation provide the channels through which employees can exercise influence. However, new participation and involvement initiatives driven by the above agenda have tended to be orientated towards individual and direct contact with employees, rather than dealing with employee collectives such as unions (Brewster *et al.*, 2007). This means that in the case of the former the voices of employees are weaker and easier to ignore: in turn, this means that such processes may be little more than window dressing.

The use of Etzioni's (1975) classic power/ involvement matrix is useful in conceiving the intended shift from the employer's traditional use of remunerative power, which resulted in calculative involvement to a more elevated plane where employer power stems from the employees' belief and identification with the organization and its aims and where the commitment is therefore more enduring. Etzioni refers to this as normative power leading to moral involvement. However, in practice, employee power has tended to be most effective when collectively expressed via unions, rather than via new forms of participation and representation (Brewster *et al.*, 2007). And, as noted earlier, firms that value the ability to flexibly adjust their workforce sizes through the regular use of redundancies or sub-contracted labour are rarely likely to be able to engender much loyalty amongst employees. Loyalty is a two way street, and if an organization is disloyal to its staff, it is likely that its staff will, in turn, be disloyal to the organization.

Strategy, HR and reward

The 1980s marked a turning point in people management. The rise of the concept of 'human resource management' centred on an increasing awareness of the perceived need for a strategic approach to the management of employees. Earlier chapters have traced the change from personnel management to human resource management and indicated the main differences between these approaches. The old image of the personnel management function, cast in the role of mediator or 'referee', aiming to bring agreement between workers and management, has long been exchanged for a HRM function, whose unitary perspective is firmly rooted in the organization's strategic goals. In the case of the administration of pay and reward systems, the previous operation, in accordance with set rules and procedures, has been revolutionized to accommodate the maintenance of a high performance, committed workforce in the context of a dynamic, competitive environment. Many firms have realized that their employees may be their greatest resource and as such, their retention is important. High quality knowledge workers, with their detailed technical understanding of their organizations and their markets, may be difficult to replace, certainly in the short run. At the same time such employees provide rich fishing grounds for head hunters from rival organizations: generic tertiary skills can make moving around a lot easier.

Retention of workers, particularly key knowledge workers, becomes an important strategic issue in the drive for sustained competitive advantage. The loss of continuity and, in many industries, particularly service industries, the break up of well nurtured relationships between employees and customers, threaten competitive ability. When added to the costs of wasted training (plus the expense of recruitment and induction training for replacements), it is understandable that many employers are anxious to retain their human capital. Hence the way organizations treat their employees, the way HRM initiatives impact at the individual level, particularly the reward system, is crucial as these employees may prove the basis of success in challenging circumstances.

Fundamental to strategic HRM is the interrelatedness of all HRM practices in line with the overall strategic goals. Strategic HRM should be flexible, devolved and decentralized to create the best fit with changing circumstances and to secure the involvement of all organizational members. HRM practices and systems are not features to be imposed on an organization but rather are developed to meet particular requirements. In this context, the reward system, geared to securing employee effort and commitment to the achievement of organizational goals, is a core component in any inclusive HR strategy.

Different pay strategies

There are various pay strategies and the dominant approach has varied over time. Pay strategies may differ in form and this is complicated by the fact that they may exist on an individual or collective basis. It is possible to identify two main types of pay system. First, there is output based pay: here the emphasis is based on a measure of production in its widest sense. On an individual level, this might relate to piecework or other forms of individual payment such as commission and individual bonuses. Pioneering work by Frederick Taylor led to the development of his system of scientific management: basically, this centred around clear hierarchies, with line jobs being broken up into their simplest component tasks. In turn, this meant that it would be easier to measure output, and pay individuals accordingly (Thompson and McHugh, 1999). This system focused on maximizing output, and minimizing shirking; it discounted the importance of intrinsic rewards, in terms of the pleasure of performing the job itself; scientific management is associated with dreary and oppressive production line work, and an emphasis of easily measurable quantity over quality production. The decline of traditional manufacturing in Britain might suggest that Taylorist methods have gone out of fashion. However, many low value added service sector jobs, ranging from call centres to fast food, lend themselves to this method: high staff turnover rates, and visibly poor quality have done little to deter many firms from the usage of such methods. More generally speaking, there has been a rise of individual performance related pay since the early 1980s in Britain. Whilst most commonly in the form of traditional Taylorist methods, more sophisticated alternatives include measured day work, team-based pay, and in the use of profit sharing and gain sharing schemes for employees.

Second, there is input-based pay: here the payment system rewards the competencies or skills the employee brings to the organization. Skill based, merit and competency pay all are relevant. In other words, employees are paid in terms of what they can potentially offer the organization. Such rewards could include 'golden hellos', up-front rewards to encourage individuals to join the firm. Payments to knowledge-based workers on the basis of their particular expertise represents a good example of input-based pay: knowledge workers embody the buying in of specialized and advanced professional and technical knowledge. Time spent working in an organization may add a layer of specialized knowledge, transcending actual technical or professional prowess. For example, knowledge relating to important clients and how to conduct successful negotiations with valued customers gained through inter-personal relations over time is precious to organizations. Often undocumented but highly prized for strategic success, such knowledge makes retention of these core workers essential, with attractive payment packages acting as inducements. At the same time, there is also an element of out-put assessment in the pay of such knowledge workers, in that the value of their knowledge needs to be repeatedly reflected in successful outcomes, often accompanied by corresponding bonuses.

But, who is responsible for administering the reward system, whether input or output based? There has been a growing tendency in many firms to decentralize reward systems to line management. This reflects contradictory pressures: to make pay and reward more strategic on the one hand, and on the other to link it more closely to actual performance and/or the quality of customer service (Lado and Wilson, 1994). This may indeed reflect the reality of HRM – people management is often fragmented, with the management of rewards rarely being linked to HR strategies, let alone the general organizational strategies, in a coherent way (cf. ibid.).

Traditional approaches to pay

Job evaluation

Job evaluation is a method by which employers, often in consultation with unions, have attempted to reward different jobs according to their worth or value. Two basic forms of job evaluation may be distinguished. The 'non-analytical' approach ranks jobs as a whole against others. The more sophisticated analytical form entails a detailed study of component factors and elements of each job. Points are awarded, for example for aspects such as the level of skill and training required, the level of responsibility, whether others are managed, the nature of the work environment. Dependent on the total points awarded, jobs are placed into various payment bands. The Equal Value (Amendment) Regulations (1983) to the

Equal Pay Act (1970) saw many employers resorting to job evaluation as a means of avoiding outside legal intervention relating to decisions on pay, following the test case of Hayward v. Cammell Laird Shipbuilders Limited, where a female cook claimed equal pay for work of equal value, making comparisons with male occupations including joiner, painter and insulation engineer. This test case ended with a House of Lords ruling in 1988 in favour of Hayward, confirming the principle of equal pay for equal work.

Criticisms of job evaluation schemes

A key criticism is that payment under a job evaluation scheme is based on the job and not on the performance of the individual job holder. It has been argued that a guaranteed rate for a job may lead to inertia as there is no assessment of how the job is conducted and no reward for effort and quality of execution.

Further criticism relates to the static nature of job evaluation schemes. While the nature of work and hence particular jobs is constantly changing, the job evaluation scheme remains cast in terms of its last review, if indeed it has been reviewed at all. In the past, this led to many anomalies where, for example, changes in technology had simplified a particular work process, but the payment structure had not been modified to reflect such changes.

In the 1980s, the underlying justice of many job evaluation schemes was still in question, as it was argued that many schemes unfairly rated typically 'masculine' job characteristics, such as heavy lifting, to a high degree and tended to undervalue the 'softer' caring skills fundamental to many female dominated occupations. A good example of attempts to build greater fairness into the ratings of job characteristics, traditionally perceived as 'male' or 'female', is found in the national job evaluation scheme for local authority manual workers, ratified in 1987 and covering over a million workers in 512 local authorities. The outcome here saw the ascendancy in the final pay awards for typical 'feminine' occupations such as home help and care assistant (Richbell, 1988).

Advent of New Pay

'New Pay' is a term first introduced by Lawler (1990). The concept signifies something of a revolutionary change in that it is aimed at a fluid approach where pay can respond to the changing demands of a dynamic environment. But it is about more than just flexible systems for, at its heart, is the mission to unify individual aims and objectives with those of the organization through a culture of commitment or 'moral' involvement (Etzioni, 1975). Implicit in this is a recognition that the adaptability and co-operation of the work force is essential in today's competitive environment.

The reward strategy is the vehicle which drives effort to achieve both individual and organizational goals. The emphasis of new pay is on performance, usually in relation to targets and objectives, pre-agreed with management in line with the overall strategy of the organization. The belief is that this competitive strategy will secure justice for (and the continued employment of) high performers and, at the same time, other staff will be encouraged to raise their own levels of achievement.

Lawler (1990) does indicate that New Pay need not always occasion the implementation of radical change and much will depend on existing practices and the extent to which they facilitate an organization's strategic objectives. The focus on performance does not mean that the total salary package rests on this component. Pay would incorporate a fixed base element necessary to attract and maintain employees and other aspects such as competency-based pay may feature. However, it is the variable element that is regarded as the spur to high achievement. The popular approach has been to centre on individual performance with the 'best' performers identified and rewarded. However, the variable performance-related payment can be collectively based, for example in terms of team performance or pitched at an organizational level, using profit sharing or gain sharing schemes.

Underlying new pay is the belief that firms can become more flexible through being able to adjust rewards; the existing body of literature on new pay heeds little attention to collective bargaining, focusing instead on the net worth of an individual to an organization, and in line with prevailing market realities. In practice, many firms in Britain have chosen not to adopt new pay, owing to a continued commitment to more traditional evaluation-linked reward systems, and the fact that many managers remain committed to long-standing systems that are well-established, enjoy legitimacy, and are founded on a body of implicit understandings with employees (see Marsden, 1999). Moreover, anti-discrimination legislation means that firms may have to justify any imbalances in the courts; this may discourage the use of subjective measures to vary pay.

Nonetheless, a recent CIPD survey (2008) discovered that, in the private sector, general pay awards were fast disappearing, with increasing moves to link pay to personal performance. This trend was also gathering pace in the public and voluntary sectors. There was some recognition of the need to also reward collective employee contributions but here there was variation in approach; the private sector favouring bonus plans or recognition schemes while the public and voluntary sectors moving more towards the use of non-cash recognition schemes.

Criticisms of New Pay

It has been argued that the rationale behind the model is too simplistic. The assumptions rest too closely to rational economic man and the link between the pay package and the level of performance may be less directly related (Lewis, 1996). Certainly, the earlier discussion of classic motivation theories highlights the importance of intrinsic factors and Vroom's (1964) expectancy theory emphasizes the individual and complex nature of the cognitive processes central to motivation and performance.

The variable component of New Pay is based on performance and the measures for judging the level and quality of performance relate to set objectives, which in turn tie performance to overall strategic objectives (Lewis, 1996). On the one side, this is perceived as the strength of performance related pay, in that it encourages and focuses effort and ability directly towards strategic aims. However, in a turbulent environment, where change is the only constant. This approach could be seen as a weakness in that the setting of specific objectives, whether they are individual or group, introduces an element of rigidity into the situation. Individuals may become locked into achieving set targets and objectives even if changing circumstances mean that other actions are more appropriate. Ultimately, the flexible approach at the heart of competitive edge may be lost as aspects of initiative, adaptability and creativity are surrendered to a more static concentration on set criteria for performance.

All these schemes assume that pay policies and practices are ultimately something to be dictated by management (Heery, 1996). Moreover, new pay shifts more risk onto employees: a proportion of pay is shifted into bonuses, etc., allowing the firm to reduce wages in line with perceptions of performance, and, indeed, any external pressures to cut wages (Heery, 1996). Despite all the rhetoric of objectivity and of scientific approaches, invariably pay is calculated at least in part due to soft ratings, and/or perceptions of customer satisfaction (ibid.). However, if rewards are seen as unfair, more employees will leave (Scott and Dean, 1992). Hence, employee discontent may also stem from the process of judging performance, usually via some form of appraisal. Issues of subjectivity and fairness may colour perceptions of justice in the process and may spill over into employee/management relations. For further discussion of appraisal see Chapter 11.

In many organizations, new pay has directed the variable component to rewarding individual performance. Where individuals have previously enjoyed a more open approach to pay with a structured and often agreed pay scale, this introduces an element of secrecy into the situation. Individuals, performing the same work, may now receive differing salaries and be left wondering what variations exist.

Further criticism arises from the potentially divisive nature of individual performance related pay when imposed on work situations which involve group work or at least co-operative behaviours between employees. Indeed, this reflects the nature of much modern day work. In such situations, to pick out and reward one individual runs the risk of causing the patterns of behaviour outlined in Adam's equity theory. In short, fellow employees may withhold effort and co-operation or manifest other withdrawal indices if they feel their efforts are undervalued.

It would seem that a more inclusive approach to performance related pay with judgements on a group or organizational level would avoid some of the above criticisms. Certainly, such an approach would erase the above concerns. The potential conflict then would come from 'easy riders', those individuals who failed to meet accepted levels of performance. This is where the test for the success of culture change would be apparent. Could group norms and, indeed, organizational norms lift the performance of deviants when backed by a high commitment culture?

Conclusion

Like any other area of HRM, managing reward is a complex business that is difficult to approach objectively; ultimately, subjective interpretations of employees (either individually or collectively) and supervisors make it difficult to impose 'scientific' systems. This means that, for most organizations, pay setting is likely to be bound up with the institutional setting and its own history. Firms are likely to adopt practices broadly in line with its peers, regional and/or national norms and rules, both to adhere to the law and to lower transaction costs (Marsden, 1999). By the latter it is meant that the 'indeterminate exchange' will work better if a body of unwritten rules and conventions are taken for granted.

Heightened competitive pressures and the decline of unions has in many liberal market economies resulted in firms placing a greater priority on individually orientated performance based reward systems. On the one hand, reward is about both pay and a host of intangibles. On the other hand, the more gung-ho HR literature appears somewhat naïve at times (see Blundell, 2000). In the end, the modern employment contract is about pay and pay related factors; all manner of hot air about caring, communication, belonging and all manner of other 'soft motivators' is likely to be meaningless to employees unless they can count on a decent wage and proper job security.

References

Adams, J. S. (1965). 'Inequity in social exchange', in L. Berlowitz, (Ed.) *Advances in Experimental Social Psychology*, Vol. 2. New York: Academic Press.

Armstrong, M. and Stephens, T. (2005). *A Handbook of Employee Reward Management and Practice.* London: Kogan Page.

Blundell, J. (2000). McJob, McCheque, McWonderful'. *Economic Affairs*, 20(1): 44–6.

Brewster, C., Wood, G., Croucher, R. and Brookes, M. (2007). 'Collective and individual voice: convergence in Europe?', *International Journal of Human Resource Management*, 18(7): 1246–62.

Burawoy, M. (1979). *Manufacturing Consent.* Chicago: University of Chicago Press.

CIPD (2008). *Reward Management: Survey Report 2008.* London: CIPD.

Cappelli, P. (Ed.). (1999). *Change at Work.* Oxford: Oxford University Press.

Donovan Commission (1968). *Report of the Royal Commission on Trade Unions and Employers Associations*, 1965–68, Cmnd. 3623. London: HMSO.

Dure, R. (2000). Stock Market Capitalism: Welfare Capitalism. Cambridge: Cambridge University Press.

Etzioni, A. (1975). *A Comparative Analysis of Complex Organisations.* New York: Free Press.

Heery, E. (1996). 'Risk, reward and the new pay', *Personnel Review*, 25(6): 54–65.

Herzberg, F. (1966). *Work and the Nature of Man.* Cleveland, Ohio: World Publishing.

Hyman, R. (1989). *The Political Economy of Industrial Relations: Theory and Practice in a Cold Climate.* London: Macmillan.

Lado, A. and Wilson, M. (1994). 'Human resource systems and sustained competitive advantage,' *Academy of Management Review*, 19(4): 699–727.

Lawler, E. E. (1990). *Strategic Pay.* San Francisco, Calif: Jossey Bass.

Lewis, P. (1996). 'Exploring Lawlers new pay theory through the case of Finbanks reward strategy for managers', *Personnel Review*, 29(1): 10–32.

Maslow, A. (1954). *Motivation and Personality*, New York: Harper Row.

Richbell, S. (1988). 'Equal value through job evaluation: perspectives on recent British experience', *Equal Opportunities International*, 7(2): 21–9.

Rousseau, D. (1998). 'The problem of the psychological contract', *Journal of Organisational Behaviour*, 19, 665–71

Rousseau, D. (2001). 'Schema, promise and mutuality: the building blocks of the psychological contract', *Journal of Occupational and Organisational Psychology,* Vol. 74, 511–41.

Royle, T. (2000). Working for McDonald's in Europe. London: Routledge.

Scott, S. and Dean, J. (1992). 'Integrated manufacturing and human resource management: a human capital approach', *Academy of Management Journal*, 35(3): 467–504.

Thompson, P. and McHugh, D. (1999). *Work Organizations*. London: Macmillan.

Toynbee, P. and Walker, D. (2008). *Unjust Rewards*. Cambridge: Granta.

Vroom, V. H. (1964). *Work and Motivation.* New York: John Wiley.

13 Human resource development

Irena Grugulis

Introduction

Human resource development is like many other virtues in that those who advocate it easily outnumber actual practitioners. Some organizations do indeed do a great deal in this area and do it extremely well. And the principles of training, knowledge, skills and development have few detractors, yet, particularly in the market driven economies of the USA and Britain, there are still many firms which operate on the basis of zero skills in which labour is a cost to be minimized. What this chapter seeks to do, in common with the others in this text, is sift the realities of labour market practice from the rhetoric of enthusiasm about the idea of development. It considers the advantages of skill, the way skills are changing and the difference that various work environments can make.

What is human resource development?

John Storey, one of the first researchers in Britain to focus seriously on the nature of human resource management and write about the development of resourceful humans, was careful to distinguish between the training workers received and the realities of the workplace. A distinction also observed by his interviewees (Storey, 1992: 8):

> It's indoctrination isn't it? Nobody wants to go on all these courses, people find them very boring. We go because we have to, there's no choice. They are just something you have to get through. Even the trainers are bored. They go through the same lines time after time, using the same scripts and even the same jokes. What a waste of time! They gave us little lapel badges with 'TC' on them and told us anyone wearing one of these would be approached by interesting people in the pub.
>
> *Well, what did you do with yours? Did you wear it?*
>
> [Laughs] No! I threw it away. It's not just me either. There are 20 in my team. Not one of them has started wearing the badge. They'd be too embarrassed to now.

> *So what is going on? What is the meaning of total quality to you and all of the other changes we've been talking about?*
>
> As far as I'm concerned it's about getting us all to work harder. It means sacking half the blokes and getting the other half to work twice as hard.

But as Storey went on to point out:

> behind this impasse on attitudes, there had been, even in this case, substantial changes in work patterns and behaviour. Productivity was higher, the range of responsibilities shouldered was much wider.

It seems that human resource development and developing resourceful humans is not solely about the activities of corporate training departments (although these may certainly play a part). Rather it involves the skills, knowledge, expertise and experience that individuals possess; the way firms choose to compete, set out their strategies and design jobs; and the way individual workers are seen by society (Cockburn, 1983).

It is that perspective on the nature of work and the way work impacts on skills and skills impact on work which this chapter presents. It starts by considering the way people are prepared for work in various countries through education and vocational training, reviews the very different ways work can be designed, describes the impact of gender and race on perceptions of skill then explores the ways that definitions of skills are changing. It concludes with a brief discussion on the future of work. In the skills arena, predictions often focus on one of two, diametrically opposing, scenarios. The first, optimistic, one is that we are heading towards a 'knowledge society' (Leadbeater, 2000), that work is becoming more intellectually demanding, and firms and nations are competing on the basis of innovation and bespoke services with routine jobs effectively automated away. The second prediction is pessimistic. It argues that, as employers seek ever more control over the work process, deskilling is inevitable (Braverman, 1974) and that work is becoming more routine and more alienating for those doing it. Clearly each of these has very different implications for skill development.

Developing the workers

The terms training and development can cover a multitude of activities and it is important to distinguish between some of these. Our main focus is, after all, on skills development and we should not assume that all training will increase or improve skills. We need to consider the activities involved, the duration of the training and the extent to which either employee or employers benefit from the process. Some courses, like the short workshops described so critically by Storey's (1992) interviewee, convey information about a new management initiative and keep workers informed but do little to raise skill levels; others, like the tips on voice control described by Callaghan and Thompson (2002), benefit the employer rather than the employee; while the games played by call centre workers that Nick Kinnie and his colleagues (2000) describe, have little to do with building skills and are simply concerned with helping employees to have fun to distract them from the realities of dull, tightly controlled and alienating work. At the other extreme some activities, such as the three-year work and study based training served by accountants, are challenging, held in high regard and add a significant premium to participants' salaries (Anderson-Gough *et al.,* 1998). Each of these activities are very different, and have a very different effect on those who participate in them. Neither the developmental process workers go through, nor its impact, are generic.

Attempting to separate training that builds skills from that which does not is difficult at the national level but there are some worrying indications. In the USA employers frequently complain that much of their training spend is remedial (Rubery and Grimshaw, 2003), while in Britain two of the top three training activities funded by employers were health and safety and induction (Self, 2008) with temporary workers, who by definition are regularly in need of induction training, receiving more training than permanent ones (Heyes and Gray, 2003). This is not to argue that remedial education, health and safety training and induction are not worthwhile activities. They are, but they do little to enhance the skills base.

Areas of excellent practice do exist. In the USA, firm level training is erratic but there are pockets of high skills elites in sectors such as financial services, aero engineering, entertainment, biotechnology and software, supported by excellent educational programmes (Rubery and Grimshaw, 2003; Crouch, 2005). In Britain, while some industry sectors do have strong traditions of workplace learning these represent pockets of excellence. Governments of all persuasions have intervened repeatedly, but national vocational training initiatives have not been an unqualified success (Grugulis, 2003). Set against this, the proportion of young people staying on at school and progressing to further and higher education has increased markedly and this provision may well incorporate areas covered by employers elsewhere (Keep and Ashton, 2004). But the number of workers with qualifications and the level of those qualifications have both increased impressively such that, by 2006 some six million workers were qualified to degree level, 2.7 million held equivalent professional qualifications and 6.4 million were qualified to intermediate level (Felstead *et al*., 2007b: 44).

But the USA and Britain are liberal market economies where most forms of state intervention are discouraged, many organizations are funded by shareholder capitalism and inter-firm collaboration is strongly discouraged. In co-ordinated market economies, such as Germany, France and the Nordic countries, relations between capital, labour and the state are very different (Ashton, 2004). In these regulated nations employer-groups collaborate to foster innovation and maintain skill levels, organizational capital is more 'patient' and less focused on short-term profits and industrial relations systems tend to be co-operative rather than adversarial (for a fuller discussion of this see Whitley, 1999; Thelen, 2004).

Such intervention encourages national provision which is linked to rigorous workplace activity, and often leads to prestigious qualifications and regulation ensures that employers train and that training is satisfactory. In Germany just over two-thirds of the workforce have successfully undertaken apprenticeships in the area in which they work and jobs tend to be designed to make best use of the skills workers possess (Mason *et al.,* 1996; Rubery and Grimshaw, 2003). Taiwan provides extensive technical education and training through the education system (Green *et al*., 1999). French employers are required to support training or pay a levy of 1.5 per cent of turnover plus an apprenticeship tax of 0.5 per cent of turnover to the state (Steedman, 2001). According to Harcourt and Wood (2007), while an initial survey of the amount of training reveals little international difference, more detailed enquiry demonstrates that, in co-ordinated economies, training is of both higher quality and longer duration.

Clearly the distinction between regulated (or co-ordinated) and liberal (or unregulated) market economies is a simplistic one. Few nations are prepared to completely abandon the idea of all economic intervention and even regulated states will not legislate for every activity. Even the USA, which has little to no regulation of skills at workplace level, funds an excellent national and state education system from which skilled workers are drawn (Whitley, 1999). The British and Australian governments intervene extensively in attempts to improve the supply of skills (Buchanan *et al.,* 2004; Keep and Ashton, 2004). German apprenticeships provide high quality and widely recognized qualifications for young people but, after that, much continuing development is as *ad hoc* and variable as in market economies (Culpepper, 1999). And it is difficult to apply either label to Japan, where there is little regulation but extensive economic co-ordination by large firms, which affects both their internal labour markets and that of their clients and suppliers (Thelen, 2004).

Perhaps what is most significant is that both market-based and regulated training can be successful. Some elites fare well in the US where challenging tasks, links to prestigious universities and professional contacts all help to develop expertise (Finegold, 1999). However the majority are often ill-served or neglected. When training is regulated a great deal of effort is focused on ensuring that the majority of workers are covered, provision is of high quality, workers are challenged to develop valuable skills and programmes are very relevant to the long term needs of industry sectors. But when most activity is targeted at intermediate level qualifications or activities, experts may fare less well.

Developing the work

But education and training is only part of the process, 'skill in the job' (Cockburn 1983: 311) is also key to workplace learning. Challenging projects, opportunities to exercise judgement, discretionary space and contacts with informed colleagues all help to develop skills, just as routine work, tightly timed activities, rules for decisions and limited contact with others restrict them (see Grugulis, 2007). Two contrasting examples may serve to illustrate this. Robertson *et al.* (2003) describe 'ScienceCo', a company that specialized in scientific innovations and patenting new work where 116 of the 140 employees were scientists (most with PhDs), where project teams were unstructured with leaders, who were often relatively inexperienced consultants, 'emerging' for each project. Personal and divisional revenue targets were set and employees described as both compe titive and combative but there was no onus on them to account rigorously for their time so they could, if they chose, work through weekends and take extended holidays of two or three months or work for 24 hours solid and take a couple of days off. Work was documented so that the firm could gain patents but most learning took place through experimentation (see also Grugulis, 2007; McKinlay *et al.*, 2000).

At the other end of the spectrum McDonald's famously competes on the basis that a Big Mac is the same, wherever in the world it is bought and that French fries served in Paris are the same as those provided in Dublin, Birmingham and New York. Yet to achieve this, they strip out employee skill and discretion from every aspect of the work process. The Operations and Training Manual (known to staff as 'the Bible') provides detailed prescriptions for every aspect of working life. Its 600 pages include full colour photographs illustrating the proper placement of ketchup, mustard and pickle on every type of burger, set out the six steps of counter service and even prescribe the arm motions that should be used in salting a batch of fries. Kitchen and counter technology reinforce these instructions as lights and buzzers tell workers when to turn burgers or take fries out of the fat, ketchup dispensers provide measured amounts of product in the requisite 'flower' pattern and lights on the till remove the need for serving staff to write out orders as well as prompting them to offer additional items (Leidner, 1993; Ritzer, 1996; Royle, 2000). Nor is this codification of work restricted to fast food operatives. Workers on the line in manufacturing companies find their actions timed and monitored to a tenth of a second (Pollert, 1981; Garrahan and Stewart, 1992; Delbridge, 1998); call centre employees are told what to say and how to say it, with calls tightly timed and performance data displayed on public view during shifts (Taylor and Bain, 1999; Taylor *et al.*, 2002); and fitness instructors can work to scripts and choreographed routines so that a keep fit enthusiast could attend a 'BodyPump' or 'BodyStep' class anywhere in the world and be sure of knowing exactly what to expect (Felstead *et al.*, 2007a). Even 'knowledge work' such as computer programming can be broken down into its constituent parts and cheaper 'coders' hired who need to (and do) know nothing about the whole system but simply write, rewrite and paste their lines of code (Barrett, 2004).

Fuller and Unwin (2004) describe this process as a choice between *expansive* and *restrictive* working environments (see Table 13.1). In an expansive environment, where learning, development and skills are encouraged workers are more likely to be members of multiple 'communities of practice', with knowledgeable colleagues in the workplace and appropriate professional contacts outside. They may have planned time off the job, skills are valued and opportunities exist for career progression. In a restrictive environment workers are likely to be confined to a narrow range of tasks with limited opportunities for professional contacts, technical skills may be taken for granted, only key workers have their skills developed, expertise is imposed from the top down and innovation is not considered important.

Table 13.1 Approaches to workforce development

Expansive	*Restrictive*
Participation in mutiple communities of practice inside and outside the workplace.	Restricted participation in multiple communities practice
Primary community of practice has shared 'participative memory': cultural inheritance of workforce development	Primary community of practice has little or no 'participative memory': no or little tradition of apprenticeship
Breadth: access to learning fostered by cross-company experience	Narrow: access to learning restricted in terms of tasks/knowledge/location
Access to range of qualifications including knowledge based vocational qualifications	Little or no access to qualifications
Planned time off-the-job including for knowledge-based courses and for reflection	Virtually all on-the-job: limited opportunities for reflection
Gradual transition to full, rounded participation	Fast–transition as quick as possible
Vision of workplace learning: progression for career	Vision of workplace learning: static for job
Organizational recognition of, and support for, employees as learners	Lack of organizational recognition of, and support for, employees as learners
Workforce development is used as a vehicle for aligning the goals of developing the individual and organizational capability	Workforce development is used to tailor individual capability to organizational need
Workforce development fosters opportunities to extend identity through boundary crossing	Workforce development limits opportunities to extend identity: little boundary crossing experienced
Reification of 'workplace curriculum' highly developed (e.g. through documents, symbols, language, tools) and accessible to apprentices	Little reification of 'workplace curriculum', patchy access to reificatory aspects of practice
Widely distributed skills	Polarized distribution of skills
Technical skills valued	Technical skills taken for granted
Knowledge and skills of whole workforce developed and valued	Knowledge and skills of key workers/ groups developed and valued
Team work valued	Rigid specialist roles
Cross-boundary communication encouraged	Bounded communication
Managers as facilitators of workforce and individual development	Managers of controllers of workforce and individual development
Chances to learn new skills/jobs	Barriers to learning new skills/jobs
Innovation important	Innovation not important
Multidimensional view of expertise	Unidimensional top-down view of expertise

Taken from Fuller and Unwin (2004).

Yet the way work is designed is not set in stone. Rather, it is a matter of choice exercised by employers. Take retail workers. In Britain this is considered an unskilled job. Staff are rarely required to know much about products sold other than their location and recruitment often focuses primarily on availability for shift work, with single young women who live with their parents near the store preferred over other candidates. It is, as Gadrey (2000: 26) describes 'tantamount to a personnel strategy based on zero competence', zero qualifications, zero training and zero career. But this is not the case everywhere. In France customers demand product knowledge of the people who serve them (McGauran, 2000, 2001), in Germany two and three year retail apprenticeships train staff in product knowledge, sales, retail management and other aspects of the work, which makes them invaluable 'anchor workers' on the shop floor (Kirsch *et al.*, 2000) and in British and American owned outlets in China the combination of high pay, 'frighteningly well educated' applicants, demanding customers and rapid promotion ensure a ready supply of skilled workers (Gamble, 2006). Even for ostensibly simple jobs, there are different ways of designing work and using labour effectively.

Given this, it should be, and is, possible for a firm to change the way it uses labour, the problem is that few organizations take this as their primary focus. Enda Hannon's (2005, 2006) work in the Irish dairy industry assesses the impact of an official initiative which helped firms to switch from selling milk (an unprocessed staple good) to more 'value added' production. The dairies he studied started manufacturing specialist baby foods, cheese sticks for children and 'functional foods' such as yoghurts or pro-biotic drinks. These certainly helped the companies become more profitable. But the changes to the products did not necessarily increase workers' skills. Most of the knowledge intensive activities were concentrated at managerial and technical levels and large numbers of research and development jobs were created but few shop-floor workers benefited and one firm actually deskilled its operatives by moving to full automation. High specification products do not always require high specification work. Increases to the customer service levels in service industries are often achieved by a simple increase in the number of people employed rather than any rise in skill levels. Even industries with extensive investment in research and development, such as pharmaceuticals, combine small numbers of highly skilled knowledge workers who develop and test new treatments with much larger numbers of un- or semi-skilled operatives on the factory line producing the pills.

Managing to discriminate

Together with skill in the person and skill in the job we should also consider what Cockburn (1983: 113) describes as 'skill in the social setting', the tendency for factors which have nothing to do with skill, such as gender, race, age or appearance, to be used as a proxy for judgements on ability, capacity and achievements. This is not peculiar to skills (see Collinson *et al.,* 1990, for an account of gendered recruitment practices), rather skills are subject to such judgements because they are common in wider society and the status in which a particular group is held generally impacts on the skills they are deemed to possess. To the extent that Green and Ashton (1992) argued that there was little point in asking employers whether particular jobs were skilled or unskilled, since the only conclusion the researchers could reach on this evidence was the gender of the workers employed, as men's work was consistently rated as skilled and women's unskilled.

These gendered and racialized assumptions are of more than historical significance. A hospital in Carlisle was taken to the European courts for systematically devaluing the skills of women workers so that the (predominantly women) cleaners, nurses and cooks were paid less, and enjoyed less favourable terms and conditions than male cleaners, carpenters and plumbers (see an article by A. Browne in *The Observer*, 15th July 2001). One American bank chose to restructure along highly gendered lines, effectively demoting its many women managers and promoting male staff (Skuratowicz and Hunter, 2004). High flyers are also affected. According to McGuire (2000: 518):

> Few white women or people of colour occupy the types of managerial positions . . . in which they can perform extraordinary tasks, for which they are likely to acquire the label of *high potential*. [Emphasis in original]

It seems that, as Reskin and Roos (1990) argue, the labour market is effectively a 'labour queue' in which white men precede both women and black and ethnic minority workers, with judgements often legitimized by being labelled skills.

'New' skills and new opportunities?

This three-fold definition of skills, skill in the person, skill in the job and skill in the social setting, is a useful one. It captures the different aspects of skill well and brings out the way that skill in one area (say, skill in the person) may not necessarily be translated to practice (skill in the job, because of the way work is carried out) or may not be widely recognized (skill in the social setting, because of the gender or race of the person possessing the skill).

It is also useful, when considering how skilled a group of people are, to review the way skills are changing. Traditionally, the word skill was associated with technical work which resulted in physical products. Plumbers, bricklayers, welders and carpenters were (and are) all skilled trades and an individual's skill could be demonstrated by fixing a leak, building a wall or carving out decorative patterns on furnishings. But as Payne (1999) and Keep (2001) observe, in recent years the term skill has been used to describe much more intangible attitudes and attributes. It has effectively been extended to incorporate (among others) communication, problem solving, customer service, team-working, discipline, punctuality, friendliness and ability to fit in. The lists of desirable qualities are lengthy and vary, from the 'style' labour markets of boutiques and glamorous hotels demands for a persona that is 'passionate, stylish, confident, tasty, clever, successful and well-travelled' (Warhurst and Nickson, 2001: 14) to the more mundane getting on with work mates (Payne, 1999).

To a certain extent, this focus on attitudes is not new. Employers have always been interested in the 'type of people' employees are. Ford Motor Company's famous $5 a day was paid only to virtuous employees (Beynon, 1975) while Oliver and Turton (1982: 199) dubbed the emphasis on 'stable', 'reliable' and 'responsible' workers the Good Bloke Syndrome. It may be that labour market changes have simply brought this into sharper relief. The dominance of the service sector and the increasing use of team-working in manufacturing have both changed the nature of work. In service work the process of being served is as much a part of the purchase as any physical product (Noon and Blyton, 2007) so an employee's appearance, their feelings about work and the feelings they stimulate in others are now part of the wage-effort bargain to be managed rather than a personal and private matter of no concern to the employer. As a result flight attendants are expected to be slender, nurturing, attentive and flirtatious, debt collectors 'create alarm' to persuade debtors to pay (Hochschild, 1983), and call centre workers must establish rapport then, just as quickly, emotionally disengage (Korczynski, 2001). Work is about appearing and feeling as much as doing.

However, while such attributes have been part of work in the past, they have not previously been labelled as skills. It may be that such a shift is not significant, that what matters is the substance of workplace practice, rather than the label attached to it but this relabelling does have two clear disadvantages. First, it individualizes responsibility for the skills. Issues that might previously have been considered part of the remit of the human resource department (demotivation caused by pay rates or poor management practice, high turnover, poor communications) now become problems with individual workers with any reciprocal and relational aspects ignored. Second, it conveys the impression that such skills are generic. Yet this is far from being the case. Effective communication, problem solving or team-working depend on what is being communicated, solved or worked on as well as who is doing it. The person who could communicate the rules of cricket extremely well might struggle to convey those of American football, bridge or ice hockey, not because they had become a less able communicator but because they knew little of what was involved in the games.

With this in mind it is instructive to see what happens with soft and social skills in practice. Amongst those who are already highly educated and highly skilled it seems to be an advantage. In computing, greater pay premiums are available when technical knowledge is combined with soft skills and IT experts are able to problem solve or put systems into practice (Green *et al*., 2007). Most of the main accountancy firms (including KPMG, Coopers and Lybrand and Ernst and Young) hire image consultants to advise their professional staff (PriceWaterhouse extends this to advice on dining etiquette for prospective partners). The Law Society publishes guidelines on the way that solicitors should dress and Barclays Bank provided grooming sessions for all employees when they introduced a new uniform (Anderson-Gough *et al*., 2000; Wellington and Bryson, 2001). The problems occur when these new 'soft skills' are not accompanied by technical skills. Despite repeated claims of skill shortages in key areas (such as customer service) there is no pay premium for soft and social skills (Bolton, 2004) and there is some evidence that technical skills training is being sidelined by the focus on attitudes. So in Canada and the USA return to work training has become a zero sum game with a 'combination of harsh discipline and hokey motivational seminars' (Butterwick, 2003; Lafer, 2004: 120), replacing more substantive content. Low skilled workers are effectively being denied access to the traditional career ladders which used to help them out of low paid jobs.

This concentration on soft skills and neglect of technical skills causes organizational problems too. When London's Heathrow airport launched its prestigious terminal 5 the effort that had gone into designing the £4.3 billion project was not matched by technical training for the staff. Repeated workshops showed inspiring computer generated images of the future of air travel, popcorn was distributed and staff were given mock boarding cards asking 'Are you up for it?' But in the end employee enthusiasm and commitment were not enough. On the day the terminal officially opened staff (including senior executives) found that they could not park in the terminal, get into the building, work the computer terminals nor understand the building layout. Flights were cancelled, thousands of people lost their luggage (to the extent that several insurance companies refused to cover items passing through terminal 5) and both companies involved, BA and BAA, were roundly condemned. Part, though by no means all, of the problem, was that technical and practical training was marginalized and limited to a few days, management refused to meet with unions to discuss their concerns and large numbers of experienced staff took voluntary redundancy before the opening (Doward, 2008; Radio 4, 2008).

How much knowledge and skills do we need?

It seems that the developmental picture is a mixed one. Work based training varies in the extent to which it equips workers with new, valuable skills. Work may assist the learning process but it can also restrict it, confining employees to repetitive and routinized tasks. And social judgements based on an individual's gender or race can both enhance the skills they are assumed to possess and diminish them. Recent changes to the way the word skill is used are just as confusing. Focusing on an individual's attitudes and attributes can provide those who are already highly technically skilled with effective ways of putting their technical skills into practice but it may also deprive those who lack technical skills of opportunities to develop them and access better paid work.

These complexities reflect the realities of the workplace, where knowledge jobs exist side by side with unskilled work. But they are often ignored by enthusiastic optimists who claim that work is changing and that the new economy will be dominated by knowledge-intensive jobs. If this is true, if *iMac* jobs are set to outnumber and possibly eliminate *McJobs* (Warhurst and Thompson, 1998) then such a change will have significant implications for both work and skills so it is worth assessing both existing data and the extent to which we can observe any indications of change.

There are certainly grounds for optimism. The number of people with qualifications is rising and some jobs seem to be becoming more demanding. In Britain in 1986 22 per cent of jobs required more than two years of preparatory training, by 2006 this figure had increased to 30 per cent. At the other end of the work spectrum, the proportion of jobs which needed less than one month's training had shrunk from 27 per cent to 19 per cent (Felstead *et al.*, 2007b: 53–4). But while the trend is encouraging, the overall data does not really support predictions about the knowledge society. Rather, with just under 15 million jobs requiring level four qualifications (a broad category including degrees and professional qualifications) and 13.6 million requiring none or the most basic (p. 37) it would seem that this is an 'hourglass economy' (Nolan and Slater, 2003: 78) in which jobs have polarized. Worldwide this trend is more marked, with the number of unskilled jobs growing rapidly and far outstripping knowledge work (Green, 2006). Nor does it seem likely that this growth is temporary, a transition phase as the number of well paid knowledge jobs grows. Rather, the existence of knowledge work makes many of the unskilled jobs necessary as people outsource their coffee making, childcare and cleaning to others. Unlike routine work in manufacturing, person-to-person services are almost impossible to automate.

There are also some areas for concern. In Britain, the growth in employee skills and qualifications has not been matched by an equivalent growth in skill demand by jobs. This is an important point since too often economists assume that labour markets operate like markets for currencies with instant 'closure', in which demand and supply meet at the right price so imbalances (in appropriate skills or the number of willing workers) will naturally be corrected. This is not the case for the very simple reason that labour markets are different to currency dealing and here, imbalances between the supply and demand of skills have been growing over the past 20 years. As a result, some 40 per cent of workers are now overqualified for their jobs (Felstead *et al.*, 2007b: 83). More than six million graduates are competing for 4.9 million graduate jobs (in 1986 these figures were roughly in balance) and while 7.4 million jobs exist which demand neither skills nor qualifications from their holders only 2.5 million people are unqualified (p. 44). Not only has boosting supply failed to stimulate demand but consistently, throughout the labour market, people are more qualified than their work requires. This is not because, as Braverman (1974) argued, jobs are being deskilled. Rather, it is that 'some low skill jobs cannot be further deskilled because they already call for so little skill' (Rose *et al.*, 1994: 8). What are the implications of this? They could be positive. Enhancing the skills and capacity of employees may mean that they are able and willing to take on more demanding tasks, that there will effectively be a grass roots skills revolution in which workers 'grow' their jobs.

However, for that to happen, the jobs need to have discretionary space so that workers can make decisions over work quality, how to do tasks, setting priorities and so on. Such space allows workers to exercise and develop their skills, undertake problem solving and so on. Yet this space is becoming more and more restricted. In 1986 72 per cent of professionals reported having a great deal of discretion over the way they did their jobs. By 2001 this figure had shrunk to 38 per cent (Felstead *et al.*, 2007b). There is some evidence that this is also happening elsewhere. Green (2006) observes similar declines in discretion in

Belgium, Denmark, Italy, Ireland and Portugal (although interestingly Austria and Germany seem to have escaped this general trend). This decline in discretion stopped, just as the increases in skill stopped, in 2001 and the figures remained stable but while the decline has not continued there is little evidence that it will be reversed. If more jobs are becoming as tightly codified as call centres and McDonald's then it is difficult to see how an increase in qualifications will enable individuals to grow their jobs. It may be that we are simply ensuring that more qualified people become more frustrated at the limits set on their talents. That would be extremely unfortunate.

References

Anderson-Gough, F., Grey, C., and Robson, K. (1998). *Making up Accountants: the organisational and professional socialisation of trainee chartered accountants*. London: Ashgate.

Anderson-Gough, F., Grey, C., and Robson, K. (2000). In the name of the client: the service ethic in two professional service firms, *Human Relations,* 53(9): 1151–74.

Ashton, D. (2004). The political economy of workplace learning, in H. Rainbird, A. Fuller and A. Munro (Eds), *Workplace Learning in Context*. London and New York: Routledge.

Barrett, R. (2004). Working at Webboyz: an analysis of control over the software development labour process, *Sociology,* 38(4): 777–94.

Beynon, H. (1975). *Working for Ford*. Wakefield: EP Publishing Ltd.

Bolton, S. C. (2004). Conceptual confusions: emotion work as skilled work, in C. Warhurst, I. Grugulis and E. Keep (Eds), *The Skills that Matter*. Basingstoke: Palgrave Macmillan.

Braverman, H. (1974). *Labour and Monopoly Capital*. New York: Monthly Review Press.

Buchanan, J., Watson, I. and Briggs, C. (2004). Skill and the renewal of labour: the classical wage-earner model and left productivism in Australia, in C. Warhurst, I. Grugulis, and E. Keep (Eds), *The Skills that Matter*. Basingstoke: Palgrave Macmillan.

Butterwick, S. (2003). Life skills training: open for discussion, in M. G. Cohen (Ed.), *Training the excluded for Work*. Vancouver and Toronto: UBC Press.

Callaghan, G. and Thompson, P. (2002). We recruit attitude: the selection and shaping of routine call centre labour, *Journal of Management Studies,* 39(2): 233–54.

Cockburn, C. (1983). *Brothers: Male Dominance and Technological Change*. London: Pluto Press.

Collinson, D., Knights, D. and Collinson, M. (1990). *Managing to Discriminate*. London and New York: Routledge.

Crouch, C. (2005). Skill formation systems, in S. Ackroyd, R. Batt, P. Thompson and P. S. Tolbert (Eds), *The Oxford Handbook of Work and Organization*. Oxford and New York: Oxford University Press.

Culpepper, P. D. (1999). The future of the high-skill equilibrium in Germany, *Oxford Review of Economic Policy,* 15(1): 43–59.

Delbridge, R. (1998). *Life on the Line in Contemporary Manufacturing*. Oxford: Oxford University Press.

Doward, J. (2008). Lovely airport, Willie, shame it doesn't work, in *The Observer*. London.

Felstead, A., Fuller, A., Jewson, N., Kakavelakis, K. and Unwin, L. (2007a). Grooving to the same tunes? Learning, training and productive systems in the aerobics studio. *Work, Employment and Society*, 21(2): 189–208.

Felstead, A., Gallie, D., Green, F. and Zhou, Y. (2007b). *Skills at Work 1986–2006*. Oxford: SKOPE and ESRC.

Finegold, D. (1999). Creating self-sustaining, high-skill ecosystems, *Oxford Review of Economic Policy,* 15(1): 60–81.

Fuller, A. and Unwin, L. (2004). Expansive learning environments: integrating organisational and personal development, in H. Rainbird, A. Fuller and A. Munro (Eds), *Workplace Learning in Context*. London and New York: Routledge.

Gadrey, J. (2000). Working time configurations: theory, methods and assumptions for an international comparison, in C. Baret, S. Lehndorff and L. Sparks (Eds), *Flexible Working in Food Retailing: a Comparison Between France, Germany, the UK and Japan*. London and New York: Routledge.

Gamble, J. (2006). Multinational retailers in China: proliferating 'McJobs' or developing skills?, *Journal of Management Studies,* 43(7): 1463–90.

Garrahan, P. and Stewart, P. (1992). *The Nissan Enigma: Flexibility at Work in a Local Economy*. London: Mansett.

Green, F. (2006). *Demanding Work: the Paradox of Job Quality in the Affluent Economy*. Princeton and Oxford: Princeton University Press.

Green, F. and Ashton, D. (1992). Skill shortages and skill deficiency: a critique, *Work, Employment and Society,* 6(2): 287–301.

Green, F., Ashton, D., James, D. and Sung, J. (1999). The role of the state in skill formation: evidence from the Republic of Korea, Singapore and Taiwan, *Oxford Review of Economic Policy,* 15(1): 82–96.

Green, F., Felstead, A., Gaillie, D. and Zhou, Y. (2007). Computers and pay, *National Institute Economic Review,* 201(1): 63–75.

Grugulis, I. (2003). The contribution of NVQs to the growth of skills in the UK, *British Journal of Industrial Relations,* 41(3): 457–75.

Grugulis, J. (2007). *Skills, Training and Human Resource Development: a Critical Text*. Basingstoke: Palgrave Macmillan.

Grugulis, I., Dundon, T. and Wilkinson, A. (2000). Cultural control and the culture manager: employment practices in a consultancy, *Work, Employment and Society*, 14(1): 97–116.

Hannon, E. (2005). Prospects for the upskilling of general workers in liberal market economies. Presented at *British Universities Industrial Relations Association*, 7th–9th July, Northumbria University.

Hannon, E. (2006). Interrogating the skills consequences of a strategic industrial policy: case study evidence from the Irish dairy processing industry. Presented at *24th International Labour Process Conference*, 10th–12th April, London.

Harcourt, M. and Wood, G. (2007). The importance of employment protection for skill development in co-ordinated market economies, *European Journal of Industrial Relations* 13(2): 141–59.

Heyes, J. and Gray, A. (2003). The implications of the national minimum wage for training in small firms, *Human Resource Management Journal*, 13(2): 76–86.

Hochschild, A. R. (1983). *The Managed Heart: Commercialization of Human Feeling*. Berkley: University of California Press.

Keep, E. (2001). If it moves, it's a skill. Presented at ESRC Seminar on The Changing Nature of Skills and Knowledge, 3rd–4th September, Manchester.

Keep, E. and Ashton, D. (2004). The state. Presented at *SKOPE High Skills Vision Conference*, 28th–29th October, Lumley Castle.

Kinnie, N., Hutchinson, S. and Purcell, J. (2000). Fun and surveillance: the paradox of high commitment management in call centres, *International Journal of Human Resource Management,* 11(5): 67–85.

Kirsch, J., Klein, M., Lehndorff, S. and Voss-Dahm, D. (2000). The organisation of working time in large German food retail firms. in C. Baret, S. Lehndorff and L. Sparks (Eds), *Flexible Working in Food Retailing: a Comparison Between France, Germany, the UK and Japan*. London and New York: Routledge.

Korczynski, M. (2001). The contradictions of service work: call centre as customer-oriented bureaucracy, in A. Sturdy, I. Grugulis and H. Willmott (Eds), *Customer Service: Empowerment and Entrapment*. Basingstoke: Palgrave.

Lafer, G. (2004). What is skill?, in C. Warhurst, I. Grugulis and E. Keep (Eds), *The Skills that Matter*. Basingstoke: Palgrave Macmillan.

Leadbeater, C. (2000). *Living on Thin Air*. London: Viking.

Leidner, R. (1993). *Fast Food, Fast Talk: Service Work and the Routinizations of Everyday Life*. Berkeley and Los Angeles: University of California Press.

Mason, G., Van Ark, B. and Wagner, K. (1996). Workforce skills, product quality and economic performance, in A. Booth and D. J. Snower (Eds), *Acquiring Skills*. Cambridge: Cambridge University Press.

McGauran, A.-M. (2000). Vive la différence: the gendering of occupational structures in a case study of Irish and French retailing, *Women's Studies International Forum,* 23(5): 613–627.

McGauran, A.-M. (2001). Masculine, feminine or neutral? In-company equal opportunities policies in Irish and French MNC retailing. *International Journal of Human Resource Management,* 12(5): 754–71.

McGuire, G. (2000). Gender, race, ethnicity and networks: the factors affecting the status of employees' network members. *Work and Occupations,* 27(4): 501–23.

McKinlay, A. (2005). Knowledge management, in S. Ackroyd, R. Batt, P. Thompson, and P. S. Tolbert (Eds), *The Oxford Handbook of Work and Organization*, Oxford and New York: Oxford University Press.

Nolan, P. and Slater, G. (2003). The labour market: history, structure and prospects, in P. Edwards (Eds.), *Industrial Relations: Theory and Practice*. Oxford: Blackwell.

Noon, M. and Blyton, P. (2007). *The Realities of Work*. Houndsmills: Palgrave.

Oliver, J. M. and Turton, J. R. (1982). Is there a shortage of skilled labour?, *British Journal of Industrial Relations,* 20(2): 195–200.

Payne, J. (1999). All things to all people: changing perceptions of 'skill' among Britain's policy makers since 1950s and their implications. in *SKOPE Research Paper No.1*. Coventry: University of Warwick.

Pollert, A. (1981). *Girls, Wives, Factory Lives*. Basingstoke: Macmillan.

Radio 4 (2008). File on Four: A Terminal Failure.

Reskin, B. F. and Roos, P. A. (1990). *Job Queues, Gender Queues: Explaining Women's Inroads into Male Occupations*. Philadelphia: Temple University Press.

Ritzer, G. (1996). *The McDonalidization of Society*. Thousand Oaks, California and London: Pine Forge Press.

Robertson, M., Scarbrough, H. and Swan, J. (2003). Knowledge creation in professional service firms: institutional effects, *Organization Studies (after Jan 1, 2003),* 24(6): 831–57.

Rose, M., Penn, R. and Rubery, J. (1994). Introduction, the SCELI skill findings, in R. Penn, M. Rose, and J. Rubery (Eds), *Skill and Occupational Change*. Oxford: Oxford University Press.

Royle, T. (2000). *Working for McDonald's in Europe: the Unequal Struggle*. London: Routledge.

Rubery, J. and Grimshaw, D. (2003). *The Organization of Employment*. Basingstoke: Palgrave Macmillan.

Self, A. (2008). *Social Trends*. Basingstoke: Palgrave Macmillan and Office for National Statistics.

Skuratowicz, E. and Hunter, L.W. (2004). Where do women's jobs come from? Job resegregation in an American Bank, *Work and Occupations,* 31(1): 73–110.

Steedman, H. (2001). *Benchmarking Apprenticeship: UK and Continental Europe Compared*. London: Centre for Economic Performance, LSE.

Storey, J. (1992). *Developments in the Management of Human Resources*. Oxford: Blackwell.

Taylor, P. and Bain, P. (1999). An assembly line in the head: work and employee relations in the call centre, *Industrial Relations Journal,* 30(2): 101–17.

Taylor, P., Mulvey, G., Hyman, J. and Bain, P. (2002). Work organisation, control and the experience of work in call centres, *Work, Employment and Society,* 16(1): 133–50.

Thelen, K. (2004). *How Institutions Evolve: the Political Economy of Skills in Germany, Britain, the United States and Japan*. Cambridge: Cambridge University Press.

Warhurst, C. and Nickson, D. (2001). *Looking Good, Sounding Right*. London: Industrial Society.

Warhurst, C. and Thompson, P. (1998). Hands, hearts and minds: changing work and workers at the end of the century, in P. Thompson and C. Warhurst (Eds), *Workplaces of the Future*. London: Macmillan.

Wellington, C. A. and Bryson, J. R. (2001). At face value? Image consultancy, emotional labour and professional work, *Sociology,* 35(4): 933–946.

Whitley, R. (1999). *Divergent Capitalisms: the Social Structuring and Change of Business Systems*. Oxford: Oxford University Press.

14 Industrial relations and human resource management

Gilton Klerck

Introduction

The aim of this chapter is to consider the analytical purchase of the concept of 'industrial relations' and the explanatory power of its key expressions. Industrial relations (IR), conceived in narrow terms as a study of the institutions and processes of 'joint regulation', is increasingly regarded as an outmoded residue of modernity and industrialism. Developments in managerial thinking, such as human resource management (HRM), allegedly constitute a serious challenge to IR as a 'discipline'. Godard and Delaney, for instance, regard HRM as a 'new industrial relations paradigm' replacing 'research on unions and collective bargaining as the field's core' (cited in Bacon, 2003: 72). The postulated eclipse of IR by HRM is premised on an unduly restricted definition of employee relations. Rather than repeat the detail of HRM's impact on 'conventional' IR, the focus of this chapter is principally on the key features of a broader conception of IR. The latter contradicts many of the cosy assumptions about strategic integration, employee 'involvement', 'high commitment' management, and so on found in the HRM literature. In contrast to this literature, which is driven by an employer's agenda, the approach adopted here highlights the uncertainties, contradictions and tensions associated with the realignment of the local and the global, the shifting balance between incorporation and marginalization in the labour market, and the changing links between capital accumulation and social regulation. The chapter commences with an outline of the employment relationship as a historically contingent exchange relation that is socially embedded and dependent on institutional mediation for its reproduction. It then examines the 'crisis' of IR in practice, briefly considers theoretical critiques of IR by subjectivist and action-orientated approaches, and outlines some of the pitfalls in HRM as revealed by a focus on labour regulation. The chapter concludes by highlighting some of the challenges confronting the future of IR research.

The employment relationship

Industrial relations, as Edwards (2003: 338–9) observes, is 'a field of study rather than an academic discipline . . . [that contains] some distinctive perceptions which are more than the sum total of individual disciplines'. The origins of institutionalized IR lie in a public policy commitment to achieve and maintain a balance between the problems of social welfare and social control in industry (Hyman, 1989). Bain and Clegg (1974: 95) defined IR as 'the study of all aspects of job regulation – the making and administering of the rules which regulate employment relationships – regardless of whether these are seen as being formal or informal, structured or unstructured'. With some notable exceptions, however, most IR research can be located within a narrower definition of the field than the one identified by Bain and Clegg. While important conceptual innovations arose from the research on the institutions of 'job regulation', the literature was characterized by fact-finding and description rather than theoretical generalization. The analytical debate that took place centred largely on the need to establish a conceptual framework for the predominantly pragmatic and empirical concerns of IR, to clarify the boundaries of teaching and research, and to establish some degree of intellectual respectability vis-á-vis other applied fields of study and social science disciplines. Winchester (1983: 101–2) cites a number of indicators of this trend: examples of successful multi-disciplinary research are rare; most research still focuses on workplace and plant studies in private manufacturing industry; a fairly eclectic approach to methodological issues is common; and assumptions of policy relevance still characterize much of the literature.

Underlying the concept of 'job regulation' in orthodox IR theories is the notion of equilibrium: regulatory mechanisms tend to be in perfect harmony with their environment and the process of regulation itself is predictable, stable and seemingly trouble-free (Dabscheck, 1993). Historically, the bulk of IR research concentrated on the form of institutions and ignored the processes through which they are reproduced. The focus was on the status of institutions rather than the maintenance of relations. There is a growing consensus that research in IR needs to go beyond a largely functionalist description of the dynamics of job regulation to a theoretically informed analysis of the expanded reproduction of the inherently unstable and conflict-ridden relationship between capital and labour. Edwards (1995: 13–16) identifies three levels of analysis within the analytical perspective on rules. The first level concerns the immediate balance of cooperation and conflict in the workplace. To avoid the stark choice between whether employers and employees have interests that are shared (human relations theories) or that conflict (labour process theories), there is an acknowledgement that both are integral components of the employment relationship. The second level focuses on the broader policies underlying the management of the employment relationship. These policies are usually explored in terms of the association between strategic choice and technological determinism. The third level concerns the fundamental nature of the employment relationship. Here there is an attempt to move beyond simply noting that both conflict and cooperation are important.

The object of inquiry

The fundamental object of inquiry that defines the field of IR is not trade unions, management or industrial conflict, but the relationship that generates these phenomena – i.e. the *employment relationship*. The purpose of IR, as Edwards (1995) points out, is the control, adaptation and adjustment or regulation of the employment relationship. Likewise, Salamon (1998: 3) regards IR as 'a set of phenomena, both within and outside the workplace, concerned with determining and regulating the employment relationship'. It is possible to discern, Blyton and Turnbull (1998: 28) argue, a growing tendency

> to focus on and define the distinctive characteristics of the *employment relationship*; to locate that relationship within the broader *nature of economic activity*; to analyze the *structural bases* of conflict and accommodation between employer and employee; to consider the influence of the *wider society*; and to develop an *interdisciplinary approach* using concepts and ideas derived from sociology, economics, psychology, history and political science.

The employment relationship is one of the great innovations that lie behind the rise of the modern business enterprise. It revolutionized the organization of work, providing managers and workers with a very flexible method of coordination and a basis for investing in skills (Marsden, 1999). In its most basic form, every employment relationship is an economic exchange (an agreement to exchange wages for work) and a power relation (the employee 'agrees' to submit to the authority of the employer). While Braverman's (1974) seminal work has been widely criticized, what must be retained from his analysis is a rejection of the view of the employment relationship as merely an exchange relationship, as primarily a site of bargaining rather than of exploitation. In the 'hidden abode' of production, 'labour and capital come together in a way that is at once a market transaction, a labour process, and a scene of daily life: that is the employment relation' (Storper and Walker, 1989: 168). The employment relationship may be defined as 'the set of conditions determining the exchange, use and reproduction of the labour force' (Michon, 1992: 224). This conception of the employment relationship clearly goes beyond the traditional concerns of IR research. On this view, collective bargaining is merely one aspect of IR.

The employment relationship is not an abstract notion, but one of 'practical significance, being the basis of the parties' own interactions and the relationship upon which all other aspects of employee relations develop' (Blyton and Turnbull, 1998: 5). It encompasses the processes through which employees are recruited, rewarded, motivated and disciplined, as well as the ways in which the key actors in the labour market respond to these processes. Unlike other factors of production, the employer cannot precisely specify the quantity and quality of tasks to be performed by an employee in advance. Every workplace must therefore solve an implacable dilemma at the heart of the employment relationship – i.e. the conversion of labour power into actual labour – through the negotiation of order between employers and employees. The key point about the indeterminacy of the labour contract and strategies of labour control is that

> managers and workers are locked into a relationship that is contradictory and antagonistic . . . There is thus a relation of 'structured antagonism' between

> employer and worker. This term is used to stress that the antagonism is built into the basis of the relationship, even though on a day-to-day level cooperation is also important (Edwards, 1995: 15).

The employee's claim to wages and the employer's claim to performance involve an asymmetrical reciprocity. Management therefore has to find ways and means of legitimating its authority in the eyes of the workers if it is to gain their cooperation and release their creativity. This encourages management to introduce a 'rule of law' in the form of negotiated policies, practices and procedures of selection, training, appraisal and payment that supplement or replace the direct control by individual managers and the technical controls of machines (Sisson and Marginson, 2003: 161–2). To be sure, employers require the consent of their employees, but this need has to be tempered by the demands of profitability and the requirements of overall direction of the labour process. The managerial control necessary to regulate the employment relationship and to establish order in the workplace creates a force over and against employees. However, there are practical limits to how far the employer can subordinate the employee, as well as definite disadvantages in the form of potentially reduced levels of worker initiative and collaboration. That is, managerial authority and worker obedience are never absolute and always fluid and open to renegotiation. Any form of stability that does arise in the workplace is thus actively created and sustained. The labour exchange must in effect be renewed and re-negotiated in an ongoing and continuous manner.

Such is the intractability of the diverse interests in the workplace, that no matter how many managers are appointed, how many rules are formulated, and how many organizational changes are made, the problems of productive labour deployment and utilization will remain. Since a formal employment contract cannot define the relationship between wages and performance in detail and cost control must be continuously emphasized and achieved, the detail of the wage-effort bargain that underlies the employment relationship is subject to on-going and often tacit negotiation. The contract of employment is thus a *social* contract, endowed with implied expectations and embedded in relations of trust and reciprocity (Streeck, 1992). An important consequence of this open-ended character of the employment contract is that the shaping of the labour market is itself a part of the process of cultivating labour productivity (Brown and Nolan, 1988). Given the enormous difficulty in anticipating all the problems that may arise in providing customers with the goods and services they desire, the flexibility of the employment relationship which builds on workers' agreement to be available to undertake certain types of work as and when their employer directs, is a great advantage. Yet, few workers would agree to giving their employers unlimited powers over work assignments. The rise of the employment relationship owes much to 'the development of job rules that square the apparent circle of providing employers with flexible job allocations and employees with limited liability to follow their employer's instructions' (Marsden, 1999: 3–4). Insofar as the employment relationship provides a relatively stable framework for collaboration in the workplace, it reflects the struggles over forms and degrees of control and the nature and extent of autonomy under which people work.

Labour regulation

Orthodox approaches to IR generally regard employment as a largely self-contained sphere of social activity that leads to a clearly bounded set of labour 'problems' (Hyman, 1994a: 121). In reality, however, the expanded reproduction of the employment relationship is dependent on a whole ensemble of social structures and practices (such as the law, government policy, collective bargaining, social security, behavioural norms, education and training systems) to mitigate the contradictions inherent in capitalist accumulation. As a set of laws, institutions, practices and customs that control the use of labour, the employment relationship forms an integral part of the wider mode of social regulation (Boyer and Saillard, 1995; Whitley and Kristensen, 1997; Burchell *et al.*, 2003; Rubery and Grimshaw, 2003). The employment relationship is a product of not just one overarching causal logic, but of the indeterminate intersection of several generative structures. The roots of these generative structures can be traced to three sets of social processes: the processes of production and the structuring of labour demand; the processes of social reproduction and the structuring of labour supply; and the forces of regulation (Peck, 1996). The ensemble of institutions that regulate the employment relationship produce and reproduce social relations, connect the processes of production and social reproduction, and mediate conflicting interests inside and outside the workplace. The sites and patterns of regulation are characterized by considerable diversity and contingency. In the *régulation* approach, as Peck (2000: 68) argues, there is 'nothing theoretically pre-ordained or fixed . . . about the scale at which regulatory functions are sited'. Labour regulation can take place at more or less mutually coordinated levels (national, sectoral, workplace and occupational group) and is comprised of more or less mutually integrated forms (market, social and statutory).

As Hyman (1994b: 170) observes, the *régulation* approach has become 'a particularly influential source of innovation in industrial relations analysis in recent years'. The central insight of this approach – that the *relative* stability of specific cycles of capitalist accumulation is secured through the interplay of a whole series of regulatory mechanisms that yields a variety of different propensities and casual liabilities – highlights the recurring instabilities in the processes of valorization, rooted in antagonistic features of the employment relationship and expressed in imbalances between investment, production and consumption. The *régulation* approach posits a strong relationship between: (a) the *rapport salarial* – the general configuration of the employment relationship in relation to the exchange, utilization and reproduction of the labour force; and (b) the *fait salarial* – the specific institutional form exhibited by the employment relationship in particular industries, regions and countries (Boyer, 1994). The attributes of a particular mode of labour regulation emerge from the intersection of a localized *fait salarial* with the broader processes of uneven development in the *rapport salarial*. While there is no simple matching process, there is 'a functional concordance between the accumulation system, the mode of social regulation, and the mode of labour regulation' (Littler, 1993: 323). Of course, no regulatory system comprises a stable, unified, functionally integrated totality, but always reflects the antagonistic and contradictory logic of the capital-labour relation (Jessop, 1991: 157). Underlying this conception of regulation, according to Elger and Edwards (2002: 185), are a series of analytical arguments, which may be summarized as follows.

- The capitalist employment relationship is structured as an antagonistic relationship with a perennial potential to generate conflict.
- Capitalist development is premised on the more or less successful management of this antagonism through a variegated combination of domination and accommodation, freedom and compulsion.
- Labour regulation most directly involves the institutional structuring of the production process, the labour market, collective representation within and beyond the workplace, and the political representation of labour.
- The state is implicated in most forms of regulation, not as a neutral agency or the successful agent of the 'needs' of capitalists, but as a more or less adequate manager of the processes of capitalist accumulation.
- Labour regulation remains persistently incomplete, recurrently contested and intrinsically contingent, and reflects the complex and varied character of labour utilization and managerial control.

Labour regulation plays the role that it does because the employment relationship is structured in the way that it is. Since it is inherently open-ended, contested and contradictory, the employment relationship is dependent on regulatory mechanisms capable of generating the social rules and conventions necessary for its cohesion and durability. At the heart of the employment relationship is a trade-off between effort and wages, control and autonomy, resistance and accommodation, efficiency and equity. This trade-off, however, is realized and reproduced in a differentiated manner across time and space. The various historical and institutional forms of the employment relationship presuppose distinctive, concomitant modes of social regulation. The competitive capitalism of the nineteenth century was associated with an employment relationship characterized by the primacy of price and market mechanisms. The subsequent development of a monopolistic regulation, based on mass production and consumption, is associated with the stabilization of earnings, rising state intervention, and close ties between production and consumption norms (Michon 1992: 224–5). The regulatory functions of the institutions associated with organized, permanent, full-time employment have come under considerable strain with the deepening of the crisis of Fordism and the proliferation of employment forms that depart from the 'standard' employment relationship.

The 'crisis' of industrial relations in practice

Orthodox approaches to IR tend to place considerable emphasis on the collective regulation of employment conditions by management and trade unions.

Common features of collective workplace relations include a history of mutual antagonism between union and management; strong shopfloor organization that relies on traditional patterns of negotiation underwritten by a formal framework of procedural agreements; the existence of few or no consultative mechanisms; and constant disagreements about union rights and management style (Smith, 1994). The processes of collective bargaining are not only extraneous to the experiences of a growing proportion of workers, but always contained a number of inherent limitations. The latter relate to its role as a potential source of managerial control and to the way in which it institutionalizes conflict, thereby giving it a greater predictability (Sisson, 1987). Collective negotiations also occur within the context of managerial strategies that are *not* part of the bargaining agenda (Hyman, 1975). Collective bargaining, on its own, is seldom capable of decisively influencing the production, investment and location decisions of capitalist enterprises. The day-to-day management of labour is conducted through different forms of regulation to those involved in wage-determination. In particular, collective bargaining is not geared towards or designed for managing the organization of work. The complexity of daily production issues are incapable of regulation by collective agreements given the contingencies, emergencies, and so on that invariably arise. As Bélanger (1994: 62) puts it: 'even in the context of a unionized workplace and once a collective agreement has been struck, shopfloor management and employees still have to make arrangements on the contours and the nature of the numerous tasks to be included in a given job, as well as the volume and quality of actual work to be performed on every shift'.

Unravelling of the post-war social contract

The standard employment relationship of indefinite duration – which came to dominate the labour market in the advanced capitalist economies under relatively favourable economic conditions of continuous growth and full employment during the post-war era – underpins conventional models of IR. This relationship was consolidated at a time when industry commanded the greatest share of overall employment; powerful labour movements sustained industry-wide bargaining; governments were committed to a corporatist governance of macro-economic policies; industrial organization was based on more or less stable, predictable and protected domestic markets; and the nation-state enjoyed considerable autonomy in national economic and fiscal policies. The bureaucratic controls associated with Fordism, as Burawoy (1985: 263) shows, established 'constraints on the deployment of capital, whether by tying wages to profits or by creating internal labour markets, collective bargaining and grievance machinery which hamstrung management's domination of the workplace'. Inasmuch as these constraints stem from the statutory regulation of the labour market and the power of the trade unions, employers and governments increasingly regarded them as unwarranted and unacceptable under conditions of increasing global competition. Overly protective employment policies and extensive trade union controls, it is argued, have had the effect of curbing competition in the labour market. This prevented the downward adjustment of terms and conditions of employment, leading to employment 'rigidity'. Consequently, employers found it difficult to adjust the quantity and the quality of labour supply to rapid changes in labour demand.

Since the 1980s, the 'regionally variable processes of deindustrialization and disinvestment were pitching "capital against community" in ways that threatened to undermine the post-war social contract' (Herod *et al.,* 2003: 181). The standard employment relationship came under increasing pressure as institutionalized IR faced unparalleled challenges and drastic changes unfolded in the regulatory framework of the labour market. As Hakim (1990: 167) states in her review of workforce restructuring, strategies varied from one country to the next and followed different paths, 'but all pointed in the same general direction of increasing . . . segmentation of the labour market and exploring new forms of differentiating wage/labour relations'. The rise of non-standard employment relationships is therefore part of a wider process of de-collectivization and fragmentation in IR. Far from simply being a rational response to changing economic imperatives, the decisions concerning the restructuring of the employment relationship are political in origin and outcome. The redistributive effects of these decisions involve a diversion of the costs of restructuring onto the least politically and economically entrenched groups in society.

The crisis of Fordist production

By the 1990s, the employment relationship increasingly manifested the signs of the growing internationalization and volatility of economic activity. Changes in the way that production is organized ruptured existing arrangements in labour regulation by shifting the competitive position of the firm, altering the types of skills and aptitudes required, changing the bargaining power of the parties, and so on. These changes can be explained in large measure as involving a shift in the extent to which the market mediates employment relationships. As Streeck (1992: 66–7) argues:

> [t]he decomposition of the pluralist–corporatist regulation of industrial relations can be interpreted as a decay of the specific balance between status and contract that had underlain the Fordist–Keynesian mode of regulation . . . [This entails] a polarization in two opposite directions . . . within national societies between industries, within industries between enterprises, and within enterprises between groups of employees, with the emergence of 'good', that is, status-secured, jobs coinciding with growing disparities with a secondary labour market for 'poor', marginal and uncertain employment relationships . . . [T]he status-type safeguarding of 'core workforces' not only does not rule out the marginalization of a fringe workforce kept disposable through short-term contracts, but indeed economically presupposes it.

The standard employment relationship was not only rooted in the IR regimes of post-war Europe and North America, but was also closely linked to the

Taylorist–Fordist organization of production that prevailed during this period. The mass production of standardized, price-competitive goods for protected domestic markets was characterized by high degrees of capital intensity; the detailed demarcation of jobs and competencies; the vertical integration of production; the centralization of management; and the bureaucratization of the organization. The alleged shift from economies of scale (mass production) to economies of scope (flexible production) necessitated a greater emphasis on employee cooperation, multi-skilling and a delayering of the managerial hierarchy. The concerted efforts by employers to circumvent shop stewards as a channel of representation and deal directly with the workforce through individualized forms of direct participation, generated informal assumptions and modes of behaviour, which put a premium on consultative managerial styles and a non-antagonistic IR climate. The establishment of quality circles, just-in-time inventories, semi-autonomous work groups, and so on are presented as a move away from the alienating and deskilled employment associated with Fordism towards new forms of employee involvement and high trust relations in the workplace. Recent managerial approaches increasingly

> emphasize individualism (rather than collectivism), unitary (rather than pluralism), consultation (rather than negotiation and agreement), flexibility (rather than uniformity), employee commitment (rather than simple compliance) and empowerment and 'responsible' autonomy (rather than direct control). This can be seen as a reassertion of managerial prerogative . . . particularly in so far as employees are expected to be committed to management's organizational objectives . . . and the process of regulation emphasizes consultation which provides greater management freedom to 'set the agenda' and make decisions (Salamon, 1998: 220–2).

Despite the lack of robust empirical evidence, the proponents of 'new' IR regard the employment relationship as increasingly based on polyvalent skills, functional adaptability and high levels of discretion and commitment by employees. For conventional IR scholars, the changes that are unfolding are the product of attempts by employers to reassert their control and to intensify the work process in the context of trade union weakness, rising unemployment, and the rapid spread of micro-electronic technologies. According to Hyman (1991), these changes merely consolidate or extend the core principles of the traditional patterns of IR. Sengenberger (1992: 139) also notes that 'new opportunities for participation' are accompanied by 'the spectre of new forms of dependency, hierarchization and unilateral decision-making'. Some of the regularities, patterns and relationships currently emerging are consistent with the post-Fordist elements catalogued in the literature. These developments, however, are best viewed as tendencies rather than achievements, occurring within a context of change *and* continuity. To some extent, these developments are simply a manifestation of the inherent tendencies of capitalism towards crisis, to revolutionize the forces of production, and to extend the division of labour (Pollert, 1991). 'New' IR policies are therefore largely a reactive measure to cope with the uncertainties generated by the economic crisis rather than a proactive means to overcome the crisis itself. As such, employment 'flexibility', 'lean' production and the like are symptoms of, rather than solutions to, the crisis.

Theoretical critiques of industrial relations

Since IR is an area of study with a range of disciplinary inputs, theoretical shifts that occur in these disciplines can have profound implications for the conduct of research into IR matters. Within IR, we can discern a basic contrast between (a) systems approaches that give precedence to information about patterns and entail an almost exclusive concern with form and universality; and (b) behavioural approaches that prioritize information about processes and embody an overriding commitment to content and variability. While we cannot accept structural and behavioural approaches equally without contradiction, there is room for combining some of their insights. A coherent theoretical synthesis involves not the simple 'joining' of conflicting approaches, but rather their transcendence into a new approach in which the whole is greater than the sum of its parts. For example, in their attempt to 'complete the systems framework', Kochan *et al.* (2002: 74) tend to reify the economic structures of society and to endow management with an inordinate capacity for strategic action. As such, they end up combining, rather than transcending, the errors of determinism and voluntarism.

Essentialism and social constructionism

Industrial relations scholars, as Edwards (2003: 355) points out, insist that the 'outcomes of policies depend on specific contexts . . . [and that] there are continuing features of the employment relationship which hold true across historical eras'. Contrary to the claims of post-modernists, the study of IR does not preclude an understanding of instability, fragmentation, uncertainty, identity, consumerism and lifestyle (Eldridge, 2003). Post-modernists, under the guise of anti-essentialism, counterpose essentialism to social constructionism. While realists can accept weak social constructionism (i.e. the socially constructed nature of knowledge and institutions), they do not admit its stronger version that the objects or referents of knowledge are nothing more than social constructions (Bhaskar, 1989). If the world is purely a product of our social constructions, it should be relatively transparent. For realists, the world is relatively inaccessible precisely because it is not reducible to, or a construction of, our concepts of it. If references are unstable, it does not follow that referents are. Hence, the epistemological position of fallibilism or anti-foundationalism sits more comfortably with realism than with a strong (post-modernist) version of social constructionism. Moreover, recognizing the socially constructed nature of social phenomena is not a licence for the kind of voluntarism that makes them merely discursively revisable. Social institutions have a structural integrity, which limits and enables what they can and cannot do. In other words, the choice is not simply between a deterministic ontology of essences (empiricism) and one of endless difference (post-modernism).

Instead of relying on an overburdened notion of 'essence', Sayer (1997: 460) argues that the use of the realist concept of causal powers possessed by objects can avoid: (a) implying that any object has a single essence; and (b) raising expectations that we can simultaneously deal with the different question of what is unique or specific to a particular kind of object. Essentialism need not necessarily be associated with a non-relational ontology in which all objects are discrete and merely externally related to one another (Sayer, 1997: 461). The real dispute is over which essences we should accept as important, not whether essences can entirely be dispensed with. A moderate form of essentialism is necessary for both a coherent social ontology and a sustainable politics of emancipation. The post-modernist rejection of *any* reference to essential properties amounts simply to an inversion of essentialist assumptions. As Sayer (1997: 462) puts it:

> [i]t is dogmatic and illogical to insist that because examples of context-dependent and positional phenomena such as gender and identity are impressive that we must insist on a restrictive ontology which makes *everything* of this kind and refuse any claim that some things do have essences. Conversely, it would be equally dogmatic and illogical to argue that because objects like water or bureaucracies have essences, everything does. Moderate essentialism and criticisms of cases of misplaced essentialism are therefore quite compatible.

The post-modernist proclivity for ascribing a primary role to individual values and beliefs will invariably result in granting the strategic dimensions of IR a degree of autonomy that they rarely posses. An emphasis on individual behaviour as the driving force of IR marginalizes the underlying structural determinations of conflict and accommodation. The assumption is that management simply chooses between clearly marked solutions to the problems of labour regulation. By neglecting the material basis of labour regulation and adopting a voluntaristic model of social action, post-modern approaches cannot account for wider structural determinations and hence fail to reveal the complexities, tensions and uncertainties of choice. What is needed is a broader, materially grounded conception of regulation that is consistent with both the emphasis on rule-guided behaviour in systems theories and the stress placed on the role of human agency in strategic choice approaches. In line with a commitment to critical realism, the processes of labour regulation are viewed as tendencies that may be realized in a variety of ways in different concrete situations, adding another layer of determination to the idea of the employment relationship as a 'synthesis of multiple determinations'.

Levels of abstraction

Many of the obstacles that confront the development of theory in IR are, at least in part, 'problems of integrating different levels of generality' (Hyman, 1989: 135).

The post-modernist rejection of 'meta-narratives' simply compounds these problems. The level of generality of abstractions appropriate to determining an adequate explanation will depend on the nature of the structures or mechanisms that are really responsible (Lawson, 1997). Post-modernists are rightfully critical of the inclination to reduce a mode of regulation to national configurations. This has encouraged a tendency to reduce intra-national variability (i.e. the forms of regulation associated with particular industries or regions) to a contingent variability around dominant historical-national models. There is a need to bring sub-national regulation out of the shadows, 'not in ritual celebration of diversity and difference but in order to understand *of what* national systems are constituted' (Peck, 1996: 99). To strike a balance between micro- or meso-institutional analysis and the macro-economic focus of the *régulation* approach, labour regulation at regional or industrial level should be understood not only on its own terms, but also in terms of its articulation with broader national and global regulatory structures. Regional and local systems of regulation cannot be understood simply as derivations from a dominant national model: the latter is itself constituted of a series of regional systems. Hence, to avoid an eclectic combination of analyses, we must recognize the complementarities as well as the tensions and conflicts between micro and macro approaches.

By combining a critical realist interpretation of the relationship between labour market processes and space with a regulationist interpretation of the distinctive ways in which labour markets and their regulatory institutions interrelate at the local level, Peck (1996) demonstrates how local labour markets are both constructed (in terms of the concrete working out of generative mechanisms underpinning them) and socially regulated (in terms of the distinctive 'regulatory milieux' formed in and around them) in locally-specific ways. If each local labour market represents a unique geographic conjuncture of regulatory processes, it follows that the institutional form of the employment relationship will also take on a locally distinctive character. A meso-level theorization of the local labour market is an indispensable component of any explanation of the disjuncture between general processes of social regulation and the variety of local outcomes. The concept of labour regulation is thus an important mediation between the theoretical insights of an abstract analysis based on the law of value and a concrete empirical reality, as revealed using the methods of social scientific analysis. The dynamics of capitalism define the basic tendencies and counter-tendencies, structural contradictions, strategic dilemmas, and overall constraints that shape and are in turn shaped by the specific institutional and organizational forms associated with a mode of regulation (Jessop, 1991). In general, a regulatory mechanism at one level presupposes other, more foundational levels. The regulation of the employment relationship would be impossible in the absence of wider processes and structures of societal regulation such as the state, the family, schools and the courts. As a site of regulation, however, the workplace is ontologically constituted by sets of relations that are irreducible to these wider processes of social regulation.

Labour regulation, understood as the mediation of power relations, takes place at multiple levels and each dimension of the employment relationship may be regulated at one or more of these scales. As Bowles and Gintis argue: 'power is heterogeneous, wielding a variety of weapons, yielding to a host of counterpressures, and obeying no single logic' (cited in Spencer, 2000: 556). At the most basic level, we can distinguish between two different planes: the internal and external regulation of the employment relationship. The reductionism in conceptions that emphasize either exogenous or endogenous factors can be avoided once it is recognized that there can be no *a priori* prioritization of one level at the expense of the other. Whether exogenous or endogenous factors predominate is contingent on a whole host of factors that include the varying degrees to which different regulatory regimes are socially embedded and institutionally mediated. There is a constant tension between the institutionalization of the employment relationship through collective regulation and the continuous process of negotiating order within the workplace. While the dividing line between internal and external regulation is often blurred, many of the contemporary changes in the workplace can be understood as a shift in the balance between external and internal regulation of the employment relationship.

Industrial relations and human resource management

The term 'HRM' became increasingly popular from the 1980s onwards although its roots can be found in the human relations approach of 1950s and 1960s. HRM shares with the human relations approach a concern for the internal dynamics of the workgroup; a desire to create social cohesion and value consensus through corporate culture; an attempt to integrate personnel issues within the overall business strategy; and an effort to generate higher levels of employee commitment and involvement. The importance of HRM to IR, according to Salamon (1998: 19), lies in its association with 'a strategic, integrated and highly distinctive managerial approach to the management of people'. It is closely tied to managerial interests and has strong unitarist overtones in its approach to employees as a collective. Storey (1989: 9) suggests that 'it eschews the joint regulative approach . . . places emphasis on utilizing labour to its full capacity or potential . . . [and] is therefore about . . . exploiting the labour resource more fully'. In fact, Fowler questions whether supporters of HRM are 'genuinely concerned with creating a new, equal partnership between employer and employed, or are they really offering a covert form of employee manipulation dressed up as mutuality' (cited in Salamon, 1998: 19).

Conceptions of HRM range from inclusive (all forms of labour management are included within the broader study of HRM) to exclusive (HRM is contrasted to other forms of labour management) definitions (Storey, 2001: 5). Whereas the former accepts the continued relevance of IR as a study of the collective aspects of employee relations, the latter postulates the eclipse of IR. Exclusive definitions clearly constitute a greater challenge to the continued relevance of IR. On this view,

> HRM comprises a set of policies designed to maximize organizational integration, employee commitment, flexibility and quality of work. Within this

model, collective industrial relations have, at best, only a minor role (Guest, 1987: 503).

Several attempts have been made to distinguish HRM from personnel management and IR (Blyton and Turnbull, 1992; Storey, 1992; Legge, 1995; Bacon, 2003). Edwards (2003: 341) suggests that several possible relations between HRM and IR can be identified.

- HRM and IR can be regarded as co-equal with IR handling collective bargaining and HRM dealing with personnel administration.
- HRM can be regarded as the generic term, with IR being a subordinate and possibly waning sub-set.
- HRM can challenge IR by claiming to be more proactive and even strategic.
- IR can retain analytical dominance, with HRM being regarded as one particular technique to manage the inherent contradictions of the employment relationship.

Rhetoric and reality

Insofar as HRM represents a distinctive approach to labour management, it relies primarily on direct communication with employees through mechanisms such as quality circles rather than indirect communication through collective bargaining with trade unions. Despite significant continuities between HRM and personnel management there are several differences between these two approaches. It is, however, important to bear in mind that personnel management depicts actual practices, while HRM largely portrays normative prescriptions. As Applebaum and Batt report in their extensive study of workplace reforms: 'despite the reported gains in performance and the apparent acceleration of experiments with innovative practices, the overwhelming majority of US workplaces are traditionally managed' (cited in Milkman, 1997: 144). A significant problem with much of the discussion on HRM is the persistent failure to distinguish between prescription and description. The prescriptive aspect is, by definition, open to the challenge that it does not have any bearing on reality. In practice, the emphasis on team working and employee involvement often coincides with conventional forms of authority relations overtly based on an assertion of managerial control (Geary and Dobbins, 2001; McKinlay and Taylor, 1996). In many cases, these new work arrangements could only be established through a more aggressive and hostile managerial style (Steward, 1997).

Many, if not all, of the personnel practices associated with HRM (e.g. psychological testing, appraisal, performance-related pay, quality circles and teamwork) are design to shape employees' beliefs and attitudes, and to emphasize individualism. A vital part of HRM is a concerted attempt to avoid, remove or minimize IR practices, such as negotiations with trade unions, in an effort to shift the balance between individualism and collectivism (Storey and Bacon, 1993).

These strategies have struck a sympathetic chord with employers given the context of rising economic instability and uncertainty. Such are the times when cost cutting is prioritized, the scope for compromise is reduced, and the unions are generally on the defensive. A significant shortcoming in much of the literature on HRM is a failure to canvas the views of employees. A study in the British automobile sector found that most workers perceived the changes associated with 'new' IR as 'concrete mechanisms of labour subordination' (Danford, 1997: 109). Quality control and team working contain a strong control function aimed at disciplining employees – namely, 'management through blame' (Delbridge and Turnbull, 1992). Teamworking, as Garrahan and Stewart (1992: 106) also point out,

> is a process in which workers control one another's actions. It is this which gives to the autocratic internal regime a spurious air of employee participation and control in work.

The superficial nature of cooperation and empowerment underlying HRM means that the actual experiences of workers will reinforce existing low trust and adversarial IR. The ideology of employee 'involvement' is circumscribed by the real imperative of HRM: namely, getting employees to work harder. There is a perpetual tension under capitalism between treating workers as commodities to be hired and fired, and harnessing their ingenuity and cooperativeness. The emphasis on employee 'involvement' in HRM strategies does not spell the end of control in the workplace, but rather signals its reconfiguration. Hence the paradox: 'as workers were given more autonomy they were increasingly coming under tighter managerial control' (Geary, 1994: 648). Achieving and maintaining a balance between control and autonomy in the workplace depends less on the relatively simple task of meeting employees' comparative wage aspirations, than on 'the endlessly demanding one of creating and maintaining the institutional forms that will maximize their willingness to work efficiently' (Brown and Nolan, 1988: 353). The rhetoric of commitment and cooperation built up around HRM is readily exposed under close empirical scrutiny. The effectiveness of an enterprise depends on the contingent amalgamation of a whole myriad of mediating processes that include managerial style, job demarcation and coordination, the distribution of information, the encouragement of learning and innovation, and the mobilization of consent and cooperation among employees. In their efforts to convert labour power into actual work performance, managers are confronted by a complex set of constraints and opportunities, and have access to numerous mechanisms of control and coordination. As Edwards (1986: 41) argues,

> [f]irms will develop their practices of labour control with whatever materials they have available. They are unlikely to have explicit strategies and more likely to react to particular circumstances as best they can. Even when they have fairly clear goals they are unlikely to follow a policy which conforms to an ideal-type: they will proceed according to their own needs. In particular,

> they are likely to use a variety of means of controlling the labour process and tying workers to the firm.

No matter what strategy it pursues, management's basic objective remains a stable, predictable and cost-effective workforce. Hakim's (1990) research shows that employers rely on a blend of IR policies with few sharp distinctions and considerable overlap between types, and some ambiguity and variation within types. There is thus no single, clear division between strategies, but rather many gradations. Hence, it is necessary to move down a level of abstraction in order to consider the more concrete dynamics of labour regulation. Descending from the abstract level of analysis means coming to grips with the complexity and indeterminacy of policy change and institutional restructuring. Empirically, strategies may be combined, and the particularities of each case will reflect institutional legacies, conjunctural conditions, the balance of class forces, and so on. Even firms with sophisticated HRM policies rely on negotiation to establish what the rules actually mean and managers depend on workers to interpret their instructions intelligently (Edwards, 1994; Marsden, 1999). The negotiability of order in the workplace depends, therefore, on the willingness of workers to interpret the intent of managerial instructions. The need to elicit active cooperation from employees through the provision of material and symbolic rewards stems from the fact that 'no system of regulation is comprehensive enough to achieve complete control over the system to be regulated' (Tsoukas, 2000: 39). In other words, labour power must always in part be self-regulating. This underlying contradiction inherent in management's control over labour decisively qualifies management's capacity for strategic action.

Conclusion: the future of industrial relations

A problem that HRM fails to address relates to the fact that management's capacity for strategic action is caught on the horns of a dilemma: 'solving' problems of employee involvement and commitment raises problems of managerial control and authority (and vice versa). It is therefore not a matter of 'choosing' between control and autonomy, but rather the terms of their resolution. While employers have a general interest in their employees displaying a certain degree of willingness to cooperate, there are definite limits and risks involved in the extent of autonomy that management can concede to any sector of the workforce. IR research has consistently emphasized the conflict, uncertainty and opposition associated with the managerial function. As Edwards (2003: 339) points out:

> the management of labour entails the two principles of control and consent. In particular, any concrete 'industrial relation' will have elements of both, and these elements are necessarily in contradiction . . . An IR system can never be in equilibrium because it rests on the need to manage actively these contradictory pressures.

The so-called 'crisis of IR' is merely a crisis of a particular conception of employee relations: one that is narrowly focused on mass production and revolves largely around the experiences of organized, permanent (typically male) workers. In contrast to such a restricted view, a labour regulation approach can and has been applied effectively to account for non-traditional IR issues such as non-union firms, non-standard employment, quality circles and networked organizations (Bélanger *et al.*, 1994; Peck, 1996; Gallie *et al.*, 1998; Lind *et al.*, 2004; Davies and Ryner, 2006). As we noted above, a regime of labour regulation is realized, or partially realized, through a complex amalgam of regulatory mechanisms geared towards the mediation of conflicting objectives and the management of antagonistic social forces. For instance, important aspects of labour regulation are shaped through informal workgroup relations, unofficial custom and practice, and tacit negotiations. Whereas the traditional concerns of IR are closely associated with 'formal' mechanisms of coordination, 'informal' mechanisms are frequently viewed in static and undifferentiated terms. This may be avoided by conceptualizing the distinction between the formal and informal aspects of IR in terms of different sites and forms or methods of labour regulation that will, by virtue of their respective structures and objects, vary in the extent to which they are based on coercion or consent, are resisted or accepted, and so on. Informal practices, such as individualized pay bargaining, underscore 'the pervasiveness of custom and indeterminacy within the employment relationship' (Ram *et al.*, 2001: 847). The research conducted by these authors shows that all firms combine formality and informality just as they combine control and consent, with the balance varying as conditions differ.

'Resolving' a crisis of regulation involves a process of restructuring the employment relationship to reassert the priorities of accumulation. That is, the restructuring of production is always also the restructuring of the employment relationship. In the process of restructuring, as Peck (1996: 240) points out, 'the contours of labour control are [continuously] reworked and remade'. It is in this light that we should view the attempts by management to introduce, albeit selectively and partially, aspects of HRM such as team briefings, quality circles and semi-autonomous workgroups. These mechanisms are geared towards increasing employees' sense of loyalty and commitment to the organization; changing their attitudes towards management's objectives and priorities; enhancing their willingness to accept change; and encouraging them to display greater initiative and self-discipline. However, the tentative nature of changes in a period of transition means that identifying the directions of change involves more than simply measuring the extent of empirical change. A wide range of potentially disparate changes, for example, does not add up to a shift in the overall direction of employee relations. We need to identify the types of change involved, determine the reach and pace of these changes, trace the connections between them, and then assess which of the changes (if any) are the more robust or decisive.

The claim that the capitalist labour market's inherent and systematic capacity for self-destruction necessitates state or more broadly social regulation should not be confused with a crude functionalism in which effective institutional responses are somehow always materialized. Nor are the dilemmas of labour regulation soluble in an absolute sense once an 'appropriate' institutional and policy framework is established. Pressures for regulation do not necessarily result in effective regulation: the effects of institutional interventions simply cannot be guaranteed. Functionalism is avoided by acknowledging, first, that there are a host of potential institutional responses to the same regulatory dilemma. Second, the form that regulation assumes and the dynamics that it displays are determined in large measure by the structures and propensities of the object of regulation. The contradictions of the employment relationship under capitalism are systemic and ultimately 'resolvable' only in terms of temporary institutional containment. That is, the institutional framework of the employment relationship, while necessary for its continued reproduction, does not fully resolve its underlying contradictions, which are logically (though not temporally) prior to institutional responses (Peck, 1996: 42). Once established, labour market institutions acquire their own bureaucratic and political momentum, which will only fortuitously happen to coincide with the shifting regulatory requirements of the employment relationship. Although the latter is dependent on some form of social regulation for its reproduction, such interventions are always inherently unstable, partial and contingent on the simultaneous operation of a range of other mediation mechanisms. According to Jessop (2001: 12),

> an adequate account of regulation must not only consider the material preconditions of, and constraints upon, reproduction . . . but must also take account of the different modes of calculation and the orientations of the various social forces involved in economic and social regulation. An important theoretical development in this context would be a more explicit concern with the 'spatio-temporal fixes' within which capitalist reproduction and regularization occur.

Absent from the prescriptions of HRM is an adequate explanation of the processes that constrain or facilitate a diversification in regulatory forms. The proponents of HRM have been quick to generalize their findings across occupations, industries and regions, thereby ignoring the constraints and opportunities created by particular forms of mechanization and labour market structures. By contrast, IR scholars have long placed the issue of sectoral and occupational variations in workplace restructuring at the centre of their research. The enduring diversity of national and regional spaces is a product of the 'intricate intertwining of the effects of disparate regulatory regimes and production regimes' (Waddington, 1999: 14). Employers and employees have to act in 'social formations which have already developed distinctive ways of governing work and firms' (Kristensen, 1997: 6). In other words, economic transactions are embedded in different social relations between (as well as within) countries so that they find distinct trade-offs between competition and cooperation, efficiency and equity, exclusion and integration. Current industrial restructuring is far more problematic for both capital and labour than the technical-organization discourses of HRM suggest.

The wide divergence in working practices and the management of labour across time and space reflects the social embeddedness of the employment relationship. Labour regulation is a conjuncturally specific phenomenon that only coalesces under certain spatio-temporal conditions (Peck, 1996). Given the social nature and institutional dependence of labour's production and reproduction, changes in the mechanisms through which it is incorporated, allocated, controlled and reproduced are always partial, contested and highly context-dependent. As Gallie and White (1994: 107) point out, current restructuring is characterized by slow and cautious changes on a trail-and-error basis; a limited and discontinuous search for new employment strategies; a status quo bias in the need to maintain worker commitment and legitimate managerial authority; and an *ad hoc* and piecemeal renewal of policies in response to specific pressures. Managements' attempts at restructuring the workplace are therefore far less conclusive, uniform and purposeful than implied by the proponents of HRM. There is a need for a greater appreciation of the open-ended and complex nature of changes in the workplace. The path dependency of changes in regulatory systems means that regulatory solutions that are effective in one context may not be readily supplanted into others. Establishing a durable form of labour regulation is a contingent process dependent on experimentation and chance discoveries. As a complex and contingently realized 'fit' between social mediation and capital accumulation, labour regulation is inherently unstable and manifested in a myriad of mediation mechanisms. According to Michon (1992: 227), the societal variability of the forms taken by the employment relationship reflects 'the multiple levels that play a significant role in the structuring of the system and that reflect the heterogeneity of economic and social space'.

The conception of IR as a study of the ways in which the employment relationship is regulated is a welcome departure from the voluntaristic overtones of HRM approaches, which tend to treat structures in the workplace as simply the product of conscious human activities. Grounding an analysis of IR in the *régulation* approach provides a methodological footing that avoids the twin errors of voluntarism versus reification and an abstract determinism versus an ever-contingent empiricism. By drawing on this approach, we can conceive the drive for profits as the underlying force for change in the workplace, while recognizing that it will assume various forms depending on the impact of mediating institutions such as occupational groups, trade unions, employers' associations, regulatory agencies, and the like. That is, actors in the labour market regulate the employment relationship in ways that are constrained but not determined by the fundamental features of a capitalist society. This approach also encourages a greater sensitivity to the intractability of the object of regulation in IR. Durable regulation, in the form of an essentially stable employment relationship, is unattainable since industrial conflict can never be 'resolved' in any final or absolute sense. In practice, labour regulation is a dialectical and continuous process of challenge and response, cooperation and conflict, control and autonomy. HRM is simply one way of managing these contradictions, not a means to evade or eliminate them.

References

Bacon, N. (2003). Human resource management and industrial relations, in P. Ackers and A. Wilkinson (Eds), *Understanding Work and Employment: Industrial Relations in Transition*. Oxford: Oxford University Press.

Bain, G. S. and Clegg, H. A. (1974). A strategy for industrial relations research in Great Britain, *British Journal of Industrial Relations*, 12(1): 91–113.

Bélanger, J. (1994). Job controls under different labor relations regimes: a comparison of Canada and Great Britain, in J. Bélanger, P. K. Edwards and L. Haiven (Eds), *Workplace Industrial Relations and the Global Challenge*. Ithaca: ILR Press.

Bélanger, J., Edwards, P. K. and Haiven, L. (Eds), (1994). *Workplace Industrial Relations and the Global Challenge*. Ithaca: ILR Press.

Bhaskar, R. (1989). *Reclaiming Reality: a Critical Introduction to Contemporary Philosophy*. London: Verso.

Blyton, P. and Turnbull, P. (1992). *Reassessing Human Resource Management*. London: Sage.

Blyton, P. and Turnbull, P. (1998). *The Dynamics of Employee Relations*. London: Macmillan.

Boyer, R. 1994. Labour institutions and economic growth: a survey and a 'regulationist' approach, *Labour*, 7(1): 25–72.

Boyer, R. and Saillard, Y. (Eds), (1995). *Régulation Theory: the State of the Art*. London: Routledge.

Braverman, H. (1974). *Labor and Monopoly Capital: the Degradation of Work in the Twentieth Century*. New York: Monthly Review Press.

Brown, W. and Nolan, P. (1988). Wages and labour productivity: the contribution of industrial relations research to an understanding of pay determination, *British Journal of Industrial Relations*, 26(3): 339–61.

Burawoy, M. (1985). *The Politics of Production. Factory Regimes Under Capitalism and Socialism*. London: Verso.

Burchell, B., Deakin, S., Michie, J. and Rubery, J. (Eds), (2003). *Systems of Production: Markets, Organisations and Performance*. London: Routledge.

Dabscheck, B. (1993). Industrial relations and theories of interest group regulation, in R. J. Adams and N. M. Meltz (Eds), *Industrial Relations Theory: its Nature, Scope, and Pedagogy*. Lanham: IMLR Press and The Scarecrow Press.

Danford, A. (1997). The 'new industrial relations' and class struggle in the 1990s, *Capital and Class* 61: 107–12.

Davies, M. and Ryner, M. (Eds), (2006). *Poverty and the Production of World Politics: Unprotected Workers in the Global Political Economy*. Basingstoke: Palgrave Macmillan.

Delbridge, R. and Turnbull, P. (1992). Human resource maximization: the management of labour under just-in-time manufacturing systems, in P. Blyton and P. Turnbull (Eds), *Reassessing Human Resource Management*. London: Sage.

Edwards, P. K. (1986). *Conflict at Work: a Materialist Analysis of Workplace Relations*. Oxford: Basil Blackwell.

Edwards, P. (1994). Discipline and the creation of order, in K. Sisson (Ed.), *Personnel Management: a Comprehensive Guide to Theory and Practice in Britain*. Oxford: Blackwell.

Edwards, P. (1995). The employment relationship, in P. Edwards (Ed.), *Industrial Relations: Theory and Practice in Britain*. Oxford: Blackwell.

Edwards, P. (2003). The future of industrial relations, in P. Ackers and A. Wilkinson (Eds), *Understanding Work and Employment: Industrial Relations in Transition*. Oxford: Oxford University Press.

Eldridge, J. (2003). Post-modernism and industrial relations, in P. Ackers and A. Wilkinson (Eds), *Understanding Work and Employment: Industrial Relations in Transition*. Oxford: Oxford University Press.

Elger, T. and Edwards, P. (2002). National states and the regulation of labour in the global economy: an introduction, in J. Kelly (Ed.), *Industrial Relations: Critical Perspectives on Business and Management*, Volume III. London: Routledge.

Gallie, D. and White, M. (1994). Employer policies, employee contracts, and labour-market structure, in J. Rubery and F. Wilkinson (Eds.), *Employer Strategy and the Labour Market*. Oxford: Oxford University Press.

Gallie, D., White, M. Cheng, Y. and Tomlinson, M. (1998). *Restructuring the Employment Relationship*. Oxford: Clarendon Press.

Garrahan, P. and Stewart, P. (1992). Management control and a new regime of subordination, in N. Gilbert *et al.* (Eds), *Fordism and Flexibility: Divisions and Change*. London: Macmillan.

Geary, J. F. (1994). Task participation: employees' participation enabled or constrained?, in K. Sisson (Ed.), *Personnel Management*. Oxford: Blackwell.

Geary, J. F. and Dobbins, T. (2001). Teamworking: a new dynamic in the pursuit of management control, *Human Resource Management Journal*, 11(1): 3–23.

Guest, D. (1987). Human resource management and industrial relations, *Journal of Management Studies*, 24: 503–22.

Hakim, C. (1990). Workforce restructuring in Europe in the 1980s, *International Journal of Comparative Labour Law and Industrial Relations*, 5(4): 167–203.

Herod, A., Peck, J. and Wills, J. (2003). Geography and industrial relations, in P. Ackers and A. Wilkinson (Eds), *Understanding Work and Employment: Industrial Relations in Transition*. Oxford: Oxford University Press.

Hyman, R. (1975). *Industrial Relations. A Marxist Introduction*. London: Macmillan.

Hyman, R. (1989). *The Political Economy of Industrial Relations. Theory and Practice in a Cold Climate*. London: Macmillan.

Hyman, R. (1991). *Plus ça Change?* The theory of production and the production of theory, in A. Pollert (Ed.), *Farewell to Flexibility?* Oxford: Blackwell.

Hyman, R. (1994a). Changing trade union identities and strategies, in R. Hyman and A. Ferner (Eds), *New Frontiers in European Industrial Relations*. Oxford: Blackwell.

Hyman, R. (1994b). Theory and industrial relations, *British Journal of Industrial Relations,* 32(2): 165–80.

Jessop, B. (1991). Polar bears and class struggle: much less than a self-criticism, in W. Bonefeld and J. Holloway (Eds), *Post-Fordism and Social Form. A Marxist Debate on the Post-Fordist State*. London: Macmillan.

Jessop, B. (2001). *Capitalism, the Regulation Approach, and Critical Realism*. Department of Sociology, Lancaster University. www.comp.lancs.ac.uk/sociology.

Kochan, T. A., McKersie, R. B. and Cappelli, P. (2002). Strategic choice and industrial relations theory, in J. Kelly (Ed.), *Industrial Relations. Critical Perspectives on Business and Management*, Volume I. London: Routledge.

Kristensen, P. H. (1997). National systems of governance and managerial prerogatives in the evolution of work systems: England, Germany and Denmark compared, in R. Whitley and P. H. Kristensen (Eds), *Governance at Work: the Social Regulation of Economic Relations*. Oxford: Oxford University Press.

Lawson, T. (1997). *Economics and Reality*. London: Routledge.

Legge, K. (1995). *Human Resource Management: Rhetorics and Realities*. London: Macmillan.

Lind, J., Knudsen, H. and Jørgensen, H. (Eds), (2004). *Labour and Employment Regulation in Europe*. Brussels: P.I.E.-Peter Lang.

Littler, C. R. (1993). Industrial relations theory: a political economy perspective, in R. J. Adams and N. M. Meltz (Eds), *Industrial Relations Theory: its Nature, Scope, and Pedagogy*. Lanham: IMLR Press and The Scarecrow Press.

Marsden, D. (1999). *A Theory of Employment Systems: Micro-foundations of Societal Diversity*. Oxford: Oxford University Press.

McKinlay, A. and Taylor, P. (1996). Power, surveillance and resistance, in P. Ackers, C. Smith and P. Smith (Eds), *The New Workplace and Trade Unionism*. London: Routledge.

Michon, F. (1992). The institutional forms of work and employment: towards the construction of an international, historical and comparative approach, in A. Castro, P. Méhaut and J. Rubery (Eds), *International Integration and Labour Market Organisation*. London: Academic Press.

Milkman, R. (1997). *Farewell to the Factory. Auto Workers in the Late Twentieth Century*. Los Angeles: University of California Press.

Peck, J. (1996). *Work-Place: the Social Regulation of Labor Markets*. New York: The Guilford Press.

Peck, J. (2000). Doing regulation, in G. L. Clark, M. P. Feldman and M. S. Gertler (Eds), *The Oxford Handbook of Economic Geography*. Oxford: Oxford University Press.

Pollert, A. (1991). The orthodoxy of flexibility, in A. Pollert (Ed.), *Farewell to Flexibility?* Oxford: Blackwell.

Ram, M., Edwards, P., Gilman, M. and Arrowsmith, J. (2001). The dynamics of informality: employment relations in small firms and the effects of regulatory change, *Work, Employment and Society*, 15(4): 845–61.

Rubery, J. and Grimshaw, D. (2003). *The Organization of Employment: an International Perspective*. Basingstoke: Palgrave Macmillan.

Salamon, M. (1998). *Industrial Relations: Theory and Practice*. Hemel Hempstead: Prentice Hall.

Sayer, A. (1997). Essentialism, social constructionism, and beyond, *Sociological Review*, 45(3): 453–87.

Sengenberger, W. (1992). Intensified competition, industrial restructuring and industrial relations, *International Labour Review*, 131(2): 139–53.

Sisson, K. (1987). *The Management of Collective Bargaining. An International Comparison*. Oxford: Basil Blackwell.

Sisson, K. and Marginson, P. (2003). Management: systems, structures and strategy, in P. Edwards (Ed.), *Industrial Relations: Theory and Practice* (2nd edition). Oxford: Blackwell Publishing.

Smith, A. (1994). New technology and the process of labor regulation: an international perspective, in J. Bélanger, P. K. Edwards and L. Haiven (Eds.), *Workplace Industrial Relations and the Global Challenge*. Ithaca: ILR Press.

Spencer, D. A. (2000). The demise of radical political economics? An essay on the evolution of a theory of capitalist production, *Cambridge Journal of Economics*, 24: 543–64.

Steward, P. (1997). Striking smarter and harder at Vauxhall: the new industrial relations of lean production?, *Capital and Class*, 61: 1–12.

Storey, J. (1989). Introduction, in J. Storey (Ed.), *New Perspectives on Human Resource Management*. London: Routledge.

Storey, J. (1992). *Developments in the Management of Human Resources*. Oxford: Blackwell.

Storey, J. (2001). The meaning of strategy in human resource management, in J. Storey (Ed.), *Human Resource Management: a Critical Text*. London: Thomson Learning.

Storey, J. and Bacon, N. (1993). Individualism and collectivism: into the 1990s, *International Journal of Human Resource Management*, 4(3): 665–84.

Storper, M. and Walker, R. (1989). *The Capitalist Imperative: Territory, Technology, and Industrial Growth*. New York: Basil Blackwell.

Streeck, W. (1992). *Social Institutions and Economic Performance: Studies of Industrial Relations in Advanced Capitalist Economies*. London: Sage Publications.

Tsoukas, H. (2000). What is management? An outline of a metatheory, in S. Ackroyd and S. Fleetwood (Eds), *Realist Perspectives on Management and Organisations*. London: Routledge.

Waddington, J. (1999). Situating labour within the globalization debate, in J. Waddington (Ed.), *Globalization and Patterns of Labour Resistance*. London: Mansell.

Whitley, R. and Kristensen, P. H. (Eds), (1997). *Governance at Work: the Social Regulation of Economic Relations*. Oxford: Oxford University Press.

Winchester, D. (1983). Industrial relations research in Britain, *British Journal of Industrial Relations*, 21(1): 100–14.

Section III

The international context of HRM

15 Human resource management in emerging markets

Frank M. Horwitz and Kamel Mellahi

Introduction

This chapter evaluates the extent and nature of diffusion of human resource management (HRM) practices in emerging market economies, including Asia and Africa, considering diversity of practices both cross-culturally and within countries. Whilst there is much recent research on HRM in MNCs in Asian countries like China (Warner, 2008), Japan and Korea, the focus is predominantly on foreign MNCs with their home country origins and head office located in developed Western markets. 'The role of the multinational corporation (MNC) as a vehicle by which dominant HR policies and practices may be transported across national boundaries and institutionalized within local contexts is presently one of the most significant lines of enquiry in comparative research' (Morley *et al.*, 2007: 17).

There is little published work on HRM in emerging market MNCs, which this chapter seeks to explore. The case for such an investigation is to understand the distinctive versus universalistic nature of human resource management (HRM) strategies as they are diffused cross-culturally in an era of heightened skills shortages and growth of emerging market MNCs. This enquiry is important in the context of Antoine van Agtmael's (2007: 10–11) prediction that 'in about 25 years the combined gross national product (GNP) of emergent markets will overtake that of currently mature economies causing a major shift in the centre of gravity of the global economy away from the developed to emerging economies'. Emerging markets account for more than 50 per cent of global economic output. Indeed, emerging market MNCs like Tata, Infosys and Wipro of India, Exarro Resources, Naspers, SABMiller, Sasol and Sappi in South Africa, Haier in China, Embraer and CVRD in Brazil, and Hyundai and Samsung in Korea, are now global players. UNCTAD's (2005) World Investment Report reported that five out of the six most attractive business locations in 2005 were emerging economies, namely China, India, Russia, Brazil and Mexico. Van Agtmaal (op. cit.: 12) predicts that by the middle of this century, emerging markets in aggregate will be nearly twice as large as the current developed economies.

There is wide agreement that emerging markets are not a homogeneous group. They are at different stages of economic development, they have different regulatory environments and the educational and skills level of the population, as well as national cultures vary dramatically from one emerging market to another.

Luo and Tang (2007: 482) define emerging market as countries 'whose national economies have grown rapidly, where industries have undergone and are continuing to undergo dramatic structural changes, and whose markets hold promise despite volatile and weak legal systems'. Emerging markets are undergoing 'rapid institutional adaptation to free-market ideologies' (Elango and Pattnaik 2007: 541). South Africa (SA) for example, has experienced a dramatic transition in the post-apartheid era. Socio-legal and political context is particularly important in labour relations, given different regulatory systems, collective bargaining institutions, collective bargaining institutions, and relative power of stakeholder interests. While these factors are not static or immutable in time, they may impede or enable change in a particular cultural and industry context. Trade unions in South Africa retain a relatively important influence over the choice and implementation process of HRM practices; more so than in China where they may be considered, in part, as organs of the state. Labour legislation in India and South Africa is protective of worker interests in respect of organizational rights, collective bargaining and the principle of unfair labour practices such as arbitrary dismissal and unfair employment discrimination; though the caste system in India perpetuates certain employment inequalities. Statutory institutions in South Africa, such as bargaining councils, the labour court, and the Commission for Conciliation, Meditation and Arbitration (CCMA), play a prominent role in the conduct of industrial relations. The regulatory context is an important mediating variable and co-contributing factor in limiting the arbitrary introduction of HRM practices by MNCs and enabling hybrid outcomes. Some South African MNCs have introduced productivity measures successfully learnt in the African context, most of which are adapted from lean manufacturing, TQM and other Japanese practices.

Drawing on comparative examples from several emerging market countries this chapter thematically explores emergent themes in HRM, considering (1) the extent to which HRM practice is converging, (2) reasons for this, including globalization and (3) contextual factors which limit this.

HRM in emerging markets: an Afro-Asian emerging market framework

A large and expanding body of research has looked at best HRM practices in emerging economies and suggests that a strong fit between HRM practices and the context within which they operate is required for high effectiveness. For example, in South Africa, the importance of family and community are seen in the network of interrelationships, extended family and mutual obligations. This results in a sense of communalism. Some advocate African 'ubuntu' (see Mbigi and Maree, 1995) as a basis for fostering an Afrocentric managerial culture with regiocentic HRM practices (Mbigi, 2000). The notion of 'ubuntu' literally translated, means 'I am who I am through others'; this in contrast to the Western tenet of 'cogito ergo sum' – 'I think therefore I am'. It is this contrasting of a form of communal humanism with individualism and instrumentalism which has a normative appeal for advocates of an African economic and cultural renaissance, and is posited as having the potential to build competitive advantage (Mangaliso, 2001; Jackson, 2004).

Jackson (2004: 20–2) proposes a typology of western instrumentalism and African humanism and East Asian attributes as a useful analytical framework. The latter concept reflects values such as sharing, adherence to social obligations, collective trust, deference to rank and seniority, sanctity of commitment and good social and personal relations. As discussed above, these arguably reflect a conceptual proximity to Confucian humanism and Chinese Quanxi, with social cohesion and cooperative rather than adversarial and competitive relations. Jackson submits that a nascent African management approach with roots in a humanistic tradition could reflect a potentially positive contribution to global HRM. His typology has been extended to identify important HR dimensions. However, there is a danger in presenting both African and east Asian systems in this way. An unrealistic, idealized or indeed romanticized conception may not have significant empirical or managerial support. Second, there is a latent assumption of both homogeneity and unique distinctiveness, which obfuscates the reality of inter-regional, inter-country and inter-ethnic diversity. Hence a cross-divergence perspective is important.

A second node of analysis considers not which of convergence or divergence prevails, as this is over simplistic, but examines the conditions under which hybrid or cross-vergent models are developed in practice in a particular context. It appears that the adoption of east Asian HRM in southern African firms derives from both increased investment and the consequent influence these firms have in Africa, and an emergent managerial belief in southern African firms, that there is much to be learned from Indian, Chinese and Japanese managerial practices, particularly as these might have a higher likelihood of adoption in the African cultural context. Whilst it may be argued that Chinese HRM other than in outside MNCs may tend to not be based on the ILO notion of 'decent work'. Large Indian emergent market MNCs like the Tata Corporation, ICICI Banking and Mittal Steel, and Korean MNCs, such as Hyundai, have become significant direct investors in other emerging markets such as South Africa; while South African MNC, SAB Miller, has become the second largest brewing MNC globally with operations in Eastern Europe, China, USA and elsewhere; and other South African MNCs such as Exarro Resources (mining and iron ore) and Naspers (media communications) have significant operations in China. Murray and Roberts, a construction and property development MNC, has significant interests in the Middle East. This may, however, be a somewhat normative belief. Whilst there are indeed some similarities between African and east Asian cultures, there are also fundamental differences between them. In this section we attempt to formulate a rationale for a more critical analysis of the diffusion of practices between these two regions.

An enduring theme in the literature on developing countries is the appropriateness of Western management principles and practices. Many authors have challenged the tendency by MNCs, as well as local managers, to adopt practices with little consideration as to the suitability and relevance of such practices. Some have identified the limitations of concepts formulated in the West, while others have offered empirical evidence on the nature of extant practices, pointing to their appropriateness or lack thereof (Nzelibe, 1986; Mangaliso, 2001; Kamoche *et al.*, 2004). This growing critique has highlighted the need to understand the African and Asian MNC context as well as the indigenous thought system and in particular the perspective of workers in these diverse economies. Thought systems in Africa and Asia variously include features such as: a high degree of harmony in social relations, use of symbolism to make sense of the world, and a strong emphasis on family and the immediate community. This importance of family and collective solidarity is seen in the network of interrelationships, extended family and mutual obligations, not dissimilar to the paternalism found in Chinese, African and Taiwanese MNCs. In the case of certain African MNCs, this results in a sense of communalism and traditionalism (Nzelibe, 1986; Horwitz *et al.*, 2002), which is not unlike the Confucian influence on East Asian MNCs culture.

This has led some authors like April and Shockley (2007), Jackson (2004), and Mangaliso (2001) to propose an epistemological shift away from the predominant Western management theories to alternative ones based on Asian and African perspectives in MNCs from these economies. Maruyama proceeds to identify epistemological aspects in which both Asia and Africa share some common ground. These include cultural heterogeneity as a source of mutually beneficial win–win cooperation, a polyocular vision with regard to what constitutes 'objective' truth, the mental connectedness the worker shares with group members, the idea that the individual assumes a relational existence and identity whose *raison d'etre* is located within the community to which he/she belongs.

Given the salience of differences of Malay and Thai cultures, for example, human resource strategies in MNCs from these countries should not be assumed to be identical across different managerial functions, and a blind application of a regiocentric approach should be avoided (Paik *et al.*, 2000). Just as the African notion of 'ubuntu' is not widespread in parts of modern Africa, so too are the tenets of Confucianism not hegemonic in East Asia. In Malaysia and Indonesia, Muslim cultural beliefs are more extensive. However, it is the precepts of Confucianism which advocates of African 'ubuntu' tend to equate with African values. Caution is however, necessary in potentially confusing a desired future vision with current empirical reality. Several east Asian countries are further along a transition continuum in respect of economic development and growth than most African countries. The socio-economic context of management therefore differs from that of African countries, most of whom have high levels of unemployment, poverty and illiteracy. At the same time, like east Asian countries, there is a high needto develop people (Kamoche *et al.*, 2004). These contextual overlaps suggest avenues for further research.

Managerial styles, culture and high performance work practices in emerging economies

National cultural context factors may also limit or assist the adoption of HRM practices such as performance related pay and merit promotion, where deference to seniority, service and age remain important in Japan and countries where family control of large enterprises remains strong, e.g. chaebols in South Korea and Malawian firms in Africa. In contrast, meritocratic values and individual goal orientation evident in Singapore (Chew and Horwitz, 2004), Hong Kong and to a slightly lesser degree in South Africa, would permit greater flexibility in adopting performance appraisal, merit pay and promotion, and financial incentive schemes. Yet within a country and national cultural context, variation between MNC and local firm propensity to adopt HRM occurs (Horwitz and Smith, 1998: 590). This study found that MNCs in South Africa used numerical forms of flexibility, such as outsourcing and sub-contracting to a larger extent than South African owned firms. However, MNC influence may extend beyond HRM. In Engen, South Africa, a large petroleum company, its former owner Petronas of Malaysia had key Malaysian staff members in the South African operation's strategic planning department responsible for charting the future direction of the company. This supports the proposition that MNC influence on global integration and work practice standardization, may reveal cross-cultural convergence of HRM practices within MNCs through adoption of 'best global practice', compared with a higher degree of divergence in local firms.

HRM practices

Human resource departments are concerned with both remuneration and measures to improve performance management through pay incentives. Increasingly the former is being outsourced and/or replaced with technology as IT and new software packages are designed to do pay administration. For more progressive organizations, this will allow HR functions to concentrate on aligning HR policy and measures with organizational strategy to optimize performance. The use of job evaluation by HR departments in medium and large organizations is common practice for establishing the relative worth of jobs and ranking jobs as a basis for designing a grading structure. Job evaluation systems, for example, were introduced in the mining and beer brewing industries in the early 1970s in South Africa. As organizations restructure and de-layer hierarchies, job evaluation systems have to adapt to deal with processes such as broad banding and multi-skilling. Job analysis and work process redesign are increasingly important facets of HR work in emerging market MNCs. Research shows that although Western MNC HRM practices have prevailed for decades in African countries there is an increase in firms adopting Japanese and east Asian practices (Faull, 2000; Horwitz *et al.*, 2002). This is particularly evident in the use of Japanese MNC (such as Toyota and Nissan which have assembly plants in SA) lean manufacturing, just-in-time methods and other operations management measures to reduce product defects, stock holdings, inventory and waste. These measures have also increased in the manufacturing sector where firms have introduced kaizen, kanban methods, Nissan type green areas, Toyota Total Quality Management (TQM) and production systems and quality improvement teams. However, the adoption of east Asian work practices is seen by many as unworkable.

There is case study evidence of forms of functional and numerical flexibility in firms such as Pick n Pay Retailers, SA Nylon Spinners and Sun International

Hotels (Horwitz and Townshend, 1993). However, these practices are less common (under 10 per cent) in relation to use of cost–effective numerical flexibility such as downsizing and outsourcing, and temporal flexibility types such as part-time, temporary and casual, short term work (Allan *et al.*, 2001). Use of flexible work practices, including functional forms of flexibility such as multi-skilling and performance based pay, is more common in MNCs than in local firms (Horwitz and Smith, 1998: 590–606). African organizations tend to emphasize collective and procedural relations, whereas Asian MNCs have more distinctive, often diffused, HRM practices based variously on group cohesion, individual relations and, in cases of Chinese and Taiwanese clothing and textile firms, low-cost work practices and employment practices; this, especially with the recent growing influence of Chinese state-run enterprises and Taiwanese MNCs in other emerging markets in Africa such as Angola, Sudan and South Africa.

Mediating contextual factors in adoption of HRM have been found in African countries. Consequently, managing diversity, job design, training and development, and performance management seem to be dominant HRM functional areas driving the agendas of both local and MNC firms.

Managerial styles

Managerial styles reflect organizational and national cultural patterns. In South Africa, whilst achievement is valued, group and organization conformity is also important. Whilst there is a paucity of empirical research on managerial culture in southern African firms a masculine dominance is evident across ethnic groups (Horwitz, 2000: 217), underlined by individualist values and a relatively large power distance between groups. This supports Jackson's (2004) framework and is based on historical racial and ethnic disparities. However, an emergent black middle class has begun to occupy decision making roles. Class mobility is likely to have an impact on managerial culture and inform strategic choices about appropriate organizational culture, business and HRM practices in the African context. There is some evidence therefore for elements of an African renaissance approach. Managerial ideologies in Chinese, Korean and Indian MNCs often tend to reflect unitarist ideas – the organization as a 'happy family' or cohesive team emphasizing loyalty and conflict avoidance, notions similar to the Japanese notion of 'industrial familism'. However, organization and national culture in many African countries tend to reflect considerable diversity and pluralism, with procedural regulation of conflicts in South Africa particularly. The latter lends support for the post-instrumental model in Jackson's framework. The advent of democracy, especially in South Africa, and 'glasnost' effect of global competition begs the on-going question as to the inevitability of HRM convergence and global hegemony of 'best practice' over local exigencies. In practice, hybrid models appear more likely.

Managerial styles in many Western MNCs in emergent markets reflect both Western values based on individualism, meritocracy and an authoritarian legacy of apartheid and colonialism. These are often rooted in high masculinity cultures (Hofstede, 1980). Indigenous models of leadership and organization emphasizing the notion of 'ubuntu' or humaneness, group decision making, and interdependence, struggle to assert in the face of a converging global business orthodoxy (Mbigi, 2000). These notions may be similar in concept to the Confucian emphasis on family Guanxi networks/social capital and cohesion found in Chinese firms. Notwithstanding increasing globalization of emerging market economies struggling with International Monetary Fund (IMF) and World Bank debt repayment policies, investment in southern Africa by east Asian firms and local interest in Japanese work methods, has occurred. There has been a resultant reassessment of organizational strategies and increased experimentation with Japanese work methods such as self-directed teams, employee empowerment through task-level participation and multi-skilling in local southern African firms, but has also seen the diffusion of low-cost HRM practices in Chinese firms. However, Wells (2003) notes that there are differences between African and Asian MNCs in that their competencies are developed in countries that have distinct disadvantages due to erosion of natural resources, insufficient investment in infrastructure, including physical and human capital.

Patterns of diffusion of HRM practices

The diffusion of HRM may show an uneven pattern in respect of the extent or degree of adoption and actual modification/adaptation of these practices for successful implementation. Practices may be adopted 'as is', or with some modification, or comprehensively redesigned to suit local conditions. It is important that IHRM research focuses more closely on the nature and process of adaptation and implementation. This requires more organizational level research, especially of a qualitative nature. This will enable research to move beyond descriptive evaluation of the extent and type of HRM diffusion, and convergence/divergence debate, by requiring a more rigorous and critical assessment of the variables and processes affecting success or failure in HRM diffusion and hybridization. Hybrid forms of HRM may occur in nomenclature, design, content and implementation processes. In South Africa, indigenous African terms are now being given to adapted east Asian practices, often in preference to using Japanese terminology, for example, the Zulu term 'Indaba' groups for TQM teams or 'sebenza' problem solving teams. 'Indaba' refers to 'debate in groups'. The latter term means work or workplace. Horwitz and Smith (1998: 590–8) found that, although consultation and employee involvement occurred in introducing these practices, MNCs were more likely than local firms to involve employees in both design and implementation processes.

In the southern African and Chinese contexts it appears that 'as is' adoption is rarely effective and that either some or extensive modification occurs, thus reflecting the need for sensitivity to local circumstances and support for the notion of cross–vergence. For example in most of the above cases where performance-based pay and variable pay were introduced, these tended to be work group or team-based schemes rather than individually based; this especially so in unionized firms. In South Africa, in over 85 per cent of the cases reviewed, the HRM practices were of Japanese origin, though Malaysian and Taiwanese firms have also implemented home-based policies and practices. In the latter case, however, managerial practices are somewhat traditional, based on low labour cost/cost reduction methods, and cannot be considered 'high performance'. There is some evidence of reverse diffusion. South African Breweries' jointly owned breweries in Poland have successfully implemented best operating practices and management know-how on systems, process and technology based on Japanese practices and its experience in emergent economies, and South African indigenous restaurants in Singapore draw on home-country practices. Similarly, the South African based consultant firm Competitive Capabilities (CCI), using Japanese world class manufacturing and operations methodologies and building on its African experience, has extended these precepts into its work in Australia and Singapore. Identical HRM practices cannot be transferred intact. A degree of cross–vergence appears inevitable and indeed necessary.

Skills retention and migration in emerging market MNCs

Van Agtmael (2007 op. cit.: 227–47) refers to a revolution in 'cheap brainpower' in discussing emergent market examples of Infosys, India's leading software exporter, with a market value of over $18billion in 2005, and with over 49,000 employees. Infosys recruits less than 1 per cent of the more than one million job applicants annually in clearly a very selective recruitment and hiring process. It has consistently been rated the best employer to work for in various surveys in India. Ranbaxy Laboratories Limited, with experienced international mangers in its leadership team and focusing on both developed and emerging markets, has become the biggest manufacturer of antibiotics in India with plants in seven countries and exports to 70 others. Countries like India and Taiwan have invested heavily in human resource development to address the brain drain or indeed to reverse it, as appears to be occurring in India in the technology field. Whilst China has been dubbed the world's manufacturing hub, some are calling India the back office of the world. 'Brainpower hub might be a better name' (van Agtmael, op. cit., p. 233). India graduates over 100,000 highly qualified engineers a year, many with software skills, with a substantial number of these working in Bangalore. The establishment of country-wide institutes of technology has gone some way to increasing the supply of skilled and professional labour market entrants in India and Taiwan. Large-scale science parks with closely-linked training institutes have been developed in countries like Brazil, China, India, Singapore, Taiwan, and Malaysia, as these countries seek to make education and skills development a national competitive advantage and endeavouring to reverse the 'brain drain' in creating new white-collar jobs in emergent markets.

This so-called 'war for talent' is not therefore unique to some emergent markets like South Africa or Hong Kong. It must be accepted that an increasing level of labour mobility in international labour markets as high economic growth in emergent markets like China, India, South-East Asia, Dubai and other Middle East emergent markets reflects a massive demand for scarce skills at premium wage prices (Horwitz, 2007). 'Despite its booming economies and huge numbers of people,

Asia is suffering a shortage of skills. And it is about to get worse', stated *The Economist* on 16 August 2007 – and it has undoubtedly made many leaders around the world sit up and take note. When one looks at new research emerging to support this claim, an image is forming of a global market increasingly in need of skilled labour. *The Economist* argues that it seems odd when one considers the case of Asia – that in 'the world's most populous region the biggest problem facing employers is a shortage of people', and that 'businesses are being forced to reconsider just how quickly they will be able to grow, because they cannot find enough people with the skills they need'. Emerging markets like India and South Africa have become 'a fertile global hunting ground for other countries to pursue a strategy of replacment recruiting in a global village offering an open market for employment and career opportunities for scarce skills' (Ray, 2007). Though China and India appear to have deepened their shallow talent pools, South Africa has been less succesful, resulting in a rising 'churn' as more executives, professionals and skilled technical people job-hop. This creates an artificial demand in the labour market and could be eased by more effective motivation and retention strategies.

'Yet the demand for qualified staff continues to outstrip supply in most emerging economies. Turnover is higher, poaching is rampant and pay packages often overheated. Retaining talented staff means that their pay packages are sometimes more generous than those of comparable positions in the developed world' (Pacek and Thorniley, 2007). The 2007 Economist Intelligence Unit (EIU) Corporate Network Survey obtained the opinions of 600 chief executives of multinational companies with businesses across Asia. In China, the number one concern was a shortage of qualified staff, while in Japan it is seen as the second biggest threat. In India, it was rated as the fourth highest concern. The EIU study in Asia is but the latest body of global research adding weight to the reality of skills shortages. A recent World Bank survey also revealed that a shortage of skills was the factor most identified by management in the over 800 firms questioned as strongly retarding their further development (*Economist,* 2007; Horwitz, 2007).

The global skills shortage challenge poses a number of lessons from the collective experience of business, government and public sector leaders, as they try to address this critical component for competitiveness and service delivery. According to Hermann (in Samodien and Bailey, 2007) of the trade union Solidarity (in South Africa), service delivery is hampered by a 40 per cent shortage of artisans in the country, with only 10 per cent left of the number of qualified artisans available 20 years ago, and with one engineer for every 3,200 people compared with other emergent markets such as China and India, where the ratio is 1: 150. On the supply side, whilst technical skills shortages are partly to blame, only 1,440 apprentices registered in 2005, compared to 33,000 in 1975 (Keating, 2007). This is similar to a 'systematic shrinkage of skills', which may require importing certain high priority skills in the short term (Abedian, 2007). Poor knowledge and education about the opportunities for technical training, together with perceptions that artisan and technical work is somehow of a lesser status to graduate qualifications, continue. Abedian estimates there are currently at least 500,000 skilled jobs that need to be filled to support South Africa's growth trajectory.

While improving the supply side production of graduates, technicians, artisans, and health–care professionals from emerging market tertiary education institutions is critical, for corporate leaders the challenge lies in attracting, motivating and retaining intellectual capital. There are a number of key factors to addressing this challenge, which organizations are now beginning to understand and respond to. Some, in so doing, are becoming an employer of choice in their industry. By creating a unique value proposition and managing talent well, organizations will then be in a better position to manage their valuable knowledge and enhance their capacity to execute strategies and service delivery. In addition, companies could take greater advantage of the incentives offered to them to train and develop people internally, such as the skills levy/grant system – yet less than 20 per cent of businesses are using the system at present. Talent management research in South Africa and East Asia shows that professional workers at high skill levels in knowledge intensive industries rate the following as critical to work motivation, effective utilization and retention (Sutherland and Jordaan, 2004; Horwitz *et al.*, 2006; Sutherland, 2006):

- autonomy and opportunity to plan and control their own work
- challenging, 'stretching' and stimulating work
- collegial peer and boss relations
- career development and personal growth
- competitive, flexible remuneration
- an 'engaging' culture with direct, informal communications, work-life balance and 'decent work'.

Skills requirements in organizations should also be closely aligned with an organization's strategy. As positive indications of economic growth are now occurring, concomitant social development and service delivery is clearly dependent on an ability to motivate and retain scarce skills; this given that sub-Saharan Africa is especially short of specialized and professional skills. Getting to this point though begins with understanding and addressing the unique needs of scarce skills knowledge and professional workers today, which include:

1. ***Competitive market-based and flexible pay, benefits, and employment practices*** (e.g. flexible contracts).
2. ***Intrinsic work factors*** such as autonomy and job satisfaction, planning and control over work, recognition and reward.
3. ***Opportunity to do challenging work*** that is exciting and stimulating and at the leading edge in an industry or sector.
4. ***Growth and skills development.*** According to the EIU survey, raising pay to above market rates was only the fourth most effective HR strategy amongst Asian firms. The top three all revolved around personal growth: increased training was first, using a mentoring system second, and personal-development road maps or plans third. In South Africa, it was in this area of opportunities for growth that many firms would appear to be failing. The Deloitte National Remuneration (2007), showed that in regard to staff turnover, most South African workers

quit their jobs because of a lack of career advancement and effective utilization of their knowledge and skills.

5 ***Social networks***, peer group relations, and organizational context. These include an open and engaging culture with peer interaction that creates opportunities for collegial learning, values diversity as essential for innovation, high quality relations with the organization's leadership, and fair employment practices. Workplace contextual factors such as unfair discrimination – explicit or often subtle, but still with the net result of under utilization – lack of job satisfaction and resultant under-performance is often rationalized along racial or cultural lines. Recent Deloitte research, 'Connecting People to What Matters Most', describes three keys to creating a high-performance work environment and culture:

- ***Connecting people to people*** (people rely heavily on the knowledge and insight of others, which means personal relationships are more important than ever);
- ***Connecting people to purpose*** (actively build and sustain a sense of personal and organizational mission); Connect people to resources (managing knowledge, technology, and time in ways that enhance performance and adaptability;
- ***Connecting people with the right resources***. (Confucian 'Guanxi' and African 'Ubuntu').

Ultimately, skills development is a national and organization challenge and not purely a functional one. Senior line and HR executives in MNCs are called to create a new vision and plan for talent management. It is a shared challenge in emergent markets from Asia to Africa. Organizations that take the lead will undoubtedly steal a march on the competition, in terms of people and profits. However, a purely market driven approach to skills development is not likely to be effective in emergent markets. The notion of a developmental state occurring in emerging markets such as China, Korea and South Africa, as well as in more developed Asian states such as Singapore, committed to developing the country's human resources in partnership with the private sector and organized labour can remove the many constraints to international competitiveness such as skills development and better education (Soko, 2007).

Conclusions

There is a an adaptive mix of HRM and managerial systems in the emerging market MNCs, highlighting the extent of similarity or divergence and potential cross–vergence of hybrid models where elements of Asian low cost, high skill practices, African renaissance and Post instrumental practices may occur (Jackson, 2004). This supports the more realistic idea of a hybrid model which is not an exclusive ideal type of any one of these frameworks, and adds credence to the need for adding the construct of cross–vergence to the convergent/divergent analytical framework (Horwitz *et al.*, 2002). There is sufficient scope to theorize the diffusion of work practices between East Asian and African regions and other emerging markets, given both the apparent similarities in contextual circumstances and current expansion of business links between them. It is hoped that lessons can be learned from previous efforts to transfer management practices in order that managers might adopt a more eclectic approach and that researchers will approach this emergent field with an open mind.

Human resource development and education in skills and competencies needed in an emerging market MNCs will be critical to their global competitiveness. Several sectors need both high and low level skills. The former are in the information economy and high value adding occupations, while the latter are in services sectors such as hospitality. Hybrid forms of HR based on MNC and local form practices may occur in nomenclature, design, content and implementation processes. There is some evidence of reverse diffusion. SAB Miller's (South African Breweries owns the US beer company Miller) jointly owned breweries in Poland have successfully implemented best operating practices and management know-how on systems, process and technology based on Japanese practices and its experience in emergent economies. A balance will need to be struck between indigenous responses to past discrimination and the clear need for high performance practices.

This conclusion is consistent with Aguilera and Dencker (2004), who note differing levels of integration across countries, ranging from no integration, to partial integration, to full integration. For example, firms in the US and the UK integrate their subsidiaries to a greater extent than do firms in Japan, Germany and France. Aguilera and Dencker (2004), in positing a strategic fit framework, argue that although at a broad level practices such as pay-for-performance systems are common across market economy types, at a refined level there are non-trivial differences that HR has to manage. For example, a compensation system in the BP Amoco merger had to be redesigned because they differed significantly and a new job structure framework was established. Thus, even firms in countries within the same market economic type will experience some degree of localization in HRM practices and policies and therefore need to adjust the role of HRM accordingly.

Given the diverse ethnic demography of many emerging markets, with a large underclass in African, Indian and Chinese markets, organizations including MNCs will need to shift from compliance to a commitment model that has an organizational culture reflecting the notion of African 'ubuntu' – collective social identity and capacity building, or Chinese Quanxi as vital for both competitiveness and social cohesion in the workplace. MNCs in emerging markets may face a double transitional challenge – to redress historical inequalities by building a democracy based on human rights and tolerance, and to simultaneously and speedily develop its human capital capacity to compete in a harsh global economy. Skills formation and entrepreneurial development are vital, especially in countries with huge transitional challenges such as South Africa, China and Russia (Horwitz *et al.*, 2005). These can be summed up in one word – 'development'. National skills policies in South Africa have introduced mechanisms such as a 1 per cent of payroll levy to finance human resource development in order to meet national, sector and organizational development objectives. Large-scale labour absorption into a shrinking formal labour market is unlikely, given the shift of employment to service and informal, non-core work mainly outside the ambit of employment equity legislation. The priority of practical policy initiatives by government, private sector firms, labour market institutions such as sector training authorities and bargaining councils, must be large scale initiatives to train and retrain for enhancing employability in the changing labour market.

This is supported by Gomez and Sanchez (2005) who conclude that human resources can play a strategic role in building social capital in the process of balancing local and global forces. They argue that HR can be critical in helping MNCs deal with local differences while also helping the company implement practices that are critical for its global strategy and local development needs. Globalization and localization call for different levels of MNC control and coordination of its subsidiaries. One such mechanism used by MNCs concerned with coordination/integration is the creation of social capital – the intangible resources embedded in the network of existing company relationships that assist in the accomplishment of necessary tasks; it allows MNCs to help bridge the gap between globalization and localization of strategic practices. These authors submit that HR practices can create social capital in locally adaptive ways. Even though practices are bound to differ among countries, strategically speaking, companies will want to practice some commonalities across their subsidiaries, and more specifically, those practices that are strategically aligned with the organization's mission. Companies specifically transfer organizational practices that reflect their core competencies and espouse corporate values. HR practices are associated with social capital. Practices such as human resource development, fair labour practices and standards, equal opportunity and employee empowerment and equitable wage structures and incentive schemes, cross-functional team development, performance management systems incentives and other practices differentiate firms with high levels of social capital from those with low levels. According to Aguilera and Dencker (2004) and Gomez and Sanchez (2005) certain of these practices may be more appropriate for certain cultural contexts than for others in building social capital, MNCs must take into account the cultural and institutional context in which they operate. The same HR practices, for example, performance appraisal, or those pertaining to cross-border mergers and acquisitions, that could build trust in one country context, may fail to do so in another – each HR practice that an MNC considers implementing should be filtered through a 'localization mesh' that identifies clashes with local values, resource capabilities (such as technical and managerial competencies), culture and institutional/regulatory environment. This analysis, according to the above authors, should allow for modifications that will render the practice 'culturally fit', given that 'understanding the HR-performance relationship essentially requires exploring the heterogeneities of implementation' (Khilji and Wang, 2006: 1173).

In this context, argue that it is not clear van Agtmaal (2007) and Battersby (2007), argue that it is not clear how long the paradigm of emerging markets and the developed/developing construct will be able to explain the fundamental shift of power under way. The economic primacy of the once-called West – now called the industrialized North – is no longer a given and these nations are no longer able to take unilateral decisions affecting emerging economies. It may be a matter of time before a block of emerging economies, headed by China, increasingly calls the shots on global geopolitical and economic issues. Needless to say, the human resource research agenda on emerging markets will be a rich and exciting one.

References

Abedian, I. (2007). Quoted in S. Mangxamba, 'Look East, government urged'.

Aguilera, R. V. and Dencker, J. C. (2004). The role of human resource management in cross-border mergers and acquisitions, *International Journal of Human Resource Management*, 15(8): 1355–70.

Allan, C., Brosnan, P., Horwitz, F. M. and Walsh, P. (2001). From standard to non-standard employment, *International Journal of Manpower*, 22(8): 748–63.

April, K. and Shockley, M. (2007). *Diversity in Africa: The coming of Age of a continent*. Basingstoke: Palgrave Macmillan.

Battersby, J. (2007). South Africans can show the way amid shifts in global power, *Cape Argus,* July 2: 13.

Cape Argus, August 27: 18.

Chew, I. and Horwitz, F. M. (2004). Human resource strategies: case studies in multinational firms. *Asian Pacific Journal of Human Resources*, 42(1): 32–56.

Deloitte National Remuneration Guide, South Africa (2007) and Deloitte, Touché and Tohmatsu – Survey 'Connecting people to what matters most'.

Economist Intelligence Unit (EIU) (2007). *Global Corporate Network Survey* (August 16).

Elango, B. and Pattnaik, C. (2007). Building capabilities for international operations through networks: a study of Indian firms, *Journal of International Business Studies*, 38: 541–55.

Faull, N. (2000). The Manufacturing Round Table Project. Graduate School Of Business University of Cape Town.

Gomez, C. and Sanchez, J. (2005). HR's strategic role within MNCs: helping build social capital in Latin America, *International Journal of Human Resource Management*, 16(12): 2189–200.

Heenen, D. A. and Perlmutter, H. V. (1979). *Multinational Organizational Development*, pp. 2–9. Reading, MA: Addision Wesley.

Hofstede, G. (1980). *Culture's consequences: international differences in work-related values*. Beverly Hills, CA Sage.

Hofstede, G. (1991). *Culture's and Organizations: Software of the Mind*. London: McGraw-Hill.

Horwitz, F. M. (2000). Management in South Africa, in M. Warner. (Ed.), *Management in Emergent Countries*, pp. 214–27. London: Thomson Learning.

Horwitz, F. M. (2006b). Human resource management in Africa, in J. Luiz (Ed.), *Managing Business in Africa*, pp. 137–8. Cape Town: Oxford University Press.

Horwitz, F. M. (2007b). 'Industrial relations in Africa', in M. J. Morley, P. Gunnigle, and D. G. Collings (Eds), *Global Industrial Relations,* p. 196. London: Routledge.

Horwitz, F. M. and Smith, D. A. (1998). Flexible work practices and human resource management: a comparison of South African and foreign-owned companies, *International Journal of Human Resource Management*, 9(4): 590–607.

Horwitz, F. M. and Townshend, M. (1993). Elements in participation, teamwork and flexibility, *International Journal of Human Resource Management*, 4(4): 17–31.

Horwitz, F. M., Chan, T. H., Quazi, H. A., Nonkwelo, C., Roditi, D. and van Eck, P. (2006). Human resource strategies for managing knowledge workers: an Afro-Asian comparative analysis, *International Journal of Human Resource Management*, 17(5): 775–811.

Horwitz, F. M., Kamoche, K. and Chew, I. (2002). 'Looking East: diffusing high performance work practices in the southern Afro-Asian context', *International Journal of Human Resource Management*, 13(7): 1019–41.

Horwitz, F. M., Ferguson, M., Rivett, I. and Lee, A. (2005). An Afro-Asian nexus: South African multinational firm experiences in Chinese labor markets, *South African Journal of Business Management*, 36(3): 29–40.

Jackson, T. (2004). *Management and Change in Africa*, pp. 1–48. London: Routledge.

Kane-Berman, J. (2006). Taxing challenges, *Fast Facts* (3), South African Institute of Race Relations, March: 1.

Kamoche, K., Debrah, Y., Horwitz, F. M. and Muuka, G. (eds) (2004). *Managing Human Resources in Africa*. London: Routledge, 1–18, 183–190.

Khilji, S. E. and Wang, X. (2006). Intended and implemented HRM: the missing linchpin in strategic human resource management research, *International Journal of Human Resource Management,* 17(7): 1171–89.

Luo, Y. and Tung, T. (2007). International expansion of emerging market enterprises: A springboard perspective, *Journal of International Business Studies,* 38: 481–98.

Mangaliso, M. P. (2001). Building competitive advantage from ubuntu: Management lessons from Africa, *Academy of Management Executive*, 15(3): 23–32.

Mbigi, L. (2000). Making the African renaissance globally competitive, *People Dynamics*, 18(11): 16–21.

Mbigi, L. and Maree, J. (1995). *Ubuntu: The Spirit of African Transformational Management*. Randburg, S. Africa: Knowledge Resources.

Morley, M. J., Gunnigle, P. and Collings, D. G. (2007). *Global Industrial Relations*, pp. 15–17. London: Routledge.

Nzelibe, C. O. (1986). The evolution of African management thought, *International Studies of Management and Organization*, 16(2): 6–16.

Pacek, N. and Thorniley, D. (2007). *Emerging Markets* – The Economist Book.

Paik, Y., Vance, C. M. and Stage, H. D. (2000). A test of assumed cluster homogeneity for performance appraisal management in South East Asian countries.

Ray, M. (2007). The war for talent, *Business in Africa*, February: 21–22.

Samodien, L. and Bailey, C. (2007). *Metal workers gather to join private sector strike.* Cape Argus, June 9: 3.

Sutherland, M. (2006). How do senior people attract and keep staff. The role of HR in South Africa, *MBA.co.za*, April 2–3.

Sutherland, M. and Jordaan, W. (2004). Factors affecting the retention of knowledge workers, *South African Journal of Human Resource Management*, 2(2): 55–64.

Templer, A., Hofmeyr, K. and Rall, J. (1997). An international comparison of human resource management objectives, *International Journal of Human Resource Management,* 8(4): 550–60.

Thomas, A. and Bendixen, M. (2000). The management implications of ethnicity in South Africa, *Journal of International Business Stud*ies, 31(3): 507–19.

Verberg, R. M., Drenth, P., Koopman, P. L., van Muijen, J. J. and Zong-Ming, W. (1999). Managing human resources across cultures: A comparative analysis of practices, in S. Ward, C. Pearson, L. Entrekin, and H. Winzar (1999). The fit between cultural values and countries: is there evidence of globalization, nationalism, or crossvergence?, *International Journal of Management*, 16(4): 466–73.

Warner, M. (2008). Reassessing human resource management 'with Chinese characteristics': an overview, *The International Journal of Human Resource Management*, 19(5): 771–801.

Wells, L. T. (2003). Multinationals and developing countries, in T. L. Brewer, S. Young, and S. E. Guisinger (Eds), *The New Economic Analysis of Multinationals*, pp. 106–21. Cheltenham: Edward Elgar Publishing Limited.

16 Comparative HRM

The debates and the evidence

Chris Brewster and Wolfgang Mayrhofer

Introduction

Every organization has to utilize and, hence, in some way, to manage, human resources: to that extent, human resource management (HRM) is universal. The classic texts marking the origin of HRM identified, respectively, four (employee influence, human resource flow, reward systems and work systems in Beer *et al.*, 1984) or five (selection, performance, appraisal, rewards and development in Fombrun *et al.*, 1984) areas which they imply can be used to analyze HRM in any organization anywhere in the world. These approaches, or variations of them, are used in and taught at most universities and business schools across the globe.

And yet, the way that people think about and practice HRM varies from country to country. Differences invite comparison, not only in practical, but also in academic terms. Traditionally, three distinct streams of discussion (Dowling, 1999) deal with these differences under the umbrella of international HRM (see also Chapter 17 by Collings, Scullion and Curran): a stream looking at individuals working abroad encountering differences compared to their home-country context, in particular expatriates and more recently other forms of working, such as self-initiated stays abroad (e.g. Morley *et al.*, 2006); a second stream looking at various aspects of HRM in companies operating across national borders, specifically HRM related problems of multinational corporations (MNCs) (e.g. a perspective taken by Schuler and Tarique, 2006); a third stream of research analyzing HRM in the light of national, cultural and regional differences.

This chapter focuses on the latter, i.e. comparative HRM which has developed into a discourse of its own with a firmly established place within HRM. Starting in the 1990s, early works were addressing the theoretical and methodological foundations as well as providing first descriptive results of large-scale survey studies (e.g. Brewster and Tyson, 1991; Begin, 1992; Hegewisch and Brewster, 1993; Boxall, 1995). Since then, international HRM (IHRM) has strongly developed as a field, supported by developments at the macro-level, such as increasing economic interdependencies across national borders, globalization and the rise in importance of MNCs and reflected, for example, in the growing number of participants in specialized IHRM conferences or the growth in number of issues of the *International Journal of Human Resource Management*. Comparative HRM, too, has gained in scope and depth. Major contributions in IHRM explicitly take a comparative angle and see comparative HRM as integral or core element of IHRM (e.g. Harzing and van Ruysseveldt, 2004; Brewster *et al.*, 2007; the global HRM series edited by Schuler, Jackson, Sparrow and Poole). The focus of the discussion has shifted from a primarily descriptive perspective to a more explanatory angle looking into 'why' and 'how', i.e. reasons for and processes leading to commonalities and differences in HRM between different countries and cultures (for a typical example see e.g. Kabst *et al.*, 2006 for explaining differences in financial participation across three European countries from a neoinstitutionalist perspective).

Given what is happening in the world of business and politics, we assume in this chapter that an understanding of HRM increasingly has to take an international and comparative view. Discussions of globalization are as lively in the management literature as they are in the political and cultural literature. Arguably, internationalization is a factor for all organizations. This is obviously true for MNCs, but smaller organizations in most countries (particularly in the European Union) are impacted by competition from foreign organizations, too. In the public sector, there are not only the traditional diplomatic agencies that governments have (and staff) in other countries, but the emergence of governmental and non-governmental international organizations such as the United Nations or the Red Cross. Increasingly, government departments are working with other agencies across their region or across the world. Even local authorities in the European Union now have to accept tenders from other suppliers in the EU. An increased knowledge about the specifics of management across borders, including knowledge of how human resource management issues are handled in various countries (Dickmann *et al.*, 2008), has become a prominent issue for social scientists as it has become a key issue for all kinds of managers.

Looking at HRM from a comparative angle implies decisions on how to conceive of the differences in HRM systems and approaches and then choosing an appropriate perspective. A telescope analogy is useful in this context (Brewster, 1995). Changing the focus on a telescope provides the viewer with ever more detail and the ability to distinguish ever-finer differences within the big picture that can be seen with the naked eye. None of the chosen perspectives are wrong or inaccurate, but some are more useful for some purposes than for others. HRM can be conceived of in this way. In HRM there are universals, e.g. the need for organizations to attract, pay and deploy workers, for example; there are some things that are shared within regions; some that are distinctive for certain nations; some that are unique to certain sectors; in many ways each organization or even each section of an organization is different; and some factors that are unique to each individual manager and employee. Each perspective sharpens the focus on some aspects but, inevitably, blurs others. The many (within country) studies that (accurately) find differences between sectors within a country, for example, have been extended to studies of particular sectors across countries with the implicit (but inaccurate) assumption that there will be more differences between the sectors than between the countries. Hence, when discussing comparative HRM it is important to take into account the chosen perspective and to be aware of the *missing* complexity. Much research and analysis of HRM, particularly in the UK, has been concentrated at the workplace level. The tradition of comparing HRM in organizations of different size, sector or ownership within one country remains very strong. There are also many commentators who state, or imply by omission, that their analysis is universal. As long as the level of analysis is explicitly that of local explanation or generalized assumptions these views through the telescope are different but not inaccurate; but when the former makes assumptions about generality or the latter attempts to explain practices at workplace level, there will be inevitable inaccuracies.

This chapter adopts a mid-focus position, concentrating upon comparative HRM at the country level. The main area of focus is comparisons between countries, but occasionally the focus will be changed to note differences between cultures, regional groups of countries (such as the European Union or groups within that) or differences within countries. As with the telescope metaphor, this picture is no more nor less accurate than the others: it just helps us to understand some things more clearly.

Against the backdrop of such a mid-focus position, a systematic critical analysis of comparative HRM has to address at least three questions (for a more in-depth discussion of the underlying angles for these questions see Mayrhofer, 2007). First, and most important, what are the theoretical foundations for comparative HRM? Second, which levels of analyses does comparative HRM primarily address? Third, what are the major themes and outcomes of empirical comparative HRM research? Addressing these questions allows a comprehensive overview of the arguments used in the comparative HRM discussion and the areas of interest, as well as critical issues in comparative HRM. Hence, this chapter explores, in turn, the conceptual paradigms that underlie the topic; an overview of the strengths and weaknesses of comparative HRM in terms of levels of analysis; and, as two major themes emerging, the issues of convergence and divergence raised by the notion of globalization as well as explanators advanced for commonalities and differences that are found, including not only functionalist, culturalist and institutionalist perspectives, but also the role of multinational enterprises in diffusing HRM practices across different contexts.

Conceptual paradigms

HRM is conceptualized in different ways across countries or perhaps groups of countries. Likewise, the research traditions through which it is explored are quite different. Two different (ideal type) paradigms have been classified as the *universalist* and the *contextual* (Brewster, 1999a, b). The notion of paradigm is used here in Kuhn's (1970) sense as an accepted model or theory, and with the corollary that different researchers may be using competing models or theories. This notion of paradigms, supplemented by a configurational perspective, has been applied to HRM elsewhere, in particular when analyzing the HR-performance-link (Wright and McMahan, 1992; Delery and Doty, 1996; Martín-Alcázar *et al.*, 2005; Stavrou and Brewster, 2005; see also Wood's contribution in the current volume). Other paradigms have originated in particular geographical areas; though, like the ones explored here, they will have supporters now in many countries. Thus, there is a strong Latin paradigm of research into HRM which, building on the French sociological and Marxist traditions and the focus on Roman law, is concerned with the establishment of large-scale concepts, societal level and political interactions and the nature and detail of the law. There are different approaches to the notion of HRM in Japan and so on. For our purposes here, the universalist and contextual paradigms will serve as good examples, building as they do on the significant US and northern European traditions. The difference between these paradigms, the lack of awareness of that difference and the tendency for commentators to drift from one to another, or to apply one paradigm when the other would be more appropriate, has contributed to the confusion about the very nature of HRM as a field of study, as pointed out by many of its leading figures (see e.g. Storey, 1992, 1995).

The *universalist paradigm* is dominant in the United States of America but, as noted above, is also widely used by commentators, business school academics and consultancies throughout the world. It is basically a nomothetic social science approach: using evidence to test generalizations of an abstract and law-like character. This paradigm assumes that the purpose of the study of our area of the social sciences, HRM, and in particular strategic HRM (Schuler and Jackson, 2000), is to improve the way that human resources are managed strategically within organizations. The background objective of this work is to improve organizational performance, judged either by its impact on the organization's declared corporate strategy (Huselid, 1995; Becker *et al.*, 2001), on the customer (Ulrich, 1989) or on shareholders (Becker and Gerhart, 1996). This objective will apply in all cases. Thus, the widely cited definition by Wright and McMahan states that SHRM is 'the pattern of planned human resource deployments and activities intended to enable a firm to achieve its goals' (Wright and McMahan, 1992: 298).

Research and understanding based on this paradigm has a simplicity of focus, it allows research to coalesce around a shared objective and it has a clear relationship with the demands of industry. However, it has been criticized for ignoring other levels of analysis and being inappropriately applied, for the narrowness of the research objectives and the ignoring of other stakeholders, and for its rather mechanistic explanations (e.g. Legge, 1995; Marchington and Grugulis, 2000; Brewster, 2004).

Arguably, there is greater coherence in the US in what constitutes 'good' HRM: a coalescing of views around the concept of 'high performance work systems'.

These have been characterized by the US Department of Labor (1993) as having certain clear characteristics:

- careful and extensive systems for recruitment, selection and training;
- formal systems for sharing information with the individuals who work in the organization;
- clear job design;
- participation procedures;
- monitoring of attitudes;
- individual performance appraisals;
- properly functioning grievance procedures; and
- promotion and compensation schemes that provide for the recognition and financial rewarding of high performing members of the workforce.

There have been many other attempts to develop such lists (see e.g. Storey, 1992), and they all differ to some degree, but the Department of Labor list can be taken as an exemplar of the universalist paradigm: few US researchers in HRM would argue, except perhaps in detail, with this list. Both researchers and practitioners in other countries, however, find such a list contrary to experience and even to what they would conceive of as good practice. Thus, they might argue for information being shared with representative bodies such as trade unions or works councils, for flexible work boundaries, for group reward systems. And they might argue that attitude monitoring, appraisal systems, etc. are culturally inappropriate.

Methodologically, research based on this vision of HRM is deductive: it involves generating carefully designed questions which can lead to proof or disproof, the elements of which can be measured in such a way that the question itself can be subjected to the mechanism of testing and prediction. Built into this paradigm is the assumption that research is not 'rigorous' unless it is drawn from existing literature and theory, focused around a tightly designed question which can be proved or disproved to be 'correct', and contains a structure of testing that can lead on to prediction. Testing of these hypotheses, particularly for the leading international journals, requires the rigorous use of established statistical methodologies. The research base is mostly centred on a small number of private sector, 'leading edge' exemplars of 'good practice', often large multinationals, generally from the manufacturing or even specifically the high tech sector.

By contrast the *contextual paradigm* is idiographic, searching for an overall understanding of what is contextually unique and why. It is focused on understanding what is different between and within HRM in various contexts and what the antecedents of those differences are. This is a sub-category of the generic contingent models proposed for the social sciences (Woodward, 1970; Venkatraman, 1989). Understanding HRM becomes dependent on a large number of variables and the concept of a 'best way' becomes impossible.

The research mechanisms used tend to be inductive: theory is generated from an accumulation of data collected or gathered in a less directed (or constrained) manner than would be the case under the universalist paradigm. Research traditions are different and focused less upon testing and prediction and more upon the collection of evidence. There is an assumption that if things are important they should be studied, even if testable prediction is not possible or the resultant data are complex and unclear. The policies and practices of the 'leading edge' companies (something of a value-laden term in itself) are of less interest to the contextualists than identifying the way labour markets work and what the more typical organizations are doing. Amongst most researchers working in this paradigm, it is the explanations that matter – any immediate link to firm performance is secondary. It is assumed that HRM can apply to societies, governments or regions, organizations and workplaces. At the level of the organization (not 'firm' – other major types of organization such as public sector and not for profit organizations are also included), the objectives and strategy of management are not necessarily assumed to be 'good', either for the organization or for society. The many examples where this is clearly not the case were emphasized by many of the organizations involved in the 2008 financial crisis.

As a contributor to explanation, the contextual paradigm tends to place as much emphasis on external factors or employees reactions as on the actions of the management within an organization. Thus it explores the importance of such factors as culture, ownership structures, labour markets, the role of the state and trade union organization as aspects of the subject rather than external influences upon it. The scope of HRM goes beyond the organization to reflect the reality of the role of many HR departments, particularly in Europe: for example, in lobbying about and adjusting to government actions, in dealing with such issues as equal opportunities legislation or with trade unions and tripartite institutions. This paradigm is widespread in many European countries, Australia and New Zealand and also has some adherents in North America. Furthermore, if one were to judge by the journals and newsletters put out by the HRM societies and consultancies, HRM practitioners in the United States are as interested in many of the same legislative and labour market issues as those elsewhere. Interestingly, there are increasing calls from North Americans for a contextual paradigm or, to be precise, approaches that have considerable resonance with this paradigm, to be used in the USA (see e.g. Dyer and Kochan, 1995).

The contextual paradigm is intuitively pluralistic. There is no unitary assumption that the interests of everyone in the organization will be the same; or any expectation that an organization will have a strategy that people within the organization will necessarily support. Rather, the assumption is that not only will the employees and the unions have a different perspective to the management team (Purcell and Ahlstrand, 1994), but that even within the management team there may be different interests and views (Lepak and Snell, 1999).

Many of the seminal management and HRM texts are written as if the analysis applies at all levels – what Rose (1991) called 'false universalism'. This is a major problem in relation to the US literature. The cultural hegemony of US teaching and publishing, particularly in the US and 'international' journals, mean that these texts are often utilized by readers and students in other countries. US-based literature searches, now all done on computer, of course, tend to privilege texts from this US-based literature, and hence texts in the universalist tradition. For analysts and practitioners elsewhere with interests in different sectors, countries and so on, many of these descriptions and prescriptions fail to meet their reality. It is not that either paradigm is necessarily correct or more instructive than others, but that the level and focus needs to be specified to make the analysis meaningful (Brewster, 1999a, b).

Using the contextual paradigm, researchers have attempted to explore and, if possible, explain through comparative HRM studies. In its simplest form, HRM in two different countries is compared and contrasted at a merely descriptive level. In a broader sense the criteria for comparison, derived from theoretical reasoning or closely linked to observable phenomena, go far beyond that to explore clusters of countries, or to challenge the national boundaries concept. Cultural groups do not always coincide with national borders. Hence studies such as that by Dewettinck *et al.*, (2004) who compare the way people are managed in the Walloon and Flemish parts of Belgium (with France and the Netherlands) would be claimed as comparative HRM texts. While basically using *comparative* in this broad sense, the majority of comparative HRM contributions do deal with differences across nations, culture clusters, and world regions.

Units of analysis

Comparative HRM research usually focuses on individual and collective actors of various kinds as well as the respective structures and processes linked with these actors, all of them in different countries, cultures or regions. The degree of social complexity constitutes a useful main differentiation criterion in order to group these actors according to different analytical levels. Actors are characterized by low social complexity if the emerging social relationships within these actors are either non-existent, as in the case of individuals, or have comparatively little complexity, e.g. in face-to-face groups. However, collective actors such as countries or supra-national units show high social complexity. A complex fabric of social relationships constitutes their internal environment. Between these two poles, various existing actors can be grouped (e.g. see Figure 16.1).

Looking back from early 1990s, analysis of published comparative HRM research reveals that country, organization and individual level analyses dominate

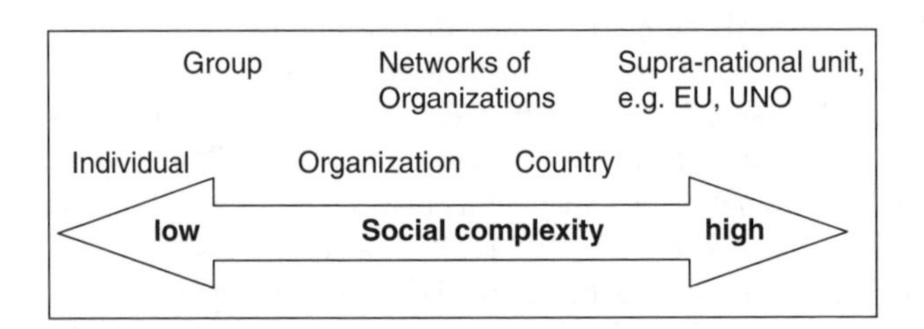

Figure 16.1 Units of analysis in comparative HRM and their social complexity.

the scene. Investigating articles published in journals that are listed in a major academic electronic database of the field, *EBSCO Business Source Premier* providing full text access to more than 2,300 journals and including more than 1,100 peer-reviewed business publications, an extensive search in all peer-reviewed articles published in the years from 1990 to 2005 was conducted (for a more detailed view see Mayrhofer and Reichel, 2009 forthcoming). Using 'comparative HRM' and a number of variations of this search term, the 'author-supplied keywords' as well as 'abstract or author-supplied abstract' section of the database was searched. In addition, two further criteria were used: articles had to be comparative in a geographical or cultural sense, excluding articles comparing different types of companies, e.g. public versus private, or regions of one country, e.g. states of the USA; in addition, there was a focus on core areas of HRM, i.e. issues of organizing and configuring HRM within the firm and major HRM practices, excluding literature not explicitly linked with HRM, e.g. comparative leadership studies. Results reveal that comparative HRM typically:

- is empirical rather than conceptual,
- focuses on country, organization or individual as the primary units of analysis,
- uses cross-sectional 'snapshot' rather than longitudinal, i.e. panel or trend study, designs and
- focuses on comparison of one or more sets of HRM practices, e.g. recruitment procedures, and/or HRM configuration such as strategic orientation or size of the HRM department rather than the link between HRM and some kind of output like satisfaction, performance, or commitment.

Overall, this shows that comparative HRM puts an emphasis on actors and respective processes and structures at a low to medium level of social complexity. Typical blind spots are networks of organizations and supra-national actors.

Developments over time: convergence and divergence

Developments over time are one of the most intriguing areas in the growing body of evidence in comparative HRM. While many studies use cross-sectional designs, panel or at least trend studies address include the temporal perspective and address questions such as: If HRM is different across countries, then what are the trends? Are the differences static or, more sensibly and assuming that almost no social systems will remain completely static, what is the direction of movement – are different units of analysis heading in the same direction, are they becoming more alike? Is HRM, like so much else, maybe even bound to become largely similar subject to forces comfortably labelled as globalization? Contributions to answering these questions – often labelled within the frame of convergence and divergence – come from theoretical, methodological and empirical sources.

From a theoretical perspective, arguments are raised for both convergence and divergence. Arguing at the macro-level, different forms of capitalism (Hall and

Soskice, 2001; Amable, 2003) as well as the importance of national business systems (Whitley, 1999) emphasize the differences in the modern world, its institutional change (Djelic and Quack, 2003) and the limits of globalization (Guillén, 2001). From the cultural perspective, national and regional cultures reflect substantial differences in norms and values (Hofstede, 1980; House *et al.*, 2004) that will also make convergence at all levels highly unlikely. On the other hand, part of the globalization literature expects converging developments. Galbraith contended that modern man's 'area of decision is, in fact, exceedingly small' and that 'the imperatives of organization, technology and planning operate similarly, and . . . to a broadly similar result, on all societies' (1967: 336). Likewise, Kerr *et al.* (1960) postulated that the logics of industrialization produce common values, beliefs and systems of organization despite different ideologies, politics and cultures. Covering both basic arguments and pointing towards synchronic developments, arguments are brought forward that emphasize the simultaneous occurrence of both converging and diverging trends (Crouch and Streeck, 1997; Inkeles, 1998).

From a methodological perspective, it is essential to have a clear understanding about what convergence and divergence actually mean. Some studies have claimed to find convergence from a single point in time analysis (e.g. Chen *et al.*, 2005). A closer look reveals that, clearly, what they have found are similarities, but not convergence, which requires a coming together over time. To be clearer about this, two major forms of convergence have been suggested (Mayrhofer *et al.*, 2002). *Final* convergence exists when units of analysis are becoming more alike, e.g. share a development towards a common end point, implying a decrease in differences between countries. To be sure, this does not imply that this endpoint will or should ever be reached. *Directional* convergence occurs when units of analysis share the same trend, i.e. they go in the same direction, regardless of their initial starting level and a common endpoint. An example would be an increasing use of Assessment Centres in management development across different countries, irrespective of different starting levels.

From an empirical perspective, hard evidence of long-term development in HRM is scarce. Arguably the most elaborate work in this area stems from Cranet, a research network dedicated to a trend study about developments in the area of HRM in public and private organizations with more than 200 employees since 1989 and conducting seven survey-rounds in currently more than 40 countries world-wide, with an emphasis on Europe (see Brewster and Hegewisch, 1994; Brewster *et al.*, 2000). Detailed evidence is available for developments in Europe (see the overview in Brewster *et al.*, 2004). Results show that in Europe many aspects of HRM show directional convergence, i.e. the trends are the same. Thus, there are increases in most countries most of the time in such issues as the use of contingent pay and the extent of communications with employees. However, contrary to the received wisdom in the universalistic texts, there is no sign of common trends in the size of the HRM department (Brewster *et al.*, 2006) nor in training and development, which is given high priority in many countries but seems to remain the first area for cuts when finances become tight. The evidence is summarized as follows: 'From a directional convergence point of view, there seems to be a positive indication of convergence. However, when one looks at the question from a final convergence point of view, the answer is no longer a clear positive. None of the HR practices converge' (Mayrhofer *et al.*, 2004: 432). It seems clear that the evidence supports those who would argue, for various reasons, that globalization might not be taking place in the clear, straightforward way of 'making things more similar'. Hence, the broader issue of factors explaining similarities and differences between HRM in different countries and their development becomes crucial.

Explanators in more detail: cost efficiency, culture, institutions and diffusion

Comparative HRM should attempt explanation as well as description (Boxall, 1995) and it is worth analyzing and trying to explain what impacts on and creates the diversity – and sometimes the lack of it – that we find between countries in their understanding of, approaches to and practices on HRM. While differences as well as commonalities of contextual influencing factors exist, it is by no means clear which factors have what effects on HRM. In broad terms, there are three partly competing, partly complementary sets of explanators: a more functionalist view linked with the universalist paradigm of HRM; and a cultural and institutional perspective asking whether differences are 'sustained because people find it repulsive, unethical or unappealing to do otherwise .... [or] ... because a wider formal system of laws, agreements, standards and codes exist?' (Sorge, 2004: 118), both rooted in the contextual paradigm. In all three perspectives, MNCs can play an important role in diffusion processes.

Functionalist perspective

Linked to a universalist perspective and tied to a functional view of the organization, there are a number of arguments emphasizing forces that support more homogeneity. At the organizational level and perhaps most pointedly, tendencies towards similarity are claimed by transaction cost economics: 'Most transaction cost theorists argue that there is one best organizational form for firms that have similar or identical transaction costs' (Hollingsworth and Boyer, 1997: 34). With different basic assumptions and theoretical reasoning, some institutionalist approaches also lean to a kind of homogeneity. For example, the world polity view (e.g. Meyer *et al.*, 1997) assumes that global rationality myths exist that lead towards converging developments across national and cultural borders. Likewise, other forms of neo-institutionalism would argue that large collective actors such as the European Union provide fertile ground for different kinds of isomorphic pressures within this unique setting, i.e. a supra-national construct that ties together politically sovereign states into a coherent and heavily interdependent union, where many national activities are governed by European regulations and organizations have a more unified context to operate in.

Cultural perspective

Both culture and institutional views emphasize heterogeneity, but differ in their arguments. Early authorities on culture argued that it is 'one of those terms that defy a single all-purpose definition and there are almost as many meanings of culture as people using the term' (Ajiferuke and Boddewyn, 1970: 154). Subsequent years and studies have added further complexity, rather than clarifying the issue. In all its various manifestations, the cultural literature assumes that variations in practices will be in line with different cultural contexts. Typically, these will reflect national boundaries, but this is by no means always the case. Whilst the 'culturalist' school is an extremely broad one, what most of these approaches have in common is that they treat culture as a given; it may be possible for a society to enhance or change its 'social capital', but it is not possible to develop social trust deliberately and systematically, nor radically to depart from established rules and norms (Fukuyama, 1995; Lane, 1989). Culture is seen as a way in which individuals can confer shared meanings, and hence make sense of, social interactions. Even if the nature of that culture may be relatively fluid and subjective, it provides a persistent boundary, horizon or 'segment' to the life-world of individuals and clusters thereof. A range of researchers have not only found geographically-based, usually national, differences in deep-seated values about what is good or bad, honest or dishonest, fair or unfair, etc. They also point to the inter-relation between cultural-level and individual-level values: each individual will be different but the aggregation of their approaches makes what is acceptable and desirable in one country different from what is acceptable or desirable in another. In addition, what happens at the organizational level is also affected by these values (see e.g. Hofstede, 1980; House *et al.*, 2004; Schwartz, 2004). These perceptions affect the way people in a country, and perhaps especially relevantly here, managers, view the world. Since HRM is concerned with interactions between people at different hierarchical levels within an organization and also the organization-context link, these cultural differences will inevitably be reflected in differences in the way people are managed.

Institutionalist perspective

Institutional perspectives, by contrast, focus on the institutions within a society as being the environmental structures that keep them distinctive. Institutions are likely to shape the social construction of the nature of organizations and will certainly structure policies and practices within them. The institutional perspective (Meyer and Rowan, 1977; DiMaggio and Powell, 1983) argues that isomorphism between organizations is determined less by cultural differences than by institutions. Adding in a cross-national element has led some institutionalists to argue that it is the economic, social and legal arrangements of societies that keep the nations distinctive (Hollingsworth and Boyer, 1997; Whitley, 1999). Thus, the general and vocational education system, the way labor markets work, employment legislation and the industrial relations system will all impact on the way that

HRM can be conducted in particular states. HRM will be a function of the country's particular institutional arrangements – the 'societal effect' (Maurice *et al.*, 1986). As with the culture effects, there seems to be a kind of societal recipe that can be violated or ignored, but only at a cost, most prominent a loss of legitimacy. Most people, or most organizations, do not choose to do so.

Perhaps a key institution underlying differences in HRM is the legal system. La Porta *et al.* (1997) distinguished between common law and civil law societies, arguing that common law, the legal system of the UK, US and most Commonwealth countries, accords an important role to the judges who make law in the courts by setting precedents. This provides stronger investor protection than the civil law system found in much of the rest of the world. They develop an argument that within the civil law family, French civil law provides the lowest levels of shareholder protection, followed by German civil law and then Scandinavian civil law. In common law countries, in order to protect ownership rights and ensure general economic prosperity, employee rights are best secured through individual litigation aimed at enforcing general common-law style legislation (Djankov *et al.*, 2003: 603). More recently, La Porta and colleagues have built on this reasoning and argued that civil law countries are characterized by the direct regulation of markets, including labour markets (Botero *et al.*, 2004: 1379).

The recognition of institutional differences is not new (Rosenzweig and Singh, 1991). Neither are these major explanatory patterns the only ones that have been addressed in the literature. Additional explanators include patterns of ownership, leading to differences in the amount of attention paid to long-term sustainability versus pressure to produce short-term profits and the incentive to drive competitors out of the market-place (Randlesome, 1994; Brewster, 2004); the relationship between national level political structures and practices; or the relative power of stakeholders at firm level, merits further investigation. Pagano and Volpin (2005), for example, suggest that the type of electoral system – a proportional or majoritarian electoral system – is a key determining factor in the levels of protection that employees and investors have and, by extrapolation, the kind of HRM found in a particular country and test this using national level data from 21 OECD countries.

Diffusion perspective

Diffusion, too, is a major approach towards explaining commonalities and differences in HRM across countries. It refers to the dissemination of tangible or intangible units within a certain frame of reference, e.g. an organization, the economic system, countries, etc. Diffusion can relate to very different phenomena like the diffusion of innovation (e.g. Rogers, 1983), of products through marketing (e.g. Schuh, 2000), of management knowledge (e.g. Alvarez, 1998) or of linguistic concepts in established local languages (e.g. Hoffmann, 2000). While diffusion of organizational concepts and practices happens through a number of channels such as organizational policies, expatriation, border-spanning educational systems, consultants, or rating agencies, MNCs and their subsidiaries are often seen as a key element, especially in HRM due to the growth in the number, reach and power of MNCs and their central role in the globalization process (Meyer, 2000). Much attention is currently being focused on how MNCs are changing local HRM practices by importing successful practices across national borders. Hence, a major question is: are the actions of MNCs reducing national differences in HRM and what is the balance between the extent to which foreign organizations bring new practices into a country compared to the extent to which they adjust to local practices (Quintanilla and Ferner, 2003)?

It has been argued that this will vary with a number of factors, most importantly with: the kind of country the MNC operates in; theories of how different types of business systems or market economies may influence HRM; the country of origin of the MNCs; the type of organization, i.e. foreign-owned MNCs, domestic-owned MNCs and domestic organizations; and with the impact of context on MNCs operating under these different conditions (Gooderham *et al.*, 1999; Ferner and Quintanilla, 2001; Almond and Ferner, 2006; Farndale and Paauwe, 2007).

Conclusion: recognizing the comparative dimension of HRM

Overall, the work in comparative HRM shows that beyond some universals, substantial differences in the meaning and practice of HRM in different countries exist. There are clear regional differences between, say, the patterns of contingent employment, anti-unionism and the role of the HRM department in the USA, Japan and Europe. And, going back to the focus-pulling analogy, within Europe different sub-regional patterns can be distinguished, reflecting the wider discussion about business systems and varieties of capitalism. Below the sub-regional level there is clearly in existence a set of broad, relatively inert distinctions between the various national contexts of personnel management that makes any universalistic models of HRM problematic. The idiosyncratic national institutional settings are so variable that no common model is likely to emerge for the foreseeable future. Our discussion of the issues of comparative HRM in general and convergence and divergence in national patterns of HRM in particular is, therefore, equivocal and perhaps needs more careful nuance than has been the case in much of the writing about HRM. HRM varies by country, sector and size of organization; by subjects within the generic topic of HRM; and by the nature of the organization (life-stage; governance; market, etc.). All this points towards the greater explanatory power of the contextual paradigm – at least in such cases.

However, comparative HRM is inevitably a complex subject. A full understanding requires drawing on a wide range of possible explanators. The current state of theory and its capacity to analyze important questions of comparative HRM is perhaps the key unresolved issue characterizing existing comparative HRM research. So far, the theoretical efforts are not coherent and only partly able to explain observed differences and commonalities. There is no coherent and widely agreed theoretical rationale for the observed comparative differences of HRM that allows an integration of the existing theoretical explanations primarily based on functional, cultural or institutional arguments. It might be too ambitious to call for a meta-theory uniting these perspectives. Yet, it is highly unsatisfactory for the field of comparative HRM research – and with it, we would argue, for much of management and cross-cultural research – to have so many different explanations of the commonalities and differences in HRM between countries, cultures and regions, but no accepted set of theoretical propositions that can unify the field.

References

Ajiferuke, M. and Boddewyn, J. (1970). 'Culture' and other explanatory variables in comparative management studies, *Academy of Management Journal*, 13: 153–63.

Almond, P. and Ferner, A. (Eds), (2006). *American Multinationals in Europe.* New York: Oxford University Press.

Alvarez, J. L. (Ed.) (1998). *The Diffusion and Consumption of Business Knowledge.* London: Macmillan Press.

Amable, B. (2003). *The Diversity of Modern Capitalism.* Oxford: Oxford University Press.

Becker, B. and Gerhart, B. (1996). The impact of human resource management on organizational performance: progress and prospects, *Academy of Management Journal*, 39: 779–801.

Becker, B., Huselid, M. A. and Ulrich, D. (2001). *The HR Scorecard: Linking People, Strategy, and Performance.* Boston, MA: Harvard Business School Press.

Beer, M., Spector, B., Lawrence, P. R., Mills, D. Q. and Walton, R. E. (1984). *Managing Human Assets.* New York: The Free Press.

Begin, J. P. (1992). Comparative human resource management (HRM): a systems perspective, *International Journal of Human Resource Management*, 3: 379–408.

Botero, J., Djankov, S., La Porta, R. and Lopez-De-Silanes, F. C. (2004). The regulation of labor, *The Quarterly Journal of Economics*, 119: 1339–82.

Boxall, P. (1995). Building the theory of comparative HRM, *Human Resource Management Journal*, 5: 5–17.

Brewster, C. (1995). Towards a 'European' model of human resource management, *Journal of International Business Studies*, 26: 1–21.

Brewster, C. (1999a). Different paradigms in strategic HRM: questions raised by comparative research, in P. Wright, L. Dyer, J. Boudreau, and G. Milkovich (Eds), *Research in Personnel and HRM.* Greenwich, CT: JAI Press.

Brewster, C. (1999b). Strategic human resource management: the value of different paradigms, *Management International Review*, 39: 45–64.

Brewster, C. (2004). European perspectives on human resource management, *Human Resource Management Review*, 14: 365–82.

Brewster, C. and Hegewisch, A. (Eds) (1994). *Policy and Practice in European Human Resource Management. The Price Waterhouse Cranfield Survey.* London, New York: Routledge.

Brewster, C. and Tyson, S. (Eds) (1991). *International Comparisons in Human Resource Management.* London: Pitman.

Brewster, C., Mayrhofer, W. and Morley, M. (Eds) (2000). *New Challenges in European Human Resource Management.* London: Macmillan.

Brewster, C., Mayrhofer, W. and Morley, M. (Eds) (2004). *Human Resource Management in Europe. Evidence of convergence?* Oxford: Elsevier/Butterworth-Heinemann.

Brewster, C., Wood, G., Brookes, M. and van Ommeren, J. (2006). What determines the size of the HR function? A cross-national analysis, *Human Resource Management*, 45: 3–21.

Brewster, C., Sparrow, P. and Vernon, G. (2007). *International Human Resource Management.* London: Chartered Institute of Personnel and Development.

Chen, S.-J., Lawler, J. J. and Bae, J. (2005). Convergence in human resource systems: A comparison of locally owned and MNC subsidiaries in Taiwan, *Human Resource Management*. 44: 237–56.

Crouch, C. and Streeck, W. (1997). *Political Economy of Modern Capitalism. Mapping Convergence and Diversity.* London: Sage.

Delery, J. E. and Doty, H. (1996). Modes of theorizing in strategic human resource management, Tests of universalistic, contingency and configurational performance predictions, *Academy of Management Journal*, 39: 802–35.

Dewettinck, K., Buyens, D., Dany, F. and Quinodon, B. (2004). Belgium and France: language, culture and differences in HR practices, in C. Brewster, W. Mayrhofer, and M. J. Morley, (Eds). *European Human Resource Management – Evidence of Convergence?* London: Butterworth-Heinemann.

Dickmann, M., Brewster, C. and Sparrow, P. R. (Eds) (2008). *International HRM: A European Perspective.* London: Routledge.

DiMaggio, P. J. and Powell, W. W. (1983). The iron cage revisited: institutional isomorphism and collective rationality in organizational fields, *American Sociological Review*, 48: 147–60.

Djankov, S., Glaeser, E., La Porta, R., Lopez-de-Silanes, F. and Shleifer, A. (2003). The new comparative economics, *Journal of Comparative Economics*, 31: 595–619.

Djelic, M.-L. and Quack, S. (Eds) (2003). *Globalization and Institutions. Redefining the Rules of the Economic Game.* Cheltenham: Edward Elgar.

Dowling, P. J. (1999). Completing the puzzle: issues in the development of the field of international human resource management, *Management International Review*, 39: 27–43.

Dyer, L. and Kochan, T. (1995). Is there a new HRM? Contemporary evidence and future directions, in B. Downie, and M. L. Coates (Eds), *Managing Human Resources in the 1990s and Beyond: Is the Workplace Being Transformed?* Kingston, Ontario: Industrial Relations Centre Press, Queen's University.

Farndale, E. and Paauwe, J. (2007). Uncovering competitive and institutional drivers of HRM practices in multinational corporations, *Human Resource Management Journal*, 17: 355–75.

Ferner, A. and Quintanilla, J. (2001). Country-of-origin, host country effects and the management of HR in multinationals, *Journal of World Business*, 36: 107–27.

Fombrun, C. J., Tichy, N. and Devanna, M. A. (1984). *Strategic Human Resource Management.* New York: Wiley.

Fukyama, F. (1995). *Trust: social virtues and the creation of property.* New York: Free Press.

Galbraith, J. K. (1967). *The New Industrial State.* Boston, MA: Houghton Mifflin (5th print).

Gooderham, P. N., Nordhaug, O. and Ringdal, K. (1999). Institutional and rational determinants of organizational practices: human resource management in European firms, *Administrative Science Quartely*, 44: 507–31.

Guillén, M. F. (2001). *The Limits of Convergence. Globalization and Organizational Change in Argentina, South Korea and Spain.* Princeton, Oxford: Princeton University Press.

Hall, P. A. and Soskice, D. (Eds) (2001). *Varieties of Capitalism. The Institutional Foundations of Comparative Advantage.* Oxford: Oxford University Press.

Harzing, A.-W. and van Ruysseveldt, J. (2004). *International Human Resource Management,* London: Sage.

Hegewisch, A. and Brewster, C. (Eds) (1993). *European Developments in Human Resouurce Management.* London: Kogan Page.

Hoffmann, E. (2000). Onymischer Wandel, in L. N. Zybatow (Ed.), *Sprachwandel in der Slavia. Die slavischen Sprachen an der Schwelle zum 21. Jahrhundert. Ein Internationales Handbuch, Teil 1 (= Linguistik International, Bd. 4)*. Frankfurt a.M.

Hofstede, G. (1980). *Culture's Consequence. International Differences in Work-Related Values.* Newbury Park: Sage Publications.

Hollingsworth, J. R. and Boyer, R. (1997). Coordination of economic actors and social systems of production, in J. R. Hollingsworth, and R. Boyer (Eds), *Contemporary Capitalism*. Cambridge: Cambridge University Press.

House, R. J., Hanges, P. J., Javidan, M., Dorfman, P. W. and Gupta, V. (Eds) (2004). *Culture, Leadership, and Organizations: The GLOBE Study of 62 Societies.* Thousand Oaks, CA: Sage.

Huselid, M. A. (1995). The impact of human resource management practices on turnover, productivity, and corporate financial performance, *Academy of Management Journal*, 38: 635–72.

Inkeles, A. (Ed.) (1998). *One World Emerging? Convergence and Divergence in Industrial Societies.* Boulder, Co: Westview.

Kabst, R., Matiaske, W. and Schmelter, A. (2006). Financial participation in British, French and German organizations: a neoinstitutionalist perspective. *Economic and Industrial Democracy*, 27: 565–85.

Kerr, C., Dunlop, J., Harbison, F. and Myers, C. (1960). *Industrialism and Industrial Man.* Cambridge, MA: Harvard University Press.

Kuhn, T. (1970). *The Structure of Scientific Revolutions.* Chicago: University of Chicago Press.

La Porta, R., Lopez-de-Silanes, F., Shleifer, A. and Vishny, R. W. (1997). Legal determinants of external finance, *Journal of Finance*, 52: 1131–50.

Lane, C. (1998). Theories and Issues in the Study of Trust. In Lane, C. and Bachmenn, R. (eds) *Trust Within and between Organizations.* Oxford: Oxford University Press.

Legge, K. (1995). HRM: rhetoric, reality and hidden agendas, in J. Storey (Ed.), *Human Resource Management: a Critical Text.* London: Routledge.

Lepak, D. and Snell, S. (1999). The human resource architecture: toward a theory of human capital allocation and development, *Academy of Management Review*, 24: 31–48.

Marchington, M. and Grugulis, I. (2000). Best practice human resource management: perfect opportunity or dangerous illusion?, *International Journal of Human Resource Management*, 11: 1104–24.

Martín-Alcázar, F., Romero-Fernández, P. and Sánchez-Gardey, G. (2005). Strategic human resource management: integrating the universalistic, contingent, configurational and contextual perspectives, *International Journal of Human Resource Management*, 16: 633–59.

Maurice, M., Sellier, F. and Silvestre, J. (1986). *The Social Foundations of Industrial Power.* Cambridge, MA: MIT Press.

Mayrhofer, W. (2007). European comparative management research: towards a research agenda, *European Journal of International Management*, 1: 191–205.

Mayrhofer, W. and Reichel, A. (2009, forthcoming). Comparative analysis of HR, in P. R. Sparrow (Ed.), *Handbook of International HR Research: Integrating People, Process and Context*. Oxford: Blackwell.

Mayrhofer, W., Morley, M. and Brewster, C. (2004). Convergence, stasis, or divergence?, in C. Brewster, W. Mayrhofer, and M. Morley (Eds), *Human Resource Management in Europe. Evidence of Convergence?* London: Elsevier/Butterworth-Heinemann.

Mayrhofer, W., Müller-Camen, M., Ledolter, J., Strunk, G. and Erten, C. (2002). The diffusion of management concepts in Europe – conceptual considerations and longitudinal analysis, *Journal of Cross-Cultural Competence & Management*, 3: 315–49.

Meyer, J. W. (2000). Globalization – sources and effects on national states and societies, *International Sociology*, 15: 233–48.

Meyer, J. W. and Rowan, E. (1977). Institutionalized organizations: formal structure as myth and ceremony, *American Journal of Sociology*, 83: 340–63.

Meyer, J. W., Boli, J., Thomas, G. M. and Ramirez, F. O. (1997). World society and the nation-state, *The American Journal of Sociology*, 103: 144–81.

Morley, M., Heraty, N. and Collings, D. G. (Eds) (2006). *New Directions in Expatriate Research*. Houndsmills, New York: Palgrave.

Pagano, M. and Volpin, P. F. (2005). Managers, workers, and corporate control, *Journal of Finance*, 60: 841–68.

Purcell, J. and Ahlstrand, B. (1994). *Human Resource Management in the Multi-Divisional Firm*. Oxford: Oxford University Press.

Quintanilla, J. and Ferner, A. (2003). Multinationals and human resource management: between global convergence and national identity, *International Journal of Human Resource Management*, 14: 363–8.

Randlesome, C. (1994). *The Business Culture in Germany*. Oxford: Butterworth Heinemann.

Rogers, E. (1983). *Diffusion of Innovations*. New York.

Rose, M. J. (1991). Comparing forms of comparative analysis, *Political Studies*, 39: 446–62.

Rosenzweig, P. M. and Singh, J. V. (1991). Organizational environments and the multinational enterprise, *Academy of Management Review*, 16: 340–61.

Schuh, A. (2000). Global standardization as a success formula for marketing in central and Eastern Europe?, *Journal of World Business*, 5: 133–48.

Schuler, R. S. and Jackson, S. E. (Eds) (2000). *Strategic Human Resource Management*. Oxford: Blackwell.

Schuler, R. S. and Tarique, I. (2006). International human resource management: a North American perspective, a thematic update and suggestions for future research, *International Journal of Human Resource Management*, 18(5): 717–44.

Schwartz, S. H. (2004). Mapping and interpreting cultural differences around the world, in H. Vinken, J. Soeters and P. Ester (Eds), *Comparing Cultures, Dimensions of Culture in a Comparative Perspective*. Leiden: Brill.

Sorge, A. (2004). Cross-national differences in human resources and organization, in A.-W. Harzing, and J. van Ruysseveldt (Eds), *International Human Resource Management*. London: Sage.

Stavrou, E. T. and Brewster, C. (2005). The configurational approach to linking strategic human resource management bundles with business performance: myth or reality? *Management Revue*, 16: 186–202.

Storey, J. (1992). *Developments in the Management of Human Resources*. Oxford: Blackwell Business.

Storey, J. (Ed.) (1995). *Human Resource Management: a Critical Text*. London: Routledge.

Ulrich, D. (1989). Tie the corporate knot: gaining complete customer commitment, *Sloan Management Review*, Summer: 19–28.

U.S. Department of Labor (1993). *High Performance Work Practices and Firm Performance,* Washington DC: US P.M. Wright, Government Printing Office.

Venkatraman, N. (1989). The concept of fit in strategy research: toward verbal and statistical correspondence, *Academy of Management Review*, 14: 423–44.

Whitley, R. (1999). *Divergent Capitalisms: the social structuring and change of business systems.* Oxford: Oxford University Press.

Woodward, J. (1970). *Industrial Organization: Theory and Practice.* London: Oxford University Press.

Wright, P. and McMahan, G. C. (1992). Theoretical perspectives for strategic human resource management, *Journal of Management*, 18: 295–320.

17 International human resource management

David G. Collings, Hugh Scullion and Deirdre Curran

Introduction

The topic of international human resource management (IHRM) has gained an important niche in the field of human resource management (HRM) and become a key issue for practitioners in multinational corporations (MNCs). Our point of departure is that managing human resources within organizations that straddle national boundaries is more than a matter of scale, and presents the field with unique and complex challenges that need to be considered carefully and critically. In this chapter we begin by introducing the topic in the context of the traditional ethnocentric view of international management and by highlighting the historical under-representation of research on the human resource function in the international management literature. Following this general introduction we illuminate a number of key themes in the field of IHRM which form the basis for structuring the remainder of the chapter. First, we consider the key issue of global staffing, we then explore the issue of standardization versus localization in the transfer of IHRM policy and practice. Third, we propose the adoption of an industrial relations perspective on the management of people in the international firm. Finally, we conclude by summarizing the main issues explored in the chapter and draw out the implications of the material for the management of people in the international arena.[1]

International human resource management in context

The issue of how organizations operating across national borders manage their foreign operations has a long history. Entrepreneurs have recognized the importance of physically relocating managers to foreign locations where business operations are based since approximately 1900 BC. Even at this stage, locals were viewed as inferior and restricted to lower level jobs while parent country nationals (PCNs) were charged with running foreign operations and afforded superior conditions, similar to modern day expatriates (Moore and Lewis, 1999: 66–7). While international trade may have been the exception rather than the rule at this time, Hirst and Thompson (1999: 2) posit 'the present highly internationalized economy is not unprecedented', rather it is 'one of a number of distinct conjunctures or states of the international economy that have existed . . . from the 1860s, indicating a long pedigree of international trade. Nonetheless, the emphasis on the role of parent country national expatriates, defined here as managers transferred from the headquarters operations to subsidiaries generally for a period of three to five years, dominated the research agenda of international human resource management for much of the latter part of the last century. Arguably, this is reflective of the ethnocentric view of multinational management adopted by many contributions, particularly from North America, to the field (Scullion and Brewster, 2001). These contributors, often implicitly, present a view that headquarters policy and practice, generally US based, is superior and that MNCs – and, indeed, their subsidiaries – will benefit from transferring this to their subsidiary operations. However, in recent years we have seen significant advancement in the literature, including a large body of European and more general non-US centric literature.

Somewhat paradoxically, for a number of years the study of MNCs focused on activities such as international marketing and strategy, international production and the like with human resource management research significantly underrepresented (Morley *et al*., 2006). This led Ondrack (1985) to argue that IHRM was one of the least-studied areas of international business, while Laurent (1986) described the field as in its infancy. We have, however, seen significant advances in recent years and there is now a good degree of literature in the area.

For some (Torrington, 1994: 4) international HRM is little more than domestic HRM on a larger scale with some additional complexities. However, we argue that international HRM is a far more complex and challenging animal and that the management of human resources in the international context is an especially complex and demanding process. In this regard Lazarova (2006) distinguished IHRM from HRM by reference to the additional layers of complexity of operation associated with operating in diverse national contexts combined with the requirement to manage three diverse groups of employees – namely home, host and third country nationals. Further, Schneider and Barsoux (2003) point to the heavy demands which internationalizing a company places on the HR function. Specifically, they point to the requirement for the HR function to have a sound understanding of the organization's corporate strategy and ensuring that HR policy is aligned with it. Second, HR must understand the cultural assumptions underpinning the organization's HR policies, as well as the subsidiary's policies. Finally, HR must have the ability to judge the antecedents and consequences of political resistance to HQ policy in subsidiaries and indeed the reasons why HQ may wish to transfer standardized policies in specific instances. Thus, HR professionals should recognize the potential to learn from the subsidiaries. In this chapter we adopt Scullion's (1995: 325) definition of IHRM as 'the HRM issues and problems arising from the internationalization of business, and the HRM strategies, policies and practices which firms pursue in response to the internationalization of business'.

Hence, in addition to regular functional HRM issues, IHRM includes a number of discreet themes including, *inter alia*: approaches to multinational management and global staffing; which explores the various strategic choices that can be made in the management and staffing of global firms; standardization versus localization in the transfer of IR/HR policies and practices, which focuses on the extent to which the MNC can implement globally standard policies and practices vis-à-vis the extent to which they must be adapted to account for local norms and traditions (Rosenzweig and Nohria, 1994; Edwards, 1998; Gunnigle *et al.*, 2002; Minbavea *et al.*, 2003); and the related theme of adopting an industrial relations perspective on the management of people in the international firm (Collings, 2008).

The breadth of topics encompassed within the field of IHRM prevents us from undertaking a full review (see e.g. Harzing, 2004; Scullion and Linehan, 2005; Briscoe *et al.*, 2008; Dickmann *et al.*, 2008; Dowling *et al.*, 2008 etc.). Therefore, in this chapter we focus specifically on the themes outlined above to provide the reader with a critical understanding of key IHRM themes and directions for further study.

Multinational management and global staffing

Given the significant impact of the parent company's international strategy and corporate top management team's beliefs on the nature of human resource policy and practice in foreign subsidiaries (Taylor *et al.*, 1996; Lazarova, 2006) we begin by considering the various orientations MNCs can have towards foreign operations. In this regard Perlmutter's (1969) contribution represents a key point of departure. In developing a model of *the multinationality* of international firms, he argued that no single criterion of multinationality was enough, nor were quantifiable measures such as percentage of foreign equity enough in themselves. Rather 'the orientation toward "foreign people, ideas, resources" in headquarters and subsidiaries, and in the host and home environments, becomes crucial in estimating the multinationality of a firm' (Perlmutter, 1969: 11). Initially he identified three approaches to the staffing of MNCs, namely: *ethnocentric*, *polycentric* and *geocentric* (Perlmutter, 1969) while in later work he developed a fourth approach, the *regiocentric* approach (Heenan and Perlmutter, 1979). We also point to linkages between Perlmutter's typology and some important literature on international strategy (cf. Bartlett and Ghoshal, 1998) and strategic international HRM (Taylor *et al.*, 1996). (For a fuller discussion of this area, including the advantages and disadvantages of each approach, see Collings and Scullion, 2006.)

As alluded to above, *ethnocentric* organizations are considered to be home country orientated. This is reflected in the fact that key positions in the HQ and subsidiaries are generally staffed by parent country nationals (PCNs). Further, home country policies, practice and people are considered superior and there are limited opportunities for host country nationals (HCNs) to be promoted to key positions or to the HQ. Similarly there is little attempt to identify and diffuse best practice from the subsidiaries. The literature suggests that ethnocentric policies are most appropriate during the early stages of subsidiary establishment, although Collings *et al.* (2008) suggest that born global firms, or firms that globalize at the early stage of their life cycles, may have limited excess managerial capability at the HQ and thus may not be in a position to deploy PCNs to subsidiaries. From a strategic

IHRM perspective, an ethnocentric orientation is similar to the Taylor *et al.* (1996) exportive approach, which emphasizes the transfer of policy from HQ with little regard for national difference. It is also consistent with Bartlett and Ghoshal's (1998) conceptualization of global companies. In this regard global companies are characterized by standardization and the promotion of organizational efficiency. They are focused on the integration of production and the development and diffusion of standardized products in a cost-effective manner. In global companies most key functions tend to be centralized and the role of subsidiaries is limited.

Polycentric organizations stand in contrast to ethnocentric ones and are primarily host-country orientated. Foreign subsidiaries are principally staffed by HCNs or managers from the subsidiary location. Perlmutter has compared these organizations to confederations, or as: 'loosely connected group[s] with quasi-independent subsidiaries as centres' (1969: 12). Subsidiaries are allowed to develop with minimal interference from HQ and are generally controlled through good financial monitoring and procedures. Polycentric staffing policies are most likely to be evident where organizations serve heterogeneous product markets and where products and services must be adapted and marketed to suit specific national tastes. The polycentric orientation is consistent with Taylor *et al.* (1996) adaptive orientation whereby policies are designed to ensure they are consistent with the local context. It is also consistent with Bartlett and Ghoshal's (1998) multidomestic organization model. The multidomestic companies are characterized by a decentralization of decision making and manufacturing driven by a desire for local responsiveness. The differentiation of products and services to accommodate local tastes and requirements is more important than the standardization which is characteristic of global firms.

Geocentric organizations are less concerned with nationality and this is reflected in the filling of positions at both HQ and subsidiary level with the 'best person for the job' regardless of nationality. Geocentric organizations are considered to represent the most complex form of organizational structure, thus requiring high levels of communication and integration across borders. The aim of the structure is to de-emphasize national culture and to emphasize an integrating corporate culture (Edstrom and Galbraith, 1997; see also Caligiuri and Stroth, 1995). This geocentric approach resonates with Taylor *et al.* (1996) integrative orientation. Taylor *et al.* argue that integrative firms attempt to use 'best practice' regardless of where it originates within the MNC. Geocentric organizations are consistent with Bartlett and Ghoshal's (1998) transnational model of organization. The transnational is characterized by flexible organizational strategy which can respond to emerging developments in the business environment. The MNC is conceptualized as an integrated network of sub-units within which expertise and resources are neither centralized nor completely de-centralized.

Finally, *regiocentric* organizations are conceptualized on a regional basis and managers are generally selected on the basis of 'the best in the region' with international transfers generally being restricted to regions. Under this structure subsidiaries within a region may have a relatively high degree of autonomy. Corporate policies and communication are generally mediated through the regional HQ.

This strategy has become more popular in recent years with many MNCs choosing to organize operations regionally. Indeed, writers such as Alan Rugman argue that most MNCs are regional rather than truly international, with the majority of their operations and sales being concentrated in their home region, thus highlighting the potential significance of the regiocentric orientation. However, based on their case research, Collings *et al.* (2008: 209) argue that 'at a corporate level regiocentric strategies may be as limiting as ethnocentric ones, in that the MNC may fail to source key talent outside of the home region, thus limiting the performance of the MNC through failing to adequately understand the peculiarities of regions outside of the home one and a failure to exploit the best talent within the MNC'. They also argue that regional structure can lead to the emergence of silo mentalities, whereby regional managers prefer to hold and protect their top talent within the region rather than allowing them to develop outside the region. Notwithstanding this, the significance of TCNs has increased significantly due to a number of factors, including: 1) the increasing significance of regional trading blocks such as NAFTA, the EU; 2) the increasing regional focus of MNCs identified by Rugman and colleagues; and the difficulties associated with implementing global strategies in MNCs.

Global staffing

A key visible measure of a MNC's orientation towards the management of their foreign subsidiaries emerges with regard to staffing decisions. These staffing decisions are encompassed under the term global staffing, which has been defined as: 'the critical issues faced by MNCs with regard to the employment of home, host and third country nationals to fill key positions in their headquarter and subsidiary operations' (Scullion and Collings, 2006b: 3).

Global staffing is considered a critical issue in IHRM for several reasons. First, the success of global business is increasingly linked to the ability of MNCs to attract and retain the quality of management talent required to effectively co-ordinate and implement global strategies (Evans *et al.*, 2002). Second, shortages of international management talent is a growing problem for many MNCs and has been exacerbated in recent years by the rapid growth of the emerging markets such as China, India, Central and Eastern Europe and South America (Dicken, 2007). This poses a significant global staffing challenge for MNCs as there will be an increasing need for international management talent with both the distinctive competences and the willingness to manage in these culturally challenging and geographically distant markets (Bjorkman and Xiucheng, 2002). In addition, there is increasing recognition of the growing importance of staffing strategies such as inpatriation (the transfer of foreign employees to work in the home country of an international organization on a temporary or permanent basis), and the use of third country nationals (Harvey *et al.*, 2000; Scullion and Collings, 2006). Finally, both the problems of expatriate performance and the challenges of localization continue to be problematic for many MNCs, including the growing numbers of SME international firms (Scullion and Brewster, 2001).

A key underlying theme in debates on global staffing concerns the reasons why MNCs use expatriates to staff their foreign operations and Edstrom and Galbraith's (1977) classic study identified three key motives for utilizing international transfers; position-filling, individual development and organizational development. In the first case expatriates are employed to fill key technical and managerial roles. In the second, assignments are used mainly for individual development purposes and in the third case assignments are used to build organizational competence at the organizational level and to promote the transfer of knowledge within the MNC network. More recently there has been an increasing awareness of the role of expatriates in controlling foreign subsidiaries, a motive for expatriation traditionally underexplored in the literature. Brewster (1991: 34) traces this traditional lack of focus to the North American origin of much of the previous research at this time combined with the tendency among managers and academics to consider control to be a relatively disreputable rationale for using expatriates. A key contribution to this latter debate was Harzing's (2001) study. Harzing identified three control roles of expatriates. First, expatriate managers can act as 'bears' in that they become the main focal point of control over the subsidiary in contrast to centralized control systems. Second, expatriates can perform as 'bumble bees' used to control subsidiaries through socialization and the development of informal networks. Finally, expatriates can act as 'spiders' seeking to achieve control through the weaving of informal communication networks within the MNC. Harzing's (2001) study goes beyond the question of why MNCs use expatriates and seeks to engage with the broader issue of how important these roles are in different situations. In this regard, her findings suggest that while expatriates tend to perform their roles as bears regardless of the situation, their roles as spiders and bumble bees tend to be more context specific. For example, the bumble bee role appeared more important in newly established subsidiaries while the bumble bee and spider roles were more significant in well established subsidiaries.

Emerging issues in global staffing

In the preceding section, we established the importance of global staffing in MNCs and unearthed the roles performed by expatriates in the MNC. However, as alluded to, global staffing issues are becoming more significant as shortages of international talent emerge as a key strategic issue for many international firms and often constrain the implementation of global strategies (Evans *et al.*, 2002). One key issue in this regard relates to the supply of such employees (Collings *et al.*, 2007). In explaining this supply issue we point to a number of key trends. First, research has highlighted the low level of female participation in international management as a key constraint on the supply of international managers and suggests that many women have restricted opportunities to expand their careers through international assignments (Linehan, 2002) therefore limiting the pool of potential incumbents for international roles. Research also shows that failure by many MNCs to adopt a strategic approach to repatriation impacts adversely on the supply of international managers, and that many MNCs continue to adopt *ad hoc* approaches to repatriation (Lazarova and Caligiuri, 2001). Thus, managers are reluctant to accept international assignments owing to the negative repatriate experiences of colleagues. A further constraint on the ability of MNCs to implement their international strategies is the growing barrier to international mobility amongst potential international assignees. Key constraints which emerge in explaining these barriers to international mobility include dual career issues, quality of life considerations, and the fear of international terrorism (Scullion *et al*., 2007).

Apposite to the decreasing supply of individuals with the competence and desire to accept international assignments, the demand for such individuals continues to grow. Collings *et al.* (2007) identify a number of demand factors in this regards. These include, *inter alia*: the emergence of new markets in China, India and Central and Eastern Europe and the increasing internationalization of small and medium enterprises.

The changing context of global staffing has resulted in organizations re-evaluating their global staffing orientations. In this regard, recent research suggests the emergence of newer, short-term, more flexible non-traditional forms of international assignments which are increasingly being used as alternatives to the traditional long term expatriate assignment (Welch and Worm, 2006; Collings *et al*., 2007). A recent ORC Worldwide survey showed that 72 per cent of firms used short term assignments in 2002 compared with only 26 per cent in 1996. The same surveys also highlighted a more than doubling of commuter assignments in the same period from 19 per cent to 46 per cent (cited in Dowling *et al.,* 2008: 128). The emergence of this 'portfolio approach' to international assignments poses considerable challenges for the HR function of the multinational firm (Roberts *et al*., 1998; Collings *et al*., 2007) Dilemmas arise for organizations regarding the role of the international human resource function in managing these global staffing arrangements. Recent research has highlighted the lack of HR support provided for staff on alternative assignments and shows that the burden of managing the impact of alternative assignments (such as the effect of unexpected travel schedules on their family relationships) is largely left with employees and their families (Mayerhofer *et al.,* 2004).

The potential benefits associated with alternative forms of international assignment from an organizational perspective include reduced costs, increased supply of potential candidates who might consider a short term or commuter assignment but may not have considered a traditional assignment, greater opportunities to develop employees in the international context, etc. Individual employees involved in alternative assignments are perceived to experience less disruption to their careers because they do not change jobs and stay in the promotion loop and they avoid the often painful re-integration phase (Collings *et al*., 2007). However, they may be involved in frequent travel and be required to develop networks and personal relationships in a wide range of different countries, putting considerable pressure on family and work commitments at home (Scullion and Collings, 2006). Further research is required to help us more fully understand how staff on alternative assignments manage the multiple demands of their lifestyle and whether assignments would be more successful for the organization and individuals if HRM policies and practices focused more on family friendly staffing arrangements (Mayerhofer *et al*., 2004).

Having considered some of the issues relating to the management and staffing of international firms we now go on to explore issues relating to the transfer of IR/HR policy and practice between the parent company and the geographically dispersed subsidiary.

MNCs and IR/HR policy transfer: Standardization versus localization

A key role of the HR function in the MNC is the development and dissemination of HR policy and practice to foreign subsidiaries where appropriate. While a complete discussion of the differing theoretical perspectives on transfer is beyond the scope of the current chapter we do focus on introducing two models which may assist in understanding the reasons why we first may wish to transfer HRM policies and practices and furthermore the factors which may retard the transfer process (for a consideration of some relevant theoretical approaches see Mayrhofer and Brewster in the current volume; Edwards, 2004).

A key point of departure in considering the transfer process is the notion that MNC's aspiration to transfer IR/HR policy and practice is driven by the desire to internalize ownership specific advantages (cf. Rugman, 1981) by replicating in foreign subsidiaries employment practices which they perceive to be advantageous in the HQ organization. We present two key theoretical contributions on the international diffusion of IR/HR policy and practice, Cooke's model and Edwards and Ferner's four influences framework. While there are a number of other theories presented in the literature, these are chosen because of their academic merit and their potential to advance theory in the field.

Cooke's framework is premised on a number of assumptions. First, MNCs seek to optimize profits on a global basis. Second, unions seek to optimize gains to workers (Cooke, 2006). Looking specifically at the IR domain, MNCs will attempt to diffuse specific IR policies and practices to their subsidiaries if they consider them to have ownership specific advantages. In other words, if the MNC perceives a specific IR practice to be a source of competitive advantage which will differentiate it in the global marketplace it will have a preference to replicate it in its foreign subsidiary. For example, a US manufacturing multinational may perceive that the operational and financial flexibility associated with its non-union status may be a key variable in its competitive success and one which competitors in other countries, with higher levels of union power, may find difficult to replicate. In this context, the MNC may well have a preference for establishing subsidiaries on a non-union basis to continue to reap the rewards of this orientation. Alternatively, a German MNC may consider its highly skilled workforce, which would have been developed through the German vocational education and training system, to be its source of competitive advantage and thus may attempt to replicate its systems in foreign subsidiaries. The gains which either party can realize are, however, bounded by the broader economic and socio-political environments within which they operate.

As noted above, however, the impact of the host context is also significant in explaining, not only the location of MNCs subsidiaries, but also the configuration of IR policies and practices in the subsidiaries. In this regard each subsidiary location offers specific location (dis)advantages. The US MNC referred to above would perceive the ability to set up on a non-union basis in a country with lower levels of institutional constraint in this regard, to be a location specific advantage, whereas the relative difficulty of setting up on a non-union basis in a more regulated country would be considered a location specific disadvantage.

The IR system within the MNC's home country, and the various host countries within which it operates, all form part of a complex interplay which influence the configuration of IR policy and practice in MNC subsidiaries (Cooke, 2003). Further, the exercise of power by both parties in the employment relationship also serves as a moderating factor in the optimization of gains (Cooke, 2006). This point is also made by Edwards *et al.* (2004), who note that since institutions are not deterministic within a given host country, key actors will have a degree of 'wriggle room' in interpreting policy and practice in the subsidiary.

The kernel of Cooke's thesis is that the parties act rationally and calculatively weigh up the potential costs and benefits associated with replicating a perceived ownership specific advantage abroad. Thus, in deciding on the final configuration of IR policy in a subsidiary, MNCs will weigh up the IR ownership advantages they enjoy and the IR location advantages available in different hosts.

An alternative theoretical framework for the analysis of decisions to diffuse HRM policies in MNCs is Edwards and Ferner's (2002) *Four Influences Framework* (see also Edwards, 2004). This framework presents a useful classification of four key influences on the nature and configuration of the transfer of employment practices across borders. The influences are inter-related and comprise of home and host country effects and the relative economic dominance or otherwise of each of them on the configuration of management practice within MNCs. Further, the impact of structural factors within the firm is considered in terms on international integration of production. We outline some of the key aspects of this framework below.

Country of origin effects

The first element of the *Four Influences Framework* is the country of origin effect. This concerns the extent to which a MNC's country of origin imprints a distinctive national effect on the management style and configuration of employment practices within a MNC. This results in a degree of embeddedness of a MNC in its home business system (Ferner, 1997). In this regard there is a growing body of literature which emphasizes the impact of a MNC's country of origin on its management practice (cf. Gunnigle *et al.*, 2002; Ferner *et al.*, 2004). The country of origin effect is often evident in the concentration of assets, key employment categories and even sales in a MNC's country of origin, reflecting the significance of the home country. Further, most MNCs fill key positions in the executive team with parent country nationals (cf. Edwards, 2004). The country of origin effect may be seen in a number of management practices within MNCs. For instance Ferner *et al.* (2004) demonstrate that US MNCs are distinctive in terms of centralized, standardized and formalized approaches towards HR policy. Similarly a large body of research across a number of countries appears to confirm that US MNCs: 'tend to show relatively little enthusiasm for institutions which accord a role for organized labour' (Muller-Camen *et al.*, 2001: 445; see also Almond *et al.*, 2005; Gunnigle *et al.*, 2005, etc). As Hayden and Edwards (2001) note, however, the country of origin does not impose a straitjacket on management, forcing all MNCs from a particular country to act in a certain way; rather many other factors, such as ownership structure, sector and the like, result in elements of heterogeneity between firms emanating from the same business system.

The country of origin effect may also be visible in terms of variations in how firms are financed. Specifically O'Sullivan (2001) draws the distinction between the fluid, arms-length relationships between managers and shareholders in the Anglo-Saxon context and the stable and co-operative relationships between the respective parties in Germany. This, she argues, is driven by the nature of stock ownership in the respective countries. In the Anglo-Saxon model stock ownership is generally concentrated in a small number of large institutional shareholders, whose primary objective is to maximize short-term profits. This has led to an emphasis on short-term management practices in firms emanating from these countries, and this is particularly pronounced in US MNCs (cf. Edwards and Ferner, 2002). Significantly, however, the country of origin effect is not fixed and rather evolves over time, particularly as firms operate in the international marketplace for longer time periods (Edwards and Ferner, 2002). Nonetheless Edwards (2004) notes that in considering the relations between different groups of organizational actors (in this case HQ and subsidiary managers), the logic of the country of origin effect is that actors in the parent country are likely to be key players in the transfer process. While acknowledging the potential impact of political considerations in the actual extent of transfer, the country of origin effect is likely to play a significant role in the determination of industrial relations policy and practice in foreign subsidiaries of MNCs.

Dominance effects

The second influence in Edwards and Ferner's framework is so-called dominance effects. The notion of dominance effects derives from the work of Smith and Meiskins (1995), who posit that at a point in time a hierarchy of economies exists within the international capitalist system and that in this context, nations in dominant positions have developed methods of structuring production or division of labour which draw emulation and interest. As Edwards (2004: 397) notes 'the logic of the "dominance effects" argument is that such transfer is not solely created by the legacy and force of institutions but is also shaped by competitive pressures at the international level'. This of course resonates with some of the tenets of new-institutionalism discussed above. In this regard Gunnigle *et al.* (2002) found dominance effects to be one of the key factors in explaining higher levels of standardization in US MNCs in Europe than in their European counterparts. They argued that the hegemonic position which the US economy had reached in recent years meant that US firms could more credibly impose standardized management practices on their foreign subsidiaries than their European counterparts. Again Edwards and Ferner (2002) remind us of the important consideration that the hierarchies of economies evolve over time. In this regard they point to the emergence of the dominance of the US economy in the mid-part of the last century, then the emergence of Japanese firms in the 1970s and 1980s threatened and indeed overtook the US position and more recently the US economy has come to the fore again. The most significant implication of dominance effects in the context of our consideration is that MNCs emanating from dominant economies may use their position to influence the adoption of company imposed models of the management of IR to subsidiaries. It is important to note, however, that the flow may of course be in the opposite direction and that MNCs may draw on the dominant position of the host countries in which it is located and transfer practices in the opposite direction (Edwards and Ferner, 2002) although the extent to which reverse transfer occurs appears to be relatively limited (cf. Edwards *et al.*, 2006).

International integration

The third element of the framework is international integration, defined as 'the generation of inter-unit linkages across borders' (Edwards, 2004). MNCs are increasingly realizing the synergistic benefits of integration of operations across national borders through advances in telecommunications and transportation technologies, combined with more homogoneous product markets and decreasing barriers to international trade. This is considered a structural influence on the diffusion of employment practices in MNCs and there is a significant sectoral effect on the extent to which it is evident within an MNC (Edwards *et al.*, 1999). International integration is reflected in the growing significance of regional divisions at the expense of country based models. There are two forms of integration which MNCs may pursue in this regard, namely, segmentation of operations across countries and standardization across countries (Edwards, 2004). The segmentation of operations is aimed at exploiting the various location advantages offered by different host locations to produce particular parts of a final product in various locales and is also termed vertical integration (Shenkar and Luo, 2004: 12) or global commodity chains (Gereffi, 1999). A key example would be the apparel or footwear industries, whereby production advantages of low cost locations mean that production is often concentrated in those locales, whereas design and marketing expertise available in more developed countries means that these functions are concentrated in higher cost locales. Alternatively international integration may be driven by standardization across different countries. In this regard MNCs aim to develop and produce relatively homogonous products, with relatively similar production techniques. A key implication of the latter would be the ability of the MNC headquarters to engage in coercive comparisons, by generating internal competition between plants and thus pressuring management and worker representatives to adopt practices favoured by HQ due to fears over production location and investment decisions (cf. Edwards *et al.*, 1999). In the industrial relations sphere Hamill (1984) has shown that higher levels of international integration lead to centralization of decision making on IR/HR issues, a finding replicated in Marginson *et al.*'s (1995) contention that it drives the development of standardized policy with regard to labour management.

Host country effects

The final element of the framework is host country effects. In particular, the concern in this regard is the aspect of the host business system which can limit MNCs in their attempts to diffuse practices to subsidiaries. Specifically, the introduction of standardized practices across MNC is clearly impacted by the institutional and cultural constraints in the host country. The higher the level of institutional constraint in the host environment the more difficult it will be for a MNC to implement standardized practices in that environment (cf. Gunnigle *et al.*, 2002). Basic HRM issues are often subject to significant legal or institutional constraint in the host environment (Young *et al.*, 1985; Ferner and Quintanilla, 1998). In the context of this discussion it is important to note 'while host institutions are not viewed as totally constraining actors . . . they pose certain limits within which action occurs' (Lane, 2003: 84). Thus many MNCs utilize threats to move production out of specific host countries and other techniques to leverage the diffusion of preferred policies with regard to subsidiary IR and HRM. For instance Ferner *et al.* (2001) note that even in highly regulated institutional contexts MNCs were able to create sufficient flexibility to preserve elements of their home style.

Frameworks such as those proposed by Cooke and Edwards and Ferner provide useful mechanisms for understanding and exploring the various influences on employment relations in MNCs by drawing out the key constraints, opportunities and pressures which MNCs are subject to in transferring IR/HR policy and practice between parent company and subsidiary.

Adopting an IR perspective on international management

In a recent contribution Collings (2008) has argued that an industrial relations perspective may help scholars and academics to understand the management challenge in MNCs. Collings (2008: 175) defines international IR (IIR) as the 'IR issues and problems, for both capital and labour, arising from the internationalization of business, and the IR strategies, policies and practices which firms, employees and their representatives pursue in response to the internationalization of business'. Thus an IIR approach advances studies in the IHRM tradition in two key ways and an IIR approach can be differentiated from an IHRM one in two further regards. This first distinction is on the basis of the substantive coverage of an IIR approach. Specifically, it engages with a range of issues which are often neglected in the international HRM literature, including trade union recognition and avoidance, collective bargaining, employee participation and involvement and the like. Second, it offers a different perspective on the areas under study which relates to the analytical approach toward the topics explored. Specifically, its consideration of the responses of other IR actors (the State, trade unions, employer organizations, European works councils, etc.) towards managerial strategies in MNCs is an important perspective omitted in many studies in the IHRM tradition. IIR approaches generally recognize the significance of collective groups of employees, often represented by a trade union, as a pluralist interest group within the firm, a perspective lacking in many unitarist studies in IHRM. Further, the consideration of power is one of the key means through which international IR research can contribute to our understanding of management in MNCs. Indeed, Edwards and Kuruvilla (2005) note the scope for organizational politics and power to shape the ways in which MNC manage their international workforces. They further note that the impact of power has also been neglected to a large degree in studies of the global–local debate in IHRM research. Arguably, an international IR perspective, with its pluralist underpinning, would help in understanding some of the challenges of managing human resources on a global scale (see Collings, 2008 for a full discussion of these issues). To a degree both of the theoretical frameworks presented in the preceding section display elements of an IIR perspective, and hence they are considered particularly appropriate examples in the context of the current volume with its emphasis on a critical perspective on HRM. Indeed, insights from an industrial relations tradition inform much of the critical content of this volume.

Conclusion

This chapter presented a number of key themes and critical issues with regard to the management of the international firm. In the international arena strategic choices need to be made about the approach taken to global management whether it is an ethno/poly/geo- or regio-centric approach. The approach adopted has direct implications regarding global staffing and the options and issues involved in staffing the international firm were highlighted here. The collaborative transfer of knowledge, policy and practice between the parent company and the subsidiary is another important determinant of the success of the international firm. In this regard we explored the motivation behind the approach taken to, and the extent of diffusion of IR/HR policy and practice across geographical boundaries. The four influences framework proposed by Edwards and Ferner offers us a schema for classifying the various approaches to the transfer of employment practices across borders. Finally, we considered Collings's (2008) proposal for adopting an IR perspective on the management of people in the international firms and argue it is justified as it allows for consideration of issues and actors otherwise neglected. It also allows for a more collective, pluralist orientation that gives due consideration to the importance of the concept of power in the employment relationship of the international firm.

The importance of IHRM is unlikely to abate in coming decades and represents a key contemporary issue in the wider field of human resource management. In adopting a critical perspective on the field, we advocate the use of a pluralist industrial relations lens as a means of looking beyond the traditional unitarist and managerial assumptions underscoring much of the extant research and thinking in the field.

Note

[1] Space restrictions prevent a thorough examination of all aspects of IHRM. For a broader discussion of IHRM issues see, for example, Briscoe *et al.* (2008), Dowling *et al.* (2008) or Scullion and Linehan (2005).

References

Almond, P., Edwards, T., Colling, T., Ferner, A., Gunnigle, P., Muller-Camen, M., Quintanilla, J. and Waechter, H. (2005). Unravelling home and host country effects: an investigation of the HR policies of an American multinational in four European countries, *Industrial Relations*, 44: 276–306.

Bartlett, C. and Ghoshal, S. (1998). *Managing Across Borders: The Transnational Solution.* Boston: HBS Press.

Björkman, I. and Xiucheng, F. (2002). Human resource management and the performance of western firms in China, *International Journal of Human Resource Management,* 13: 853–64.

Brewster, C. (1991). *The Management of Expatriates*, London: Kogan Page.

Briscoe, D. R., Schuler, R. S. and Claus, L. (2008). *International Human Resource Management Policy and Practice for Multinational Enterprises*, 3rd edition. London: Routledge.

Caligiuri, P. M. and Stroth, L. K. (1995). Multinational corporation management strategies and international human resource practices: bringing IHRM to the bottom line, *International Journal of Human Resource Management,* 6(3): 494–507.

Collings, D. G. (2008). Multinational Corporations and Industrial Relations Research: A road less travelled, *International Journal of Management Reviews,* 10(2): 173–93.

Collings, D. G., Morley, M. J. and Gunnigle, P. (2008). Composing the Top Management Team in the International Subsidiary: Qualitative Evidence on International Staffing in US MNCs in the Republic of Ireland, *Journal of World Business*, 43(2): 197–212.

Collings, D. G. and Scullion, H. (2006). Approaches to international staffing, in H. Scullion and D.G. Collings (Eds), *Global Staffing.* London: Routledge.

Collings, D. G., Scullion, H. and Morley, M. J. (2007). Changing patterns of global staffing in the multinational enterprise: challenges to the conventional expatriate assignment and emerging alternatives, *Journal of World Business,* 42(2): 198–213.

Cooke, W. N. (2006). Industrial relations in MNCs, in M. J. Morley, P. Gunnigle and D. G. Collings (Eds), *Global Industrial Relations.* London: Routledge.

Cooke, W. N. (2003). The influence of industrial relations systems factors on foreign direct investment, in W. N. Cooke (Ed.), *Multinational Companies and Global Human Resource Strategies.* Wesport: Quorum Books.

Dicken, P. (2007). *Global Shift,* 5th edition. London: Sage.

Dickmann, M., Sparrow, P. and Brewster, C. (Eds) (2008). *International Human Resource Management: A European Perspective.* London: Routledge.

Dowling, P., Festing, M. and Engle, A. E. (2008). *International Human Resource Management: Managing People in a Global Context*, 5th edition. London: Thomson Learning.

Edström, A. and Galbraith, J. R. (1977). Transfer of Managers as a Coordination and Control Strategy in Multinational Organizations, *Administrative Science Quarterly*, 22: 248–63.

Edwards, T. (1998). Multinationals, labour management and the process of reverse diffusion: A case study, *International Journal of Human Resource Management*, 9, 696–709.

Edwards, T. (2004). The transfer of employment practices across borders in multinational corporations, in A.W. Harzing and J. Van Ruysseveldt (eds) *International Human Resource Management,* London: Sage.

Edwards, T., Collings, D., Quintanilla, J. and Temple, A. (2006). Innovation and the Diffusion of Organization Learning, in P. Almond and A. Ferner (Eds), *American Multinationals in Europe: Managing Employment Relations Across National Borders.* Oxford: Oxford University Press, pp. 223–47.

Edwards, T. and Ferner, A. (2002). The Renewed 'American Challenge': a review of employment practices in US multinationals, *Industrial Relations Journal,* 33: 94–111.

Edwards, T. and Kuruvilla, S. (2005). International HRM: national business systems, organizational politics and the international division of labour in MNCs, *International Journal of Human Resource Management,* 16: 1–21.

Edwards, T., Rees, C. and Coller, X. (1999). Structure, politics and the diffusion of employment practices in multinationals, *European Journal of Industrial Relations,* 5: 286–306.

Evans, P., Pucik, V. and Barsoux, J. L. (2002). *The Global Challenge: Frameworks for International Human Resource Management.* New York: McGraw Hill/Irwin.

Ferner, A. (1997). Country of origin effects and human resource management in multinational companies, *Human Resource Management Journal,* 7(1): 19–36.

Ferner, A. and Quintanilla, J. (1998). Multinationals, national business systems and HRM: the enduring influence of national identity or a process of 'Anglo-Saxonization', *International Journal of Human Resource Management,* 9: 710–31.

Ferner, A., Quintanilla, J. and Varul, M. Z. (2001). Country of origin effects, host country effects, and the management of HR in multinationals: German companies in Britain and Spain, *Journal of World Business,* 36: 107–27.

Ferner, A., Almond, P., Clarke, I., Colling, T., Edwards, T., Holden, L. and Muller, M. (2004). The transmission and adaptation of 'American' traits in US multinationals abroad: case study evidence from the UK, *Organizational Studies,* 25: 363–91.

Gereffi, G. (1999). International trade and industrial upgrading in the apparel commodity chain, *Journal of International Economics,* 48: 37–70.

Gunnnigle, P., Murphy, K. M., Cleveland, J., Heraty, N. and Morley, M. (2002). Localisation in human resource management: comparing American and European multinational corporations, *Advances in International Management,* 14: 259–84.

Gunnigle, P., Collings, D. G. and Morley, M. (2005). Exploring the dynamics of industrial relations in US multinationals: evidence from the Republic of Ireland, *Industrial Relations Journal,* 36(3): 241–56.

Hamill, J. (1984). Labour relations decision making within multinational corporations, *Industrial Relations Journal,* 15(2): 30–4.

Harvey, M. G., Novicevc, M. N. and Speier, C. (2000). Strategic global human resource management: the role of inpatriate managers, *Human Resource Management Review,* 10: 153–75.

Harzing, A. W. (2001). Of bears bees and spiders: The role of expatriates in controlling foreign subsidiaries, *Journal of World Business*, 26: 366–79.

Harzing, A. W. (2004). Strategy and structure of multinational companies, in A. W. Harzing and J. Van Ruysseveldt (Eds), *International Human Resource Management*, 2nd edition. London: Sage.

Hayden, A. and Edwards, T. (2001). The erosion of the country of origin effect: a case study of a Swedish multinational company, *Industrial Relations/Relations Industrielles,* 56: 116–40.

Heenan, D. A. and Perlmutter, H. V. (1979). *Multinational Organizational Development.* Reading, MA: Addison-Wesley.

Hirst, P. and Thompson, G. (1999). *Globalisation in Question*, 2nd edition. Cambridge: Polity.

Lane, C. (2003). Changes in corporate governance of German corporations: convergence to the Anglo-American Model?, *Competition and Change,* 7: 79–100.

Laurent, A. (1986). The cross-cultural puzzle of international human resource management, *Human Resource Management,* 25: 91–103.

Lazarova, M. (2006). International human resource management in global perspective, in M. J. Morley, N. Heraty and D. G. Collings (Eds), *International Human Resource Management and International Assignments*. Basingstoke: Palgrave MacMillan.

Lazarova, M. and Caligiuri, P. (2001). Retaining repatriates: the role of organizational support practices, *Journal of World Business:* 36: 389–402.

Linehan, M. (2002). Senior female international manager: empirical evidence from Western Europe, *International Journal of Human Resource Management*, 13: 802–14.

Marginson, P., Armstrong, P., Edwards, P. and Purcell, J. (1995). Managing labour in the global corporation: a survey based analysis of multinationals operating in the UK, *International Journal of Human Resource Management,* 6: 702–19.

Mayerhofer, H., Hartmann, L. C., Michelitsch-Riedl, G. and Kollinger, I. (2004). Flexpatriate Assignments: a Neglected Issue in Global Staffing, *International Journal of Human Resource Management*, 15(8): 1371–89.

Minbaeva, D., Pedersen, T., Björkman, I., Fey, C. F. and Park, H. J. (2003). MNC Knowledge Transfer, subsidiary absorptive capacity, and HRM, *Journal of International Business Studies*, 34(6): 586–99.

Moore, K. and Lewis, D. (1999). *Birth of the Multinational.* Copenhagen: Copenhagen Business Press.

Morley, M. J., Heraty, N. and Collings, D. G. (2006). Introduction, in M. J. Morley, N. Heraty and D. G. Collings (Eds), *International Human Resource Management and International Assignments*. Basingstoke, Palgrave MacMillan.

Muller-Camen, M., Almond, P., Gunnigle, P., Quintanilla, J. and Tempel, A. (2001). Between home and host country: multinationals and employment relations in Europe, *Industrial Relations Journal*, 32: 435–48.

Ondrack, D. (1985). International human resource management in European and North American firms, *International Studies of Management and Organization*, 15: 6–32.

O'Sullivan, M. A. (2001). *Contests for Corporate Control: Corporate Governance and Economic Performance in the United States and Germany.* Oxford: Oxford University Press.

Perlmutter, H. V. (1969). The tortuous evolution of the multinational corporation. *Columbia Journal of World Business*, 4: 9–18.

Roberts, K., Kossek, E. and Ozeki, C. (1998). Managing the global workforce: challenges and strategies. *Academy of Management Executive*, 12(4): 93–106.

Rosenzweig, P. M. and Nohria, N. (1994). Influences on human resource management practices in multinational corporations, *Journal of International Business Studies,* 25: 229–42.

Rugman, A. M. (1981). *Inside the Multinationals.* New York: Columbia University Press.

Scullion, H. (1995). International human resource management, in J. Storey (Ed.), *Human Resource Management: A Critical Text*, London: Thompson.

Scullion, H. and Brewster, C. (2001). Managing expatriates: messages from Europe, *Journal of World Business*, 36: 346–65.

Scullion, H. and Linehan, M. (Eds) (2005). *International Human Resource Management: A Critical Introduction.* Basingstoke: Palgrave.

Scullion, H. and Collings, D. G. (2006). *Global Staffing*. London: Routledge.

Scullion, H., Collings, D. G. and Gunnigle, P. (2007). International HRM in the 21st Century: Emerging Themes and Contemporary Debates. *Human Resource Management Journal*, 17(4): 309–19.

Schneider, S. C. and Barsoux, J. L. (2003). *Managing Across Cultures*, 2nd edition Harlow: Prentice Hall.

Shenkar, O. and Luo, Y. (2004). *International Business.* Hoboken, NJ: John Wiley.

Smith, C. and Meiskins, P. (1995). System, society and dominance effects in cross national organisational analysis, *Work, Employment and Society,* 9: 241–68.

Taylor, S., Beechler, S. and Napier, N. (1996). Towards an integrative model of strategic international human resource management, *Academy of Management Review*, 21: 959–85.

Torrington, D. (1994). *International Human Resource Management: Think Globally, Act Locally.* London: Prentice Hall.

Welch, D. E. and Worm, V. (2006). International Business Travellers: a challenge for IHRM, in G.K. Stahl and I. Björkman (Eds), *Handbook of Research in International Human Resource Management.* Cheltenham, UK: Edward Elgar.

Young, S., Hood, N. and Hamill, J. (1985). Decision making in foreign owned multinational subsidiaries in the United Kingdom. *ILO Working Paper No. 35*. Geneva: ILO.

Index

A library at your fingertips!

eBooks are electronic versions of printed books. You can store them on your PC/laptop or browse them online.

They have advantages for anyone needing rapid access to a wide variety of published, copyright information.

eBooks can help your research by enabling you to bookmark chapters, annotate text and use instant searches to find specific words or phrases. Several eBook files would fit on even a small laptop or PDA.

NEW: Save money by eSubscribing: cheap, online access to any eBook for as long as you need it.

Annual subscription packages

We now offer special low-cost bulk subscriptions to packages of eBooks in certain subject areas. These are available to libraries or to individuals.

For more information please contact webmaster.ebooks@tandf.co.uk

We're continually developing the eBook concept, so keep up to date by visiting the website.

www.eBookstore.tandf.co.uk

LIBRARY, UNIVERSITY OF CHESTER